Measuring Adult Literacy

The International Adult Literacy Survey (IALS) in the European context

This research was funded by the European Commission

Edited by Siobhán Carey

Authors: Siobhán Carey
Ann Bridgwood
Margaret Thomas
Patricia Ávila

London: Office for National Statistics

First published 2000

ISBN 1 85774 368 7

TABLE OF CONTENTS

Acknowledgements

This report represents the culmination of a collaborative research project funded by the European Commission. Like any large-scale undertaking it has involved the co-operation of a large number of people and in this case across a number of countries. Without the contribution of the many individuals concerned it would not have been possible and without their enthusiasm and good humour it would not have been so enjoyable. The International Adult Literacy Survey assessment places a heavy burden on the respondent and agreement to take part is not a trivial undertaking. We are particularly indebted to the many respondents in France, Sweden, Britain and Portugal who gave of their time and enthusiasm so willingly, for the second time, in agreeing to take part in the survey.

Particular thanks are due to the project team within Social Survey Division of ONS. The management and co-ordination of this ambitious project was challenging to say the least. Specific mentions are due to Baljit Gill, Ann Bridgwood and Sampson Low who successfully steered the project through the many stages and milestones. Scott Murray and Nancy Darcovitch of Statistics Canada provided much appreciated assistance at various stages in the project. Particular thanks also to Ettore Marchetti of the European Commission for his interest and support throughout the project.

Working together with researchers in other countries over a protracted period of time offers an opportunity to develop true collaborative partnerships which will last for longer than the life of this project. We hope this project will be the foundation stone for further collaboration adventures.

This data from this study offers a rich source of information only some of which it has been possible to exploit in the context of this report. We hope that it will be widely used by other researchers to fully exploit its' value.

Siobhán Carey
Research Director
Social Survey Division
Office for National Statistics

Notes to tables

1. The following conventions have been used in tables:

-	No cases
0	Values of less than 0.5
[ ]	the numbers in square brackets are the actual numbers which are presented when the base is less than 30
..	category not applicable

2. The row percentages may add to 99% or 101% because of rounding.

3. Unless stated otherwise, changes and differences mentioned in the text have been found to be statistically significant at the 95% confidence level.

1. Introduction

1.1 Introduction

This report presents the results from a collaborative project undertaken on behalf of DGXXII of the European Commission. The objective of the project was to consider the potential for cultural bias in large scale international surveys, in particular surveys such as the International Adult Literacy Survey (IALS) which incorporates measurement from two distinct disciplines, educational and social research. Although the IALS is used as the basis for this investigation many of the underlying principles and concerns are relevant to any survey which aims to produce data on an international basis and to all those who use data from different survey sources to make comparisons.

The background to the initiation of this project was how to explain large differences between countries in the distribution of skills as found in the IALS. Two approaches to explaining these differences emerged. Analysis of the literacy measures in the international report showed clear and strong relationships between literacy as measured by IALS and characteristics such as education level, age, occupation and reading habits. One explanation of the differences between countries is that the characteristics associated with high literacy skills are distributed differently across countries therefore that there are large differences between countries in the observed skill levels should not be a surprise. Another viewpoint was that the differences between countries found in the IALS were too large to be plausible, particularly among some European countries, especially France, and therefore there must be some other explanation as to why such large differences were observed.

The project has considered three main areas of interest; the measurement methods used in large scale assessments; household survey methods and their application in the context of international survey initiatives. Thirdly, the project set out to investigate empirically the stability of the literacy measure as used in IALS. The overall objective was to establish good practice that could be implemented in future similar surveys.

1.2 The International Adult Literacy Survey (IALS)

The IALS is an international programme of surveys co-ordinated by Statistics Canada and supported by the OECD that set out to profile the literacy skills of the adult population in a number of countries. The IALS had its genesis in work carried out in the US during the 1980s; in particular the Young Adult Literacy Assessment (YAL)[1] conducted in the US in 1985. The YAL was the first survey of this type, which brought educational research measurement techniques into the context of a household survey of adults. Unlike previous studies, the YAL study did not treat literacy as a single dimension. Rather it identified three scales that represented three different aspects of literacy – prose, document and quantitative – which it was felt better reflected the diversity of literacy tasks that are encountered in daily life. The assessment in the YAL survey used open-ended rather than multiple choice assessment tasks as it more closely reflected the situation in which adults have to perform literacy tasks. The assessment tasks were taken from a broad range of contexts simulating the range of tasks that adults would encounter in everyday life.

In the US further studies followed the YAL lead, a study of job seekers[2] in 1989/90 and then the National Adult Literacy Survey (NALS) in 1992[3]. Meanwhile other countries were

---

[1] Kirsch, Irwin and Ann Jungeblut. *Literacy: Profiles of America's Young Adults.* Educational Testing Service (1986 Princeton, N.J.)

[2] Kirsch Irwin, Ann Jungeblut. *Profiling the Literacy Proficiencies of JTPA and ES/UI Populations.* US Dept. of Labor and ETS. 1992

beginning to follow the US lead. In Australia a survey of 1,500 adults[4] was undertaken using the YAL framework in 1988/9. In 1989 a similar study was undertaken in Canada[5] but with the additional dimension that it was carried out in both official languages, English and French. This was to set the scene for the birth of IALS. Against a growing interest within the US and Canada to have comparable data for their national studies, a proposal was developed to recruit countries to participate in IALS. In the IALS technical report the success of IALS was identified as being dependent on four criteria, the selection of a scientifically credible sample; the adaptation of the background questionnaire and assessment instruments while maintaining their theoretic and conceptual integrity; the administration of the survey in accordance with the prescribed protocols and the preparation of the data in a standardised format[6].

In 1994 nine countries took part in the first ever IALS – Canada, the US, Ireland, Germany, France, Sweden, the Netherlands, Poland and Switzerland. These countries worked collaboratively to develop an assessment instrument that would be used in different languages and cultures taking as the starting point the conceptual and methodological developments in measuring literacy in the US in the 1980s. The results from seven of the countries that took part in IALS in 1994 were published by the OECD in 1995[7]. A further four countries, the United Kingdom, Belgium (Flanders), Australia and New Zealand participated in the survey in 1996 and a second international report was published in 1997[8]. A number of other countries, including several European Union member countries, have just completed IALS and a third international report will be published in due course. A technical report[9] on IALS was published in 1997 which provides detailed descriptions of the survey processes.

IALS represents a new departure in large-scale survey research, characterised by multi-disciplinary measurement techniques and international effort on a grand scale. It is likely that IALS is only the first of what may turn into a long line of similar or related studies. The IALS data has been widely used both nationally and internationally, by policy makers and researchers alike. Plans are already in prospect to extend the IALS model to include new skill measures such as problem solving, teamwork, practical cognition and computer literacy through assessment or behavioural reports. It is proposed to include these new measures which are currently under development along with the prose and document literacy measures from IALS and a revised numeracy measure in the International Life Skills Survey[10]. In the context of these future likely developments it is important that every effort is made to make these surveys of the highest possible quality so that the data can be used with confidence.

---

3 Kirsch Irwin, Ann Jungeblut, Lynn Jenkins and Andrew Kolstad. *Adult Literacy in America*. National Center for Education Statistics.,1993.

4 Wickert Rosie. *No Single Measure.* Commonwealth Dept. of Employment, Education and Training. Canberra 1989.

5 *Adult Literacy in Canada Results of a National Study.* Statistics Canada1991.

6 *Adult Literacy in OECD Countries Technical Report on the First International Adult Literacy Survey.* National Center for Education Statistics: Washington 1998 p. 15

7 Literacy, Economy and Society: Results of the first International Adult Literacy Survey. OECD and Statistics Canada (1995).

8 *Literacy Skills for the Knowledge Society: Further results from the International Adult Literacy Survey.* OECD and Human Resources Development Canada. (1997). This report included data for the seven countries reported on in 1995 and the UK, Australia, New Zealand, Begium (Flanders) and the Rep. of Ireland.

9 *Adult Literacy in OECD Countries Technical Report on the First International Adult Literacy Survey.* National Center for Education Statistics: Washington 1998

10 International Life Skills Survey co-ordinated by National Centre for Educational Statistics and Statistics Canada

1.3 The IALS literacy measure

The definition of literacy adopted for IALS is that used in the YAL study. It defines literacy as

> *Using printed and written information to function in society, to achieve one's goals and to develop one's knowledge and potential.*

This definition does not treat literacy as a dichotomous condition that people either have or do not have, but rather defines literacy as a broad range of skills required in a varied range of contexts. It also implies that literacy goes beyond merely reading or comprehending text to include a broader range of skills in using information in texts. In IALS three dimensions of literacy skill are measured:

Prose literacy: the knowledge and skills required to understand and use information from texts such as prose, newspaper articles and passages of fiction. The texts have a typical paragraph structure.

Document literacy: the knowledge and skills required to locate and use information contained in various formats such as timetables, graphs, charts and forms. The texts have a varied format, use abbreviated and/informal language and use a variety of devices and visual aids to convey meaning such as diagrams, maps or schematics.

Quantitative literacy: the knowledge and skills required to apply arithmetic operations, either alone or sequentially, to numbers embedded in printed materials, such as calculating savings from a sale advertisement, working out the interest required to achieve a desired return on an investment or totaling a bank deposit slip

Each of the three scales which measure these dimensions of literacy skill is designed to range from 0 to 500 and has been grouped into five literacy levels. Level 1 represents the lowest ability range and Level 5 the highest. Each level implies an ability to cope with a particular type of task and is based on incremental shifts in the skills required to successfully complete items at different points along the scales. The underlying framework[11] describes the difficulty of an item as being associated with both the characteristics of the task and the attributes of the text. Performance on any particular task therefore reflects the interaction between the characteristics of the task itself and both the context and the format of the text.

The definition and measurement of literacy as used in IALS is not without its critics. There is a constituency of researchers who would propose both alternative definitions of literacy and alternative analysis tools for its measurement.[12]

[11] Kirsch, I. Ann Jungeblut and Peter B. Mosenthal. The Measurement of Adult Literacy. in *Adult Literacy in OECD Countries Technical Report on the First International Adult Literacy Survey*. National Center for Education Statistics: Washington 1998
Peter Mosenthal. Defining Prose Task Characteristics for Use in Computer-Adaptive Testing and Instruction. In American Educational Research Journal. 1998.

[12] See for example Brian Street. Literacy, Economy and Society: a Review in *Literacy Across the Curriculum* Vol. 12, No. 3 1996 and Mary Hamilton and Dave Barton. *The International Adult Literacy Survey: What does it really measure?* Centre for Languages in Social Life Working paper 107, 1999.

1.4 The IALS specification

The IALS is a survey of adults living in private households. Each participating country is asked to implement a common survey design using common instruments. The specification sets out a number of key design features which include:

- Probability sampling methods at each stage of sampling to ensure a representative sample of adults living in private households in their country
- A minimum sample size (3,000 is recommended) and minimum response rate
- The sampling plan submitted and agreed by the international co-ordinators
- Quality checks on the scoring of assessments by rescoring assessments within and between countries
- The use of common instruments with minimal change (background questionnaire and literacy assessment)
- Including all mandatory questions on the background questionnaire with minimum modification
- Adaptation/translation of the assessment/scoring guide with modifications limited to adaptations of text to local cultural context and usage
- Implementing the survey is a standard way according to the agreed international protocols (e.g. allowing the respondent as much time as they required, not using incentives and using face to face interviewing methods)
- Coding industry, occupation and education to standard international classifications
- Weighting the data to known population estimates and to take account of non-response

1.5 The IALS interview

The interview consists of two main elements, a background questionnaire and a literacy assessment. The background questionnaire collects information on the socio-demographic characteristics of the respondent (age, sex, employment status, occupation, education, income etc) as well as asking about their reading habits and literacy practices in everyday life and at work. The background questionnaire takes on average 30 minutes to complete.

The literacy assessment consists of a short screening assessment which seeks to identify those with very limited literacy skills. Respondents who correctly answer at least 2 of the 6 screening tasks are then presented with a more extensive assessment booklet to complete which measures three dimensions of literacy, prose literacy, document literacy and quantitative literacy. In order to ensure as broad a range of item content as possible the total number of tasks in the assessment is larger than any one individual could reasonably be asked to complete. Each respondent therefore is only asked to complete a subset of the total assessment. The assessment items are grouped into seven blocks and a Balanced Incomplete Block (BIB) design used to arrange the blocks in different combinations into seven booklets. Each booklet contained three blocks of items and each block appeared at each possible location, the beginning, middle or end of a booklet in a spiral effect. Respondents were allowed to take as much time as they required to complete the booklet. Each booklet contains about 45 questions for the respondent to answer.

The booklets are scored using a scoring guide common to all countries. The scoring guide codes data according to whether the respondent answered the question correctly, leaves the question blank or gives either a wrong answer or makes a mark/cross/stroke though the question. The data from each country is sent to the international co-ordinators for checking and editing. The scaling of the data onto the literacy scale is carried centrally for all countries by the Educational Testing Service (ETS), Princeton. The scaling techniques used for summarising the test data are those developed in the context of large scale student assessment – Item Response Theory or Models (IRT or IRM). These models are used to summarise the data to produce proficiency estimates for the population. The techniques used include complex strategies for handling missing data for both individual non-response and for item non-response.

1.6 Description of the current project

This assessment of IALS was the subject of a call for tenders by the European Commission in 1996. The project, as initially proposed, consisted of a number of strands of work which are inter-related and which sought to examine the question from a number of different perspectives. Those broad strands of work remained the same in principle throughout the life of the project although the substance of the work evolved as the project team took on board new analyses or publications or results from the early stages of the project. The four main strands of work initially were:

- A review of IALS
- Secondary analysis of the IALS data
- Re-interviewing IALS respondents
- Consideration of the future prospects for large-scale assessments in Europe

The distinctions between some of these strands became less clear as the work progressed. In particular the review of IALS and the investigation of what methodology should be adopted for such surveys in a European context seemed to reflect the same issues but for the different research specialisms. Each of the strands is described briefly in turn outlining the original concepts behind that part of the work programme, the evolution through the life of the project and the final shape and content of the project. The findings from each of the stages are reported later in this report.

1.6.1 Review of IALS

The large differences observed in skill profiles, particularly the case of France, raised concerns about the comparability of the IALS across countries. In advance of the publication of the first results from IALS a review was commissioned by the international co-ordinators of the survey[13]. In the intervening period between submitting the proposal for this project and commencing work more detail about how IALS had been conducted in the different countries had come into the public domain[14]. The starting point for the project was to review how IALS had been carried out in the different countries in order to identify possible sources of error. Because IALS represented the fusion of measurement from two traditionally separate and distinct disciplines this review was approached from both the survey methods and the educational measurement perspectives, in particular the use of IRT.

1.6.2 Secondary Analysis of the IALS data

The IALS assessment contains some 140 items which represent a broad range of contexts, subject matter and difficulty. As outlined in section 1.5, respondents in the survey are asked to complete an assessment booklet which contains a sub-sample of the total test (about 45 questions). The methodology used to scale the data in IALS is based on Item Response

[13] Graham Kalton, Lars Lyberg and Jean-Michel Rempp. Review of Methodology in *Adult Literacy in OECD Countries Technical Report on the First International Adult Literacy Survey*. National Center for Education Statistics: Washington 1998

[14] ibid

Theory models (IRT) to produce population estimates. The models used in IALS are complex and include adjustments for various types of non-response. IRT models are very specialised and are almost exclusively used in educational research and mainly in North America. The complexity and lack of transparency in the scaling technique means that for many researchers, particularly the survey practitioners who are charged with carrying out the survey and are used to more widely accessible statistical tools the scaling process requires a certain amount of trust.

IRT is one method of summarising the data from the many items the respondent has answered. As these models are highly sophisticated they are not easily replicated. The summation of the data or the 'black box' could be replaced with other methods of summarising the data which would be more accessible to more generalist researchers and statisticians. One of the difficulties that many national IALS teams had was that they were unlikely to have available the full range of skills desired for a project of this type. They tended to have either the skills and experience necessary to undertake a large and complex household survey or the survey specific statistical expertise but rarely both. The objective of the secondary analysis was to subject the IALS data to statistical methods other than IRT to establish the consistency of those analyses with the results of the IRT models. Although the French IALS data was not included in the IALS international reports, the French Ministry of Education kindly gave their permission for the French survey data to be included in the analyses for this project. The availability of the data from the French survey greatly enriched the value of the work and raised many interesting questions, some of which we hope we have been able to answer.

The progamme of secondary analysis work originally proposed was reviewed at the beginning of the project in the light of both the IALS technical report which had been published in the interim and other research that had been carried out. A report by Dickes and Fliellier[15] had addressed some of the areas that had been identified as areas of concern and focussed mainly on the psychometric aspects of the data. Meanwhile a report by Blum and Guerin-Pace[16] had identified some new possible areas of investigation, notably the adaptation/translation of the assessment used in France. From their work and from an initial analysis of the assessment items in the French assessment compared with the UK items, it appeared that for a number of the test items the tasks in the French version differed in potentially significant ways from the tasks as applied in other countries/versions of the test.

1.6.3 Survey Practice across Europe

One of the difficulties in reviewing how IALS was carried out in countries was that no one individual had sufficient knowledge about how surveys are normally carried out in those countries to be able to evaluate all the surveys. This lack of a 'benchmark' meant that while the technical report outlined differences between the surveys it was difficult to determine if these differences in how the IALS was carried out across countries simply reflected normal differences in survey practice between countries or survey organisations. In thinking about how to overcome this knowledge deficit and in thinking about how future surveys could be evaluated it was felt useful to try and produce an overview of survey practice across a number of EU member countries. The review focused on identifying the range of procedures feasible in each of the countries. It was not possible to include all EU member countries in the review but we tried to select sufficiently diverse countries to reflect the range of survey

---

[15] Paul Dickes et André Fliellier. *Analyses secondaires des données françaises de la première Enquête Internationale sur l'Alphabétisation des Adults (enquête IALS).* Université de Nancy, Novembre 1997 (unpublished).

[16] Alain Blum et France Guérin-Pace. *Analyse des disparités culturelles des réponses à l' enquête IALS.* Institut National d'Études Démographiques (unpublished) and Alain Blum and France Guérin-Pace. 'L'Illusion comparative' in *Population.* INED No. 2 1999.

custom and practice. The countries included were: Great Britain, Netherlands, Sweden, Italy, France, Portugal, Germany and Greece.

Understanding the differences between countries in how they implement surveys is useful not only for IALS but also for many other areas of research which try to produce comparative results across countries, languages and cultures.

1.6.4 Follow-up survey

This strand represented the largest single element of the project and the area that was subject to the most change over the life of the project. The initial call for tender had set the objective as 'to assess scientifically the potential for cultural bias in surveys such as IALS and in particular differences between Northern and Southern Europe'. Based on some of the arguments that had been put forward in the debate about how to explain the observed differences in IALS, the re-test element of the project as initially conceived set out to investigate whether the motivation of respondents in completing the assessment, or in doing well in the assessment differed across countries or groups of countries. For the purposes of designing the study this was expressed in terms of the use of incentives to enhance or modify respondent motivation. The design of the survey changed as information from each stage of the research was taken into account.

The follow-up survey involved research teams in 4 countries, Great Britain, France, Sweden and Portugal. Three of these countries had taken part in IALS (Great Britain in 1996, Sweden and France in 1994). A literacy survey had also been carried out in Portugal in 1994 but this took place outside the framework of IALS. This Portuguese Adult Literacy Survey (PALS) used a similar framework to that in IALS in terms of the definition of literacy and the development of literacy levels but was more simple in design and less ambitious in intent.

1.6.4.1 Stage 1: Initial Qualitative Research

The initial stage of the project involved qualitative work in all four countries to better understand the dynamics of the IALS in the different countries. Qualitative research was carried out in Britain, France and Sweden in October /November 1997. The objective of this research was to explore respondents' reactions and attitudes to the IALS assessment and to discuss with them the level of commitment they felt towards the task; their understanding of what was expected of them and to explore ways of maximising respondent motivation. It was hoped that this would give a better understanding of what it was like for someone to take part in IALS. In each country 15 former IALS respondents and 15 new respondents were interviewed. Former IALS respondents were asked to complete a shortened version of the background questionnaire from IALS and the same IALS booklet they had completed on the previous occasion. Respondents were stopped after they had spent 40 minutes on the booklet and then were asked qualitative questions on their approach to, commitment to and understanding of the tasks.

Based on this qualitative research (see Chapter 8) a need for more explicit rules, standard across countries, for introducing the booklet and for explaining how to complete the booklet was identified. There was little evidence from this qualitative research to suggest that incentive payments would motivate people any more than could be done by other means such as improved information or by establishing a 'contract' between respondent and interviewer.

Based on these albeit preliminary and qualitative results it seemed that the notion that incentives could be used to manipulate or improve respondent effort was not substantiated. The design of the next stage of the research was therefore constructed to provide more concrete evidence of whether incentives could be used to manipulate motivation, and to look at the effect on performance of other motivating factors.

1.6.4.2 Stage 2: Field trial

The next stage in the research was to conduct a small field trial to evaluate the effect of increased information and/or incentive payment on demonstrated performance on the literacy assessment. In Britain, France and Sweden 48 former IALS respondents, and in Portugal 48 former PALS respondents, were interviewed with the sample assigned to 4 treatment and control groups. The financial incentive needed to be sufficiently large in each country to maximise its potential to manipulate motivation but could vary between countries.

The sample was drawn from IALS respondents who had completed enough of the booklet in IALS to have a score calculated rather than imputed[17] and who also agreed to a recall, but excluded those estimated with the highest performance, Level 5, as they have no room for improvement. The list of case numbers of respondents who had not completed enough of the literacy assessment to be used for estimation was provided by ETS who had done the original scaling. The field trial included a background questionnaire (a shortened version of the IALS questionnaire), the same test booklet as in the original survey, a short debriefing questionnaire asking about motivation, effort, attitudes to the test and calls and outcome information about responders and non-responders. The pilot took place in Great Britain, Sweden and France at the end of January, early February 1998 and in Portugal in April 1998. A scorer training meeting was held in London in early February and the booklets from all three IALS countries were scored at the same time in order to ensure consistency.

Treatment	**Increased information: summary findings, booklet rules explained**	**No increase in information**
Incentive	Group A n = 12	Group B n = 12
No incentive	Group C n = 12	Group D n = 12

In order to ensure that each treatment group had roughly the same characteristics the treatment groups were matched on age, sex, literacy level, educational level and employment status. So for example, in Britain one group was defined as older people with low levels of education, low average prose literacy score and in the lower social class groups. Within each grouping individuals were then assigned to the different treatments.

Another objective of both the qualitative research and the field trial was to test the feasibility and acceptability of the overall project design which involved going back to IALS respondents and asking them to retake the assessment. In both the qualitative work and the field trial there were some problems in tracing those who had moved in the intervening period.

[17] In IALS where a respondent has not completed at least 5 items on each literacy scale their proficiency values were estimate. Different procedures were used depending on whether the non completion of the assessment was reported to be for literacy related reasons such as language problems or for non literacy related reasons such as not having any more time to spend on the interview. Those who had not done enough of the booklet to have their score calculated were excluded as their would be insufficient information on their proficiency from the first survey to make interpretation meaningful.

1.6.4.3 Design of the mainstage follow-up survey

Given that there was no indication from the two earlier stages of the research that motivation or effort could be manipulated by an incentive payment it was felt that more value could be gained from the study in terms of prospective recommendation by departing from the original design based on a split sample around incentive payments. An alternative design which it was felt better addressed the key issues in relation to the comparability of IALS was devised, agreed and implemented.

During the review of IALS and the initial stages of the retest a number of aspects of IALS implementation were found to vary between countries, the effects of which are difficult to estimate. Some examples of the variation that occurred were the title of the survey, the way the survey was introduced and the instructions the respondent was given about completing the booklet. These differences may have had no impact at all or may have had significant impact either alone or in combination.

1.6.4.4 The split sample design

Retaining the split sample design but replacing the incentive/no incentive dichotomy with variations which would address these issues individually was problematic. While holding everything else constant and changing one element only would have allowed for the estimation of the impact of specific individual changes, for example the administration of the test, it would not have shown whether this would have the same effect across countries or whether all these aspects contribute additively or cancel each other out. Implementing the same design in all (or at least three) of the countries would enhance the power of any analyses. Given that we were concerned at all times to identify best survey practice for future application in similar surveys only addressing some of the issues seemed unsatisfactory. A number of different alternative designs were considered. The key areas felt to be in need of investigation were:

- the stability of the literacy assessment both across countries, within countries and over time,
- the effect of the translation on performance in France,
- the impact of different survey practice in the different countries, and
- how IALS compares with a simpler survey such as the PALS.

Given that the focus of the project was to identify how such surveys might be improved for future rounds it was agreed to retain the split design but to consolidate the areas in need of standardisation into the optimal protocol, or best practice. The test design agreed was therefore similar in Britain, Sweden and France with a separate design being implemented in Portugal (see section 1.6.4.5 below). The design adopted was as follows:

Treatment	GB	Sweden	France	Portugal
IALS	300 IALS respondents doing IALS test under existing protocol	300 IALS respondents doing IALS test under existing protocol	300 IALS respondents doing IALS test under existing protocol	300 PALS respondents doing PALS test under existing protocol
Best Practice:	300 IALS respondents doing IALS test under amended protocol	300 IALS respondents doing IALS test under amended protocol	500 IALS respondents doing Swiss French test under amended protocol	1200 (new sample) respondents doing IALS test under amended protocol

The IALS sample is the control group which provides evidence of the stability of the measure over time and across countries. It allows the estimation of how much any change observed in the Best Practice sample is simply due to a different time and place. The Best Practice part of the survey involved changes in the protocols and implementation of the survey in all the areas where it was felt that greater standardisation could be achieved. It was intended to assess the impact of reducing the unnecessary variation identified e.g. the test version in France, changing introductions, guidelines, instructions, administration of the assessment. This meant that the difference in protocol between the two treatment groups would vary between countries.

In France there was one important element that needed to be tested. Given that potentially significant differences in the adaptation of the assessment items had been identified there was a need to correct those items in the French assessment that were thought to be problematic. The choice was between amending the French assessment in view of the findings or to use a different French language version of the test, i.e. the Swiss or French Canadian versions. On balance it was decided to use the Swiss version of the IALS assessment on the Best Practice sample. Because a different test version was being used for some respondents in France the psychometric properties of that test on a new population needed to be validated. The initially proposed 300 cases were insufficient to check the test for validity and so the sample size was increased to 500 for the Best Practice sample in France. As a sample of 300 was deemed the minimum to detect any variation, the sample size could not be reduced in any of the other cells to compensate for the additional costs.

1.6.4.5 Survey design: Portugal

The design in Portugal had always differed from that in the other three countries as Portugal had never taken part in IALS. At the same time as the first IALS (1994) Portugal had a undertaken literacy survey (PALS) using the IALS measurement framework. This Portuguese literacy test did not involve any complex rotation, all the items were of Portuguese origin and so did not need to be translated and the scaling involved did not use the complex IRT models. Portugal therefore offered a unique opportunity to examine measurement in a Southern European context and to test a simple measurement tool against the complex IALS technique. To do this it is necessary to establish a link between the two tests. Initial designs considered had involved rotation of the IALS and PALS blocks through a sample of respondents from the 1994 PALS survey. Based on the PALS distribution of literacy skills a follow-up of the 1994 PALS sample looked unlikely to yield sufficient data using the IALS measure to allow the test to be scaled for Portugal even if the entire sample from 1994 was followed up. At least 1,200 cases of reasonably complete booklets were needed and so an alternative strategy had to be found. Having considered a number of possibilities it was decided that the only way of achieving sufficient cases to support scaling was if IALS was carried out in Portugal on a new sample alongside a follow-up of PALS. The PALS component would provide an indication of how things might have changed in the inervening period so the linking of IALS/PALS would therefore be based around the distribution, albeit out of date.

The Portuguese IALS sample was carried out as a follow–up to the LFS. In order to maximise the volume of assessment data the sample underrepresented the lower end of the educational distribution and overrepresented those at the middle and upper education levels in the ratios 10:45:45. Because of the change in design in Portugal a small pilot had to be carried out to test the psychometric characteristics of the IALS test. A pilot of 300 was carried out in May 1998 to test the translation of the assessment and as a dress rehearsal for the main stage. The pilot survey indicated that many respondents in Portugal were quitting the survey before completing much of the assessment. In the pilot the background questionnaire included both the core mandatory questions and all the optional questions. Following the poor data yield from the pilot survey it was decided necessary to reduce respondent burden by shortening the background questionnaire to those questions essential for scaling so that a greater proportion of the available time would be devoted to the assessment booklet.

1.6.4.6 Scoring

One issue that had been identified in the report by Blum and Guérin-Pace[18] as potentially indicative of motivation was the phenomenon of respondents striking through the assessment questions or stimulus. The IALS scoring did not distinguish between an incorrect answer and a marking such as a question mark or cross beside a question on the booklet. The scoring rules are that such answers are marked as incorrect. Omit answers where the respondent has not answered or marked the question in any way, are treated differently in the scaling model, either as a 'not reached' item or as an 'incorrect' response depending on the pattern of those omit scores the answers. For the follow-up survey it was felt useful to capture the distinction between these two outcomes when scoring the booklets. The scoring codes for the retest were expanded to distinquish between 'real wrong answers' where the respondent gave an answer but answered it incorrectly and 'crossed out' questions.

Each country also scored a proportion of booklets from the original survey using the extended coding frame to check for consistency in scoring between the original IALS and the follow-up survey.

1.7 Structure of this report

This report considers each strand of the project in turn. The main elements of the project are intended to stand alone as some may be of more general interest and relevance outside the context of IALS. The first chapters consider the IALS methodology in the context of more general methodological issues of large-scale assessment and international survey attempts (Chapters 2 to 5). Chapters 6 and 7 present the analyses carried out by those involved in the secondary analysis of the IALS data. Chapters 8 and 9 document the process of redefining and developing the follow-up survey and Chapters 10 to 13 report on the reinterview element of the project. The final chapter draws together the main themes of the report and recommendations for future similar research in the European context.

The data from the project provides a rich and valuable source for better understanding the dynamics of survey research. It has only been possible to develop the main themes of interest in the context of key issues being studied in this report, however, it is hoped that the data will be more fully and widely explored through further secondary analysis.

1.8 Organisation and management of the project

The project was managed by Social Survey Division (SSD) of the Office for National Statistics (ONS) in London. SSD had carried out the British IALS in 1996[19] and had previously responded to an invitation to tender issued by the European Commission in relation to the development and co-ordination of the second IALS (SIALS). The competition in response to that invitation to tender was not pursued as concerns started to be raised about the comparability and quality of the IALS data.

This current project was the subject of a separate invitation to tender in September 1996. ONS sought to develop a proposal to address the aims and objectives of the study and to involve relevant partners and experts. The proposal was accepted and a contract awarded in July 1997. As lead contractor ONS were responsible for executing the project within the

---

[18] See 16

[19] Carey S, Low S and Hansbro J. *Adult Literacy in Britain.* London: TSO 1997.

timetable and budget and for ensuring the appropriateness of the design to meet the study objectives.

Although the project was managed and co-ordinated by ONS a large number of experts and organisations were involved across many countries. Two project groups were established, an 'Expert group' to take forward the IALS review, the secondary analysis and the survey practice review. A second group, consisting of project teams from each of the participating countries, was established to develop and carry out the qualitative research and the follow-up survey. On issues of design of the study both the international group of project managers and the expert group participated in the decision making process.

The work was managed by a series of meetings convened at appropriate points in the work programme. Work was progressed between meetings by the project teams and experts in the different countries. On the qualitative research and the follow-up survey project there was much day to day contact with the teams in the other countries with the ONS retest project manager acting as the fulcrum for that communication. The development of the instruments, protocols and general co-ordination was lead by ONS with input from the project teams in the other countries.

The timetable for the entire project was challenging and as in many other similar initiatives was less collaborative than had originally been envisaged with more of the responsibility assumed by the ONS central team for pracitcal reasons.

The expert group functioned in a very different way, the meetings were scheduled at intervals to allow discussion and review of the work undertaken so far. Most of the work of the experts was carried out independently or on a bi-lateral co-operative basis, for example, the compilation of the review of survey practice was co-ordinated and collated by one member but required the input of several other members of the team.

1.9 Staffing and partners

The project involved the co-operation and contribution of a large number of people. The following individuals/organisations were involved in the project in no particular order.

Expert Group:

Alain Blum	Institut National d'Etudes Demographiques, Paris
France Guérin-Pace	Institut National d'Etudes Demographiques, Paris
Patrick Heady	Methods and Quality Division, ONS, London
Wim de Heer	Statistics Netherlands
Lars Lyberg	Statistics Sweden
Harvey Goldstein	Institute of Education, London

Research Teams:

Great Britain

Baljit Gill	Social Survey Division, ONS
Ann Bridgwood	Social Survey Division, ONS
Michaela Pink	Social Survey Division, ONS
Dipika Ray	Social Survey Division, ONS

France

Agnès Cousin	Institut de Sondages Lavialle, Paris
Jean-Pierre Lacaille	Institut de Sondages Lavialle, Paris
Monique Laouenan	Institut de Sondages Lavialle, Paris

Portugal

João Sebastião	Centro de Investigação e Estudos de Sociologia, Lisbon
Patricia Ávila	Centro de Investigação e Estudos de Sociologia, Lisbon
António Firmino daCosta	Centro de Investigação e Estudos de Sociologia, Lisbon
Maria do Carmen Gomez	Centro de Investigação e Estudos de Sociologia, Lisbon
Daniel Santos	Institut National Estatistica, Lisbon
Maria-José Costa	Institut National Estatistica, Lisbon
Victor Garcia	Institut National Estatistica, Lisbon

Sweden

Mats Myrberg	University of Linkoping
Åsa Ericsson	University of Linkoping
Michael Söderström,	TEMO, Stockholm

Project Consultants and Advisors:

Scott Murray, Statistics Canada, Ottawa, Canada
Nancy Darcovitch, Statistics Canada, Ottawa, Canada
Irwin Kirsch, Educational Testing Service, Princeton, U.S.A
Kentaro Yamamoto, Educational Testing Service, Princeton, U.S.A
Prof. Albert Beaton, Boston College, U.S.A.

Project team: Social Survey Division, Office for National Statistics, London

Siobhán Carey
Ann Bridgwood
Baljit Gill
Sampson Low
Sharon Beishon
Linda Mortimer
Margaret Thomas
Jil Matheson

PART A

A: Review of survey and measurement procedures

Over the past 30 years there have been a number of large scale assessments carried out involving an ever growing number of countries. Many of these assessments have been carried out under two frameworks, those of the International Association for the Evaluation of Educational Achievement (IEA) and the International Assessment of Educational Progress (IAEP) (fashioned on the US National Assessment of Educational Progress (NAEP)). Most large scale assessments, particularly the international assessments, were restricted to student populations. The International Adult Literacy Survey (IALS) however brought together techniques from two distinct tradtions, that of educational assessment and that of household surveys to bring assessment out of the classroom and into people's homes. The introduction of measurement techniques that heretofore had been associated almost exclusively with school based surveys for many survey researchers brought about a new set of problems in how to interpret the results. The following chapters are concerned with the measurement problems associated with measuring literacy in a household survey context. There are two main areas to be addressed, the survey methodology and how to ensure it is of high quality and the issues surrounding educational measurement methods and techniques and their application in an international household survey context.

A.I Measurement in a survey context

Regardless of the analysis tools employed there are other factors which must be got right first since even the most sophisticated analysis tools can not compensate for poor quality data. International surveys are in their infancy and opportunities exist to continually improve their design and execution. In this section of the report the survey execution in IALS is reviewed by Lars Lyberg from Statistics Sweden (Chapter 2). Chapter 5 on Survey practices in European countries by Wim de Heer from Statistics Netherlands has identified a number of areas where attention must be made to minimise variation between countries in how the survey is implemented and sets out the basic design parameters that need to be met for future surveys of this type.

A.II Assessment techniques

The prevailing assessment methodology used in international large scale assessment is Item Response Theory or Item Response Models. These were developed in the US and are widely accepted in the US as the optimum assessment summarisation technique. All the large scale assessments in the US use this technique and it has been used in the more recent international assessments including IALS.

Table A.1 summaries the most important international assessments that have been or are currently being carried out. The taste for such assessments is unlikely to diminish, indeed, the demand for data which will support international comparisons is growing in many spheres.

The predominance of IRT models in educational assessment and their adoption for IALS does not mean that they are universally accepted. Among European countries in particular the suitability and acceptability of IRT models for assessment has been widely debated. In agreeing to participate in IALS European countries were often circumspect in the dependence of the assessment on IRT models, although this was probably more behind the scenes than a public debate, a debate which seems not to have happened in some other countries. In many European countries there was a substantial constituency who were less than enthusiastic about the methodology proposed while in other countries there was little or no debate on the acceptability of the methodology. Given that for many countries there was little opportunity to influence the development or analysis the debate was whether to participate or not. Agreeing to participate in the study meant accepting the methodology as it stood.

In this project we sought to represent both viewpoints. Chapter 3 The Importance of Item Reponse Theory (IRT) for Large-Scale Assessment is by Prof. Albert Beaton of Boston College who was project director for TIMSS and Chapter 4 IALS – A Commentary on the scaling and data analysis is contributed by Prof. Harvey Goldstein of the Institute of Education in London who has published widely his critiques of large scale assessments.

A.III Future proposals

New international surveys involving assessment are already under development. The Programme for International Student Assessment (PISA) is being carried out in some 32 countries worldwide, with the mainstage collection scheduled for Sping 2000. Like previous assessments it seeks to produce internationally comparable indicators of student achievement in reading, mathematics and science literacy. Again, as with previous studies PISA will use Item Response Theory models (IRT) as the method of summation for analysis. Proposals also exist for an International Life Skills Survey (ILSS) which is similar to IALS but which includes additional skills. The issue of the validity and acceptability of IRT as the sole measurement protocol for such assessment is therefore very pertinent in view of the continuing demand for international comparisons.

Table A.1 **International assessments**

Year	Survey	Population	Content	Commissioning organisation
1960		13 year olds in 12 countries	Mathematics, science reading, geography, non verbal reasoning	IEA
1964	First International Mathematics Study (FIMS)	13 year olds in 12 countries and students in pre university year	Mathematics	IEA
1970-72	First International Science Study (FISS)	10 and 14 year olds and students in pre university year in 19 countries	Science (plus other subjects)	IEA
1980-82		10 to 14 year olds in 10 countries	Classroom environment (mathematics, science and history)	IEA
1982-83	Second International Mathematics Study (SIMS)	13 year olds in 20 countries	Mathematics	IEA
1984	Second International Science Study (SISS)	10 and 14 year olds and pre university year in 24 countries	Science	IEA
1984-85		10 and 14 to 16 year olds and pre university year in 14 countries	Written composition	IEA
1988	First International Assessment of Science (IAEPS 1) and Mathematics (IAEPS 1)	13 year olds in 6 countries	Mathematics and Science	IAEP
1988-92				Computers
1988-95		4 year olds in 14 countries		Pre-primary
1990	Assessment of Science (IAEPS 2) and Mathematics (IAEPS 2)	9 and 13 year olds in 20 countries	Mathematics and Science	IAEP
1991		9 and 14 year olds in 31 countries	Reading	
1993-94	Thirds International Mathematics and Science Survey (TIMSS)	9 and 13 year olds in 41 countries plus last year pre university	Mathematics and Science	TIMSS
1994-98	International Adult Literacy Survey (IALS)	Adults aged 16-65 in private households in 13 countries	Literacy	Co-ordinated by Statistics Canada
1999	TIMSS repeat	13 and 14 year olds	Mathematics and Science	IEA
2000	Programme for Indicators of Student Achivement (PISA)	15 year olds in 31 countries	Reading, Mathematics and Science	OECD

2. Review of IALS – a commentary on the technical report

Lars Lyberg, Statistics Sweden

Lars Lyberg is Head of the Research and Development Department of Statistics Sweden and has served as President of the International Association of Survey Statisticians. He has a special interest in international statistics and on survey quality in particular. He has published widely on the problems of non-sampling errors in surveys. He is Chief Editor of the Journal of Official Statistics.

2.1 Aims

This review will assess the Technical Report[1] on the First International Adult Literacy Survey[2] conducted in 1994 (IALS) and provide interpretation on the value of the data in terms of reliability and comparability, particularly as it applies in a European context. More specifically, the IALS design and procedures are discussed and advice is provided as how to improve these in future adult literacy surveys. In an accompanying review a commentary on the scaling and data analysis is provided[3]. It is important to emphasize that suggestions provided should be in the spirit of continuous improvement. These kinds of multi-national surveys are still in their infancy. They have not been around long enough. Best practices have not yet been developed.

The first IALS was conducted in 1994. Participating countries included Canada the U.S.A., Germany, The Netherlands, Switzerland (German- and French-speaking parts), Poland, Sweden, France and Ireland. A pilot study was conducted in 1993. Most of the 1994 IALS countries participated in that pilot study, although some, such as Sweden, did not carry out a pilot. The 1995 survey has been succeeded by new IALS rounds with new countries participating. In 1996 the U.K., Australia, New Zealand, and Belgium (Flemish only) took part. In 1998 there was a new round with Finland, Norway, Switzerland (the Italian-speaking part), Denmark, Slovenia, Czech Republic, Hungary, and Chile. As will be argued later on it is imperative that these surveys are of a high quality.

2.2 Earlier evaluation attempts

In one of the countries that participated in the first IALS in 1994 concerns were raised regarding the international comparability of the survey data. It was therefore decided that the IALS methodology should be subjected to an external evaluation. This evaluation was conducted by three researchers (Jean-Michel Rempp, Graham Kalton, and the present author) who had not been involved in the conduct of the 1994 IALS. The report of this evaluation group is included in the Technical Report[4] which itself consists of specially commissioned chapters covering various technical issues.

The main findings of the evaluation were:

1. Considerable efforts were made to standardize the measurement process and it is concluded that the 'psychometric validity' of the survey was established. (The evaluation

---

[1] *Adult Literacy in OECD Countries Technical Report on the First International Adult Literacy Survey.* National Center for Education Statistics: Washington (1998) .

[2] Literacy, Economy and Society: Results of the first International Adult Literacy Survey. OECD and Statistics Canada (1995). *Literacy Skills for the Knowledge Society: Further results from the International Adult Literacy Survey.* OECD and Human Resources Development Canada. (1997).

[3] see Goldstein H. *IALS – A commentary on the scaing and data analysis*, Chapter 4 in this report

[4] Appendix A in the Technical Report, see 1 above.

group's expertise was in survey design and survey errors rather than psychometric issues and our view was later challenged by Professor Harvey Goldstein which led to the report mentioned above.)

2. Regarding other aspects of the survey methodology used, attempts at standardization were not successful. Methodology guidance was indeed provided by IALS coordinators, but adherence to these guidelines was not enforced. Participating countries were given too much freedom to deviate from suggested procedures.

3. Reducing and adjusting for non-response were especially problematic areas. Non-response rates are high and reduction and adjustment procedures differ too much between countries. Also sample design and execution seem more problematic than other parts of IALS.

4. National comparisons should focus on correlates of literacy rather than overall literacy levels, given the variation in procedures used across countries.

The evaluation, which was brief due to time constraints, ended with some recommendations:

- First, some additional studies regarding data quality were suggested including nonrespondent profiles, comparisons of survey estimates to benchmark data, and effects of alternative weighting schemes.
- Second, for future rounds of IALS current best practices need to be established and their implementation carefully monitored.
- Third, the national surveys should be conducted by organizations with strong track records in all aspects of survey research.

2.3 The Technical Report

When studying the Technical Report it is quite evident that the conclusions and recommendations provided in the early evaluation report still hold with the exception of Conclusion no. 1 where an in-depth treatment is provided by Harvey Goldstein. Some new concerns are raised since the Technical Report contains some material that was not available when the early evaluation took place.

It should be pointed out that multi-national surveys are important instruments for advancing the field of social and other sciences. The IALS is a very important survey and is probably at least as good as other similar studies.

Although it is recommended that standardization of practices should be an important feature in future rounds, it is not realistic to believe that the survey could be conducted in exactly the same fashion in all participating countries. The cultures of survey practice across countries differ a lot. For instance, access to methodologists, population registers and experienced survey organizations varies across nations. Also, the level of funding varies across nations which limits the possibilities to adhere to some suggested practices. The important thing is to try to avoid any *unnecessary* variation in survey procedures across nations in these types of multi-national surveys. Despite such ambitions necessary and unnecessary variation will still occur. It is therefore important that procedures used are documented so that their likely effect on the comparability of estimates can be built into the reporting process. This implies, of course, the launching of a methodological program to understand what the likely effects of variation are.

Additional analyses of IALS data and analyses of survey research capability in European countries are needed. Consequently, such efforts have started within the current project, where this review of the Technical Report is just one part.

2.4 Observations based on the Technical Report

2.4.1 General

Adult literacy is crucial to a nation's economic strength and social cohesion and there is a growing interest among governments to understand the level and distribution of literacy among their adult populations. The European Union ought to be particularly interested in studying adult literacy since inadequate levels of literacy across countries could have negative impacts on the rate of progress for the EU as an entity. Therefore it is also important to establish that measurements of adult literacy should be of high quality.

International comparisons are difficult to make. Several factors contribute to this difficulty, for instance the meaning of equivalence of survey questions and test items, cultural bias, translation, and measurement errors. Also international comparisons, especially in areas like literacy, tend to have an impact on country-specific policy decisions and in an EU context even decisions that could affect several countries. Furthermore it is quite clear that in these kinds of surveys national pride is at stake. Comparisons between countries might generate indignation and agitation. Thus, comparisons should at least be based on measurements and analyses based on sound methodology.

We can conclude that the design, execution, and analysis of multi-national surveys present severe challenges. Uniformity along these dimensions across countries is very hard to achieve in practice, but it is a state to strive for. Product quality, in terms of reliable and valid estimates for each country, is best achieved through good process quality, i.e., by using known dependable methods, preferably the best practices available. Product variation as a result of some countries using substandard methods is a very unnecessary source of variation. This does not mean that all countries should necessarily use the same methods for each survey operation. It means that all problems associated with the various survey operations should be addressed using best practices suited to each country's needs[5] When developing the design of the IALS it is obvious that most resources went to assessment and psychometric aspects of the design and less to other survey operations. This was probably not an efficient allocation for the IALS but is understandable in view of the concerns over the transferability of the testing instruments across languages and cultures.

It seems as if the collaborative procedures in developing the measurement instruments were efficient with participation from all countries in a team work fashion. Similar procedures should be used for other design aspects when it comes to future rounds. It is especially important that statisticians be represented on those teams as well as subject experts and survey practitioners.

The amount of effort required to edit and score the data files was underestimated, resulting in late delivery of clean data files.

The survey coordinators stipulated a fixed number of completed cases to save appropriate levels of analysis. Such a stipulation implies oversampling and there is a risk that non-response follow-up efforts are played down by participating countries. Despite the stipulation the number of completed cases varied between 2,000 and 4,600. Modified guidelines for achieving sufficient numbers of respondents are called for.

---

[5] Lyberg, L., Biemer, P., Collins, M., DeLeeuw, E., Dippo, C., Schwarz, N., and Trewin, D. (eds.) *Survey Measurement and Process Quality*. Wiley. (1997).

The background questionnaire provides information that can be used to connect literacy with other variables. The background questionnaire should be designed so that questions have the same "meaning" in different countries. The background questionnaire used in the IALS was very North American in its orientation. It seems as if there was no real attempt to develop individual country questionnaires that conveyed this same "meaning." Depending on who was involved in the survey in different countries and the countries' varying mix of expertise, National Project Managers felt more or less able to argue for country-specific changes in the questionnaire. As a result some countries felt compelled to include questions that were almost meaningless in their countries, e.g., a question on type of secondary education course followed. This could certainly harm the credibility of the survey and/or the organization conducting the survey to the sample units (respondents and nonrespondents) in those countries.

There were also problems associated with the background questionnaire per se. For instance, the questions on training were not sufficiently focused and generated a considerable respondent burden. Also questions on parental education are probably problematic. Respondents had difficulties distinguishing between different levels of education; often they simply did not know the answer. Some of the scales used could be improved. All these concerns should be addressed by an improved cognitive test procedure of the questionnaire. This procedure is likely to be extensive considering the problems associated with multi-language questionnaires.

2.5 Sample design

The design specifications stated that each participating country should use a high quality representative sample of individuals. "High quality" and "representative" should imply probability sampling, i.e., sample selection probabilities should be known and every member of the target population should have a non-zero probability of being included in the sample.

Evidently probability sampling was not explicitly stipulated by the IALS coordinators, rather it was highly recommended. It should be pointed out that quota sampling was described in the sampling guidelines as one potential method albeit with proper cautions included. Describing a sampling method that does not generate probability samples is perhaps an unfortunate move, since that could be interpreted as an OK to use such methods. Quota sampling was not used by any country but three countries used sampling methods that had problematic features such as random routes and replacements resulting in non-probability samples. Each country had to submit a sampling plan ahead of time. All sampling plans were eventually approved by the coordinators, but it is not clear whether these plans contained any "non-probability" features or if these were included later on.

The sampling plans are difficult to assess due to lack of detail and lack of information on the quality of master samples, replacement procedures, and non-response treatment. The technical report states that non-probability sampling might produce good results. This is indeed true, but when is that the case? It is unfortunate that the report tries to make a case for non-probability samples when probability sampling removes the need for such arguing. It is also unfortunate that a large number of interviews seems more important than random sampling and a proper non-response follow-up.

There is little reason to dwell upon the details of the sampling plans already used when it comes to recommendations for future rounds. The basic recommendation must be that future rounds should use strict probability sampling in all sampling stages. If nothing else, survey results do not have to be defended with nonscientific arguments.

2.6 Coverage

Coverage rates vary between 89 and 99%. It is not always clear how the sampling frames were constructed. The intended coverage of the surveys generally conforms well to the design specifications. The actual coverage is generally lower than the intended coverage due to deficiencies in the frame construction processes and the resulting frame per se. There are indeed coverage problems in some countries and for some population segments. As already pointed out, comparisons should be made between survey estimates and benchmark estimates. Such comparisons should be part of future IALS designs. Also frame construction processes should be visualized in all national survey plans, preferably in the form of checklists.

2.7 Survey response and weighting

The design specifications stated that the overall non-response rate should be less than 20%. This requirement also needed to be satisfied for all important strata. This is a very strong requirement but it was not associated with any guidelines as how to achieve this low level of non-response. Typically, decent non-response rates can only be achieved by administering a battery of measures like call-backs, refusal conversion, tracking respondents, incentives, interviewer training, advance letters, information material, etc. Here it is essential that future IALS coordinators provide guidance on how to perform non-response rate reduction. Such a plan would have to differ between countries depending on culture and general conditions for survey work. Common to all plans would be the multi-measure aspect.

No country met the non-response requirements. As a matter of fact, most fell well short of them since non-response rates varied between 25 and 55%. Interviewers were instructed to make call-backs but it is not clear how these were to be administered. Important considerations when developing call-back procedures include number of attempts, distribution of attempts over time, kind of refusal conversion and whether different interviewers should be used at different contact attempts. Apart from call-backs only incentives are mentioned as potential measures for non-response reduction. Countries were asked not to use incentives (two did anyway) and when it came to call-backs, the number of contact attempts actually made varied between three and ten with no data on how successful the attempts had been. Very little information is provided on how countries tried to secure cooperation.

This part of the design is very weak. Future rounds of IALS would have to require each country to work on non-response reduction according to the kind of plan outlined above. Also, a uniform definition of non-response should be applied across nations. In the current study it is not possible to confidently compare non-response rates across countries because definitions of non-response rates may differ between countries.

Differences in non-response rates between countries is a result of national differences (survey climate, general attitudes toward surveys, the sensitivity of the literacy topic, etc.) and organizational differences (fieldwork strategies, interviewer training, methodology used, etc.). We strongly believe that the latter are most important in IALS. Organizational differences are easier to decrease through standardization while national differences tend to remain over time. However one factor associated with how the survey is perceived by the public is sponsor visibility. It would be good if all countries stressed the importance of getting literacy data and the main sponsors in each country could assume responsibility to do so.

It is essential that future literacy studies enforce standardized current best methods to deal with non-response reduction. Only a well-trained field-work organization with experienced interviewers and supervisors can ensure low non-response rates in complex surveys like IALS. The high non-response rates in the 1994 IALS are indeed disturbing. At the same time there are reasons to be optimistic. If the methods for gaining participation which were used in the specific non-response study had also been used in the regular IALS, could non-response rates have been reduced by the corresponding amount?

Weighting of responding sample units is performed to compensate for unequal selection probabilities, for non-response, and for noncoverage. The countries had varying ambitions in carrying out the weighting task. All countries benchmarked to at least one of the variables age, employment, and education. It is particularly important that the base weights be adjusted as effectively as possible to compensate for non-response and noncoverage. More attention should be given to this issue in future rounds. Benchmarking, weight trimming, and post-stratification should be part of a more standardized framework for future weightings. It should be emphasized that this part of the design is not easy to standardize since external data source quality varies across countries. Even if countries submit a plan for weighting and grossing that is approved by the IALS coordinators the execution of such a plan needs close supervision, since the weighting task is technically complex and should be handled by experienced survey statisticians.

Non-response weighting needs special attention. The technical report discusses three studies on the magnitude of non-response bias in Canada, the U.S., and Sweden. Results indicate that the bias might be small in the Canadian and Swedish IALS, while the U.S. study is more careful when it comes to dismissing bias remaining after weighting. Typically, the non-response models adopted assume comparable literacy skills for respondents and nonrespondents within adjustment groups. It is not out of the question, though, that competing non-response models could yield substantially different results.

As pointed out in the technical report the non-response analysis conducted for the IALS was not as extensive or as definite as desired. Future studies should build in collection of data on nonrespondents in the design and competing non-response adjustment schemes should be administered. This should be done in every participating country.

Item non-response is a special problem. It is known, according to the technical report, that less able respondents are more likely than able respondents to leave cognitive items unattended. In other types of surveys item non-response is usually caused by some questions being sensitive, that questions are missed by the respondent or the interviewer due to unclear skip instructions or that the respondent for some reason cannot provide an answer. Only the last cause is relevant in literacy surveys unless we are talking about the background questionnaire. In IALS omitted items were scored as wrong depending on their location and sequence. This decision model should be examined carefully in future IALS. Theoretically a respondent has an opportunity to examine and answer all items positioned before an item with a valid response. The lack of answers could then be interpreted as if the respondent had been unable to answer corresponding items. That might not necessarily be the case. The respondent burden, fatigue or lack of motivation could result in respondents *not* examining items to an extent that allows informed decisions about answering items.

Common measures to deal with item non-response include making questionnaires user-friendly with easy skip patterns, being careful about including and positioning sensitive questions, avoid burdening questions, using response alternatives that respondents can identify with, and imputation. These measures apply to the background questionnaire and they are strengthened by the interview mode that is used to administer it. When it comes to the assessment items very little of this applies. Instead other factors are important, especially the need to boost motivation or commitment among respondents. Only cognitive studies of the item examination and answering process can shed some light on issues that affect motivation for different respondent groups and across countries. Such studies include qualitative studies, think-aloud protocols and focus groups. To my knowledge very few, if any, such studies have been conducted in connection with the IALS.

2.8 Data collection and processing

Although design specifications regarding data collection and data processing were provided there was a fair degree of variation in the procedures used in different countries. Variation is present in type of interviewer training, interviewer experience, average number of cases per interviewer, survey organization experience, control of field work, use of incentives, measures for reducing non-response rates, non-response coding, presentation of the study to sample persons, the administering of the booklet task (both exercise and main study), and respondent burden.

For instance, the average number of interviews per interviewer varied between 6 and 30 which means that the correlated response variance component could vary between countries. Of course, there is also variation around these averages within countries. The amount of interviewer training varied between no special training to two days. Some countries allowed respondents to use pocket calculators, others did not. In some countries interviewers were paid less for non-response cases which hardly encourages non-response follow-up efforts. Some countries gave feedback to the interviewers, others did not. A couple of countries did not present the IALS in the way prescribed.

It is difficult to imagine the effects of all this variation. One single example is that differences in data collection procedures result in different imputation proportions across countries. The obvious way to avoid speculation is to enforce a certain standardization and data collection and data processing is probably the design area where such standardization is most easily applied and monitored. The instructions necessary could be provided in the form of checklists.

The background questionnaire seems well developed. However, there are areas that could be improved. A couple of questions have an awkward wording and scales are sometimes difficult to use. A few questions could benefit from a partitioning into one initial screening question and another as a result of the screening question. Again standard cognitive test procedures are appropriate. One problem remains, however. It is not clear whether tests were administered to make the background questionnaire comparable across countries in the same or similar way as the booklet items were. Some problems with the background questionnaire have been observed (some countries collected more data than prescribed by the study design) but the basic one, whether questions convey the same meaning across countries, needs more attention. Within the European context more effort should be made to develop questionnaires that draw on existing work on harmonisation.

The procedure used in IALS for ensuring the quality of the translation is unclear. The technical report says that countries were instructed to modify each item by translating the English text to their own language and rules were provided on the item modification process. The translated items were then subject to a review to check that the conceptual associations in the text/questions were preserved after translation. No requirement was made for translation of the items back and forth to be undertaken and it is not clear if any country did do back translation.

Secondary analyses have shown that also the translation of booklet items might be problematic. As pointed out in the technical report the item development process in an international context needs to be more rigorously studied. What are the real issues in developing approximately equivalent texts and tasks across countries?[6]

2.8.1 Coding and Scoring

Each country was responsible for coding industry, occupation, and education to ISIC, ISOC, and ISCED standards at fine levels. Outgoing quality levels were set: at most 5% error rate

[6] Harkness, J. (ed.). *Cross-Cultural Survey Equivalence.* ZUMA Nachrichten, no.3. (1998).

was allowed on the one digit level. For industry and occupation this is a very strong quality requirement. Evaluation studies of I&O manual coding in the U.S., Canadian, and Swedish censuses show that this is very difficult to achieve even with specially trained staff. Some of the data collection agencies used in the IALS do not have a lot of experience coding these variables. Very little information is provided regarding the coding and any quality control procedures associated with it. The report statement that coding errors probably are random cannot be justified.

Future IALS must provide more guidance and monitoring when it comes to complex coding. Quality control procedures include extensive training and two-way independent verification with adjudication. The IALS procedures show no appreciation of known coding error structures verified by other studies.

Compared to coding it should be relatively easy to enforce 100% verification of background questionnaire data entry. Current variation ranges from no verification to 100% verification, though.

The technical report recommends that countries should document key study design features and submit those to the coordinators ahead of time and that there should be an operations audit before the main study begins. This recommendation is probably too weak. Instead, a main design should be established for this part of the IALS. Each country's deviations should be approved ahead of time, checklists developed for each country, and field checks performed on site by the coordinators. It should be noted, however, that this is a very special customer-client situation. Despite checklists, on-site supervision and support and other measures, there is a risk for non-compliance among participating survey organizations. First, it is important that organizations chosen to conduct the survey are reputable ones with lots of experience and methodological resources. That should reduce the risk for non-compliance since so much would be at stake for the organizations. Second, contracts with chosen organizations should include paragraphs on sanctions in case of serious non-compliance, for instance fee reductions that could be used for measuring the effects of them, or, in extreme cases, sanctions that could lead to a country being left out from the international comparisons.

2.8.2 Scoring

In addition to the coding, classification and data entry requirements of the background questionnaire, the assessment booklets had to be marked and the data captured. The IALS used entirely open-ended items which had to be scored according to a scoring guide. The scorers had to mark answers as correct, incorrect or omitted. Scoring rubrics should be applied in a consistent fashion within and between countries. In the 1995 IALS a group of survey managers and chief scorers clarified ambiguities not covered by the guidelines. Clarifications were incorporated in the final rubrics. A joint scoring hotline was established. Any scoring problems were resolved by the hotline group and conveyed to all national study managers. Each country undertook a 10% rescoring and countries agreed to exchange at least 300 randomly selected booklets with another country sharing the same language.

This is an ambitious quality control scheme but it raises some questions anyway. For instance, how was the statistical tolerance established for the rescoring operation? How were unreliable scorers identified? How were scoring difficulties identified in the first place? How were systematic scoring errors in countries really detected? How was the 3% difference limit decided?

Scoring is based on a scoring system and the persons performing the scoring task. Scoring variation can arise due to the system (common cause) or to the scorers (special cause). It seems as if these sources of variation are not distinguished. More emphasis should be put on the scoring system and its defects in future rounds of IALS scoring. Also there is a need to discuss whether the relatively simple scoring frame used in the IALS should be more detailed in future rounds. The quality issues associated with scoring of assessments are reviewed elsewhere in this report[7].

One issue that should be explicitly dealt with is confidentiality. Most countries have a Data Act or at least a set of rules when it comes to minimizing disclosure risks. These rules should be adhered to. Furthermore IALS designers might find it appropriate to establish specific rules or guidelines that go deeper than what is generally prescribed in a country. Since motivation can be a function of the degree of confidentiality promised, it is important that information about data protection is provided to the respondents at the outset.

2.9 Conclusions

Based on the contents of the technical report the following recommendations are made regarding future IALS rounds.

1. Future rounds should use strict probability sampling.
2. The frame construction process should be visualized in all national survey plans.
3. Each country should have a plan for gaining respondent cooperation. Typically, such a plan would contain a number of different approaches in order to achieve a decent response rate. Plans can differ between countries.
4. Future IALS coordinators need to assist countries in developing their non-response adjustment procedures.
5. Each country should submit a plan for weighting.
6. Based on the evaluation of survey practice and capability in European countries[8] main design features should be established. This will constitute a considerable effort.
7. IALS coordinators need to develop specifications of standardized methods for data collection, coding, and data entry. The coordinators should enforce the use of these methods.
8. National survey organizations should be experienced and have access to survey statisticians and well-trained interviewers. Statisticians should more often be involved in countries' contacts with IALS coordinators compared to 1994.
9. Guidelines regarding designs and survey processes should be in checklist form to avoid problems of interpretation.
10. It is essential that teamwork be established between coordinators and country representatives for all design aspects, not only the measurement part.
11. Countries should document procedures they use.
12. The background questionnaire and the booklet items should be improved by means of cognitive tests. The translation model used in 1994 needs to be examined carefully.

---

[7] See Chapter 11 of this report.

[8] see DeHeer W. *Survey practices in European countries*. Chapter 5 in this report

3. The Importance of Item Response Theory (IRT) for Large-Scale Assessments

Albert E. Beaton, Boston College

Albert Beaton is the International Study Director of the Third International Mathematics and Science Study (TIMSS) which was organized under the auspices of the International Association for the Evaluation of Educational Achievement (IEA), He is a Professor of Education at Boston College, Chestnut Hill, Mass., U.S.A.

3.1 Introduction

Educational testing and assessment have been developing dramatically over the past few years as tests and assessments have been called upon to address many demands that are complex and, sometimes, contradictory. For example, subject matter experts demand a very broad coverage of the topic being measured while school administrators insist that their students' learning time be interrupted as little as possible. Both the National Assessment of Educational Progress (NAEP) in the United States and the Third International Mathematics and Science Study (TIMSS) have had to develop complex assessment designs to address the many concerns of their constituents and potential critics, and these methods have been adapted and applied in adult literacy surveys. The many considerations in test or assessment construction have created a need for analytic methods that can extract the most important information from the resulting complex data sets. Item response theory (IRT[1]) has proven to be a very powerful tool for such national and international assessments.

The original ideas for IRT have been developed both in Europe and the United States. The basic concepts were first proposed at the University of Aberdeen by Furguson, Lawley, and Finney (see Goldstein and Wood, 1989, for more information) in the 1930s for use in bioassay studies. A complex "three parameter" model" was developed by the psychologist Lord (1952) and was used for analysis of tests in the United States. The Danish mathematician Rasch (1960) developed a simpler "one parameter" model that is now widely used as, for example, in TIMSS. The American mathematician Birnbaum (1968) extended Lord's work by developing a simpler, more manageable "three parameter" model for practical applications. Birnbaum's model is also widely used as, for example, in NAEP. As will be shown below, IRT development is continuing at a rapid pace in both the United States and Australia.

Much of the work in developing IRT has come from latent trait theory in psychology. The basic assumption is that individuals have latent traits that are not directly observable but are estimable, and that test items also have properties that are also estimable. The combination of the individuals' abilities and the test item properties produces the individual's item responses under an assumed mathematical model. It is assumed that nothing else--besides random error--affect the responses to items. From the responses of individuals to test items, the abilities of the individuals and the items' properties can be estimated. If the model and the assumptions are true, then the IRT analysis will produce useful estimates of the individual and item parameters as well as estimates of their errors.

IRT can also be looked at in a different way, without the psychological assumptions. IRT is one of many ways to summarize a set of data. Experience has shown that the basic data from an educational test tend to result in a triangular data format as shown in Figure 1, which is artificial data. The rows in the figure represent individuals who have taken the test and the columns represent test items. A real dataset would usually contain many more rows

[1] Some argue (e.g., Goldstein and Wood, 1989) that this psychometric technique would more properly be called Item Response Modeling; in this paper, the more common name will be used.

(individuals) and many more columns (items). A value of unity in a cell in the figure indicates that an individual gave a correct answer to an item and a zero represents an incorrect answer. To show the triangular format, the rows have been sorted by the number of items answered correctly; that is, the individuals with the most correct answers are at the top, and those with the fewest are at the bottom. Also, the columns are sorted so that the "easiest" items, those answered correctly by the most students, are on the left and the most difficult items are on the right. For simplicity here, we will assume that all items are scored right/wrong and that there are no items omitted and no items for which credit for partial answers was given.

Figure 3.1 Triangular Format of Testing Data

		Item																
		Easy Items													**Hard Items**			
		1	2	3	4	5	.....	21	22	23	24	25	....	46	47	48	49	50
Top Students	1)	1	1	1	1	1	...	1	1	1	1	1	...	1	1	1	0	1
	2)	1	1	1	1	1	...	1	1	1	1	1	...	1	1	1	1	0
	3)	1	1	1	1	1	...	1	1	1	1	1	...	1	1	1	1	0
	4)	1	1	1	1	1	...	1	1	1	1	1	...	1	1	0	1	1
	5)	1	1	1	1	1	...	1	1	1	1	1	...	1	1	0	1	0
											. . .							
Middle Students	1)	1	1	1	1	1	...	1	1	1	1	1	...	0	0	0	0	0
	2)	1	1	1	1	1	...	1	1	1	1	0	...	0	0	0	0	0
	3)	1	1	1	1	1	...	1	1	0	0	1	...	0	0	0	0	0
	4)	1	1	1	1	1	...	1	1	1	0	0	...	0	0	0	0	0
	5)	1	1	1	1	1	...	1	1	0	0	1	...	0	0	0	0	0
											. . .							
Bottom Students	1)	1	1	1	1	1	...	0	0	0	0	0	...	0	0	0	0	0
	2)	1	1	1	1	0	...	0	0	0	0	0	...	0	0	0	0	0
	3)	1	1	0	0	1	...	0	0	0	0	0	...	0	0	0	0	0
	4)	1	1	0	1	0	...	0	0	0	0	0	...	0	0	0	0	0
	5)	1	1	0	0	0	...	0	0	0	0	0	...	0	0	0	0	0

This triangular format makes basic sense. Some students know more about the subject matter that is tested and others know less. Finding out how much they know is why we test. Some items are more difficult for students than others, and this is well known. What the triangular format shows is that the high-scoring students get the easy items right and most of the more difficult items; the low scoring students tend to miss the easy items as well as the more difficult. It is seldom that a low-scoring student will get a very difficult item correct except by lucky guessing. This underlying order to the data collected from most tests is what makes summarization useful. With real data, the triangular format is approximate, not exact. The top scorers may miss different difficult items and the low scorers may get a few difficult items right correct, even if only by chance.

There are many ways to summarize such data. The simplest is the number of items answered correctly by each student, as has been done for many years. For many cases, this approach is sufficient but, as will be shown below, this sort of approach is not adequate for modern complex data designs. In simple testing programs, the results from number-right reporting will usually be only trivially different from the more complex IRT approaches.

It is important to recognize that any form of data summarization loses some information. To reduce the information about a student's responses to a large number of test items into a single number ignores the information about the pattern of responses to those items. This is why the triangular format is so important; it implies a regularity in the data called unidimensionality. Students who score highly on the test tend to have a higher probability of answering each and every item correctly than low scorers. Multidimensionality occurs when one group of students tends to answer one type of item correctly, but not the other items, and another group of students answers a different type correctly. In this case, the triangular format does not hold. A simple summarization, either by counting the number of correct items or by IRT, would miss important information about student performance. In such a case, it is appropriate to divide the data into separate types of items, so that each type follows the triangular format, and then analyze and report each item type separately. For example, if mathematics items do not follow the triangular format, geometry proficiency might be reported separately from algebra proficiency, if analysis of the responses so warrant.

IRT fits a mathematical model to the available data. The model expresses the probability of a student correctly answering an item given the student's ability and the properties of the item. There are several different mathematical models in use. The simplest IRT model is the Rasch model that uses only one parameter for each item, the item's difficulty. Thus, the Rasch model implies that the probability of correctly answering a particular item is solely a function of the student's ability and one parameter for that item, its difficulty. Another widely used model is called the three-parameter logistic (3PL) model that states that the probability of correctly answering an item is not only a function of the item's difficulty but also its ability to discriminate among examinees and the likelihood of answering the item correctly by chance. The discrimination parameter represents how sharply the item separates the examinees into those who can answer the item correctly and those who fail. The guessing parameter allows for the probability of a low-scoring student answering an item correctly by guessing. Using a mathematical model, IRT then fits the model to the data generating an ability estimate for each examinee and one or more parameters for each item, depending on the model.

In most practical applications, the choice of the IRT model makes little difference, but in some cases it may. This is true for most statistical models; for example, in many practical applications using the mean or median of a variable will make little differences, but in some cases it will make a substantial difference such as reversing the rank-order of subgroups. Thus, the basic fit of the model needs careful checking and IRT gives a number of ways to check the goodness of fit. Some things are obvious; the Rasch model does not account for guessing and thus does not fit well for multiple-choice tests in which there is substantial guessing. In general, the better the model fits, the better the summarization of the data. If the model does not fit well, then it is important to find out why: is the test multidimensional? are the items poorly written?

3.2 Use in Large-Scale Assessments

In the case of a single test given to all students under the same circumstances, the difference between IRT and number-right scoring is likely to be small, hardly worth the extra effort required by IRT. IRT, however, is still useful and gives helpful diagnostics to ascertain how a test is functioning.

As mentioned above, large-scale assessments have put severe pressures onto the testing process, and it is here where IRT is invaluable. Subject matter experts want broad coverage of the domain being tested and administrators want to give up as little of their students' time as possible. The result of these conflicting desiderata has been matrix sampling and, in particular, balanced incomplete block (BIB) spiraling (Messick, Beaton, and Lord, 1983). Under matrix sampling, since the coverage of the subject matter requires more student time than allowed, the subject matter is broken up into sections called blocks, and different blocks are placed in booklets and assigned to different students. Test booklets are assigned to students at random. The result is that the students in a sample take different tests. BIB spiraling breaks the item pool into smaller blocks and then rotates the blocks into booklets so that each item is paired with each other item in some booklet. BIB spiraling also assigns different tests to different students but assures that the correlation between each pair of items can be estimated.

The result of this accommodation of competing interests is a complex assessment design, a design that would not fare well if simple number-right scores were used. Since different students were assigned different test booklets that might have different numbers of items, a particular number-right score might have a different meaning depending on the booklet administered. Computing the proportion or percentage correct would not correct the problem if the booklets were not parallel in difficulty, a situation that is hard to create in the assessment context. The situation becomes even more problematic when the test is used to measure several subscales such as physics and chemistry in which case the number of items in a particular sub-area would be few. Formally equating the tests using traditional methods would be very difficult indeed. Fortunately, IRT takes this type of problem in stride and is able to produce reasonably comparable student scores even though the students have not all taken the same set of items.

Another problem of large-scale assessment has been addressed by innovations in IRT methodology. The problem is that policy-makers and others using test results want more information than simple overall mathematics scores, for example; they want to measure and understand differences in various parts of a subject area, such as algebra, geometry, and so forth. The simple approach would be to have separate tests for each sub-area or subscale, but such an approach would take more student time than is available, and so a general mathematics test must contain a wide variety of items. Given the BIB spiraling approach mentioned above, the result is that an individual student typically is assigned only a few items for a particular subscale with the result that the student's knowledge in that sub-area is poorly measured and subscale scores are unreliable.

The approach to this problem in NAEP was guided by an insight of Mislevy into the fact that individual scores were not needed for NAEP; in fact, individual scores could not be reported nor used in individual decision-making. NAEP was designed to estimate how large populations and sub-populations would perform on a test from a sample of students; accurate estimation of the performance of individual students was not important. Using this insight and the theory of missing data developed by Rubin (1987), Mislevy and his associates developed the concept of plausible values (Mislevy, Beaton, Kaplan, and Sheehan, 1992). Instead of producing an individual score for each student in a sample, this modification of IRT produces a number of "plausible values," to represent a student's performance. Usually, five such plausible values are drawn for each student. If a student's knowledge is reasonably well-measured by the test, then the plausible values will be close together; if the knowledge is poorly measured, then the plausible values may vary widely. Rubin's theory shows how these plausible values can be used to make consistent estimates of population distributions, which is the aim of NAEP and other assessments, such as TIMSS. As well as estimating the properties of population distributions, the method of plausible values also gives indicators of the accuracy of its estimates.

IRT has also helped TIMSS address the issue of whether an item means the same thing--is functioning in the same way--in different countries and different languages. If items are behaving in the same way, then their item characteristic curves--the relationships between responses to items and the estimates of student ability--should be the same for all countries; that is, the probability of answering a specific item correctly for a student with a certain level of knowledge should be the same no matter what country the student came from or the language of testing. It is important to do this without specifying that the students in all countries have the same level of knowledge since this would be throwing out the differences that TIMSS was meant to identify. IRT handles this question directly since the relationship between estimates of student knowledge and the probability of passing an item is explicit, and TIMSS was able to assure that the relationship was reasonably similar for the participating countries. TIMSS investigated the relationship in analyses of pre-test data as well as analyses of the final tests. In a few cases, the student responses for an item in an individual country were quite different from the rest of the world, and the difference could be explained by a typographical error in printing or a mis-translation; in such cases, the item was removed from the data from that particular country. The mechanisms of IRT made it easily possible to continue with analyses and international comparisons even though some countries were missing one or a few items.

Most of the early work in IRT has assumed that test items could be answered in a binary way, that is, as simply right or wrong. Subject-matter experts have insisted on including open-ended questions in addition to multiple-choice and on giving students partial credit for their responses if they were partially correct. Clearly, this insistence expands the possibilities for educational measurement. In NAEP and TIMSS, some open-ended items were assigned several points; for example, a three-point item would be assigned three points for a fully correct response, one or two points depending on how much of a correct response was given, and zero points for a completely wrong answer. Expanding the previous work by others (e.g., Samejima, 1969, Masters 1982), Muraki and Bock (1998) developed the Parscale program that allows such partial credit schemes to be incorporated into main-line IRT analyses. Adams (1997) adapted and modified this method for use in TIMSS.

Thus, the IRT method, including plausible values, has been fundamental in analyzing the complex data from large-scale assessments and addressing the competing, sometimes contradictory, assessment demands. Its main advantage is that it gives a general framework for organizing and understanding the testing process. In some cases, such as a national test in which all student are assigned the same test items, the advantages may not outweigh the costs, but in complex international studies it is hard to believe that any other method has comparable advantages.

3.3 Reporting

Reporting assessment results is a complex, never fully satisfying process. The public and policy-makers want general results, simple summarizations of the complex assessment process and, in particular, how various subgroups of the assessed population performed. Persons studying the details of the assessment--for knowledge about the curriculum, for example--want more detailed information about the subscales and, in many cases, the responses to individual items. Many different approaches have been taken, and none seems to answer all demands on assessment data. It is argued here that IRT scaling, along with the availability of the complete database, is the best available way to approach the problem.

First, let us look at publishing the statistics for all individual items. This has been tried and has failed. The early NAEP results were so published, and few, if any, were interested in the results. Each of the hundreds of items was presented along with the proportion of students answering the item correctly. In addition, the proportion answering the item correctly was given for each policy-interesting subgroup. Along with each proportion or other statistic was its standard error. Yes, a reader could find an occasional item where one group out-performed another but there was no big picture, no summary. And, most of the policy-makers who wanted to use the results had neither the time nor the background to pan the results for nuggets of wisdom. NAEP quickly moved to providing the average percentage-correct over groups of items for the various subgroups.

The IRT process results in a performance scale for each subject area, including various subscales. A scale is simply an arbitrary line on which student performance estimates--scores--can be placed. An easy way to form the line is to place the average score at zero and the standard deviation at unity, but this approach has a severe political problem: some, usually around half, of the students will have negative scores. Negative scores are difficult to explain to the public, especially if two or more grades are tested and all of the groups in the lowest grade have negative average scores. To avoid this problem, a different scale is set up to avoid negative scores. For NAEP, the scale runs from zero to 500, with few students scoring below 100 or above 400; for TIMSS, the scale runs from zero to 1,000, with few students scoring outside the 200 to 800 range. Thus, there are essentially no negative scores in either assessment.

There is an abstract interpretation of measurement scales that has not been widely used. Let us consider a hypothetical test of 1000 items where the difficulties of these items are spread evenly over the range of ability in the population being measured and a little beyond. The items in this test are selected so that they discriminate equally among students and guessing is impossible; that is, the items fit the assumptions of the Rasch model. Under these assumptions, the IRT scale scores for TIMSS are estimates of the number-right scores that the students would have received if they were administered this idealized TIMSS test. That is, the TIMSS scale score is an estimate of the number of items that a student would have answered correctly on a 1000 item hypothetical test. In addition to the estimate of the number-correct, IRT produces an estimate of the error in prediction from the fallible test that the student actually took.

Despite a rationale, measurement scales, like most scales, may be quite difficult to interpret directly, and yet can be used effectively. Temperature scales are also arbitrary, for example, the Celsius scale sets the value of zero as the freezing temperature of water and 100 at water's boiling point and then divides the interval between zero and 100 into 100 equal parts. With experience, we learn what degree on the Celsius scale corresponds to a comfortable room temperature, the temperature for a normal, healthy person, the temperature for an extreme fever, and other points that are relevant to our lives. We need to use measurement scales for a little while to get the feeling for what five or ten or a hundred points mean. Usually, a set of data will have a few hints as to "how big is big" on a particular scale; for example, in TIMSS the differences among countries at the eighth grade level can be compared to the growth over all countries between the seventh and eighth grades.

To help policy-makers and others understand what various points on the scale mean, NAEP has developed a system of scale anchoring (Beaton and Allen, 1992). The purpose of scale anchoring is to describe what a large majority of students at one point on the scale know and can do that most students at lower levels cannot. Scale points are selected so that they are reasonably distinct; for example, NAEP tries to anchor its scales at 200, 250, 300, and 350, about where most students perform. The NAEP item statistics are then reviewed and items are selected that characterize these scale points. Subject matter experts review the selected items to attempt to generalize from the particular items to classes of knowledge. At present, TIMSS is in the process of anchoring its mathematics and science tests.

Despite considerable effort, there appears to be no simple way to answer all of the needs of persons who wish to use the data from a large-scale assessment. TIMSS makes written reports, scale scores (plausible values), items, and item statistics available, but these do not answer all reasonable needs. In the end, making the basic data available, along with adequate documentation, allows any interested user to explore the data in any way he or she likes. For the skeptical, it allows the possibility of checking basic computations. It also allows anyone to try to fit different IRT or other models to the data to see if a different approach might change a data interpretation. It also gives the opportunity for anyone to explore hypotheses using the testing data and other data collected from questionnaires or other sources. It should be noted that, in making a database publicly available, the confidentiality commitments made to students or teachers must be honored.

3.4 Implementation

Implementation of IRT methodology to large-scale assessments is not simple but still quite possible. Although most of the recent developments have been in the United States and Australia, there is a substantial effort in Europe at present to explore and use IRT technology. As mentioned above, many of the original concepts were European--from Scotland and Denmark. IRT has recently bloomed in the Netherlands, and it has produced presidents of the Psychometric Society, the society that is the sounding board for new ideas and approaches. It seems to me that Europe has the interest and resources to introduce the IRT technology to European tests.

Fortunately, the developments in large-scale assessment have been compulsively and voluminously recorded. The IRT developments in NAEP have been thoroughly documented in a series of technical reports beginning with Beaton (1987) and being updated an improved regularly. Issues of the Journal of Educational Measurement (1992, vol. 29, no 2) and the Journal of Educational Statistics (1992, vol. 17, no. 2) were devoted to thorough coverage of the NAEP technology. TIMSS has also been thorough in its reporting of its methods through technical reports (e.g., Martin and Kelly, 1997) which are available on the Internet. There is also a substantial literature produced by researchers who have replicated and/or evaluated the IRT technology. Most, although not all, of the software for analysis of large-scale assessments is commercially available along with documentation.

Certainly, implementation of IRT is not trivial and will require considerable investment in intellectual resources and commitment. I would suggest starting with an existing data set (the International Adult Literacy Study (IALS), say, or the TIMSS data sets that are readily available) and attempting to work through the procedures before new data are collected. Variations on existing models could be explored. I am sure that outside expertise would be available on a teaching or consulting basis, if needed, to get such a project started or trouble-shoot various problems as they arise.

3.5 Conclusion

IRT is one way of handling complex data that has been used extensively and successfully in recent highly visible assessments. It gives a way of analyzing complex datasets in such a way as to present meaningful summaries to broad audiences, including the general public. The general audiences have accepted these summaries, seemingly without objection. The success of IRT is surely well worth copying.

And yet, IRT is not a magical system that works without thought or examination. Too often, a researcher seems to mistake an assumption for a natural law, that is, believes without evidence that the real world actually behaves in the way he or she assumes. IRT makes assumptions about the relationship between items and abilities that are reasonable and usually approximately true, as far as we can tell. But the IRT analyst must be ever alert to the possibility of exceptions that negate the model and be prepared to use other methods if necessary.

I believe that IRT is the best-known way to handle large-scale assessment date, but I do not doubt that it will be replaced in the next century with some better approach. We must always be looking for the better approach. Alternative methods such as non-linear factor analysis are being explored as a way to allow for multi-dimensional models, and these methods are promising, although to my knowledge they have not been used in large-scale assessments at this time. Perhaps these will be the better methods of the future, perhaps not.

It is important to remember that there are competing goals in any assessment. Results must be timely and comprehensible to the funders and to the general public, and yet there are many other stake-holders who want different and more detailed information from an assessment. Very complex and detailed reporting will not satisfy the legitimate needs of many policy-makers, although such analyses may contribute to our understanding of student performance. No publication can satisfy the needs of all. That there are different approaches that reflect different perspectives is normal and healthy. IRT has proven itself to be a practical and useful tool for answering many of the needs of its funders and the educational community.

References

Adams, R. J., M. L. Wu, and G. Macaskill (1997), Scaling Methodology and Procedures for the Mathematics and Science Scales; in Martin and Kelly, *TIMSS Technical Report, Volume II.* Chestnut Hill MA: Boston College.

Beaton, A.E. (Ed, 1987). *The TIMSS 1983-84 Technical Report (Report No: 15-TR-20).* Princeton NJ, Educational Testing Service

Beaton, A.E. and N. L. Allen (1992). Interpreting Scales Through Scale Anchoring. J. of Educ. Stat., Vol. 17(2).

Birnbaum, A. (1968) Some latent trait models. In F.M. Lord and M.R. Novick. Statistical theories of mental test scores. Reading, Mass.: Addison-Wesley.

Goldstein, Harvey and Robert Wood (1989). Five decades of Multiple Response Modeling. British J. Of Mathematical and Statistical Psychology, Vol. 42(2) pp. 139-167.

Martin, M. O. and D. L. Kelly, 1997. *TIMSS Technical Report, Volume II.* Chestnut Hill MA, Boston College.

Lord, F.M. (1952) A theory of Test Scores. *Psychometric Monograph No.7,* Psychometric Society.

Masters, G.N. (1982). A Rasch model for partial credit scoring. *Psychometrika, 47,* 149-174.

Messick, S.J., A.E. Beaton, and F.M. Lord (1983). *NAEP Reconsidered: A New Design for a New Era. (NAEP report 83-1).* Princeton NJ: Educational Testing Service.

Mislevy, R.J., A.E. Beaton, B. Kaplan, and K. Sheehan (1992). Estimating Population Characteristics from Sparse Matrix Samples of Item Responses. *J. of Educ. Meas.* 29(2) pp133-161.

Muraki, E. and Bock, R.D. (1998). *Parscale: Parameter scaling of rating data (Version 3.5).* [Computer program] Mooresville, IN: Scientific Software, Inc.

Rasch, G. (1960). *Probabilistic models for some intelligence and attainment tests.* Copenhagen: Danmark's Paedogogiske Institut. (Chicago,: U. of Chicago Press, 1980.)

Rubin, D.B. (1987) *Multiple imputation for nonresponse in surveys.* New York: John Wiley

Samajima, F. (1969). Estimation of latent trait ability using a response pattern of graded scores. *Psychometric Monograph Supplement No. 17.*

4. IALS - A commentary on the scaling and data analysis

Harvey Goldstein, Institute of Education, London

Professor Goldstein has been professor of Statistical Methods at the Institute of Education, University of London, since 1977. He was awarded the Royal Statistical Society's Guy medal in silver in 1998. He has published widely on the use of statistical modelling techniques in the construction and analysis of educational tests. He is probably most associated with the methodology of multilevel modelling and since 1986 has made a number of theoretical developments in this field and has written the major text on the subject. Other research interests include school effectiveness and class sizes on student achievement.

4.1 Introduction

The technical report of the International Adult Literacy Survey (IALS)[1] sets out the details of how the responses to the IALS questionnaire tasks were converted to numerical scores and subsequently analysed to provide country comparisons. In the following sections I examine the assumptions made during this process and provide a critical commentary.

4.2 Establishing psychometric validity

The authors of the Technical Report claim (p.21) to have established 'psychometric validity'. By this they appear to mean to following:

- Establishing that each of the three 'proficiencies' is unidimensional
- That verbal descriptions can be attached to particular scale scores
- That each proficiency scale can be assigned the same 'meaning' in each country.

The following sections deal with each of these issues. In particular it will be argued that the psychometric requirements imposed on IALS are too restrictive and are not sufficient to provide a secure basis for valid international comparisons. I also argue that one of the aims of surveys such as IALS is to discover *whether* literacy can indeed be taken to mean the same thing in each country; in other words the focus should be on searching for differences and attempting to understand them. The psychometric techniques used in IALS are designed to select only those elements which are common and that leads to a number of problems as discussed below.

4.3 Defining the domains of literacy

From the outset IALS considered literacy measurement in three 'domains'; Prose literacy, document literacy and quantitative literacy, the domains being based upon earlier US work. Scales were constructed and results are reported for each of these three 'measures'.

Three major US studies in the 1980s and 1990s were used to produce the three domains. This was done in each case (by ETS) using 'item response models' (IRMs) which are referred to in the report as 'item response theory' techniques. At this juncture I merely wish to point out that these studies were all carried out on the US population. Even if these studies had unequivocally established these three domains this would be no guarantee that they could be used with the same meanings for other populations. The use of IRMs is dealt with in a later section.

---

[1] *Adult Literacy in OECD Countries Technical Report on the First International Adult Literacy Survey.* National Center for Education Statistics: Washington 1998

For each domain different tasks are used. The analysis carried out by Rock[2] (Chapter 8) shows that there are high correlations (around 0.9) between the domain scores - each domain score being effectively the number of correct responses on the constituent items. The justification for the use of 3 scales rather than just one seems rather weak. Section 8.3 states that 'a strong general literacy factor was found in all 10 populations, (but) there was sufficient separation among the three literacy scales to justify reporting these scales separately'. No attempt is made in IALS properly to explore the dimensionality of the complete set of tasks. Rather, the three scales are treated quite separately, yet Heady in Chapter 7 discusses some of the reasons for expecting high correlations; such as the presence of exemplars, literality etc. The implication of this is that underneath the chosen domains there are further dimensions along which people differ. It may be the case, for example, that there are such dimensions which are common to all three domains and which are responsible for the observed high intercorrelations. In future work this is one area for research, using multidimensional item response models of sufficient complexity. The IRMs used in IALS are all unidimensional, i.e. allow no serious possibility for discovering an underlying dimensionality structure, other than by using global and non-specific 'goodness of fit' statistics.

In the next sections I discuss the consequence of relying upon unidimensionality. In the statistical appendix a precise definition of dimensionality is given and various kinds of IRM are compared.

4.4 Problems with unidimensionality

The upshot of the initial decision to use three separate domains is that these constrain the outcomes of the study, as follows.

Suppose that for a collection of tests or test items, a two dimensional (factor) model was really underlying responses (model (3) in the appendix). If a unidimensional model (for example model (1) in the appendix) is fitted then, given a large enough sample, it will be found to be discrepant with the data. Typically this will be detected by some tests or items 'not fitting'. This is what actually occurs in IALS and such 'discrepant' items are removed. This will then result in a model which better satisfies the model assumptions, in particular that there is only a single dimension. The problem is that the 'discrepant' items will often be just the ones that are expressing the existence of a second dimension. If only a minority of items are of this kind, then the remainder will dominate the model and determine what is finally left. We see therefore that initial decisions about which items to include and in what proportions, will determine the final scale when a unidimensional model is assumed. I shall discuss in more detail in the next section the procedures actually used to deal with these items by IALS, and argue that they were inadequate.

The real problem here comes not just from the decisions by test constructors about what items to include in what tests or domains, but also in the subsequent fitting of oversimplified models which lead to further selections and removals of items to conform to a particular set of model assumptions. There are two consistent attitudes one can take towards scale construction. One is to decide what to include on largely substantive grounds, modified by piloting to ensure that the components of a test are properly understood and that items poses a reasonable measure of discriminatory power. The final decision about how to combine items together in order to report proficiencies or whatever, will then be taken on substantive grounds. The other is to allow the final reporting decision to be made following an exploration of the dimensionality structure of the data obtained from a large sample of respondents. In practice, of course, a mixture of these might be used. The problem with the IALS procedure is that it falls between these, neither allowing a proper exploration of the

[2] Rock, D. Validity Generalisation of the Assessment Across Countries in *Adult Literacy in OECD Countries Technical Report on the First International Adult Literacy Survey*. National Center for Education Statistics: Washington 1998 p. 135-142

dimensionality of the data nor allowing substantive decisions to be decisive. It should also be pointed out that procedures for exploring dimensionality have existed for some time[3] yet the relevance of these is ignored in the technical report.

4.5 Item exclusion

According to Chapter 10 of the technical report, twelve of the 114 items were dropped because they did not fit very well (model (4) given in the appendix), involving a large discrepancy value in 3 or more countries. A further 46 items (Chapter 9.3) also did not fit equally well in all countries and for 14 of these (available in French and English versions) a detailed investigation was made to try to ascertain why. When the final scale was constructed, however, these 46 remained.

The conclusion in Chapter 9 is that the IALS framework is 'consistent across two languages and five cultures'. This is curious since the detailed analysis of these items reveals a number of reasons why they would be harder (that is have different parameter values associated with them) in some countries than others. It would seem sensible to carry out a detailed analysis of all items in this kind of way in order to ascertain where 'biases' may exist, rather than just the ones which do not fit the model.

An item which does not 'fit' a particular unidimensional model is providing information that the model itself is inadequate to describe the item's responses. There may be several reasons for this. One reason may be that translation has altered the characteristics of the item relative to other items for certain countries; a different translation process might allow the item to fit the model better. Of itself, however, this does not imply that the latter translation is better; a judgement of translation accuracy has to be made on other grounds. Another reason for a poor fit is that there are in reality two or more dimensions which the items are reflecting and the lack of fit is simply indicating this. In particular there may be *different* dimensions and different numbers of dimensions in each country.

If in fact these discrepancies are indicating extra dimensions in the data, then removing 'non-fitting' items and forcing all the remaining items to have the same parameter values for each country in a unidimensional model will tend to create 'biases' against those countries where discrepancies are largest.

The problem with scale construction techniques that rely upon strong dimensionality assumptions is that the composition of the resulting test instruments will be influenced by the population in which the piloting has been carried out. Thus, for cultural, social or other reasons the intercorrelations among items, and hence the factor and dimensionality structure, may vary from population to population. IALS *assumes* that there is a common structure in all populations and this drives the construction of the scale and decisions as to which items to exclude. Furthermore, since it appears that the previous US studies were included in the scaling it seems that the US data may have dominated the scaling and weighted the scale to represent more closely the US pattern than that in any other country. In this way the use of existing instruments developed within a single country can be seen to lead to the possible introduction of subtle biases when applied to other educational systems.

I am arguing, therefore, that a broader approach is needed towards the exploration of dimensionality. While I accept that for some purposes it may be necessary to summarise results in terms of a single score scale (for each proficiency) I believe that this should be done only on the basis of a detailed understanding of any underlying more complex dimensionality structure. Techniques are available for the full exploration of dimensionality and there seems to be no convincing case for omitting such analyses.

---

[3] see, for example Bock, R. D., Gibbons, R. and Muraki, E. (1988). Full information item factor analysis. *Applied Psychological Measurement* **12**: 261-280.

4.6 International comparability

It is clear from the discussion above that the existing IALS analysis and its country comparisons are at best incomplete and possibly misleading. Forcing comparisons into just three separate dimensions previously suggested by US research is unnecessarily restrictive. The analysis of potential 'biases' is incomplete, and the statistical method of comparing country scores is inefficient and unnecessarily complex.

4.7 Scale interpretations

In order to provide an indication of the 'meaning' to be attached to particular scores on each scale, the scale for each proficiency is divided into 5 levels. Within each level tasks are identified such that there is an (approximately) 80% probability of a correct response from those individuals with proficiency scores at that level. A verbal description of these tasks, based upon a prior cognitive analysis of items, is used to typify that level. Such an attempt to give 'meaning' to the scale seems difficult to justify. Any score or level can be achieved by correct responses to a large number of different combinations of items and the choice of those items that *individually* have a high probability of success at each scale position is an oversimplification and may be very misleading. What is really required for interpretations of a scale, however it may have been produced, is a description of the different *combinations or patterns* of tasks that can lead to any given scale position.

The logic of the unidimensionality assumption, however, is that since only a single attribute is being measured the resulting scale score summarises all the information about the attribute and is therefore sufficient to characterise an individual. It follows that any verbal label attached to a scale score need only indicate the attributes that an individual with that score can be expected to exhibit. Thus, for all individuals with the same (1-dimensional) proficiency score, the relative difficulties of all the items is assumed to be the same. If in fact some such individuals find item A more difficult than item B and vice versa for other individuals, then there is no possibility of describing literacy levels consistently in the manner of IALS: individuals with very different patterns of responses could achieve the same score. Thus, the issue of dimensionality is crucial to the way in which scale scores can be interpreted. If there really are several underlying dimensions the existing descriptions provided by IALS will fail to capture the full diversity of performance by forcibly ranking everyone along a single scale.

4.8 Alternatives

Chapter 11.4 of the technical report presents a comparison of the scaled average proficiencies for each country compared to a simple scoring system consisting of the proportion of correct responses for each of the three proficiency sets of items. The country level correlations lie between 0.95 and 0.97 and essentially no inference is changed if one uses the simpler measure. This result is to be expected on theoretical grounds and, *if one wishes to restrict attention to 1-dimensional models,* there seems to be a strong case for using the proportion correct as a basis for country comparisons. The model underlying the use of the (possibly weighted) proportion correct, is in fact model (1) of the appendix as opposed to model (2), and the whole IRM analysis could in principle be carried out based upon model (1) rather than model (2)[4]. In fact one might wish to argue for a summary such as the proportion correct simply on the grounds of this being a useful summary measure without any particular modelling justification.

If one wishes to carry out a multidimensional analysis then, as mentioned earlier, this could be done on the basis of fitting multidimensional models in which *all* the items would be

[4] for a further discussion see Goldstein, H. and Wood, R. (1989). Five decades of item response modelling. *British Journal of mathematical and statistical psychology* **42**: 139-167

expected to contribute to each dimension, rather than artificially being restricted to 'loading' on just one. At the very least it would be interesting to see the results of such an analysis.

It would be advantageous for a separate scaling to be done for each country. In this way differences can be seen directly (and tested) rather than concentrating on fitting a common scale. This will make the scaling procedure more 'transparent' and allow more substantively informed judgements to be made about country differences.

Another important approach is to see whether item groupings could be established for small groups of items which, on substantive grounds were felt to constitute domains of interest. Experts in literacy with a wide variety of viewpoints and experiences could be used to suggest and discuss these and a mechanism developed for reaching consensus. These groupings would then describe 'literacy' at a more detailed level than the three proficiencies used in IALS, and for that reason have the potential for greater descriptive insights. If this were done, then for each such group or 'elementary item cluster' a (possibly weighted) proportion correct score could be obtained for each individual, and it would be these scores which would then represent the basic components of the study design. Each booklet would contain a subset of these clusters, using a similar allocation procedure to that in IALS. The analysis would then seek to estimate country means for each cluster, the variances and the correlations between them. Differences due to gender, education etc could readily be built into the multivariate response models used so that fully efficient estimates could be provided. Goldstein[5] describes the analysis of such a model. In addition, multilevel analysis could be performed so that variations between geographical areas can be estimated.

In addition to reporting at the cluster level, combinations of clusters could be formed to provide summary measures; but the main emphasis would be upon the detailed cluster level information. No scaling would need to be involved in this, save perhaps to allow for different numbers of constituent items in each cluster if inter-cluster comparisons are required. This procedure would also have the considerable advantage of being relatively easy to understand for the non-technical reader. A serious disadvantage of the current IALS model-based procedures is their opaqueness and difficulty for those without a strong technical understanding.

4.9 Further analyses

In the second IALS report[6] and the technical report there is some attempt to carry out analyses of proficiency scores which introduce other individual measurements as covariates or predictors. There is little systematic attempt, however, to see the extent to which country differences can be explained by such factors. There appears to be a reluctance in the published IALS analyses to fit models which adjust for more than one, or at most two, factors at a time.

For example, in Chapter 3 of the second IALS report, literacy scores are plotted against age with and without adjusting for level of education and separately by parents' years of education, but not in a combined analysis. Yet, (P71) the report warns that because of the marked relationship with age comparisons should take account of the age distribution. (This remark is made in the context of comparisons between regions within countries but applies equally to comparisons between countries). Indeed, since countries differ in their age distributions it could be argued that *all* comparisons should adjust for age. In particular it would appear that there are interactions with age, such that there seem to be fewer differences between countries for the older age groups.

---

[5] See Chapter 4 in Goldstein, H. (1995). *Multilevel Statistical Models.* London, Arnold; New York, Wiley.

[6] *Literacy skills for the knowledge society Further results of the first International Adult Literacy Survey.* OECD and Human Resources Development Canada (1997).

It will be important, if in future multidimensonal item response models are fitted, to incorporate factors such as age and education, into these models directly. Such a model, of the kind exemplified by (3) in the appendix, could include such covariates. As Goldstein and Wood[7] point out, it is quite possible that dimensions which emerge from an analysis of a heterogeneous population could be explained by such factors.

Current re-evaluations of IALS tasks have characterised items and their various translated versions according to their contextual characteristics, such as familiarity, repetitiveness, precision etc. Such characteristics, at least in principle, can be applied to all tasks and therefore can be used in the analysis of task responses. Thus, for example, in comparing countries a measure of average familiarity could be used to adjust differences. More usefully, comparisons could be carried out at the task level to see how far country differences can be explained by such characteristics, also allowing for age etc as suggested above.

Finally there is no attempt in IALS to carry out multilevel analyses which take account of differences between education levels, geographical areas etc. These techniques are now in common use and it is well known that a failure to take proper account of multilevel structures can lead to misleading inferences, especially when carrying out analyses of relationships between scores and other factors.

4.10 Conclusions

Based on the contents of the technical report the following summary comments and recommendations are made with implications for future IALS rounds.

1. The psychometric criteria used by IALS do not provide a satisfactory basis for country comparisons. The one-dimensional models used fail properly to explore the complexity of the data with the result that the conclusions of IALS may well be oversimplifications about the state of literacy in the member countries.
2. There is a need to carry out sensitivity analyses of the assumptions made in the item response modelling. In particular, multidimensional models should be explored and rankings of item difficulties compared between countries
3. Attention should be directed at providing greater validity and recognising that absolute comparability may not be achievable. The survey data should be viewed as potentially casting light on factors which are locally specific and not amenable to simple scale comparisons between countries.
4. Country comparisons should be carried out at task or 'small task set' level with particular attention paid to translation issues and cultural differences.
5. Multilevel modelling needs to be used in all analyses of the data in order fully to explore within-country variability

4.11 Acknowledgements

This paper has benefited greatly from discussions with Lars Lyberg, Alain Blum, France Guérin-Pace, Patrick Heady and Kentaro Yamamoto.

Further references

Goldstein, H. (1980). Dimensionality, bias, independence and measurement scale problems in latent trait test score models. *British Journal of mathematical and statistical psychology* **33**: 234-246.

[7] See 4.

Goldstein, H. (1994). Recontextualising mental measurement. *Educational Measurement: Issues and Practice* **13**: 16-19.

Mislevy, R. J. (1991). Randomisation based inference about latent variables from complex samples. *Psychometrika* **56**: 177-196.

Statistical appendix

Defining dimensionality

Dimensionality refers either to a set of items, or alternatively to a set of test scores. While the detailed procedures for investigating dimensionality will differ in each case, the essential underlying models are the same. The essence is captured in the following simple unidimensional factor model for a set of test scores

$$y_{ij} = a_i + b_i f_j + e_{ij}$$
$$f \sim N(0,\sigma_f^2), \quad e_{ij} \sim N(0,\sigma_{ei}^2) \qquad (1)$$

Where y_{ij} is the score for the i-th test for the j-th individual, f_j is the underlying factor value for the j-th individual and the e_{ij} are mutually independent 'residual' terms. The intercept term a_i is often omitted if all the measured variables are standardised to have zero means. If the responses y_{ij} are replaced by a set of item binary responses then with minor modifications we can write

$$\log it(\pi_{ij}) = a_i + b_i f_j$$
$$y_{ij} \sim Binomial(\pi_{ij},1) \qquad (2)$$
$$f \sim N(0,\sigma_f^2)$$

The basic similarity resides in the fact that a single underlying variable f_j determines the response through a simple regression type relationship, apart from random variation. Both models (1) and (2) are a special kind of 2-level model in which individuals are at level 2 and tests (or test items) at level 1. In addition to the unidimensionality assumption, the independence of the e_{ij} in (1) and the independence of the y_{ij} given π_{ij}, i.e. the item coefficient values and the individual's proficiency, is a further assumption which underlies the use of significance testing of the model, construction of confidence intervals and as a basis for testing for the degree of dimensionality which may exist. It is worth noting that in section 10.4 this assumption is incorrectly described. Model (2) is precisely the model used by IALS and is often known as a 'binary factor model and is referred by IALS as the 'two-parameter logistic model', and the notation used by IALS is also slightly different (Chapter 10). A useful discussion of these models is given by Bartholomew (1998).[8]

The aim of the statistical analysis of these models is to estimate the parameters, and in particular to provide estimates of the values of f_j, one for each individual. These are known as factor or trait scores or 'proficiencies'. They are, in effect, weighted averages of the responses – in the case of test items the (0,1) responses, where the weights depend on the values of the b_i estimates. Here we shall explore a little further what the use of such a model implies substantively.

For simplicity we shall use the traditional factor model (1), but everything we say will apply in general terms to (2) also. Suppose that individuals' responses were in fact determined by two underlying responses according to the following model

$$y_{ij} = a_i + b_i f_j + c_i g_j + e_{ij}$$
$$f \sim N(0,\sigma_f^2), \quad g \sim N(0,\sigma_g^2), \quad e_{ij} \sim N(0,\sigma_{ei}^2) \qquad (3)$$
$$\text{cov}(f,g) = \sigma_{fg}$$

---

[8] Bartholomew, D. J. (1998). Scaling unobservable constructs in social science. *Applied Statistics* **47**: 1-14. Although the logistic 'link function' is commonly used, others are possible. Goldstein (1980) shows that the choice of link function can substantially affect proficiency estimates and argues that this exposes an undesirable arbitrariness of these models see Goldstein, H. (1980). Dimensionality, bias, independence and measurement scale problems in latent trait test score models. *British Journal of mathematical and statistical psychology* **33**: 234-246.

In the IALS case, such a model would be fitted for a collection of items which are assumed to reflect two domains, say prose and document literacy. IALS makes the strong assumption that for each domain the items used reflect that domain *and only that domain*. Yet the high intercorrelations observed among the proficiency scores suggests that this is very unlikely. The advantage of a full multidimensional analysis is that it would provide some insight into how any underlying domains which can be identified from the analysis predict the responses to the test items.

Section 10.3 of the Technical report describes a (MH) test for detecting individual items which have different parameter values in some countries. While one would expect the existence of more than one dimension to lead to such a situation the non-existence of such items does not imply unidimensionality. In any case, as this section points out, the test is very approximate.

5. Survey practices in European countries

Wim DeHeer, Statistics Netherlands

Wim deHeer is currently head of the department of electronic (EDI) business surveys at Statistics Netherlands. Over recent years he was responsible for the development of new surveys within Statistics Netherland in the field of social and household survey. His main interests have been in the area of problems due to non-response and the development of appropriate fieldwork strategies to minimise non-response in household surveys.

5.1 Introduction and main conclusions

In this paper survey practices in eight European countries will be described in order to find out what problems or constraints exist to create sufficient conditions for the execution of international literacy surveys. In the papers of Lyberg and Goldstein[1] the survey practices used for the International Adult Literacy Survey (IALS) in 1994 are evaluated. They concluded, that "attempts at standardisation of survey practices were not successful" and that "participating countries were given too much freedom to deviate from suggested procedures". Although they recommend more attention be paid to standardisation of practices in future international literacy surveys, they accept that it is not realistic to expect that the survey could be carried out in exactly the same fashion in all participating countries. Therefore they suggest trying to avoid unnecessary variation in survey procedures across countries. Lyberg already clarified that there is an important relation between the way survey procedures and operations are designed and executed and the measurement or observation of literacy itself. Survey outcomes can be affected by survey procedures to a great but mostly unknown extent.

The most important goal of this paper is to investigate to what extent "unnecessary variation" exists and can be "avoided". This was done by collecting descriptive information on survey practices in eight European countries. These countries were selected on the basis of two criteria: it had to be feasible to collect this information taking into account budget- and time-constraints and the countries selected must give a fairly good picture of the situation in (western) Europe. The following countries were selected: France, Germany, Greece, Italy, The Netherlands, Portugal, Sweden and Great Britain.

The next thing to do was to define the fields of interest or aspects of survey procedures, which were supposed to be very important for literacy surveys. The following aspects were defined and worked out in an item list:

- aspects related to the sample design and sample procedures to find out to what extent the requirements of probability sampling could be met;
- aspects concerning the experience and the quality of survey organisations;
- aspects of the fieldwork or data collection procedures: the strategy to contact respondents, the strategy to convince reluctant people, the conditions and support for interviewers;
- aspects concerning dataprocessing, weighting procedures, etc.

The item list was used to guide open interviews with representatives of survey organisations in the selected European countries. In selecting survey organisations to be interviewed we did not pretend to pre-select organisations that should carry out literacy surveys in future. We only wanted to establish an overview of possibilities to "avoid unnecessary variation" and to

[1] Lyberg, L. *Review of IALS – a commentary on the technical report.* Chapter 2 in this report and Goldstein, H. *IALS - A commentary on the scaling and data analysis,* Chapter 4 in this report.

discover the constraints that might prevent the improvement of standardisation across countries. Therefore not all survey institutes in a particular country needed to be interviewed, but only a selection of different types of organisations with good records in all or most aspects of survey research. In each country interviews were carried out with the national statistical institute, a private research institute and (if available) a university-linked institute. The national statistical institutes are called "public" institutes and the others "semi-public" and "private" institutes. In total 20 interviews were carried out.

The main conclusion is that there seems to be no institute in all these countries that has sufficient experience and expertise in all aspects of the survey process when it comes to literacy surveys.

One would expect that national statistical institutes could provide all the necessary expertise. This however is not the case in most countries. In general they have no specific expertise with respect to literacy and how to measure this. This expertise can be found in (semi-) public and private institutes that are active in the field of educational research. Besides that it seems that (some of) the statistical institutes do not find it easy to implement ad hoc a very complex literacy survey. Also some statistical institutes have strict rules with respect to confidentiality, dissemination of micro data and dataprocessing (imputation), which makes it difficult to co-operate in a international survey. On the other hand private institutes seem to have less expertise and experience with respect to sampling, coding, weighting, imputation and the like.

A second important conclusion and at the same time recommendation is that it seems to be necessary to form combinations or consortia of institutes per country to combine all necessary expertise and experience, in order to get the best possible survey practices and to avoid unnecessary variation.

The evidence and findings that will be reported in the following paragraphs will of course underpin these conclusions. With respect to the interviews with survey organisations we can say that organisations were very co-operative in general. Sometimes however, the willingness to answer certain questions dissolved and it looked as if some did not want to disturb the positive picture of themselves by stating that they were not able to carry out some aspects of the whole process.

This attitude must be changed when organisations have to work together and form teams in which all necessary expertise is present.

If there is insufficient openness it is not possible to decide before the start of the project whether all necessary expertise is available. This certainly will lead to (big) problems during the project. This openness is also needed when it is not possible to find all the necessary expertise in a country. Then they must rely on *an (international) team of experts* that can advise and help.

In the next paragraphs the survey practices in each country will be described and evaluated for each aspect of the survey process. Every section starts with an explanation about what minimum standards can be defined in order to standardise survey procedures. The proposed minimum standards or quality criteria are described in Italics. Every section will be concluded with a general description of the possibilities to avoid unnecessary variation and recommendations in this respect. The findings for each country are summarised in two tables (see annexes 5.I and 5.II). The heading 'public' stands for government organisation and 'private' for other semi-government, university-linked or totally private organisations.

5.2 Sample design and sample procedures

5.2.1 Minimum standards

A minimum standard for the sample design should be *probability sampling*. This also means that the principle of probability should not be weakened in subsequent stages of the sampling procedures. Probability sampling means that all elements of a target population (persons or households) have a non-zero chance to be included in the sample. These chances need not to be equal for every element, but the inclusion probabilities must be known in order to correct for unequal inclusion probabilities afterwards. Only this guarantees (as far as the sampling is concerned) that quality indicators of the survey outcomes (such as standard errors) really indicate what they are supposed to.

The quality of probability sampling depends on how the different aspects of sampling procedures are designed and executed, i.e. definition of the target population and the observational or sample unit, the quality of the sample frame (character and coverage), sample selection methods and rules (to calculate inclusion probabilities), use of substitution and proxies.

Coverage and exclusion are both sides of the same coin. The coverage rate indicates to what extent the sample frame covers the target population and the exclusion rate indicates what part of the target population is excluded.

Some groups of the population might be *excluded*, although they are covered in the sample frame. For instance 'people in elderly homes' are held in the population register and their address is known. As they are in the sample frame they can be given a chance to be sampled. But for practical reasons they are often excluded from the target population. In case of *undercoverage* not every element of the population can be given a chance to be sampled. This is often the case when telephone lists are used. People without listed numbers (no telephone at all or exdirectory numbers) have zero probability of being sampled. In theory combining the use of telephone lists with random digit dialing (RDD) can solve this problem. But in practice it seems to be difficult to construct RDD-frames, within which every possible number stands for the inclusion probability of one sample unit. Besides that the quality of this kind of sampling depends to a great extent on the penetration rate of telephone ownership. Nowadays this rate is very high in most countries, but the situation seems to change very fast with the use of mobile phones. It seems that young people tend to have only a mobile phone and not a traditional fixed-line-phone. So the need to combine telephone lists from different providers makes it more difficult to give every member of the population a chance to be sampled. However, one could search for and rely on alternative or additional sample frames, but in the end the coverage problem might not be solved for the full 100%. As long as the procedure is clear and fully documented it might be possible to (reasonably) live up to the requirements of probability sampling.

For both *undercoverage* and *exclusion*, not only is the magnitude of the group important, but also the characteristics of the groups, especially with respect to the target variables. The following can be proposed as minimum standards to reduce variation in coverage and exclusion.

If undercoverage and/or exclusion are the case a minimum requirement is that sufficient documentation should be provided with respect to the magnitudes of the groups, some important population characteristics of the groups, the rationale for exclusion and some indication of the characteristics of the groups with respect to the main variables of the survey.

If the total size of the groups not covered or excluded is too large, for instance more than 10% of the population, additional research is required in order to get a better picture of the groups characteristics with respect to the main purposes of the survey.

Mostly the excluded groups are small and known to some extent (e.g. people living in institutions, elderly homes, in prison), but in most studies nothing is said about the groups characteristics with respect to the main variables and how this might effect the estimates for the whole population. This should be and can be improved for future international literacy surveys.

Most of the time the sample frame is not a list of elements of the target population, but only an approximation of that, for example a list of addresses. Such a frame contains more elements than only those of the target population, for instance addresses of firms and addresses where no one lives. In other words there can be a lot of *overcoverage* in the frame. On the other hand some addresses can contain more than one person or household, which means that inclusion probabilities are different when addresses are used. With good instructions for interviewers and rigorous checks on what they do, this problem can be handled. Different methods can be applied to select one person within a household: the Kish-method and the so-called birthday-method are two examples. It is important that a safe and reliable method is used, but it is up to the (international) survey team to decide what are safe methods in this respect. What is important is that interviewers are giving strict and clear instructions on how to select households at an address (if necessary) and how to select a person within a household. It is also important that this is verified and controlled. It must be possible to reconstruct the procedure carried out by the interviewer. All this can guarantee that the principles of probability sampling are followed and that at the end inclusion-probabilities for all sampled persons or households are known. As a minimum standard for this part of the sample selection process the following can be formulated.

To guarantee that the principles of probability sampling are followed, strict and clear instructions for interviewers are needed with respect to the selection of households at addresses where more than one household live and the selection of persons within a household. Furthermore interviewers must be controlled to make sure that they apply the selection rules as prescribed.

In the case of area sampling much of the sampling has to be carried out in the field. *In order to fulfil the requirements of probability sampling, for area sampling at least the population size per area needs to be known, so that areas can be sampled proportional to size.* This seems to be a trivial requirement, but it nevertheless seems to be important to be explicit about this, because it is not always clear that population sizes were known and/or were accurate. If the population size per area is not known or is not updated enough, one cannot be sure that all elements of the target population will have a chance to be sampled and certainly the inclusion probabilities will not be known. When areas can be sampled proportional to size, most of the time an enumeration of eligible addresses will be carried out prior to the sampling of addresses or households. This enumeration produces lists of addresses or households; out of which addresses or households will be sampled. Sometimes no enumeration is used and interviewers are given instructions on how to select or sample addresses (e.g. random route procedure) within a particular area. This way of area-sampling cannot guarantee that every household or person has the same or a known probability of being sampled, because interviewers might try to avoid sampling certain types of addresses. This possible behaviour of interviewers can affect the quality of the data and in the end the survey outcomes. Therefore it seems to be important to avoid forms of interviewer bias at the sampling stage by introducing two separate procedures: the enumeration of blocks and addresses (and sometimes even households) by an enumerator; and the selection of households at a given address and a person within a given household by an interviewer. So organisations have to live to the following requirement or minimum standard.

In the case of area sampling the minimum quality for probability sampling can be guaranteed, if the population size per area is known or can be estimated, the enumeration of addresses is a separate part of the procedure, carried out by someone other than the interviewers and the whole procedure is monitored and controlled.

This all means that 'quota sampling' must be rejected, because quota sampling by definition means that not all elements of the target population have known inclusion probabilities greater than zero.

Substitution of persons or households, who refused to participate or who could not be contacted, most of the time violates the principle of probability sampling, because it is very difficult to control the procedures in the field. If there is insufficient control on what interviewers do, substitution might introduce 'interviewer-bias'. Besides that, allowing interviewers to substitute might weaken their motivation to try to persuade reluctant respondents and to try to reconvert refusers, even when there are strict conditions and rules for this substitution. Substitution could be accepted 'theoretically' if it could be guaranteed that the procedures to substitute are carried out properly and that it does not introduce bias. There is some research underway with respect to the effect of substitution, but this research does not seem to lead to clear conclusions. Generally the guarantee that substitution will not introduce bias cannot be given and this is *why substitution should not be accepted for an international literacy survey.*

Proxy-data means that someone else gives data on the sampled person or household. Proxies can be accepted, if they add useful information for the survey, for example information on non-respondents and missing data for respondents. Of course some conditions must be set regarding the source and character of the information. The source must be reliable, which means a related person, other member of the household and in the case of households non-response, neighbours, but that depends on the type of information. With respect to the character of proxy-data, it must be restricted to factual data. Opinions or attitudes cannot of course be measured by proxy-information. *This means that proxies are not acceptable for the literacy-assessment but can be used for information on non-response.*

5.2.2 Sample design and procedures in 8 European countries

5.2.2.1 France

In France the situation differs per institute. Governmental institutes like INSEE and INED use different sample frames compared with private research institutes. Governmental institutes can use the Census address file as a sample frame. This frame covers the whole population of France. For most of its surveys INSEE uses a multistage sampling procedure. Areas are sampled first, and then within areas households are sampled using the Census address file. Using this file might cause a few problems:

- the census data might be out of date, because people moved in between; this does not mean that people who have recently moved have lower inclusion probabilities; as long as they moved to an address in France, they will have a proper inclusion probability;
- however, new dwellings and buildings are not included in the Census address file; this really causes a coverage problem, for which there is no reliable alternative up to now; in the near future there will be a provision to update this address file;
- the Census address file contains the names of heads of households, but cannot be used as a population register with all the names of all persons; so if this file is used, a person within the household still has to be selected.

Private institutes are not allowed to use the Census address file. They can only use the telephone register. The telephone register covers only about 80% of the French population. If these institutes have to cover the whole population in France they normally design a random route sampling procedure with the listed telephone numbers and addresses as starting points.

They also design and follow strict controlling procedures (if of course the sponsor will pay for it), for instance by checking 15% of the selected households. The problem is that only responding households can be used to check what interviewers did. This means that this procedure does not give sufficient guarantee that the requirements of random sampling are not violated.

Private institutes also use "quota sampling" sometimes to be able to provide sponsors with requested data within the limits of the available budgets.

Substitution is not normally used by the governmental organisations, but only in specific surveys on very difficult to approach subgroups. The private organisations occasionally use substitution.

Proxies are sometimes permitted, but only for household-members and for data that can be easily provided by them.

5.2.2.2 Germany

In Germany private and university-linked institutes carry out most of the ad-hoc social surveys. The national statistical office (Statistisches Bundesamt) carries out continuous surveys like the Labour Force Survey, the Income and Expenditure Survey, the current Household Budget Survey, the European Household Panel Survey, Time Use Survey and a survey on tourism.

For *face-to-face* surveys carried out by private and university-linked institutes the ADM[2] electoral districts are used to compose the sample frame. ADM-districts are selected with probabilities proportional to size, which means number of households. Within selected ADM-districts interviewers have to select households according to a prescribed *random route rule.* The rules on how to select households and how many within blocks, streets and buildings are to be selected are very precise. Sometimes persons other than the interviewers do the selection of addresses or households. In any case the selection procedure is checked. Experienced interviewers have a sample of their selections checked, while all the selections of new interviewers might be checked.

It is also possible to sample persons or households from the population register. There is however no national register and one has to gain the co-operation of local authorities. Sampling from population registers means first sampling municipalities and then asking municipalities to sample persons or households. This procedure however is time consuming and very costly.

Telephone surveys are mostly carried out in Germany using a mix of probability sampling from the listed telephone numbers and additional *random digit dialing* to give unlisted secret numbers a chance to be sampled. The penetration rate of telephones is very high in Germany, 95% to 97%. Only a small part of the population is not covered, but this can be a very selective group.

When ADM-districts or the population registers are used the coverage rate is almost 100%, although institutionalised people are mostly not included in surveys.

The Statistisches Bundesamt uses so called 'master samples' based on census data. The statistical offices of the 'Länder' update these samples of addresses. The addresses of these samples are used as starting points to carry out a form of area- or cluster sampling. This means that interviewers must follow strict rules to select 6 to 12 addresses or households around this starting address. Interviewers are - checked with respect to their selection of

[2] ADM Arbeitskreiss Deutsche Markt- und Sozialforschung Instituten.

households. This method of sample generation is done to reduce fieldwork-costs, especially with respect to travel expenses.

Substitution and *proxies* are not normally used in Germany, except for proxy-data for young children, which is provided by household-members.

5.2.2.3 Greece

In Greece the only possible way to carry out household surveys seems to be by using *area sampling* with the census data to select areas with probabilities proportional to size. The next step is that interviewers update the list of households and after that interviewers themselves carry out the sampling of households. It seems that the sampling procedures carried out in the field by interviewers are not very well controlled, although there might be a difference between the National Statistical Institute and other institutes. The same person who is going to interview the sampled household should not carry out the updating of the lists of households or addresses. And of course this procedure should be checked thoroughly.

Institutionalised households are normally *excluded.*

Substitution is sometimes allowed for vacant addresses and non-response. The average substitution rate is about 5%. *Proxies* are only allowed for household members with respect to 'factual' data (e.g. employment status).

5.2.2.4 Italy

With respect to sampling there is a great difference between the national statistical institute and other institutes in Italy. The national statistical institute can make use of the municipal population registers as the municipalities have by law a certain statistical task. For all household surveys first municipalities are sampled as the Primary Sampling Unit (PSU) with probabilities proportional to size. Within municipalities, households are sampled and the addresses are given to interviewers. Substitution is only allowed for the Labour Force Survey, but the substitute household is sampled by the population register office of each municipality. The substitution rate is about 4%. Proxies are only allowed from household-members.

Other (private) institutes cannot use the population register and must carry out area sampling for face-to-face household surveys. They first select areas (with probabilities proportional to size) and to select households or persons they design a *random route* procedure. The telephone list is used to select start-addresses and interviewers are instructed how to proceed. Interviewers are checked with respect to their sample results. Substitution is allowed for refusals and non-contacts. To substitute the interviewers have to follow specific rules and checks are carried out to ensure compliance.

5.2.2.5 The Netherlands

Governmental or public and private survey organisation in The Netherlands can all use the postal address file, containing all addresses in that country. As in other countries this address file includes addresses of businesses and empty houses and addresses where more than one household live. This means that in general Dutch research institutes can fulfil the requirements of probability sampling, although execution of the sampling procedures in the field needs to be controlled more thoroughly, especially with respect to literacy surveys. Sampling persons within households, starting with the address file does not seem to be very well controlled and this might lead to the situation where the most 'literate' person in a household is selected to do the tests. Sometimes non-public research organisations use 'quota sampling', although they try to convince their sponsors to use probability sampling, which is normally more expensive.

The national statistical office (and sometimes also private organisations) not only uses the postal address file, but also the national populations register as a sampling frame. This means direct access to elements of the target population.

Substitution is not used in The Netherlands and proxies are allowed sometimes, but only for 'factual' information from household-members.

5.2.2.6 Portugal

The Portuguese national statistical institute normally uses an address file as their sample frame. This address file results from the latest census and is periodically updated. A three-step sampling procedure is used, starting with the selection of areas proportional to size. Within these areas smaller geographical areas are selected with about 300 housing units and then addresses are selected. For the selection of a person within a household the 'Kish Method' is used. Substitution is sometimes allowed under strict predefined rules. Also proxies are sometimes allowed.

Private research institutes in Portugal only seem to have telephone lists as sample frames for general population surveys. They often seem to use 'quota sampling' in order to make sure that certain subgroups are well represented in the sample and they use substitution in their 'quota sampling procedures'.

5.2.2.7 Sweden

In Sweden both public and private organisations can use the national population register to carry out probability sampling. This is done for all face-to-face surveys. For telephone surveys the private organisations use the telephone register combined with random digit dialing to give unlisted numbers a chance to be sampled. The telephone coverage in Sweden is very high, about 99%, but the share of unlisted numbers (7%) is growing.

As proper probability sampling using the population register for every survey institute in Sweden is quite feasible, there is no reason at all to use the telephone file. But the importance of thoroughly checking the sample procedures in the field must be stressed, especially for a literacy survey.

5.2.2.8 Great Britain

In Great Britain the usual sampling frame is the Postcode Address File (PAF), which is available for public and private organisations. The coverage rate of addresses is 98%. The file also contains addresses of small businesses and empty properties. The overcoverage of this kind is approximately 11% and is registered during the fieldwork. A multistage sampling design is mostly used, with postcode sectors (areas) or groups of small sectors as the PSUs. The sample of PSUs is stratified by region and within region using data derived from the Census. Within PSUs addresses are sampled and interviewers are given a list of addresses. Survey organisations in the public sector do not allow their interviewers to substitute addresses with another. In the private sector, substitution is sometimes allowed where there is a lot of overcoverage with businesses and empty dwellings. Public survey organisations give interviewers detailed instructions on how to select households at addresses where more than one household lives and also if one person per household has to be selected.

Private survey organisations commonly use quota samples; for these, the postcode sectors, but not individual addresses, are chosen randomly. Interviewers are instructed to interview the required number of people in the sampled areas who meet age, sex and socio-economic criteria.

5.2.3 Summary

First we will summarise the criteria or minimum standards concerning sample design and procedures. These minimum standards are:

- *probability sampling which guarantees that every element in the population will have a non-zero chance to be sampled;*
- *documentation on non-coverage and exclusion of certain groups and additional research if the non-covered or excluded groups are more than 10% of the population under study;*
- *when area-sampling is used the population size per area must be known and documented and enumeration of sample units and the selection of households or persons by interviewers must be separate procedures carried out by different persons;*
- *substitution of non-respondents is only allowed if there is a 100% guarantee that substitution procedures will not introduce bias;*
- *proxies are allowed to gather factual data on non-respondents and to fill in missing factual data for respondents using reliable sources;*
- *all procedures must be sufficiently checked and documented in a way that procedures can be reconstructed if necessary.*

In three countries (The Netherlands, Sweden and Great Britain) there seem to be no severe problems in carrying out high quality probability sampling for public and private organisations. The necessity of designing and executing strict controls with respect to the sample selection procedures in the field however has to be emphasised and improved. Special attention is needed to ensure that non-covered and excluded groups are documented.

In Germany there would not be a problem if the population registers of municipalities could be used. Both public and private institutes can do this. If the population register is not used then both types of institutes have to rely on area sampling. In Germany unnecessary variation can be avoided only by using the population registers, but this involves more money and time. In France, Italy and Portugal it is not possible to carry out high quality probability sampling if the national statistical institutes are not involved because only they have access to (updated) census-data or population registers. If these national institutes are not involved, the only way to carry out a face-to-face literacy survey is by using area sampling. The only way to overcome variation in sampling procedures for these countries is to gain the co-operation of the national statistical institutes. In Greece the only way to carry out surveys is by use of area sampling. The procedures need to be improved however to meet the minimum requirements. This can be done with the help of an external expert team as proposed in Section 5.1.

5.3 Experiences with social or household surveys.

5.3.1 Minimum standards

A survey institute must have substantial experience of social surveys in order to be able to carry out literacy surveys at an acceptable level. The main reason for this is that literacy surveys require a lot of effort from the interviewer, the household and the selected person. Two aspects are of great importance here. The first aspect is to obtain co-operation, i.e. an acceptable response level. This is only possible if the survey organisation is aware of the non-response problem in that country, knows how to handle this (see also paragraph 5.4) and is able to evaluate the 'survey climate'. The second aspect has to do with the interview or observational process itself. The organisation and interviewers of the organisation must be able to create sufficient conditions to carry out literacy tests within the social and private environment of a household. This means that interviewers must have sufficient social capabilities and must know how far they can go in being 'social' and not violating the conditions to carry out an interview and literacy tests. They must be capable to distinguish between 'being social and explaining what has to be done' and 'carrying out the interview and observing the process'. As it is very important to be able to observe respondent's behaviour while doing the tests, it might be of great help that the survey organisation has experience and expertise in qualitative and cognitive questionnaire testing.

This is why we think that institutes must have enough experience with respect to the execution of large population or social surveys. This means that they should have successfully carried out at least 5 household surveys in recent years, face-to-face and nation-wide, each with a sample size of at least 3,000 sample elements.

They must also have experience of different data-collection methods (CATI, CAPI, telephone and face-to-face surveys) and be able to carry out the whole survey process.

These two requirements have to do with the ability to assess what various data-collection methods and data-collection procedures might contribute to data quality of the survey. A final indication for sufficient experience is that organisations have documents or reports, which show their experiences.

Organisations must be able to document their experiences in order to show that they master all aspects of survey operations

5.3.2 Experiences with social survey in different countries

5.3.2.1 France

In France it seems that governmental and private organisations have substantial experience of social surveys. INSEE, the national statistical institute carries out a number of large nation-wide surveys, such as the Labour Force Survey, Expenditure Survey, a Survey on Income and Wealth with sample sizes of 15,000 to 90,000 sample elements per year. CAPI is mostly used as the data-collection method, but CATI is also possible. Participation in these surveys is mostly mandatory. INSEE can handle the whole survey process. Although questionnaires are tested before they can be used to collect data, there is no special unit for qualitative questionnaire testing and for carrying out multilingual surveys. Other governmental institutes like INED only carry out smaller specific surveys (sexual behaviour, homelessness), but they also are able to handle the whole survey process. They have limited fieldwork capacities, but have experience of multilingual surveys and have facilities for qualitative questionnaire testing.

Private organisations seem to have less experience of nation-wide general population surveys than the INSEE, but they have quite a lot of survey-experience with respect to specific issues like travel, consumption, media, etc. They also have the facilities to use different modes of data-collection and some agencies have facilities for qualitative questionnaire tests. They are also able to carry out surveys totally by themselves

It does not seem to be easy to evaluate the survey climate in France. Although many surveys are carried out in France the 'survey burden' does not seem to be too high. On the other hand the response results seem to indicate that the survey climate is vulnerable. For the Labour Force Survey the response rate is about 90% and appears to be decreasing, which is not very high for a mandatory survey. The response level for face-to-face surveys carried out by private organisations is about 60%. If the governmental surveys were not mandatory much lower response rates could be expected.

5.3.2.2 Germany

As already stated, most ad-hoc social surveys in Germany are carried out by university-linked institutes and private institutes. These institutes have sufficient experience of nation-wide social surveys on socio-economic topics and topics like politics, travel, media, education, health, etc. Sample sizes vary from 3,000 to 10,000 households or persons. They are capable of using all kinds of data-collection instruments (CAPI, CATI) and methods (questionnaires, diaries, tests) and they can cover the whole survey process. Participation in these surveys is voluntary, but in contrast participation in the Mikrocensus (Labour Force Survey) of the Statistisches Bundesamt is compulsory. The response rates for face-to-face surveys by university and private institutes is about 55% to 60%, which indicates that the survey-taking climate in Germany seems not to be very strong and, according to the informants, is worsening because of growing telemarketing activities. Both types of survey organisations have facilities for testing questionnaires (qualitative and quantitative) and some of them are able to carry out multilingual surveys.

The 'Statistisches Bundesamt' carries out six nation-wide social surveys periodically and sometimes ad-hoc surveys. Sample sizes of these surveys are very large (about 370,000 households for the Labour Force Survey, 60,000 households for the Income and Expenditure Survey).

So there seems to be sufficient survey experience in Germany, but because of the survey climate special attention is needed with respect to the data-collection part of the survey.

5.3.2.3 Greece

In Greece there seems to be a difference between the National Statistical Institute (NSSG) and the National Institute for Social Research (EKKE). The former carries out nation-wide social surveys, using CAPI, questionnaires and diaries, which are compulsory. The latter only carries out surveys on a regional scale, only face-to-face. Both can handle the whole survey process. Although questionnaires are tested before fieldwork starts, there are no specific testing facilities. The 'survey burden' seems to be low but response rates differ between the two organisations, because governmental surveys of the national statistical institute are considered to be more serious than other surveys.

With respect to nation-wide survey experience there seems to be not much choice in Greece. Co-operation from the NSSG seems to be necessary.

5.3.2.4 Italy

The large nation-wide social surveys (Labour Force, Expenditure, Living Conditions, Socio-economic) are normally carried out by the national statistical organisation (ISTAT). Sample sizes vary from 7,000, 20,000 to 200,000. Data-collection techniques and methods are face-to-face home interviews, CATI and postal surveys. For the most part questionnaires are thoroughly tested, but there is no specific Questionnaire Laboratory or testing facilities. Surveys are carried out in two languages, for most of the country of course in Italian, but in German for a part of northern Italy. The survey climate is considered to be positive, because people seem to be very interested in the surveys. However, participation in surveys of ISTAT is usually compulsory, although this is not explicitly stated in the introductory letter. The letter refers to a specific law, but what this law is about is not explained. Response rates vary from 60% to more than 90%.

Private institutes also carry out nation-wide surveys, but on a relatively small scale with sample sizes of about 2,000 to 3,000 elements. These surveys are carried out face-to-face or by telephone (CATI). CAPI is not used on a broad scale. These institutes also carry out surveys in two languages (Italian and German) and some of these private institutes are so called 'full-service' institutes. According to these institutes, the survey climate is getting more difficult, especially with respect to contacting respondents. Response rates for face-to-face and telephone surveys are about 60%.

So in Italy also the survey climate demands specific attention when it comes to fieldwork procedures, because the mandatory character of the surveys of ISTAT might show an exaggerated positive picture.

5.3.2.5 The Netherlands

Private and public survey agencies have enough experience of social surveys in The Netherlands. Statistics Netherlands in general carries out surveys with sample sizes varying from a few thousand to 90,000 per year. Private institutes have surveys with relatively small sample sizes, about 3,000 to 6,000 approximately. All three kinds of institutes have nation-wide CAPI and CATI facilities and can handle the whole survey process. Questionnaire testing (qualitative) is possible at Statistics Netherlands and some private institutes have special testing facilities.

The survey climate does not seem to be very positive in The Netherlands. The average response rate for CAPI-surveys is about 60% and for CATI-surveys about 70%, although there is great variation between institutes and types of surveys. On the other hand it has been shown, that higher response rates can be obtained for face-to-face surveys (75% for the Housing Demand Survey), but this requires all possible efforts.

5.3.2.6 Portugal

The National Statistical Institute in Portugal carries out most standard nation-wide surveys, including: Labour Force, Expenditure, European Household Panel, Health, and Crime/Victimisation. Sample sizes for these surveys are quite large. The Labour Force Survey has a yearly sample size of more than 80,000 elements. Mostly the data collection method used is CAPI and there is sufficient experience in all aspect of the survey process. Questionnaires are designed by the statistical departments and tested before use in the field. Participation in the Census is compulsory, but the National Statistical Institute does not usually declare a survey compulsory.

Private institutes in Portugal also carry out nation-wide surveys, but sample sizes are smaller (about 8,000) and sometimes very small (1,000 to about 400). Whether private institutes have sufficient experience and capacity to carry out larger nation-wide complex surveys like a literacy survey is questionable.

5.3.2.7 Sweden

In Sweden both the national statistical institute (SCB) and private research companies carry out nation-wide social surveys, with sample sizes varying from 5,000 to 35,000 and more. They all have facilities to do home-interviews, telephone interviews and mail surveys. CATI seems to be the most popular data-collection instrument. Face-to-face surveys usually have smaller sample sizes and private organisations do not use CAPI. They all seem to have good facilities to test questionnaires. Although the survey climate is judged to be fairly good, response seems to have decreased over the years. Besides that there seems to be a great difference between the SCB and private organisations with respect to response results. Response results of private organisation are much lower (60% - 70%) than the results of the SCB (80% - 90%).

5.3.2.8 Great Britain

In Great Britain the national statistical institute (ONS), other private institutes and market research bureaus all carry out nation-wide social surveys, although the private market research bureaus do more surveys of public opinion, 'media' and 'consumer goods'. Sample sizes vary between surveys, but all kinds of organisations carry out small and large surveys.

All these institutes have CAPI and CATI facilities and usually test their questionnaires, although not all institutes have specific testing facilities.

Surveys are voluntary in Great Britain. Only the Census is compulsory. The survey climate is getting worse, which means that more effort is needed to keep response results at a stable level. Response results differ between organisations, 70 - 85% for ONS to 60% – 70% for private (commercial) organisations.

5.3.3 Summary

The minimum standards or indicators that an institute has sufficient experience are:

- *Experience with at least 5 large household surveys in recent years*
- *Experience with different modes of data collection*
- *Expertise to carry out the whole survey process*
- *Ability to document experiences and expertise.*

In most countries public and private institutes seem to have sufficient experience and expertise to carry out larger surveys. Only in Greece and Portugal is there some doubt as to whether private organisations can do this, as they seem to have much less experience with large complex surveys. Experience and expertise with the parts of the survey process that comes after the data collection stage will be discussed in section 5.5.

5.4 Response, non-response and fieldwork procedures

5.4.1 Minimum standards

Response and non-response vary across countries and surveys. There are of course different survey practices and different cultures but the aim must be to avoid unnecessary variation in survey and fieldwork procedures and to stimulate improvement in procedures. It is certainly not enough to aim at a specified response rate.

It is far more important to stress the need to use all kinds of response improving measures (the so-called 'battery' for non-response reduction) and to ask for justification and supporting documentation if the 'battery' (or parts of it) is not used. Unnecessary variation in response can only be avoided if organisations use the battery as much as they can, resulting in an optimal response level given the possibilities in a particular country.

A minimum quality level of fieldwork procedures is necessary in order to carry out an international literacy survey. This minimum quality level can be obtained if the battery of non-response reducing measures is used as described in this paragraph.

Different factors can affect response rates. Roughly these factors can be subdivided into the following groups:

- Survey and sample design
- Fieldwork operations
- Organisational aspects
- Survey taking climate.

This paragraph shall describe those aspects of fieldwork operations that are important in establishing a minimum standard. The basic idea is that the survey organisation masters the data collection process. This means that the organisation knows what is happening in the field, can explain why procedures are designed and organized as they are and is able to provide a full report on the data-collection and to what extent data-quality is affected (negatively or positively) by these procedures.

This also means that earlier attempts to master the non-response problem must be documented and that attempts must be made to gather data on non-respondents.

The most important strategies for controlling data collection or fieldwork procedures are:

- The strategy for contacting intended respondents
- The strategy for convincing reluctant respondents
- The professionalism of the interviewer force
- The way support, supervision and monitoring of the fieldwork is organized.

In some countries non-contact rates are increasing. In other countries non-contact rates seem to be stable, but more effort is needed to maintain them. In general it seems to be much more difficult to find people at home. So a well-designed and formulated *contact strategy* becomes more and more important to keep the non-contact rate as low as possible and to avoid 'non-contact bias'. With respect to the 'contact strategy' the battery at least must contain the following measures:

- An *advance letter* to let people know that an interviewer will try to get in touch with them and to 'prepare' the first contact;
- The *number of contact attempts* an interviewer must or is allowed to undertake must not be too limited; limiting the number of attempts might give interviewers the wrong signal, i.e. they might think that finishing all addresses is more important than good response results;
- *Spreading contact attempts* over different times of the day and days in the week is also very important as people generally seem to have stable patterns of being at home or not; spreading contact attempts increases the chance finding people at home;
- If organisations have a well formulated contact strategy they must also be able to *document* their experience regarding to the best interview hours per weekday and weekend.

Refusal rates are also increasing in most of the countries reviewed. It is not so self-evident that people will decide to participate. A survey organisation must be aware of that and must instruct the interviewers on how to convince reluctant respondents. Besides that there are other strategies to keep the refusal rate as low as possible. It is known that many people refuse because of temporary reasons or because they will not always participate in surveys. Therefore it may turn out to be very useful to try to convert refusals into respondents. For this a well-defined *persuasion strategy* can be formulated with at least the following elements:

- *Refusal conversion*, which means that people who have already refused to participate will be approached again after a appropriate time interval and (sometimes) by another interviewer to ask for participation again; in general about a quarter to one-third of the 'initial refusers' can be converted into participants during follow-up actions;
- *Special letters* to let people know that the survey organisation wants to try again to convince them, these letters also express an understanding of the legitimacy of peoples reasons for refusing, but also knowing that many refusals are temporary.
- *Incentives* for respondents, which mostly mean small gifts, will help to persuade reluctant people. From the literature, it is known that prepaid incentives have the best effects,

because that expresses the confidence of the survey organisation in the respondent's decision.

In order to be able to carry out the contact and persuasion strategy as intended it is necessary to improve *the professionalism of the field force* as much as possible. This means that all interviewers must know how to use these strategies and also are able to 'tailor' all these ingredients in different situations. Aspects of the quality of the field force are:

- Number of years of *experience*. Most professional behavior must be learned in the field; an interviewer needs a few years (2 – 3 years) to gain experience with respect to all important aspects of the fieldwork.
- The *workload* can also be seen as an aspect of the professionalism of the field corps. If interviewers are involved regularly and for a substantive amount of work they will be more likely to evaluate their interview work as being a professional job and be more willing to invest in it. Besides that the workload must be reasonable, i.e. interviewers must have enough time to carry out all the procedures that are needed to obtain optimal response rates.
- Therefore *the way interviewers are paid* seems to be very important. If interviewers are paid per interview they tend to get the interviews done as quickly as possible and not spend enough time trying to find people at home and convincing reluctant respondents
- The *form, length and depth of the training* of interviewers express what the survey organisation expects from their interviewers and gives the interviewers opportunities to learn the necessary skills. A combination of 'in-office' training and 'on-the-job' training and intensive support and evaluation during the first months in the field can be seen as minimum training requirements. The training should not only focus on the questionnaire and the interview, but also on the contact and persuasion strategy.
- *Rewarding good performances* also indicates what the survey organisation expects from the interviewers with respect to results and fieldwork quality.
- *Employment conditions* might indicate for interviewers how important the survey organisation thinks they are, and of course provide the conditions to do a good job or not.

As already stated a good survey organisation must know what happens in the field, not only to make sure that interviewers do their job as expected, but also to get a view on the quality of the data that are gathered in the field. Therefore *support of interviewers and supervision, as well as monitoring* of how things are going is very important. It is also important to register what has happened in order to be able to evaluate data and procedures. Important aspects and minimum measures belonging to the battery are:

- The way the *support, supervision and monitoring is organized*, which has to do with the grip the survey organisation has on the process in the field; some organisations are very active in this respect; others wait for reactions from their interviewers. When supervision is organized on a regional level the distance between the organisation and the interviewers can be shortened; on the other hand, decentralized supervision does not always mean that distances between institutes/researchers and interviewers are short.
- Organisations which are very active will organize *frequent meetings with their interviewers*; when this is done in a decentralized setting, this will prove to be very positive, because interviewers' problems can be solved very quickly and directly.
- To keep track of the quality of the fieldwork the work of interviewers must be *checked individually* by re-approaching and re-interviewing a (small) part of the assigned sample

cases and of course it must be checked in the field how *they carried out the sampling instructions*.

Information was gathered on all these aspects in the different European countries reviewed, in order to evaluate to what extend survey organisations already work according to this minimum quality standards or will be able to do this.

5.4.2 Response results and fieldwork procedures in European countries

In Annex 5.I an overview is given of these aspects per country. It shows that in most cases the public organisations (mostly statistical organisations) have better response results than private organisations. This can be explained partly by the mandatory character of survey participation (4 countries), how the survey organisation is sponsored (public or private financial resources) and of course by the fact that people are more willing to participate in governmental surveys than in commercial surveys.

5.4.2.1 France

In France public and private survey organisations seem to be able to live up to the minimum quality standards for the data-collection process as described in paragraph 5.4.1. However it seems that more attention is needed with respect to the support and supervision of interviewers, especially when it comes to specific ad-hoc surveys like a literacy survey. The central statistical office has decentralized offices to support and supervise the fieldwork, but it seems that this has more to do with the physical distances in a big country and less with shortening the distance between researcher and interviewer. To improve this relationship it would be better to have regular meetings with interviewers to keep track of their problems and the way they carry out their work. This also holds for private organisations in France, who only seem to have centralised telephone contact with their interviewers.

5.4.2.2 Germany

The central statistical office in Germany has to rely on the statistical offices in the 'Länder' in order to be able to carry out a nation-wide ad-hoc survey. These regional offices also decide by themselves how to design the fieldwork strategy, because they are responsible for the data collection in their region and provide the budget for this. Only when the central office is able to provide financial resources are they in the position to dictate how the fieldwork is carried out. Normally there is a close consultation between the central and regional offices and there are no big differences with respect to fieldwork strategy. The 'Länder' in Germany seem to be able to live up to the minimum requirements with respect to fieldwork-strategy as can be seen in Annex 5.1. Other public and private organisations also seem able to carry out fieldwork strategies according to minimum standards. However it seems to be very difficult to carry out 'refusal conversion', because by law people in Germany have a right to refuse and institutes are obliged to respect this individual right. Nevertheless there seem to be ways of improving the 'persuasion strategy' without violating the law.

Besides that the professionalism of the interviewer corps needs to be improved, in particular the way interviewers are trained, the way they are contracted and the way they are paid. In Germany interviewers are paid per interview, which seems not to be sufficient motivation to put more effort in trying to convince reluctant respondents and to contact persons or households.

The 'survey climate' in Germany seems to be poor. Only the Labour Force Survey achieves a high response rate (97%) but this is a mandatory survey. The response level for other surveys from public and private firms is about 55% to 60%. For a telephone survey a response rate of 70% can sometimes be obtained.

5.4.2.3 Greece

It seems to be very difficult for organisations other than the statistical office in Greece to live up to the minimum quality requirements with respect to fieldwork strategy. This has much to do with the fact that they have no permanent interview organisation which also means a lack of experience with respect to fieldwork strategies, interviewer corps and the way interviewers should be supported, supervised, trained and paid.

5.4.2.4 Italy

Private organisations in Italy seem able to improve their fieldwork strategies. They are aware of the fact that lack of resources prevents them from improving their work. They try to keep in control of the fieldwork within the limited resources they have. For the public organisations, especially the statistical organisation (ISTAT) there is a very peculiar situation. They do not use special 'persuasion strategies' and there is no interviewer corps, as one would expect. In Italy, all regions, provinces and municipalities are by law obliged to contribute to the national statistical system. This also means that all these public organisations have a specific task in collecting data. In fact civil servants of municipalities carry out two-thirds of the interviews. As a consequence it seems to be very difficult to keep track of fieldwork procedures and what really happens in the field. The relationship between researchers and interviewers needs to be improved by giving the central office more direct control of the interviewers and the fieldwork. In the present situation there are three other organisational levels between the researcher and the interviewers: there are 20 regional offices, 103 provinces and the municipalities, who all have a task in the survey process, especially for the data-collection part. Besides that most of the interviewers (two-thirds) are municipal civil servants, who carry out interviews as a (small) part of their job. The question is whether these civil servants behave like an interviewer or more as a representative of the local authority and how people see them. These are not ideal circumstances to carry out surveys in general and certainly are not good conditions to carry out a specific survey like a literacy survey. For such a survey with very specific procedures and conditions, another way of organising a survey is necessary, to give the researcher full control of all parts of the survey process.

5.4.2.5 The Netherlands

As can be seen in Annex 5.1, the obtained response rates for public and private organisations in The Netherlands seem to be the same in general. Both public and private organisations seem to be able to obtain higher response rates, and occasionally they do, but in general they do not use fieldwork strategies which are totally in accord with the described minimum standards. They could, but they don't. A single private organisation uses a well-defined contact-strategy, but this is not common practice in The Netherlands. In particular, the persuasion strategy used in The Netherlands seems to be very weak. 'Refusal conversion' is normally not used because survey agencies seem to be afraid of being intrusive. They try to avoid people lodging complaints against them, which in turn also might worsen the survey climate. As in Germany it must be possible in The Netherlands to formulate an appropriate 'refusal conversion' strategy, which respects the legitimate reasons people have for not co-operating, but at the same time uses the experience that many people refuse because of temporary reasons. The professionalism of the interviewer force needs also to be improved. Interviewers work part-time, are self-employed and are not trained 'on the job', which means that the relationship between survey organisations and their interviewers is weak. This also means interviewers see their interview-work as a temporary and as a 'low-status' job and at the same time they are looking for better rewarded jobs. Especially recently all survey organisations in The Netherlands have 'suffered' from the very good labour market situation when it has been very difficult to recruit new interviewers and at the same time many interviewers left the corps. Also the supervision of the interviewers should be improved. 'Strict checks on how interviewers work' and 'frequent meetings with interviewers to understand the field-problems' are not always carried out, which means they are not standard procedures.

The survey climate in The Netherlands seems to be comparable with the survey-climate in Germany. The obtained response results for voluntary surveys are more or less the same and the survey climate seems to have deteriorated in recent years due to an increase in telemarketing and direct sales.

5.4.2.6 Portugal

The Portuguese NSI is able to obtain relatively high response rates. The fieldwork-strategy seems to be very important for this. The contact- and persuasion-strategy seem to be in accordance with the minimum requirements. Interviewers have no contract, are paid per interview, which means that their professionalism can be improved. On the other hand support and supervision seem to be very well organized. The fieldwork organisation of the NSI seems to be in control of what happens in the field. This does not appear to be the case for private organisations as Annex 5.1 shows.

5.4.2.7 Sweden

Public and private organisations in Sweden differ with respect to the obtained response rates. This of course has to do with the status of the organisations (public or private), but it seems also that the professionalism of the interviewer corps of private organisations can be improved: interviewers work part-time, are self-employed, paid per interview and seem to be trained less intensively.

5.4.2.8 Great Britain

The difference in response rates between public and private survey organisations in Great Britain seems to be relatively small. It appears that only the status of the organisation makes the difference. There are only few aspects on which both organisations differ from each other: 'years of experience', 'way they pay interviewers' and 'employment conditions'. But all organisations seem to be very well able to carry out fieldwork procedures according to the described standards.

5.4.3 Summary

The battery of minimum measures to improve response rates and to avoid unnecessary variation consists of the following elements:

- *Contact strategy (advance letter, unlimited number of contact attempts, variation of contact attempts in time);*
- *Persuasion strategy (refusal conversion, special letters, respondent incentives);*
- *Professionalism of the interviewer corps (experience, workload, hourly payment, training, rewards, employment conditions);*
- *Support, supervision and monitoring (active support and supervision, fieldmeetings, individual checks).*

In general the use of the battery with minimum measures must be improved and this seems to be quite possible. This also means that any unnecessary variation in fieldwork strategy can be reduced.

The contact strategy for most non-public organisations must be improved. Also the persuasion strategy must be improved in Germany, Italy, The Netherlands and for the non-public organisations in Greece and Portugal. The professionalism of the interviewer corps must be improved in Germany, Italy, The Netherlands, and Portugal and for the non-public organisation in Greece and Sweden. The support and supervision of interviewers must be improved in all countries with a decentralized field organisation, most private organisations and the Netherlands.

Nevertheless an 80% response target for an international literacy survey in Europe does not seem possible unless national statistical offices carry out the survey and are allowed to proclaim survey participation as mandatory or at least people think that participation is compulsory. In most countries, where these national offices carry out nation wide surveys, the 'mandatory' character of survey participation seems to help obtain high response rates (France, Germany, Greece, Italy, and Portugal). It is questionable whether these organisations would be able to obtain such high response rates if people knew that participation was not compulsory.

Although a high response rate (at least 80%) does not seem realistic, decent response rates do seem possible, if 'current best methods' (the 'battery') are used in all countries and their use is monitored. This also means that in France and Italy the researcher or survey manager at the central office should have better instruments to control and monitor the fieldwork procedures.

5.5 Dataprocessing, weighting and analyses

5.5.1 Minimum requirements

It is very difficult to establish high quality international procedures for data-entry, coding, weighting, etc. The checks in questionnaires (CATI, CAPI) and data-entry programs, coding procedures and quality level, weighting methods and procedures must be well formulated and documented beforehand in a design for the whole survey process. For future international literacy surveys there is a lot of co-ordinated guidance and monitoring needed. However, clear plans and good guidance can only work if survey organisations are really capable of doing the job. This means that these organisations must have substantial experience with respect to all aspects of the survey process.

They must have at least a *few experienced mathematical statisticians and survey methodologist in their staff.*

In order to improve weighting procedures to compensate for non-response, organisations should *collect data on non-respondents* as an integrated part of the survey design and use these data in competing non-response adjustment procedures.

Organisations should also have *well trained coders* and procedures to monitor coding processes and of course documentation on the quality of their coding procedures.

Especially for literacy survey it would be better if organisations have the ability or experience to *print questionnaires and testbooks* properly and have *qualified translators* available. The last aspect seems to be important because the international comparability of an international literacy survey must be secured and there seem always to be difficulties in translating questionnaires and testbooks.

If organisations cannot live up to these requirements, there will be a great risk that literacy survey procedures will not be carried out as they should, no matter what guidance, co-ordination and sanctions there will be.

In order to evaluate whether survey organisation are able to handle all aspects of the survey process, especially concerning the stages after data are collected, information is gathered on the following items:

- *computer assisted questionnaire design, data-entry and data-editing,*

- *coding of industry, occupation and education according to ISIC, ISOC, ISCED classifications,*
- *imputation of missing data,*
- *weighting to compensate for unequal selection probabilities, non-response and noncoverage,*
- *calculation of standard errors,*
- *analyses of the data.*

5.5.2 Dataprocessing, weighting and analyses in European countries

In Annex 5.II an overview is presented on dataprocessing, weighting and analyses in different European countries. As can be seen there seems to be a difference between the statistical/public organisations and the private organisations, in general. Private organisations do not always use sophisticated statistical methods like imputation and weighting. When they do, they use simple standard methods most of the time, because in general they don't have statisticians or survey methodologists in their organisations to do this work.

Data on non-respondents are only collected by the public agency in Great Britain. In all other countries these data are not collected or available and it seems to be questionable whether the organisations in these countries could use these data in alternative weighting schemes.

In general survey organisations by in or contract out printing and graphic design facilities and if needed qualified translators. It need not to be necessary to have these expertise within the own organisation, but institutes must avoid using non-professional printers and translators because of budget problems.

In **France** the difference between public and private organisations appears to be small. Private organisations also use imputation, weighting and standard error calculation to improve their data quality, but they don't have statisticians. There might be a danger that private organisation promise more than they can realize. Data on non-respondents are not collected, but the public organisations have more data that can be used to correct for non-response.

The private organisations in **Germany** seem to have pretty good capabilities to carry out all the necessary steps with respect to dataprocessing, weighting, etc. The same holds for the central statistical office and other public organisations.

In **Greece** the situation seems to be less positive. The public organisations might be able to meet the requirements, but it is not certain that they can. The private organisation certainly cannot. They have no substantial experience (only ad-hoc) with respect to data-entry, and coding. They sometimes use simple standard methods for imputation and calculation of standard errors and they do not normally reweight their data.

In **Portugal** the NSI is very well able to carry out all necessary statistical procedures to improve data quality, although the number of auxiliary variables to reweight the survey data is limited. The Portuguese NSI has statisticians and methodologists within the staff and they also co-operate with universities if necessary. The non-public organisations in Portugal do not seem well equipped to carry out these parts of the survey process.

The private organisations in **Italy** seem to be able to carry out most of the tasks with respect to dataprocessing, but they don't use imputation. They correct for missing data (for key-variables) by going back to the respondent (by phone or mail). They 'sometimes' reweight, and calculate standard errors, but they don't have statisticians in their own organisations. They do not seem to have much experience with complex statistical techniques. The public organisations in Italy seem to be able to carry out all the tasks. The only peculiar thing is that the statistical organisation in Italy hires other organisations to carry out data-entry.

In **The Netherlands**, **Sweden** and **Great Britain** there seems to be a comparable situation. The statistical organisations have all the experience they need available within their own organisations. The private organisations have some expertise, but it is limited and only used when sponsors will pay for it. There are specialized organisations, which can do parts of the job (e.g. imputation) very well, but there seem to be no private organisation who is able to carry out all the tasks involved to a high standard.

5.5.3 Summary

It seems to be very difficult to find private organisations that will be able to carry out dataprocessing, weighting and analyses according to the minimum standards. Some certainly are able in principle, but they will not have substantial experience on the quality level that is needed. So there will always be some risk that they will deliver inferior quality. If the statistical agencies do not carry out the international literacy survey, private institutes have to look for co-operation with other organisations (maybe statistical institutes) to make sure that all the expertise that is needed will be available.

5.6 General Conclusions and Recommendations

The purpose of the inventory of the reported survey practices was to evaluate the possibility of avoiding "unnecessary variation in survey practices" in order to improve quality and comparability, which is judge to be extremely important for a survey that will be used for international comparisons and policies.

1. *Reduction of variation possible:* The first conclusion is, that there seems to be a lot of variation. But most of this variation is not necessary, which means that the existing variation can be reduced for most:

   - With respect to sampling design and procedures, the requirements of probability sampling can be met if National Statistical Institutes can be involved in the survey, either by doing the whole survey or by doing the survey in co-operation with others.
   - When it comes to experience and expertise, public institutes seem to have great experience with respect to large and complex, but continuous and ongoing survey, while private organisations are experts in small ad-hoc survey. Literacy surveys are large or complex and ad-hoc. Also public organisations have more expertise and experience of dataprocessing, coding, weighting, imputation, etc. while other institutes in most countries have specific expertise with respect to literacy. This also points at the necessity of co-operation between the different types of institutes.
   - There is a lot of variation between countries and between institutes within countries in fieldwork and data collection procedures. This variation can and should be reduced by the use of the 'battery' of minimum measures to reduce non-response. Budget constraints should not limit the use of this battery.
   - When a new international literacy survey is designed and planned it is not useful to aim at a high and unrealistic response rate. It is better to encourage the use of the 'battery' and provide the necessary budgets for it and to encourage research on non-response bias.

2. *Reduction of variation possible, but co-operation necessary:* there seems to be no institute in all the investigated countries that has sufficient experience and expertise in all aspects of the survey process when it comes to literacy surveys. Therefore it seems to be necessary to form combinations or consortia of institutes per country or for institutes to buy in the necessary expertise. This will combine all necessary expertise and experience in order to get the best possible survey practices and to avoid unnecessary variation. This

also means that organisations must have the right attitude to work together and form teams in which all necessary expertise is present. This demands an open attitude and willingness to be open about what expertise organisations have and what they have not.

3. It is not clear whether different policies and regulations concerning confidentiality and data protection will hamper co-operation of organisations within a country and of organisations in different countries to carry out an international literacy survey. This aspect is not covered is this inventory as the need for co-operation was not so clear when this inventory started. *Therefore it would be good to investigate whether data-protection acts and policies can set limits to the proposed co-operation.*

4. *An international expert team is necessary, if all necessary expertise in a particular country is not available.* This also demands an open attitude of organisations. Such a team can advise organisations and support them on aspects of the survey process for which these organisations themselves have not sufficient expertise. The team can help them also to find and select the expertise that is needed. Such a team can also function as a *quality assessment team* in order to evaluate whether all expertise and experience is available in countries and can specify in more detail what quality and expertise is needed.

5. But all this will not work if the budget that is available to carry out a literacy survey is too tight and forces organisations to look for economies. These mostly will be found at the weakest parts in the survey process, which also tend to be the parts that must be strengthened. *Therefore the budget needed to carry out a high quality international literacy survey properly* must be based on experiences with complex surveys which are carried out according to the (minimum) requirements as described in this report.

Annex 5.I Overview of fieldwork strategy

Aspect	*France*		*Germany*		*Greece*		*Italy*		*Netherlands*		*Portugal*		*Sweden*		*UK*	
	Public	Private	Public	Private	Public	Private	Public	Private	Public	Private	Public	Private	Public	Private	Public	Private
Mandatory participation	Yes	No	Sometimes	No	Yes	No	Yes	No	No	No			No	No	No	No
Response % (average)	90	60	97/60	55-60	90	?	90	60	60	50-60	80-90	?	80-90	60-70	70-85	60-70
Contact strategy																
- use of letter	Yes	Yes	Yes	Yes	Yes	Yes	Yes	?	Yes	Yes	Yes + Adds	No	Yes	Yes	Yes	Yes
- # contact attempts	no limit	no limit	No limit	3-4	No limit	Depends	2-3	3-4	No limit	(No) limit	No limit	Limited	No limit	No limit	No limit	No limit
- spread contacts	Yes	Yes	Yes	Yes	Yes	No	No	Yes	Yes	Yes/no	Yes	Yes	Yes	Yes	Yes	Yes
Persuasion strategy																
-refusal conversion	Yes	Yes	No	No	Yes	No	No	No	No	No/yes	Yes	No	Yes	Yes	Yes	Yes
-special letters etc…	No	No	No	No	No	No	No	No	No	No/yes	?	No	Yes	Yes	Yes	Yes
- resp. incentives	Yes	Yes	Sometimes	No	No	No	No	Yes	No	Yes/no	No	No	No	Yes	Yes	Yes
Interviewer corps																
-# years experience	5-10	5-6	6-10	6-7	1-5	?	?	4-6	5-10	4-6	6	?	?	10	5	2
-workload	Part/full	Part	Part	Part	Full	Part	Full	Part	Part	Part	Part/Full	Part.	Full	Part	Full	Full
-rewards	Yes	No	No	Yes	Yes	Yes	No	Yes	No	No/yes	Yes	No	Yes	Yes	Yes	Yes
-more days training	Yes	Yes	Yes	Yes	Yes	Yes	No	No	Yes	No/yes	Yes	No	Yes	No	Yes	Yes
-training on the job	Yes	Yes	No	Yes	Yes	No	No	No	No	No	Yes	No	Yes	Yes	Yes	Yes
-retraining	Yes	Yes	Yes	No	No	No	No	No	No	No	Yes	No	Yes	No	Yes	Yes
- way of paying	Hourly	Hourly	Per Interview	Per Interview	Per Interview	Per Interview	Hourly	Per Interview	Per Interview	Hourly	Per Interview	Per Interview	Hourly	Per Interview	Hourly	Per Interview
-employment conditions	Contract	Contract	Self	Self	contract	Self	Empl.	Self	Self	Self	Self	Self	Empl.	Self	Empl.	Self
Support/supervision																
-central/decentralized	Region	Central	Region	Both	Region	Central	Region	Central	Central	Central	Region	Central	Central	Central	Region	Region
-meetings	No	No	Yes	Yes	Yes	No	Yes	No	No	No	Yes	No	Yes	Yes	Yes	Yes
-individual checks	Yes	Yes	Yes	Yes	Yes	Yes	Yes	Yes	Yes	Yes	Yes	Yes	Yes	Yes	Yes	Yes
-checks at resp. home	Yes	Yes	Yes	Yes	Yes	Yes	Yes	Yes	Yes	Yes	Yes	Yes	Yes	Yes	Yes	Yes

Annex 5.II Overview dataprocessing, weighting and analyses

Aspect	*France*		*Germany*		*Greece*		*Italy*		*Netherlands*		*Portugal*		*Sweden*		*UK*	
	Public	Private	Public	Private	Public	Private	Public	Private	Public	Private	Public	Private	Public	Private	Public	Private
Experienced group for data-entry/data-editing	CAPI	Yes and hired	CAPI	Yes	Yes	No	No (hired)	Yes	CAPI/ CATI	CAPI/ CATI	CAPI/	Yes	CAPI/ CATI	Some-times & hired	CAPI/ CATI	CAPI/ CATI
Experienced group for coding/automated cod.	Yes	Yes	Yes	Yes	Yes	No	Yes	Yes	Yes	Yes	Yes	No	Yes and automa-ted	Some-times	Yes and automa-ted	Yes
Use of imputation	Yes	Sometimes	Yes	Yes	Yes	Some-times	Yes	No	Yes	Someti mes	Yes	No	Yes	No	Not usually	No
Use of weighting meth.	Yes, (Calmar)	Yes, (Quan-time)	Yes (Bascula)	Yes (Quan-time)	Yes (own softw.)	Usually not (SPSS)	Yes (own softw.)	Some-times (Quanti me)	Yes (Bascula)	Yes (Westva r,Bascul a)	Yes (call-jack)	Yes	Yes	Yes (stan-dard)	Yes (SPSS, Calmar)	Yes (Quan-time)
Purpose of weighting	Inclusio n, nonresp onse	Inclusion	All purpose s	All purposes, if data available	Nonres-ponse	n.a.	All purposes docu-mented	All purpose s	All purpose s	All purpose s	All purpose s	Inclusion probabili-ties	All purposes	All purposes	All purposes	Mainly nonres-ponse
Standard weighting variables	Age,sex, family type, area, professi on	Popula-tion variables	Age, sex, 2nd homes, citizens hip	Popula-tion variables		n.a.	Age,sex,hs h size, munici-pality	Age, sex region	Age, sex region, househo ld	Age, sex, region, househo ld	Age,sex	Age,sex, region		Popula-tion va-riables	Age, sex region	Age, sex region
Calculation standard error	Yes (jacknif e)	Yes (jacknife)	Yes (Ypsilon -Yfanal)	Yes (jacknife)	Yes (Horwit z&Th.)	Yes (stan-dard)	Yes (lineair)	Some-times	Yes (jacknif e)	Yes (jacknif e)	Yes (Jack-nife)	Yes (Jack-nife)	Yes	Some-times	Yes (Taylor Series)	Some-times
Data on nonrespon-dents	Normall y not	No	No	No	No	No	No specific data	No	No	Some data	Some data	No	No	No	Yes	No
Involved in analyses	Yes	Yes	Yes	Yes	Yes	Yes	Yes	Yes	Yes	Yes	Yes	Yes	Yes	Yes	Yes	Yes
Experienced metho-dologists available	Yes	No	Yes	Yes	Yes	Yes	Yes	No	Yes	Few	Yes	Few	Yes	Few, coopera-tion universi-ty	Yes	No

PART B

Secondary analysis and follow-up survey

This second part of this report presents the results from the both the secondary analysis and from the follow-up survey. The direction of the secondary analysis changed as work progressed and as more information became available with the publication of the IALS technical report in 1998. See chapter 1 for an outline of the programme of work.

B.I Secondary Analyis

Chapters 6 and 7 present the results from secondary analyses of the IALS data set. Chapter 6 focuses on the effect of translation on the performance of items. Chapter 7 is concerned with the balance between sophistication and complexity on the one hand and the benefits of simplicity on the other.

B.II Qualitative research

The first stages in this study were to try and understand more about the dynamics of the IALS interview and to find out more about respondent commitment to the request and the underlying motivations to try hard or to do well. Qualitative research was carried out in the three IALS countries involved in the project, Great Britain, France and Sweden. Chapter 8 reports on the findings from this research. Chapter 9 looks at a small trial of financial incentives on the engagement of respondents in the task.

B.III Follow-up survey

The largest single strand in the programme of work was the follow-up survey of IALS respondents in France, Sweden and Great Britain and of respondents in Portugal to the Portuguese Adult Literacy Survey. The methodology of the follow-up survey is documented in Chapter 10.

The results from the follow-up survey in France, Britain and Sweden are presented in Chapter 11 which looks at the individual items along with two overall measures of proficiency, the scaled score and the proportion correct. This chapter also considers differences between countries in the data completeness and on the problems of establishing consistency in scoring.

As part of the overall interview information was collected on the environment in which the respondent was completing the booklet and following the assessment booklet the respondent was asked some debriefing questions on their experience. These are reported in Chapter 12.

Chapter 13 looks at the PALS follow-up survey and the results from the IALS carried out in Portugal as part of this study. This chapter looks at items and summary measures in both surveys and reprises the issue of simplicity versus sophistication from Chapter 7.

Chapter 14 attempts to draw together the main strands of the project and consider how such surveys might be improved.

6. Weaknesses and defects of IALS

Alain Blum and France Guérin-Pace, Institut National d'Etudes Démographiques, Paris

6.1 Introduction

The results of the IALS survey (1995) suggest that three quarters of the French population have an ability level in terms of 'literacy' which prevents them handling the normal matters of everyday life: reading a newspaper, writing a letter, understanding a short text, payslip etc. Based on the scales proposed by the originators of the IALS survey, 75% of French adults have a 'literacy' level estimated at 1 or 2 for comprehension of prose texts, whereas 46% of Americans, 40% of Dutch and 28% of Swedes are at this level. For comprehension of schematic texts the percentages are 63%, 50%, 36% and 25% respectively and finally for comprehension of texts with a quantitative content the percentages are 57%, 46%, 35% and 25% respectively. When the highest level of ability is considered (level 5), only 11 French people have the skills required for this level.

The extent of the differences between countries on the one hand and the discrepancy between this and other data available on France on the other have led to considerable suspicion about the validity of this type of survey and the international comparisons resulting from it[1].

The first assumption put forward is one of a lack of equivalent difficulty in the questions asked once they have passed through the translation filter. A second assumption of bias that we also examine concerns the attitude of the people questioned towards a survey of this kind. Comments from the interviewers on the ground would suggest that in some regions, particularly in the south-west of France, the survey was very badly received and the people interviewed showed their lack of interest in and disapproval of this kind of questioning. Without re-examing the different contexts applicable to each of the countries, it is sufficient to say that the presence of the heading 'Ministry of National Education', on each page of the French questionnaire made the survey sound very much like school and put off a large number of the people interviewed.

The question of the interviewee's motivation when faced with a questionnaire which is long and also intended to test the ability of each is naturally crucial. Is it possible to hypothesise uniform behaviour of populations at regional and national level? This bias associated with people's attitudes towards the survey can be established by an interpretation of the missing answers or the speed and care given to the answers.

Here we shall focus our attention not on the conditions under which the survey was carried out in the various countries, which are the subject of a large part of this report, but on the validity of the comparisons made, examined on the basis of the individual data and general results provided by the survey in 13 countries: the 9 countries in the first wave of the survey, i.e. Canada, the United States, France, Germany, the Netherlands, Poland, Sweden, Switzerland and Ireland, and four countries in the second wave, Great Britain, New Zealand, Flemish-speaking Belgium, and Northern Ireland.[2].

[1] Because the methodologies and forms of definition of illiteracy are extremely diverse, it is virtually impossible to compare the various assessments that exist. We merely note that according to INSEE 5.4% of the adult population « has at least one of the manifestations of illiteracy » and the definition of illiteracy given by INSEE corresponds in large part to the concept of literacy (Bodier and Chambas, 1996). According to a survey of conscripts, 8% of young people aged from 16 to 24 years have reading difficulties (Bentolila and Fort, 1994).

[2] These countries were chosen from the ones in the second wave of the survey only, on the basis of availability of data.

6.2 Comparison of the item percent correct hierarchy in the different countries

Firstly, for France we looked at the coherence between the classification of items by the percentage of right answers and the ranking defined a priori by the score allocated to each item. Each item is given a score defining a theoretical difficulty scale proposed by the originators of the survey (Figure 6.1). The success hierarchy observed corresponds to the item classification from the most to the least successful, measured by the percentage of right answers. If the main hypothesis of the survey is verified, i.e. that the questions are psychometrically independent among social groups and linguistic groups, then the item success profile must be independent of the language of the questionnaire. Large permutations between the actual and theoretical hierarchies suggest that there is a discrepancy between the theoretical difficulty of the questions and the actual difficulty in a given country.

Figure 6.1 **Score and theoretical rank**

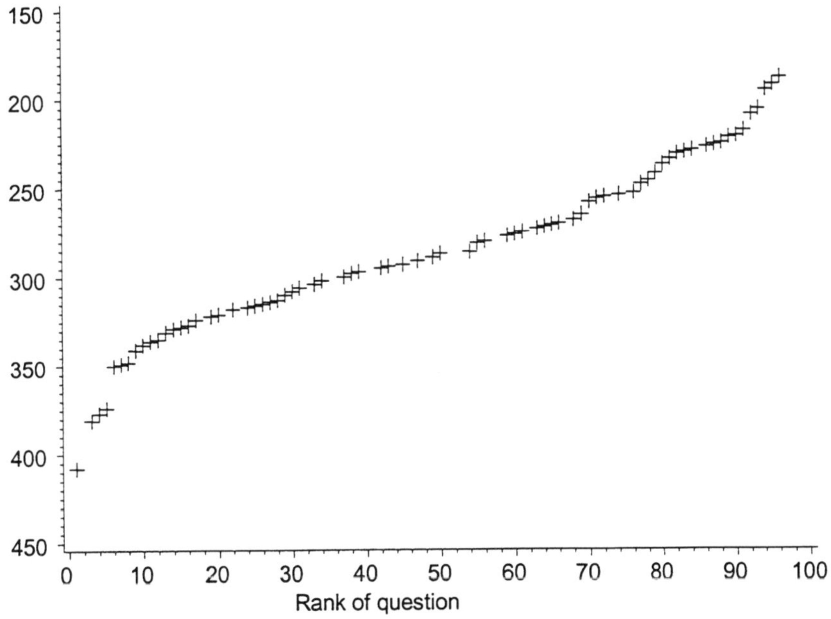

The IALS survey had two main objectives: 'to establish scales which would enable useful comparisons to be made [...] of people with different abilities. If such an assessment proves possible, the objective is then to describe the reading and writing abilities which people have in different countries.'[3] Thus the validity of the survey is based on a strong hypothesis of the existence of an identical difficulty scale of questioning between cultures and languages.

Translations of the questionnaires and documents were done in each of the countries concerned and checked by Statistics-Canada, the international co-ordinators of the survey. Three versions of the questionnaire exist in French: Canadian, Swiss and French. Similarly, the British questionnaire differs from the American one and the one for English-speaking Canada.

The translation had to be both high quality and faithful to the original text. However, no precise accuracy criterion was defined and, as some authors have commented (Kalton et al., 1995) the usual rule of back translation (new translation into English of the translated text and comparison with the original) was not followed. As emphasised by Goldstein and Wood (1989), this procedure is essential even if it is unsatisfactory.

[3] Development of human resources in Canada and OECD, 1997.

We examined whether the difficulty of the questions could actually be considered equivalent in each of the languages. This is a matter of judging not the quality of the translations but the consequences of translation of a document and questions related to this on the level of difficulty of each of the items and the mechanisms used by the interviewees to respond. Equivalence in terms of difficulty is actually defined more by the complexity of the documents than by their type or content and cannot be based directly on a comparison of the percentages of success in different questions. A difference in success rate for a given item may simply reveal a difference between the literacy levels of the two populations concerned. However, a necessary (but unsatisfactory) condition of equivalence of the difficulty levels is compliance with the difficulty hierarchies. A question, which is more difficult than another one in the Canadian English questionnaire, must remain so in the French version of the questionnaire.

Two areas of investigation can be followed to examine this hierarchy compliance. The first is to compare the hierarchy supplied a priori by the originators of the survey with the hierarchies observed in the various countries. The difficulty hierarchy of the questions is established from the 'score' allocated to each question of between 0 and 500 - the questions with the highest scores being considered the most difficult. This present score is calculated using a series of criteria, taking into account the complexity of the document to which the question refers and the complexity of the link between question and document (Kirsch et al., 1998).

The correlation between the question difficulty, indicated by the score, and the success observed, measured by the percentage of right answers, is not satisfactory in France (Figure 6.2).

Figure 6.2 **Percentage of right answers as a function of the score and item level, France**

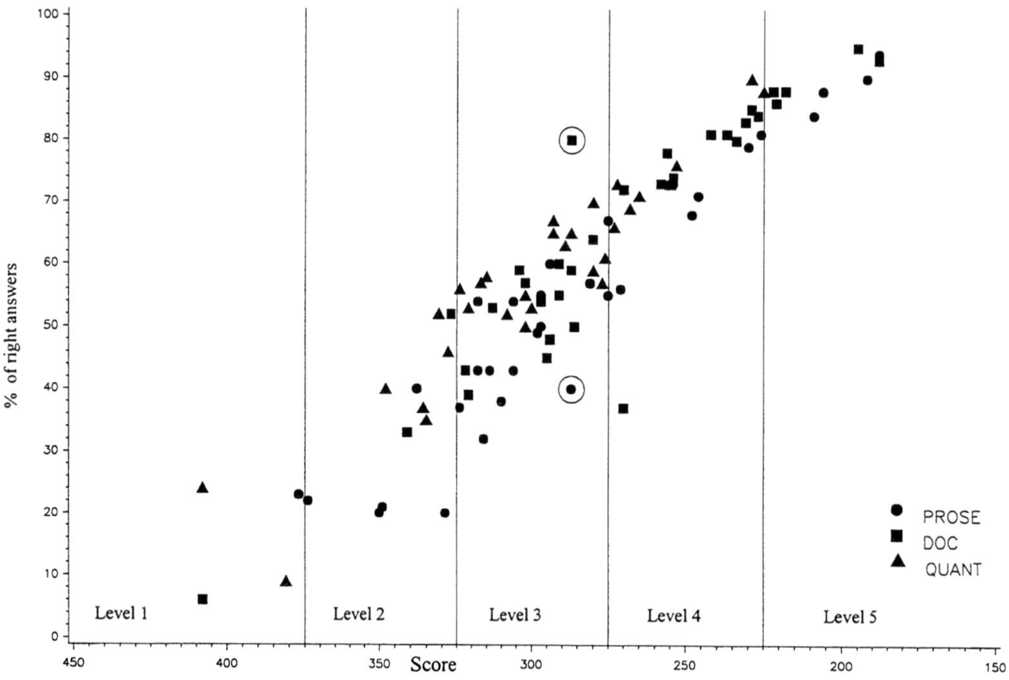

The dispersion of the cluster illustrated shows that the levels of difficulty defined a priori are far from being reflected in the success in the various items. For example, this figure shows two questions with the same difficulty score (points circled on the graph), for which the success rate varies from 40 to 80%. Moreover, although the scale of difficulty is built up on the basis of a logistic type relationship between the percentage of right answers and the score, the relationship observed in France appears to be linear and dispersed. In the United States the relationship is closer to a logistic function but the dispersion around the trend remains high (Figure 6.3).

Figure 6.3 **Percentage of right answers as a function of the score and item level, USA**

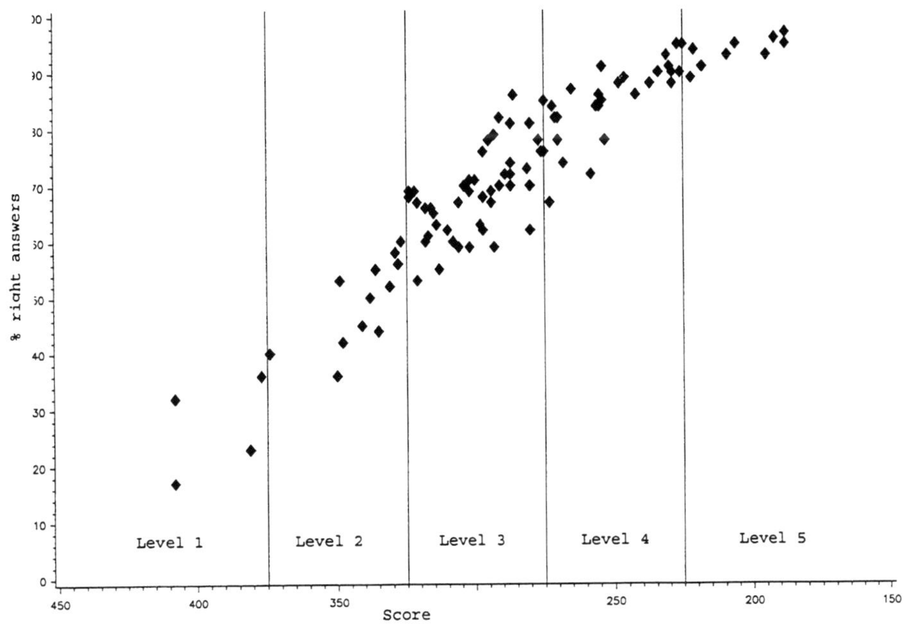

A comparison of the difficulty observed for each of the questions with the preset difficulty is not sufficient to understand the basis for the divergences in terms of language. To examine this point more deeply, we compared the success rates observed question by question, in the countries looked at two by two. If the questions are presumed to be of equivalent difficulty in two countries considered, the graphic representation of the percentage of right answers to each of the questions will then approximate to a straight line with a gradient which is a function of the total literacy level. However, examination of the graphs shows clusters in dispersed form in most cases. From a comparison between the success percentages found in France and English-speaking Canada – the questionnaire on which the French translation is based – we recorded a set of questions for which the success rate variations were high and attempted to understand these divergences (Figure 6.4). We did not use any particular quantitative criterion for this but based our findings on observation of the figure, making allowance for the relative deviation between the success percentages.

6.3 Problems associated with translation of the items

Initially, we compared the way the questions were formulated in the two languages and found that there were significant differences in the translations. On a broader scale, we examined the whole questionnaire to establish the questions where the wording was not 'equivalent' in French and English. We found 35 questions (circled in Figure 6.4) where the translations differed and analysed these divergences under three headings.

Figure 6.4 **Comparison of percentage of right answers, France and English-speaking Canada**

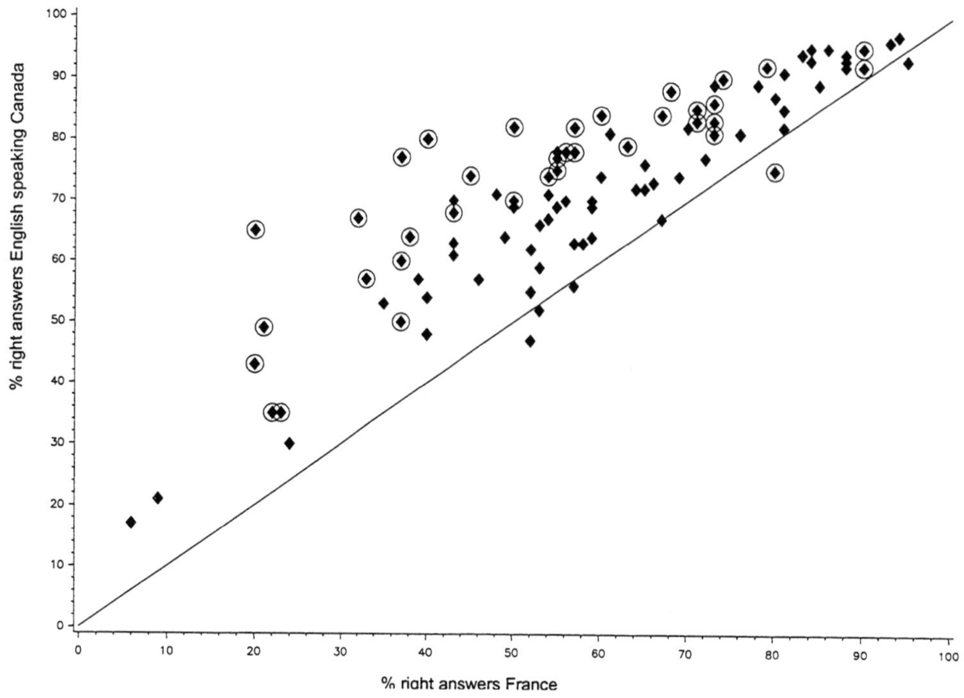

6.3.1 Omission of repetition of terms

Repetition of a term in the question in the accompanying text adjoining the answer is more frequent in the original documents (English) and forms the first source of bias. For example, in a question referring to the use of 'couches jetables', the phrase containing the answer uses the term 'changes complets'. In the Anglo-Canadian questionnaire the term 'disposable diapers' is repeated. The respondent is drawn in English more easily towards the phrase containing this term and therefore to the right answer, whereas in French the reader has to understand that these terms are equivalent before being able to answer. On several occasions in the French questionnaire a different term which has the same meaning is used in the answer. The resultant bias considerably increases the difficulty of the questions in French.

6.3.2 Greater precision of English terms

As a general rule, the questions are drafted in a more precise form in English. For example, one question rendered in English by 'What is the most important thing to keep in mind?' is translated into French as 'Que doit on avoir à l'esprit?' [What must be kept in mind?]. However the sentence containing the answer reads in English 'the most important thing' and in French 'la chose la plus importante' [the most important thing]. The link is therefore easier to establish in English. Another task is defined in English as 'List all the rates'. It is translated into French as 'Quels taux' [What rates], omitting to state 'all the rates'. This omission frequently led French interviewees to state only one rate instead of the list required for the answer to be considered correct.

6.3.3 Translation errors

Some translation errors may be relatively unimportant from a strictly linguistic point of view but become important in relation to comprehension. Three examples are particularly characteristic. In an article on transmission of allergies, the English phrase 'from an allergy sufferer's mother' is translated as 'hérité de la mère allergique' [inherited from the allergic mother] instead of 'hérité de la mère du malade allergique'. The question refers to the way in which the allergy gene is transmitted and becomes ambiguous for a French reader. Similarly, from a weather map showing the forecast for the weekend the task is to note what the weather will be like 'durant la semaine' [during the week] whereas the original text said 'during the week-end'. We were able to verify that many French interviewees tried to extrapolate maps according to flows indicated by arrows in order to attempt to forecast the weather for the week and therefore answered the question wrongly. A question rendered in French as 'soulignez la phrase indiquant ce que les Australiens ont fait pour ...' [underline the sentence indicating what the Australians did to...] is linked to a text worded: 'Une commission fut réunie en Australie' [A commission was set up in Australia]. In English the question is 'What the Australians did to help decide...', the corresponding wording being 'The Australians set up a commission'. The answer is ambiguous in French because the place is given instead of the people.

6.3.4 Other sources of error

Sources of error, which are less widespread, nevertheless reveal the complexity of a definition of difficulty equivalence between items expressed in different languages. The example below is typical and can be interpreted in terms of 'cultural bias'. The task required is to work out which are the comedies in a review covering four films. In two of these reviews, in both English and French, the term comedy appears, which makes the question easy. In France, however, we find that many interviewees gave as their answer a third film, which from the description is obviously not a comedy. The only possible explanation is the presence in that film of the actor Michel Blanc, who is well known for his roles in many comedies but is little known abroad. Here, association predominated in the answering process to the detriment of careful reading of the reviews.

However, we could find no obvious reasons for some items and conversely other questions, although fewer in number, have approximately the same success rates in both countries although the translations are not equivalent. In summary, one third of the items are more difficult in the French version of the questionnaire. In Table A6.2 in appendix to this chapter we give a detailed list of these questions and the explanations which can be given, in accordance with the scale defined above.

6.4 Classification of countries by the item success profile

Divergences between the level of difficulty of the questions defined in advance and their success can also be seen in countries other than France. Various measurements of the degree of similarity of the hierarchies show that even with a high degree of association they differ quite significantly from one country to another. We systematically calculated the values of the correlation factors between the success hierarchies observed in each of the countries, defined by the percentage of right answers, and the mean correlation ratio between the ranks (Kendall's coefficient). Although all are significant, the correlation factors are stronger between the hierarchies relating to questionnaires in the same language (American and Canadian English) (Table A6.1 in the appendix to this chapter). The values are between 0.65 and 0.86. For example, the correlation is 0.86 between English-speaking Canada and the United States and between English-speaking Canada and the United Kingdom but only 0.67 between English-speaking Canada and Sweden. This result confirms the bias associated with translation of the questionnaires, which changes the scale of difficulty of the questions. It also suggests the existence of a cultural bias, which is more difficult to demonstrate but is reflected in a greater or lesser degree of difficulty of the questions in the different countries depending on the subject covered by the documents.

To demonstrate a more systematic correlation between the different translations and the similarities to be found between different countries, we classified the countries in different groups according to their item's success hierarchy.

6.4.1 Classification of countries by item success level

We established a partition of countries by a cluster analysis according to the profile of success in the various questions, measured by the percentage of right answers or by the rank[4]. The first cluster analysis is based on the logit of percentage correct in the questions in each country[5].

Figure 6.5 **Classification on logit of percentage of right answers exluding dropped questions**

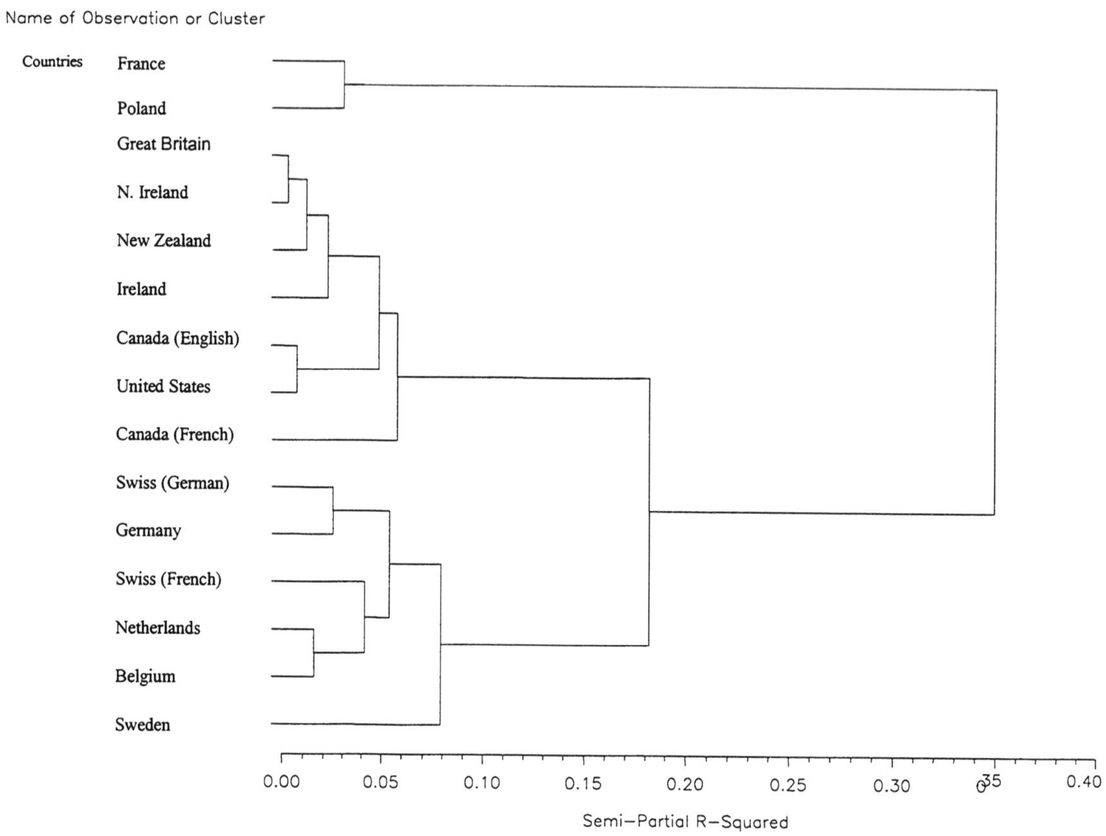

The form of the classification tree and the inertia loss variation suggest a breakdown of the countries into three classes (Figure 6.5). The first group consists of France and Poland, the second is all the English-speaking countries plus French-speaking Canada and the third is countries speaking a language of the Germanic type (German, Flemish and Dutch) plus Sweden and French-speaking Switzerland. The data used here incorporate the general success rate in the survey, resulting in the same group for France and Poland which have the lowest results. However, the other countries in which the literacy level distribution is closer are grouped by a combination of linguistic and geographic criteria.

6.4.2 Classification in ranks

To place the emphasis on the similarities in terms of relative success in the questions regardless of the percentage of right answers to each of the items, we set up a classification by

---

[4] The rank of each item is given by the proportion of correct answers (rank 1 having the highest proportion of success).

[5] All the cluster analyses are of the hierarchical ascendant type. The first was carried out on the *logit* table of success rate percentages for each of the items, i.e. on the matrix: $M(i, j) = (\log(p_{ij}/1\text{-}p_{ij})$ in which i is the item, j the country (or the country and the language) and $p_{i,j}$ the item success rate percentage i in the country j.

the rank of each of the questions in the success hierarchy[6]. Irrespective of the population distribution by levels of literary, among the various countries a correlation can be seen between the ranking of the questions, the language of the interview and the country in which the survey was carried out.

Two countries are then put in the same class if the difficulty hierarchy is similar in both, irrespective of the general success rate. France is thus grouped with French-speaking Switzerland, as we shall see below, despite a very high variation in the population distribution in the five literacy levels in the two countries.

The initial classification is established on the basis of all 97 items[7]. The results of this classification confirm the conclusions from the classification of the item success rate percentages.

The contents of clusters show that the parallels established are based on a combination of geographic proximity and linguistic proximity (Figure 6.6). All the English-speaking countries are grouped in one class. Thus the USA is first grouped with English-speaking Canada and then New Zealand; Great Britain, Northern Ireland and the Republic of Ireland form a class. These latter countries have the same version of the questionnaire. The two groups are combined and then form a single class with French-speaking Canada. Another class includes the non English-speaking European countries, divided according to the language of the questionnaire. France and French-speaking Switzerland form one class, Germany and German-speaking Switzerland another and Flemish-speaking Belgium and the Netherlands another. Sweden remains isolated before being added to the class formed by Germany and German-speaking Switzerland.

This overall result goes strongly against the foundations of the protocol of this survey, which are based on the fact that performance is independent of the language of questioning. Could the speaking of a common language be the expression of a stronger cultural proximity which could generate these groupings?

6.4.3 Classification of countries by removing the questions with a specific parameter

To confirm with certainty the results we have demonstrated, we carried out another breakdown of the countries on a restricted number of items. For this analysis we used the items which were not 'detected' as posing a problem by the assessment procedure developed by IALS. The originators of the survey actually designed methods of locating the questions for which the success profiles differed significantly in one or more countries (Yamamoto, 1998). For these questions, 'unique' parameters were estimated. It is assumed that once these questions are withdrawn, the linguistic aggregation effect does not apply in the distributions. The estimation of the unique parameters should correct any bias resulting from the translation process itself or from specific linguistic characteristics.

We carried out this study on the group of countries surveyed in the first wave only, that is the United States, English-speaking Canada, French-speaking Canada, the Netherlands, Sweden, Poland, France, French-speaking Switzerland, Germany and German-speaking Switzerland, to which we also added Great Britain[8]. After removal of the questions with a unique parameter in more than one country, 63 questions remained. Use of the reduced body of questions does not change the conclusions of the previous classification (Figure 6.7) and confirms the stability of the classes based once again on geographic and linguistic criteria.

---

[6] That is $r_{i,j}$ the rank of item *i* (from the most to the least successful) in country *j* ; the cluster analyses are made on the table $R(i,j) = (r_{ij})$

[7] The questions dropped do not appear in the analysis.

[8] As we did not have parameters for all the countries at the time of this analysis, we were forced to use only the countries surveyed in the first wave.

Figure 6.6 **Classification tree of countries by success hierarchy excluding dropped questions**

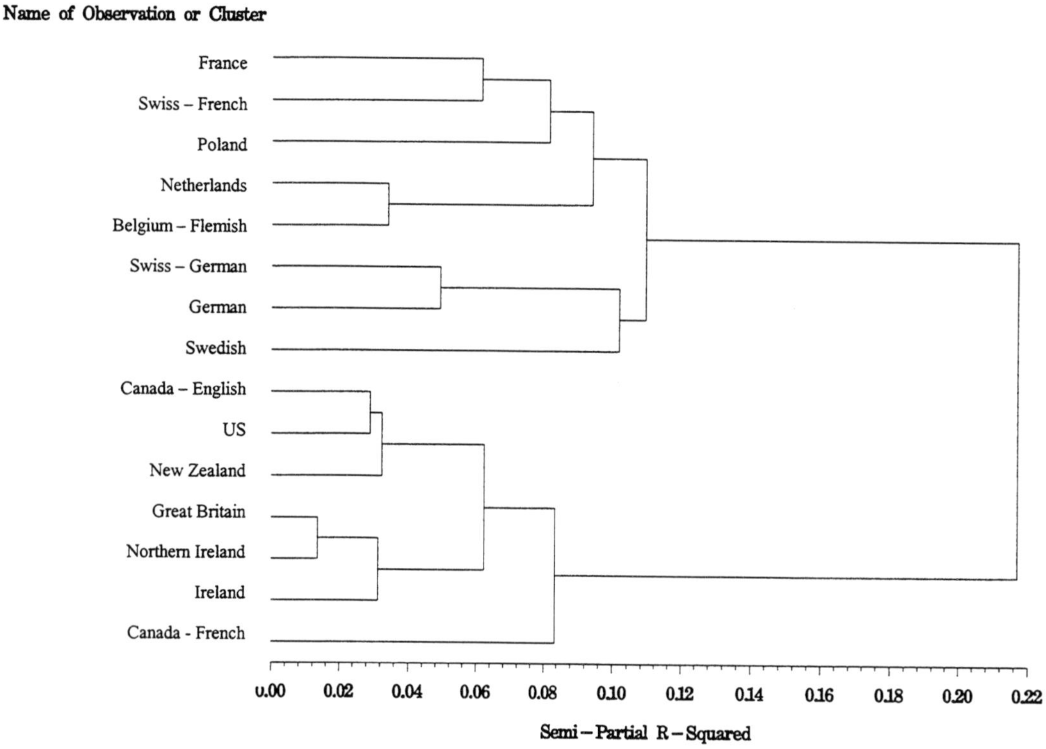

In order to define the cause of the similarities between countries, we identified the questions that contribute to formation of the classes. Table 6.1 shows the number of questions in each class where the average rank deviates significantly from the average rank in the whole sample, at thresholds of 5% and 10% respectively [9].

Table 6.1 **Classification by items with common parameters**

Class	Number of significant questions at threshold of*: **5%**	**10%**
France, French-speaking Switzerland, Poland	10	11
Sweden	3	9
Germany, German-speaking Switzerland	9	15
English-speaking Canada, United States, Great Britain, Netherlands	6	16
French-speaking Canada	6	9
All classes**	3	20

*number of questions where the rank in the class concerned differs significantly at the 5% or 10% threshold from the mean rank in the countries as a whole

** The same question may appear in more than one class, which explains why the total number observed is not the sum of the numbers observed in each of the classes.

By this method, 20 items of the 63 with common parameters (or approximately one third) have an average rank differing significantly from the average rank in the countries as a whole. The English-speaking countries class is the one in which the hierarchy differs most from the average hierarchy. Given that there is a bias associated with translation, we have to ask ourselves whether these are the questions where the wording is most sensitive to translation, whatever the language into which they are translated. The correlation between the formulation of a question, the wording of a text and its sensitivity to translation would then have to be checked in more detail.This in-depth examination would require a precise linguistic analysis.

[9] The average rank of a given item in a class is compared with the average rank of the item for all the people questioned, by means of a Fisher test.

Figure 6.7 **Classification tree of countries by success hierarchy excluding items with a unique parameter in two or more countries**

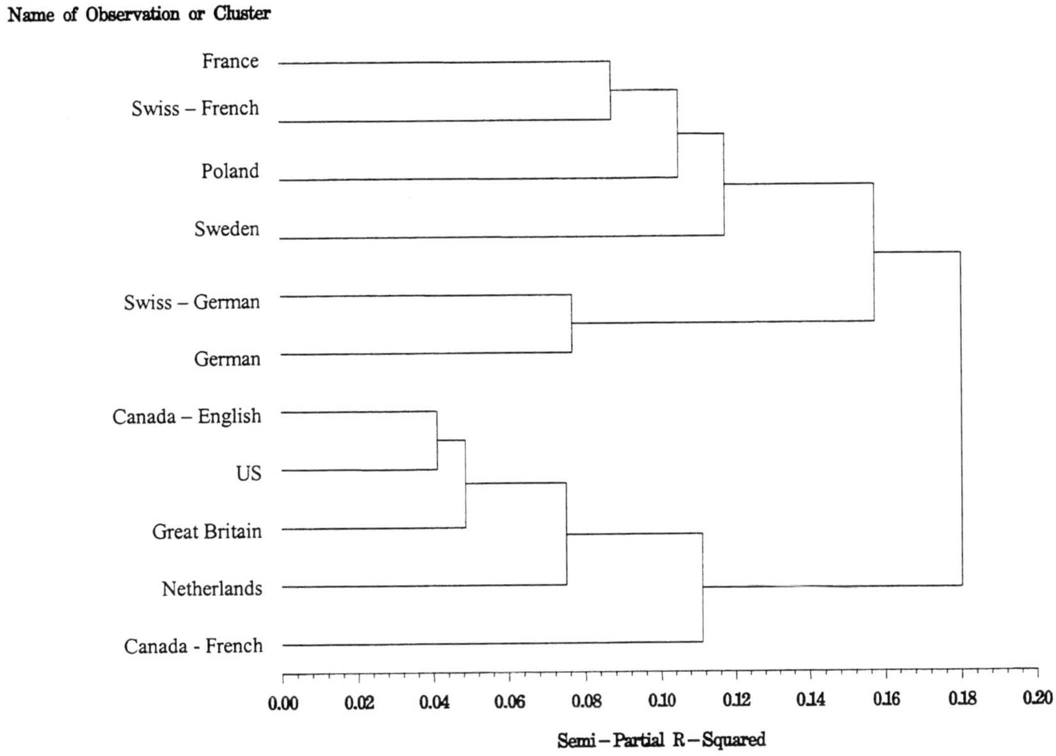

6.4.4 Conclusion

These results indicate that the item success rate is strongly determined by geographic and linguistic factors, which totally contradicts the hypothesis of comparability which underpins this survey. We have not been able to quantify the consequences of such similarities and differences on the population distribution in terms of level but it is clear that these results make a comparison of the countries impossible.

Therefore, identification of the non-equivalent items is insufficient to prevent geographical and linguistic grouping of the countries according to their profile of success in the various questions. The statistical procedures used to compensate for this bias prove not to be effective. As mentioned by André Flieller 'The systematic bias affecting all the items equally cannot be identified by the check methods used in IALS because these methods are intended to indicate any item group interactions, which do not exist in the case of systematic bias' (Dickes and Flieller,1997). Further on he says 'A systematic advantage or disadvantage of this kind could occur if, for example, people's motivation for the test were systematically higher or lower in one country than in the others.'. We shall now examine this question of motivation on the part of interviewees.

6.5 Analysis of missing answers

The consequences of inattention and lack of interest on the part of interviewees towards a long questionnaire requiring real concentration were not discussed in the reports published by the originators of the IALS survey. Nevertheless, the results in the various European and North American countries suggest that this question is important. The percentage of the population in literacy levels 1 and 2 varies between 28 % (in Sweden) and 77 % (in Poland) for the tasks associated with prose texts. These percentages are considerable, not just in France but in the other countries as well: being in level 1 means that one can 'pinpoint an element of information contained in the text which is identical to or synonymous with the information given in the instruction' and in level 2: ' pinpoint one or more elements of information in the text, which may contain a number of distracting elements, or the reader may have to make low-level deductions'[10]. At the other end of the scale of ability, the percentage of people in level 5 is particularly low, so low in fact that it was not published: levels 4 and 5 were grouped in the same class in all the publications issued by IALS and in the database distributed. A level 5 task 'requires the reader to search for information in a dense text which contains a number of plausible distracting elements'. In France, out of a sample of nearly 3000 people there are 11 in level 5 for the prose texts, 8 for the schematic texts and 16 for the questions with quantitative content, although 648 of them were educated to a level higher than the 'baccalauréat'! In the Netherlands 16 people are in level 5 for the prose texts out of a sample of nearly 3000 people. Sweden, which has the best results, has 121 people at this level for prose texts out of a sample of just over 2500 respondents.

These surprising results point us towards a more detailed analysis of how seriously the people interviewed responded to the survey. We do not claim to have carried out a systematic study of this question here but we have followed a path which demonstrates its importance unambiguously. We carried out this study using the French data, by examining the consequences of this lack of interest on the regional differentiations. The subject studied is as follows: Can different attitudes to the survey be detected in the different regions of France?

We explored the theory of unequal interviewee motivation by region, reflected in different behaviour in the way the questions were answered. For example, when faced with a question which is not understood or perceived as difficult, some interviewees try to give an answer, even if wrong, while others ignore the question and move on to the next one. If an interviewee omits a question because of its difficulty, it is desirable for the omission to be considered as a wrong answer, as the reason for the omission is doubtless the expectation of failure. However, not every omission can be interpreted in this way because some of the people interviewed freely choose not to answer because of either lack of interest or laziness, but not due to lack of understanding.

Two approaches were followed by the authors of the IALS survey to try to overcome this pitfall. The instructions supplied to the interviewers state that the people questioned should be told as soon as they read a question that if they do not know how to answer they should put some kind of mark on the question (put a cross, cross through the lines for the answer etc.). The answer is then considered to be wrong. There should be no such mark if the question is actually omitted, i.e. if interviewees do not look at the document because they have given up.

This instruction was supplemented at the codification stage by introducing specific rules. We are not discussing here the possible consequences of these rules, which have been analysed in detail elsewhere (Darcovich et al., 1998). However, we are attempting to understand how a comparison between the factors explaining the 'omissions' (an item not completed), partial omissions (several consecutive questions not completed) and quitting before finishing the test might reveal the attitude of interviewees towards questioning of this kind.

6.5.1 Codification and treatment of omissions

The omissions were reprocessed for inclusion in the final calculation of the individual score. The originators distinguished between 'items omitted' and 'items not reached'. The former are questions not answered but followed in the same block by at least one item which the interviewee has answered. The latter correspond to questions not answered and not followed in the same block by items answered (National Centre for Education Statistics, 1998). The items omitted were recoded as wrong items and the items not reached were not included in the calculation of the interviewee's individual score.

[10] Literacy, Economy and Society (op.cit.), p.36.

A final rule was applied to the people who only completed the basic questionnaire containing the socio-demographic characteristics, or only the preliminary booklet, or, finally, only answered a small number of questions. In this case the socio-demographic characteristics of the interviewee were used to determine the person's score by allocating the missing data in accordance with the answers obtained from individuals with the same socio-demographic characteristics.

An examination of the partial interruption or quitting before finishing the test provides initial evidence of a diversity of attitude (Table 6.2). Out of 2,996 people interviewed in France, 1,544 answered the whole of the questionnaire, which is slightly over half; 958 answered it partially (32%). 2502 questionnaires were therefore at least partially completed[11]. The lack of interest marks are numerous, but in the comparison between countries no correlation was demonstrated between the lack of interest mark and the success rate (Darcovich et al., 1998).

Does this mean, as suggested by the conclusion of this latest study, that the treatment of the stops has no effect on the assessment of individual ability levels? This is far to have been demonstrated.

Table 6.2 **Partial and final stops**

	Canada English	**Canada French**	**France**	**Germany**	**Nether-lands**	**Poland**	**Sweden**	**Switzer-land French**	**Switzer-land German**	**United States**
Scale	**Partial stops: Mean percentage of questions omitted by type of document**									
Prose	2.0	4.3	5.8	4.1	3.7	10.0	8.5	3.9	4.1	3.5
Document	1.5	4.2	4.2	1.9	2.6	7.8	5.3	2.4	2.6	1.7
Quantitative	1.4	4.1	4.6	2.5	3.0	7.8	6.9	2.1	3.0	2.5
	Final stops: Questions at the end of a block, not reached									
	19	30	32	15	10	44	15	21	32	34

Source : Yamamoto, *op.cit.*, 1998, p. 184-186.

We then tried to identify what could be interpreted as omissions included as wrong answers. As we have seen, a single document is used as the basis for several questions. The document and the questions referring to it are located opposite each other. An examination of the questionnaires completed by interviewees in France often reveals whole pages crossed out, even in the questionnaires filled in successfully elsewhere. It is likely that some of the answers coded as 'wrong', are in fact expressions of lack of interest and motivation rather than lack of ability.

To study this, we refined the existing codification and singled out what we call 'refusals' by pinpointing the exercises (containing at least three questions) for which all the answers are coded 'wrong'. We put forward the hypothesis that this provides us with an indicator of the pages of the questionnaire that were totally crossed out[12].

The map of the omissions corresponding to the partial omissions or quitting before finishing the test is unexpected (Figure A6.1). A large number of regions have a very small number of omissions (less than 6) and four regions have a high average number of omissions. No particular regional configuration can be detected. In contrast, the map of 'refusals' (Figure A6.2) is more homogeneous and adjacent regions have less contrasting values. More surprisingly, these two maps are complementary, which nothing could have led us to assume. The South West and Auvergne regions have a large number of answers 'crossed out' and a small number of no answers. The reverse is true for Alsace, the Limousin and the Provence-Alpes-Côte d'Azur region. This finding suggests that the answers 'crossed out' actually

[11] The following reasons are given for the unanswered questionnaires: 69 people refused the joint booklet, 154 were eliminated by the joint booklet, 229 refused to fill in the questionnaire after the joint booklet and 341 were eliminated for other reasons (language problems, mental handicap etc.).

[12] The likelihood of « recovering » exercises that are completely wrong due to lack of ability is in fact low.

correspond to a form of no answer, but it might also be assumed that this distribution is the result of structural factors, particularly differences in literacy level between the regions.

However, an analysis of the factors determining these kind of wrong answers due to refusals shows that this is not the case. In order to check this, we researched the determinants of the various types of answer using different logistic regression models. In this model each of the three variables - number of 'wrong answers' per interviewee, number of 'refusals' and number of omissions - was explained as a function of the following individual characteristics: region of residence, age, qualifications, score for the question and time taken to complete the questionnaire.

Table 6.3 **Effect of logistic regressions on the importance of "refusals", "wrong answers" and omissions**

	Odd ratio of explanatory variables		
Variables to be explained	Number of "refusals" > 10	Number of "wrong answers" > 10	Number of omissions > 10
Explanatory variables			
Level of individual (Reference = level >= 3)			
Score (level < 3)	0.96	0.99	0.98
Regions (Reference = Rhone-Alps) – Only the regions recorded as significant in at least one of the models are listed			
Aquitaine	3.56	1.6	0.52
Ile de France			2.84
Alsace			3.83
Auvergne	5.87		
Burgundy	2.77	2.0	0.41
Brittany		1.5	
Limousin			3.44
Languedoc-Roussillon			2.61
Lorraine	3.09		
Midi-Pyrenees	5.03		
North	1.81	1.5	
Poitou	2.65		
Centre	4.71		0.37
PACA			2.71
Mean time per question (Reference = University)			
Time (time < mean)		0.63	2.35
Qualifications (Reference = University)			
Qualification < CAP-BEPC [*]		3.1	
BEPC qualification [**]	1.72	3.3	
Baccalauréat		1.9	
Age (Reference = 25-55)			
Age < 25		0.7	
Age > 55		1.3	

[*] CAP = Vocational training certificate, BEP = Technical school certificate
[**] BEPC=GCSE equivalent

In this way we built up three models in which the variable explained is the probability that each of these variables is greater than 10. The results show that the 'refusals' cannot be explained by the same determinants as the 'wrong answers' (Table 6.3). Like the omissions, the determinants of the 'refusals' are essentially geographic. For example, living in the Midi-Pyrenees region increases by almost a factor of five (odds-ratio = 5.03) the odds of having a number higher than 10 of 'refusals' compared with the reference region[13] (Rhône-Alpes) and

[13] The reference region corresponds to the « average » situation.

living in the Limousin multiplies by more than three (odds-ratio = 3.44) the odds of having a large number of omissions.

The determinants of the wrong answers have a more demographic and social origin, with qualifications having a significant influence[14], along with age. The 'refusals' variable is closer to the 'omission' variable than to the 'wrong answer' variable.

To confirm these results – using a single model with a number of answer modalities –we carried out a joint analysis of the determinants of the various possible answers: 'right answer', 'wrong answer', 'refusals', and 'omission' (Guérin-Pace, Blum, 1999).

Here we have a real regional bias which no doubt expresses a cultural bias and is associated not with the difficulty of the questions or problems with translation of the questionnaire but with the general attitude of the interviewees towards it. The decision taken by the originators of the survey to consider many omissions as a 'wrong answer' then causes a major problem because it fails to make allowance for either the diversity of attitudes or the motivation of the interviewees.

Our analysis demonstrates that there is no reason to assume homogeneous attitudes within the same country and therefore even less between countries. We did not make these assessments for the other countries but it is probable that differentials are introduced for the same reasons, again leading to doubts about the comparative nature of the survey. The variations of motivation from one individual to another, become a strong element of bias in itself that changes the estimated literacy level for each individual. Many of the failures are probably the result of lack of seriousness or lack of interest when faced with a long survey.

6.6 Follow-up survey and translation effects – preliminary results

As described in the follow-up survey procedure (chapter11), a sample of French individuals interviewed in 1994 have been interviewed again in 1998. About half of the sample (300 respondents) was questioned with the original French questionnaire while the other half (422 respondents) has been interviewed with the Swiss questionnaire[15]. The main purpose of doing this is to estimate the impact of using a different translation, knowing that some of the problems found in the French questionnaire are not present in the Swiss version.

6.6.1 Variability between 1994 and 1998

First of all, differences in response profile between 1994 and 1998 show a strong instability of the results. For instance, about 40% of the responses scored "incorrect" in 1994 for the common block[16], are correct in 1998, whatever the questionnaire is (Table 6.4). Moreover, omissions are very unstable too: almost half of them (whatever the questionnaire is) become correct answers in 1998. However, when using the French questionnaire, we have a greater proportion of responses which remain "omission" (16%) than with the Swiss version (7%). Overall, the comparison of the response profile for the two samples, considering the whole set of questions of the common block, does not show strong differences.

At individual level, the comparison between 1994 and 1998 can be done by representing the proportion of correct answer, for each interviewee in 1994 and in 1998. Even if the proportions of correct answers are slightly higher in 1998, the variability between these two

[14] Thus, « not having a degree » multiplies by 10 the probability of having a number of omissions greater than 10 compared with the people who have a university degree.

[15] A first analysis shows that the two samples are almost similar, in terms of their socio-demographic structure. Using weights computed on the basis of each sample does not affect the response profile of items.

[16] Each individual had one block in common with 1994 and two new blocks of questions.

dates is very important, whatever the questionnaire used in 1998 is[17] (Figures 6.8 and 6.9). This important variability raises the question of the reliability of the literacy measure.

Table 6.4 **Comparing responses profile between 1994 and 1998 (on items of the common block)**

1994	**1998** Omission	Skipped, X, DK or comments	Correct responses	Incorrect answer	Total*
French questionnaire					
Omissions	16	5	47	29	97
Correct responses	2	0	81	15	98
Incorrect answer	12	4	39	43	98
Base (300 respondents, 4594 responses)					
Swiss questionnaire (422 respondents, 6994 responses)					
Omissions	7	11	49	31	98
Correct responses	1	2	78	17	98
Incorrect answer	5	11	42	42	100
Base (422 respondents, 6994 responses)					

* The total is not 100%, because we have dropped score 2 and 8.

Figure 6.8 **Proportion of correct answers for each individual in 1994 and 1998 (Swiss questionnaire in 1998)**

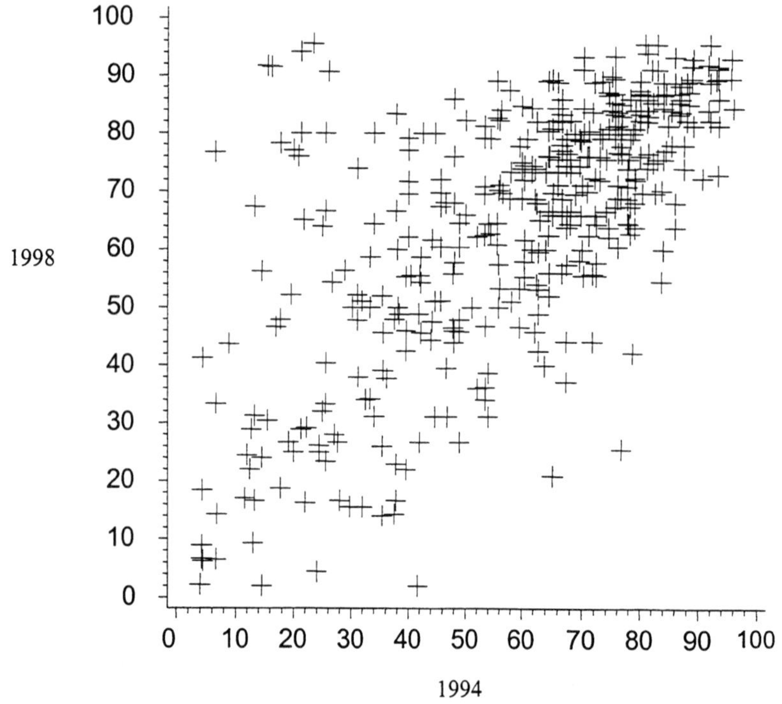

[17] These proportions have been computed on the basis of all the items, but the relation is very similar for the common block.

Figure 6.9 **Proportion of correct answers for each individual in 1994 and 1998 (Swiss questionnaire in 1998)**

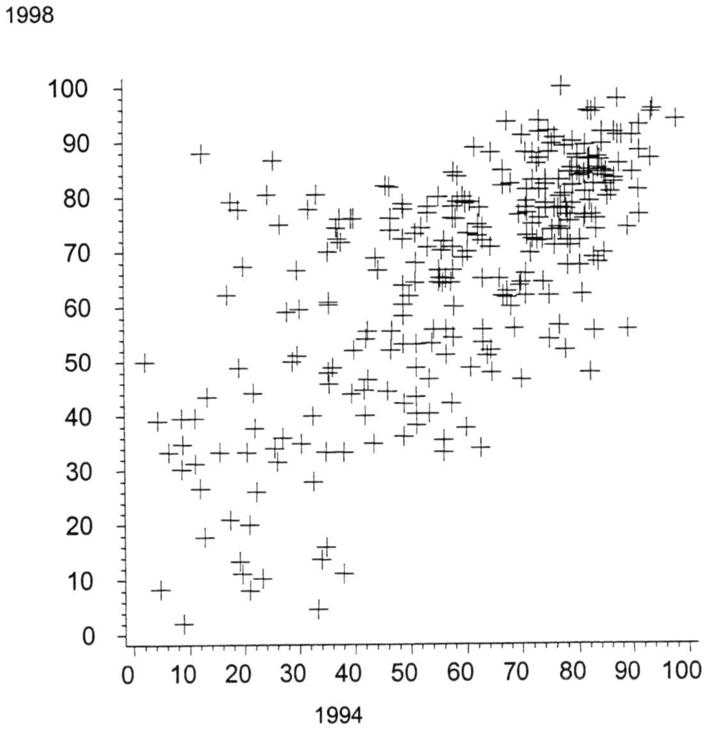

Figure 6.10 illustrates for each item this effect of translation. We have represented the proportion of correct answers in 1998 with the Swiss questionnaire, against the proportion of correct answers in 1998, using the French questionnaire, for all items. We have circled items having a problem in the French questionnaire, which have been solved in the Swiss questionnaire. Triangles items are those having both problems in the French and the Swiss questionnaire (same or different problems). Lastly, squares items are those that we have identified, having no translation problem in the French questionnaire, but in the Swiss questionnaire. All these items and the reasons of the problem are listed in appendix in the Table A6.3.

This figure clearly shows that for almost all items, the proportion of correct answers is much more important using the Swiss questionnaire than using the French one. We notice that almost all circled questions are above the diagonal (11 items among 12 black circled items), with an increase of proportion which reaches 34 % (item 6.9). The item 7.15 is the only one of this type, which is below the diagonal, for unknown reason. On the other hand, all the triangled items, which have both problems in the questionnaires, are on the diagonal or below it. Finally, we have looked at some items, which are located much above the diagonal, (for instance item 1.12) and we have found explanations for it (square items). Finally, for the 25 items with problems in France, 13 items are correct in the Swiss questionnaire, 6 items have the same problem in both questionnaires and 6 items have a different problem in the Swiss questionnaire.

Figure 6.10 **Comparing proportions of correct answers for each item in 1998 between the two samples, French or Swiss questionnaire.**

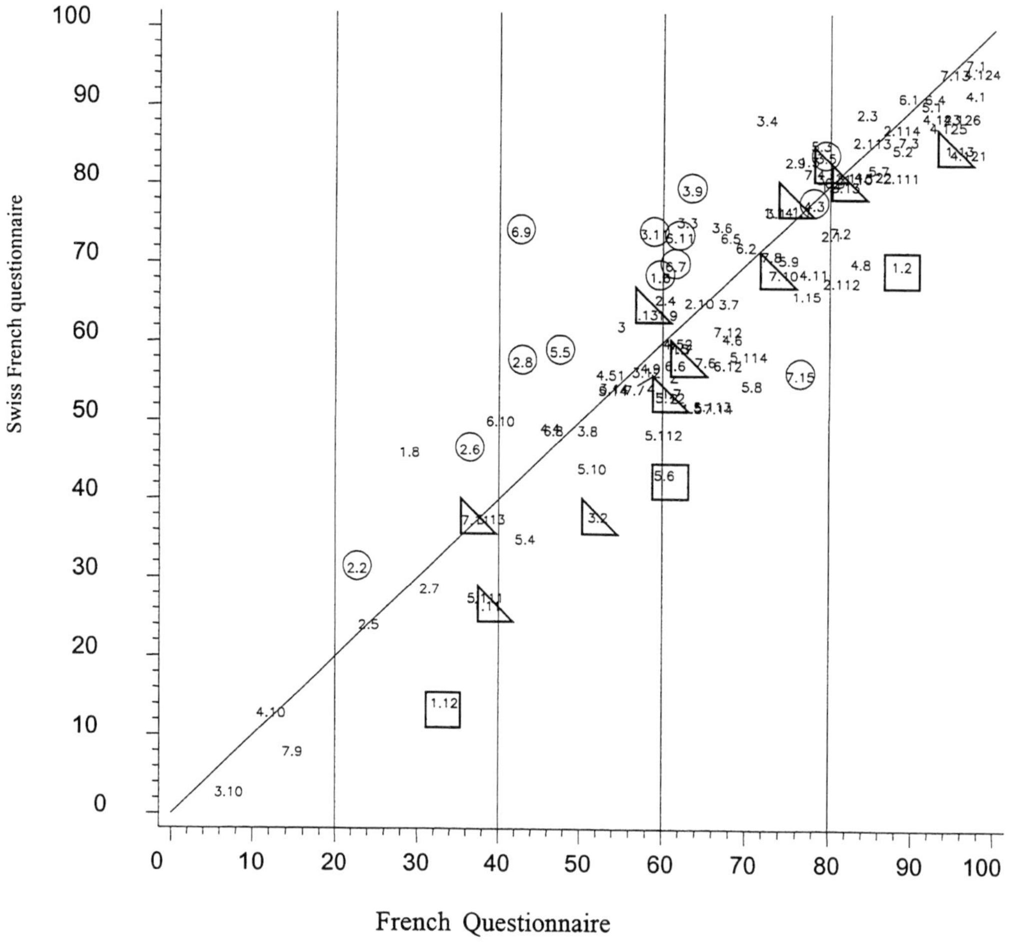

Circles = items with problems in French questionnaire, solved in Swiss questionnaire
Triangles= items with problems in both questionnaires
Squares=problems in Swiss questionnaire only

To confirm the role of translation on the results, we have built a regression model (Table 6.6). This regression model explains the proportion of correct answer for an item in 1998 as a function of the proportion of correct answer for the same item in 1994, the type of item (with translation problem or without translation problem) and the questionnaire used in 1998 (Swiss or French). The proportion of correct answer in 1994 is highly significant, and there is a general increase of the proportion of correct answer between 1994 and 1998 (12%). If the questionnaire used is the Swiss one, for an item with problem then the proportion of correct answer for this item in 1998 is increased significantly (7.9%).

Table 6.6 **Explaining the proportion of correct answers by item in 1998**

Linear Regression models

Linear regression:

P(1998;i,q) = Proportion of correct answer in 1998 for item *i* and for sub-sample, with questionnaire *q* in 1998 *(q=Swiss or French);*

P(1994,i,q) = Proportion of correct answer in 1994 for item *i* for sub-sample, with questionnaire *q* in 1998 *(q=Swiss or French);*

$I_{[Swiss,\ Prob]}(i,q)$ = 1 if *q=Swiss* and if item *i* has a problem with French translation;

$I_{[Fr,\ Prob]}(i,q)$ = 1 if *q=French* and if item *i* has a problem with French translation;

$I_{[Swiss,\ No\ Prob]}(i,q)$ = 1 if *q=Swiss* and if item *i* has not a problem with French translation;

Results of the regression models:

$$P(1998;i;q) = 12{,}1\% + \underset{(0.02)^{**}}{0{,}93}\ p(1994,i,q) \underset{(2.1)^{**}}{+7{,}9}\ I_{[Swiss,Prob]}(i,q) \underset{(2.1)}{-0.8}\ I_{[Fr,Prob]}(i,q) \underset{(1{,}0)^{**}}{-2.9}\ I_{[Swiss,No\ Prob]}(i,q)$$

*Standard error is indicated between brackets; ** means significant value at 0.01%*

We have also verified this effect at an individual level, on the basis of a second regression model (Table 6.7). It describes the individual probability to give a correct answer in 1998 to any item *i*, knowing the individual gave an incorrect answer in 1994 to the same item, as a function of the type of question (with problem or without problem) and of the questionnaire (Swiss or French). If the item had a problem in the French version, then the odds of giving a correct answer in 1998 using the Swiss questionnaire is multiplied by 1.53 higher than for an item without problem.

The previous analyses demonstrate a significant positive effect of the translation on the proportion of correct answer per individual. In other words, using the Swiss questionnaire in 1998 instead of the French one, increases significantly the probability to give a correct answer for an item that had a translation problem in the 1994.

Table 6.7 **Explaining the change at individual level (incorrect answer in 1994 and correct answer in 1998)**

Logistic regression Variables	**Coefficient**	**$P > X^2$**	**Odds ratio**
Questionnaire in 1998 [reference=Swiss]			
French questionnaire in 1998	0.1	0.08	1.12
Type of question [reference= question without problem]			
question with problem in French questionnaire	0.2	0.19	1.19
Interaction Questionnaire* type of question			
[reference= French questionnaire in 1998; question without problem in French questionnaire]			
Swiss questionnaire in 1998 and question with problem in French questionnaire	0.35	0.01	1.53

6.7 Conclusion

6.7.1 Illusion of comparison

The IALS survey was carried out to compare adult literacy levels in different countries. In the introduction to the report 'Literacy, Economy and Society' it was stated 'the objective then was to describe and compare the reading and writing abilities of people in different countries. This second objective posed the challenge of comparing the reading and writing abilities between cultures and languages'. The authors of the survey then endeavored to formulate questionnaires which could be considered equivalent between countries and languages, in other words one in which the difficulty of the various items would be the same everywhere. They then drew up procedures to identify the non-equivalent items, which led to some items being withdrawn from the assessment and the assessment being corrected for other items and some countries. When these corrections had been made, the authors of the survey considered it justifiable to make a comparison between the different countries.

The various approaches followed in this report show that the results could by no means be considered comparative:

The translations of the various questionnaires are not equivalent. The comparison between the French questionnaire and the English-speaking Canadian one has shown the different degrees of bias associated with translation of the questionnaires that make about a third of the questions asked in France more difficult. This bias associated with the translation that affects the whole of the population surveyed is not identified by the statistical procedures used in the IALS.

This lack of equivalence is not simply a factor in the French questionnaire. The various translations, classified according to the proximity of the difficulty hierarchies observed, form groups under geographic and linguistic criteria. Countries with the same language have item success classifications which are more similar than two countries with different languages. In countries with the same language, countries that are geographically close are the ones where the hierarchy is most similar. As a result, a combination of cultural bias (measured by the association of geographically close countries) and bias associated with translation can be observed.

6.7.2 Unequal motivation and results of the IALS survey.

Observation of the distribution of individuals under the 5 levels established by the authors of the survey arouses more general doubts about what this survey measures. The number of individuals in level 5 is extremely low, much lower than the number of people who have been in higher education. We might expect an individual with this level of education who took the survey seriously to be in level 5. The most difficult questions were easy to answer with a minimum of attention for a person mastering the basics of a language. On the other hand, the number of people interviewed whose level is estimated at 1 or 2 is considerable, reaching 70% of the total in some countries and generally exceeding 40%.

The surprising nature of these assessments which is due not just to the comparability of the results from one country to another but also to the validity of the survey for any country taken in isolation, led us to have doubts about the procedure followed to allow for the missing answers. It is difficult enough to process missing answers in a conventional survey, but the bias is not usually very high. In a survey of literacy, a missing answer may signify a refusal as well as ignorance. Treatment of the missing answers is therefore of great importance. If they are considered to be a mark of lack of interest, the overall results will be over-evaluated. If they are considered to be a mark of ignorance, however, the results will be under-evaluated.

An analysis carried out on the French data for the questions coded as 'wrong' has enabled us to demonstrate that many 'wrong answers' should in reality be considered as omissions. In some regions respondents wishing to ignore a set of questions crossed them out. In other regions the interviewees merely omitted them without putting any marks on the questionnaire. These answers were judged to be wrong in the first case and omissions in the second. The results are therefore significantly biased. Our analysis has demonstrated that this bias was actually geographical and had a major influence on the assessment of ability levels. Some of the disparities found, in terms of success in the survey, do not directly reflect differences in ability; they reflect different attitudes towards the survey which are not allowed for in the codification, although they affect the calculation of the individual score.

This bias is also reinforced by the procedure used by the authors of the survey to process questions omitted. If an interviewee omitted a question, the answer was allocated by taking at random an individual with similar socio-demographic characteristics. The bias found by us (due to the lack of equivalence between questionnaires and in particular the lack of motivation leading to 'refusals') is then reinforced by a cumulative process which is hard to control because allocation is done at random on the basis of biased answers.

6.7.3 Conclusion: A non-comparative survey which contains many measurement uncertainties.

The IALS survey can certainly not be considered reliable at national level and even less on an international scale, as the bias revealed does not occur in the same way in the various countries. Firstly, the instability of the item success hierarchies due to a combination of linguistic and cultural bias shows that the survey cannot be used as a comparative basis. Secondly, the codification and procedures for processing of the omissions in the IALS survey result in a biased assessment of the ability levels due to unequal motivation on the part of interviewees which is not taken into account.

On the basis of our analyses, it is not possible to assume that IALS measures only literacy. It seems to measure a combination of different factors: literacy abilities, but also motivation in the different ways of filling the questionnaire: crossing the answers, trying to find quickly the answer by pointing words which are both present in question and document or, on contrary, reading carefully the document before answering the question, etc. One could think that this last differences could be interpreted also as some kind of literacy. But, different attitudes can change depending of the context, and are related to the motivation of interviewed, during the questionnaire.

Then, the synthetic measures (individual scores, levels, repartition of national population according to 5 levels of literacy) are a mixture of these different factors, and no method has been proposed to distinguish the relative effect of each of them. Comparisons between countries are then strongly biased, and it is not possible to interpret them as differences in terms of literacy levels.

References

Darcovich, N., M. Binkley, J. Cohen, M. Myrberg and S. Persson (1998), « Non-response Bias » *in* National Center for Education Statistics, op. Cit..

Développement des ressources humaines Canada, OCDE (1997), *Literacy Skills for the knowledge society, Further Results from the International Adult Literacy Survey*, Paris, 195 p.

Dickes, P. et A. Flieller (1997), Secondary analysis of the French data from the International Adult Literacy Survey *(IALS), Université* Nancy 2, *mimeo.*

Goldstein H. et R. Wood (1989) : « Five decades of item response modelling », *British Journal of Mathematical and Statistical Psychology*, vol. 42, pp. 139-167.

Jouvenceau P., A. Desclaux et J.-P. Lacaille (1996), *Variation de résultats aux tests de compétences : les résultats de quatre expériences menées par la France*, Rapport d'expertise, OCDE, Paris, *mimeo.*

Kalton G., L. Lyberg et J.-M. Rempp (1998), Review of methodology in Adult Literacy in OECD Countries in NCES, op. Cit. Kirsch I, A. Jungeblut et B. Mosenthal (1998), « The Measurement of Adult Literacy », in National Center for Education Statistics, op. cit., ch.7.

National Center for Education Statistics (1998), *Adult Literacy in OECD Countries, Technical Report on the First International Adult Literacy Survey,* U.S. Department of Education, Office of Educational Research and Improvement, Washington, p. 215 et annexes.

Rémond, M. (1996), « Enquête internationale sur les savoir-faire en situation de vie quotidienne, International Adult Literacy Survey (IALS) - Complexité et ambiguïté des items de mesure des compétences : Quelques réflexions sur les items de « prose » et « document » qui amènent à s'interroger », *rapport d'expertise*, OCDE, Paris, *mimeo.*

Yamamoto, K. (1998), « Scaling and Scale Linking », in National Center For Education Statistics, *op. cit.*, ch. 10.

Statistique Canada, OCDE (1995)- *Littératie, Economie et Société, Résultats sur la première Enquête internationale sur l'alphabétisation des Adultes*, Paris, 218 p.

Appendix

Tables A6.1 – A6.3

Figure A6.1 – A6.2

Table A.6.1 **Correlations (Kendall) between the item success hierarchies**

	France	Canada-E	Canada-F	Switz.-G.	Switz.-F	Germany	USA	Netherl.	Poland	Sweden	GB	Ireland	N.Ireland	Belgium	New Z.	Theoret.
France	1.00	0.71	0.71	0.74	0.78	0.73	0.71	0.74	0.72	0.69	0.74	0.73	0.75	0.76	0.71	0.77
Canada-E	0.71	1.00	0.76	0.70	0.74	0.72	0.86	0.76	0.70	0.67	0.82	0.85	0.81	0.74	0.83	0.82
Canada-F	0.71	0.76	1.00	0.66	0.75	0.66	0.78	0.70	0.66	0.67	0.77	0.76	0.76	0.67	0.76	0.76
Switz.-G.	0.74	0.70	0.66	1.00	0.78	0.82	0.69	0.76	0.70	0.72	0.73	0.71	0.72	0.75	0.70	0.78
Switz.-F	0.78	0.74	0.75	0.78	1.00	0.78	0.74	0.77	0.72	0.72	0.76	0.75	0.77	0.76	0.73	0.82
Germany	0.73	0.72	0.66	0.82	0.78	1.00	0.71	0.78	0.72	0.70	0.71	0.73	0.72	0.79	0.69	0.79
USA	0.71	0.86	0.78	0.69	0.74	0.71	1.00	0.74	0.70	0.68	0.81	0.82	0.80	0.74	0.84	0.80
Netherl.	0.74	0.76	0.70	0.76	0.77	0.78	0.74	1.00	0.75	0.72	0.77	0.76	0.76	0.86	0.76	0.83
Poland	0.72	0.70	0.66	0.70	0.72	0.72	0.70	0.75	1.00	0.72	0.72	0.69	0.72	0.73	0.70	0.76
Sweden	0.69	0.67	0.67	0.72	0.72	0.70	0.68	0.72	0.72	1.00	0.76	0.73	0.72	0.68	0.70	0.74
GB	0.74	0.86	0.77	0.73	0.76	0.71	0.81	0.77	0.72	0.76	1.00	0.86	0.91	0.75	0.86	0.79
Ireland	0.73	0.85	0.76	0.71	0.75	0.73	0.82	0.76	0.69	0.73	0.86	1.00	0.85	0.74	0.82	0.80
N.Ireland	0.75	0.81	0.76	0.72	0.77	0.72	0.80	0.76	0.72	0.72	0.91	0.85	1.00	0.76	0.85	0.79
Belgium	0.76	0.74	0.67	0.75	0.76	0.79	0.74	0.86	0.73	0.68	0.75	0.74	0.76	1.00	0.74	0.80
New Z.	0.71	0.83	0.76	0.70	0.73	0.69	0.84	0.76	0.70	0.70	0.86	0.82	0.85	0.74	1.00	0.79
Theoret.	0.77	0.82	0.76	0.78	0.82	0.79	0.80	0.83	0.76	0.74	0.79	0.80	0.79	0.80	0.79	1.00

<table>
<tr><th colspan="6">Table A6.2a Repetition of terms not respected in French - comparison of English (Canada) and French questionnaires –version</th></tr>
<tr><th>ITEM</th><th>Scale /Level</th><th>% correct answers in France</th><th>Rank of item in France</th><th>% correct answers in English -speaking Canada</th><th>Rank of item in English -speaking Canada</th></tr>
<tr><td>B7Q15</td><td>Prose – 2</td><td>67</td><td>62</td><td>84</td><td>71</td></tr>
<tr><td colspan="6">What new legislation would help to fight fires ? The answer requires a search for the term “extinguisher”.
The word extinguisher does not refer directly to the term fire, whereas the English wording says “fire extinguisher” and includes the word fire.</td></tr>
<tr><td>B1Q4</td><td>Quant – 3</td><td>63</td><td>57</td><td>79</td><td>60</td></tr>
<tr><td colspan="6">This question is on the cost of couches jetables [disposal diapers] over a four-week period. The sentence containing the answer gives the cost of “changes complets”.
In the question in English the cost of “disposable diapers” is asked for; the document refers to “disposable diapers”.</td></tr>
<tr><td>B1Q11</td><td>Prose - 5</td><td>23</td><td>7</td><td>35</td><td>4</td></tr>
<tr><td colspan="6">“List two methods used by the CIEM to provide assistance to employees who are threatened with redundancy because of a restructuring of their department”.
“List two ways in which CIEM helps people who will lose their job because of a departmental reorganization”
The phrase “two methods to provide assistance” is present al the start of the French test: “[CIEM] helps employees who seriously expect to change their job” ; this sentence is followed by a series of actions taken by CIEM. Interviewees are therefore pointed toward these actions which in reality do not specifically relate to people made redundant and are therefore considered wrong. This reference does not exist in English (the corresponding phrase is “CIEM supports employees”) and
the interviewee is not directed to the wrong list.
Explanation confirmed by examination of the questionnaires: the majority of errors consist answers such as “Database” etc. which are elements from the first list</td></tr>
<tr><td>B2Q3</td><td>Prose - 2</td><td>79</td><td>78</td><td>92</td><td>84</td></tr>
<tr><td colspan="6">In French, “What happens when the plant is exposed to a temperature of 1,?C or below ?”, The sentence for the answer is “When the temperature falls to 12-14°, the plant loses its leaves and won't bloom any more”. In English, “What happens when the impatiens plant is exposed to temperatures of 14 ° or below ?”. The answer is “When the plant is exposed to temperatures of 12-14°C, it loses its leaves and won't bloom anymore.” The term exposed is repeated in English but not in French.</td></tr>
<tr><td>B7Q10</td><td>Prose – 2</td><td>56</td><td>44</td><td>78</td><td>57</td></tr>
<tr><td colspan="6">This question mentions “three kinds of information you would expect to find in a of offer”.
The French answer backup text mentions “small ads” but the term job offer never appears. In English the term “job advertisement” is mentioned in both the question and the answer.</td></tr>
<tr><td>B7Q11</td><td>Prose - 4</td><td>24</td><td>5</td><td>49</td><td>9</td></tr>
<tr><td colspan="6">Same reason as B7Q10. Also, the question in French is “Using the pamphlet, name at least three things you should mention in...”. The text with the answer begins with “Present these ...”.
In English the question is rendered as: “Using the information in the pamphlet, list three things you should mention.”.
The text begins with “Mention ...”. The term is repeated.</td></tr>
<tr><td>B3Q9</td><td>Prose – 3</td><td>40</td><td>17</td><td>80</td><td>61</td></tr>
<tr><td colspan="6">This question refers to “the purpose of the postinterview” based on a text describing an interview for a vacancy. The answer is given in a paragraph headed “After the interview” but the sentence which contains the answer does not mention the term “interview” .
In English the question is “What is the main purpose of the postinterview review” and the answer includes the word review, which is not the case in the French questionnaire. The English reader can find the answer more easily-</td></tr>
<tr><td>B1Q6</td><td>Prose - 3</td><td>50</td><td>28</td><td>70</td><td>38</td></tr>
<tr><td colspan="6">The question refers to “ecological concern” but the sentence containing the answer reads “concerned for the environment”. Also, the term “ecological concern” is mentioned elsewhere in the text.
The question in English mentions the word “environment” and the correct answer also mentions this word-</td></tr>
<tr><td>B3Q11</td><td>Prose – 3</td><td>57</td><td>46</td><td>78</td><td>57</td></tr>
<tr><td colspan="6">Cycle instructions. “How should you make sure the seat is correctly adjusted”. In English, “How should you check, to make sure the seat is in the correct position ?” In French the sentence giving the answer reads : “Check the position of the seat by adjusting it up and down, . . .”
In English, “Check the seat position, adjusting it up and down so that with …”
The verb “check” is directly repeated, but in French the verb “s’assurer” [make sure] is replaced in the text by “vérifiez” [check] and “correctly adjusted” is not repeated.</td></tr>
<tr><td>B1Q15</td><td>Quant-2</td><td>71</td><td>67</td><td>83</td><td>69</td></tr>
<tr><td colspan="6">One question refers to calculation of the “Total cost of swimming lessons for one adult and two children”. The document mentions “Young people up to 15 years”.
In English the question refers to calculation of the “total cost for swimming lessons for one adult and two children” and the document gives the cost for“Children & youths” The exact term is repeated in English</td></tr>
</table>

Table A6.2b **Comparison of English (Canada) and French questionnaires – Greater precision of English terms**

<table>
<tr><th>ITEM</th><th>Scale /Level</th><th>% correct answers in France</th><th>Rank of item in France</th><th>% correct answers in English -speaking Canada</th><th>Rank of item in English -speaking Canada</th></tr>
<tr><td>B1Q1</td><td>Doc-3</td><td>60</td><td>54</td><td>84</td><td>71</td></tr>
<tr><td colspan="6">Refrigerator maintenance manual: In French the question is "Name two things the manual suggests you check for if ice forms on your frozen food". The answer is given in a table, on the line "Frost or deposits of ice on the frozen food". In English it is worded "Name two things the manual suggests you check for if your frozen food develops ice crystals". The line on the table is worded "Frost or ice crystals on frozen foods". The term is quoted more directly in English (ice crystals, as against deposits of ice instead of "ice forms" in French). In any case ice crystals is more specific than the word ice.</td></tr>
<tr><td>B1Q13</td><td>Doc - 2</td><td>80</td><td>79</td><td>75</td><td>51</td></tr>
<tr><td colspan="6">Swimming pool opening hours : In French the question is"At what time are the last entry tickets for the swimming pool sold" ; in English, "What is the latest possible time you could enter to go swimming?".
It is mentioned in the text that the last entry is 1 hour before closing. On Mondays the pool is open from 6.30 to 12.30 and 16.00 to 21.00. Interviewees who said "11.30 on Mondays, 20.00 on Mondays and other days" gave a wrong answer. This answer is impossible in English because the term"latest time" refers to the time and not the entry.</td></tr>
<tr><td>B3Q2</td><td>Doc - 4</td><td>33</td><td>10</td><td>57</td><td>16</td></tr>
<tr><td colspan="6">One document gives a breakdown (in %) in graph form of oil consumption in the United States in different economic sectors. In French the question reads: "Summarize in one or two sentences the way in which the different uses of oil in the United States have changed between 1970 and 1989".
Question in English: "Write one or two sentences that summarize how the percentages of oil used for different purposes in the United States have changed between 1970 and 1989?".
The question in English refers to the percentages ("how the percentages") shown on the graph. The question is much simpler than the French translation, which is more abstract ("the way in which the different uses")..</td></tr>
<tr><td>B3Q5</td><td>Doc – 2</td><td>73</td><td>70</td><td>81</td><td>62</td></tr>
<tr><td colspan="6">The subject of this question is a bus timetable: "At what time can you catch the last bus to Amiens Station ...". The list of destinations starts with "Amiens Bapaume", then "Amiens Jules-Barni", then "Amiens Pigeonnier" i.e. three stops beginning with Amiens. Then come two stops with names net including Amiens, then the stop "Amiens Station". In English the timetable begins with three stops with names starting with Springfield, then two other stops with different names, then Harrison St which is less open to confusion.</td></tr>
<tr><td>B3Q15</td><td>Prose – 2</td><td>71</td><td>67</td><td>85</td><td>73</td></tr>
<tr><td colspan="6">This question reads "In the article about the British explorers, underline the sentence that tells in what way the explorers crossed Antarctica?". The English question reads "Underline the sentence in the article about the British explorers that tells how the explorers travelled across Antarctica). As well as the right answer "... after a 95-day walk during which they dragged sledges...", the French newspaper text includes the sentence "... after cutting short an attempt to beat the record for trekking across Antarctica" earlier on in the article. In the corresponding English text the first sentence reads "after cutting short a record-breaking trek &cross Antarctica" and the sentence which is the right answer "... decided to end their target after a 95-day walk during which they dragged sledges ...".
Both answers are appropriate in French but the first is considered to be wrong (a "trek"). In English, the "how" is more difficult to relate to the answer "trek" and therefore easier to relate to the right answer.</td></tr>
<tr><td>B4Q3</td><td>Quant – 2</td><td>73</td><td>70</td><td>86</td><td>75</td></tr>
<tr><td colspan="6">Aspirin instructions tell you to take "1 or 2 tablets every 6 hours". The question is "How many tablets can be taken maximum in 24 hours?". In English the question is "What is the maximum number of tablets that can be taken in 24 hours?". Answers giving "4 or 8 tablets" are wrong. The English version is more precise "is" excludes the plural) and leads more easily to the correct answer.</td></tr>
<tr><td>B5Q3</td><td>Quant – 4</td><td>37</td><td>12</td><td>50</td><td>10</td></tr>
<tr><td colspan="6">This question refers to instructions for seat belts. The instructions make a distinction between what should be done for babies, young children, children up to 12 years and children over 12 years. In English these terms are translated as Infants (or Babies), Toddlers, Children Up to 12 years and Children Over 12 Years. The question relates to "the maximum weight for a baby". The French term "babies" may refer to young children (it would have been better translated as "nourrison" [infant, unweaned baby]), which could cause confusion. The existence in English of the word "toddler" limits this confusion.</td></tr>
<tr><td>B5Q4</td><td>Prose-4</td><td>20</td><td>3</td><td>43</td><td>6</td></tr>
<tr><td colspan="6">Same reason as question B5Q3</td></tr>
<tr><td>B5Q5</td><td>Prose – 3</td><td>37</td><td>12</td><td>60</td><td>20</td></tr>
<tr><td colspan="6">" According to the pamphlet, what must be kept in mind when children are using an adult seat belt?". The wording of the answer mentions "The most important thing is ...."- In English, "According to the pamphlet, what is the most important thing to keep in mind when children are using a normal adult seat belt?". In the English text the term "The most important thing..." is repeated, limiting the scope for giving any other answer. A reading of the answers shows that French people frequently give an answer found earlier in the text and considered to be incorrect because the subtle element "the most important thing" does not appear in the French question.</td></tr>
<tr><td>B5Q11-1</td><td>Quant – 4</td><td>37</td><td>12</td><td>50</td><td>10</td></tr>
<tr><td colspan="6">The interviewee is asked to complete a table and total a number of hours distributed over the week.
In French this box is headed "Weekly report", the meaning of which is ambiguous (a report is not a total). In English it is called "Weekly summary", which defines the task to be carried out less ambiguously. A reading of the answers shows that this box is rarely filled in in French although the rest of the question is answered correctly.</td></tr>
</table>

Table A6.2b cont. **Comparison of English (Canada) and French questionnaires – Greater precision of English terms**

<table>
<tr><th>ITEM</th><th>Scale /Level</th><th>% correct answers in France</th><th>Rank of item in France</th><th>% correct answers in English -speaking Canada</th><th>Rank of item in English -speaking Canada</th></tr>
<tr><td>B6Q6</td><td>Doc – 3</td><td>50</td><td>28</td><td>82</td><td>65</td></tr>
<tr><td colspan="6">Newspaper article on nuclear energy. French : “Why were these ten countries chosen to appear on this chart?”
“Why were the ten countries shown on the chart .... ?.”.
The pronoun “ces” [these] is ambiguous in French. It could be understood to refer to the previous question, which only includes European countries. Thus, some questionnaires have the answer“because they are in Europe” (answer to the previous question).</td></tr>
<tr><td>B6Q8</td><td>Prose - 3</td><td>38</td><td>15</td><td>64</td><td>26</td></tr>
<tr><td colspan="6">Newspaper article.- “Which film had the worst review ?”. In French the review says that the director “has not succeeded” [..] “in making this comedy at all entertaining”.
In English the wording is “fails to” “make even minimally entertaining”.. The words used in the review in English are more negative and the choice between the two films is easier. The answers confirm this. In Great Britain 67% give the right film and 6% “Sister Act”. In France 39% give the right film and 23% “Sister Act”.</td></tr>
<tr><td>B6Q9</td><td>Doc - 2</td><td>37</td><td>12</td><td>77</td><td>54</td></tr>
<tr><td colspan="6">“You want to invest 100 F over 20 years. What rates in this table will pay you more than 500 francs interest,...?
In English, “list all the rates...”...
The information given in English is more precise, “list all the rates...” In French you have to take note of the plural “What rates ?”. Many answers actually contain only one rate and are considered to be wrong.</td></tr>
</table>

Table A6.2c **Comparison of English (Canada) and French questionnaires – translation errors**

<table>
<tr><th>ITEM</th><th>Scale /Level</th><th>% correct answers in France</th><th>Rank of item in France</th><th>% correct answers in English -speaking Canada</th><th>Rank of item in English - speaking Canada</th></tr>
<tr><td>B3Q13</td><td>Prose – 3</td><td>55</td><td>40</td><td>77</td><td>54</td></tr>
<tr><td colspan="6">The question in French is “How is the genetic mutation transmitted ?” and in English “How is the mutated gene inherited ?”. The meaning of “genetic mutation” and “mutated gene” is not the same. The question is more difficult in French because the reference is to a process (mutation) (Rémond, 1996). Also the translation of the corresponding document is incorrect: “from an allergy sufferer’s mother” is translated as “inherited from the allergic mother” instead of “inherited from an allergy sufferer’s mother”.</td></tr>
<tr><td>B6Q11</td><td>Doc – 3</td><td>54</td><td>37</td><td>74</td><td>47</td></tr>
<tr><td colspan="6">This is a question referring to a table showing the interest earned on capital investment. In French the question reads “If you want to at least double your capital in less than 5 years, what rate of interest do you need, according to the table?” and in English it reads : “If you wanted to more than double your principal within five years, what rate of interest on this table would you need?”
The table in French has two errors. Firstly, the English word “principal” has not been translated in the document, which makes the question hard to understand (as this word is translated in the question). Secondly, the question reads “in less than 5 years” whereas in English it says “within 5 years”. Strictly speaking (and we have confirmed this in a number of questionnaires, there is no answer to the question in French on the corresponding table. Those people who answered “impossible” were right but their answers are coded as wrong.</td></tr>
<tr><td>B2Q8</td><td>Doc – 3</td><td>43</td><td>20</td><td>68</td><td>34</td></tr>
<tr><td colspan="6">Newspaper with weather map. The weather map is headed “The Weather” but the questions instructs you to look at the meteorological map. The question incorrectly states “during the week” when the map covers the weekend. The word “precipitation” in the question is repeated in the key but also shown in it, is snow, which may be considered as precipitation. These ambiguities do not exist in English. The word “Weather” is easier to interpret than “meteorological map” which in any case does not appear in the newspaper.</td></tr>
<tr><td>B2Q6</td><td>Prose - 4</td><td>20</td><td>3</td><td>65</td><td>29</td></tr>
<tr><td colspan="6">Newspaper (Freezing embryos). The question is “Underline the sentence indicating what the Australians did to ...”; the answer is “A commission was set up in Australia”. In English the question is: “What the Australians did to help decide ....” and the answer in the document: “The Australians set up a commission”. In French the place appears, “Australia”, instead of the people, “the Australians”, introducing great confusion. The sentences underlined in the questionnaires are those in which a subject actually performs an action.</td></tr>
</table>

Table A6.3 **Comparison of French and Swiss questionnaire in retest for items with a problem in French version**

Item	Problem	Using the Swiss version the problem is...	Proportion answers correct French Version 1998 (n. cases)	Proportion answers correct Swiss Version 1998 (n. cases)
B1Q1	scoring	Not solved	76% (115)	77% (188)
B1Q4	question 'couche jetable' answer 'changes complets' SUISSE Question and answer :' couches jetables' Other problem:' un paquet par deux semaines' is a Swiss expression and the word 'approvisionnement' in the question is not often used in French.	Other problem	80%(115)	80% (188)
B1Q6	Question : 'souci écologique' and answer 'concernés par l'environnement' SUISSE Question and answer : 'soucier de l'environnement'	Solved	60% (114)	69% (188)
B1Q11	Problem : The verb 'aider' in the document is a distractor SUISSE : same problem	Not solved	39% (114)	27% (187)
B1Q13	'A quelle heure a lieu la vente des derniers billets?' instead of 'Dernière entrée' SUISSE 'Jusqu'à quelle heure peut-on acheter un billet pour aller se baigner?' Other problem: 'heure limite d'admission' on the document is more difficult to understand than 'dernière entrée'	Other problem	96% (114)	85 % (187)
B2Q2	Question: .. '...bonnes plantes pour avoir chez soi ?' The sentence 'décorant la maison et le jardin' in the document is a distractor. SUISSE Question : 'plantes intéressantes à cultiver' Document : 'enjolivent l'interieur des maisons' is not a distractor because the question asks to find 'plants interesting for cultivating'	Solved	23% (141)	31 %(181)
B2Q6-	Error of translation'Une commission fut réunie en Australie' instead of 'Australians set up a commission'. . *SUISSE*'Pour étudier la question les Australiens ont constitué un comité qui a publié....'	Solved	36% (140)	47% (180)
B2Q8	Problems : Question : 'bulletin météorologique', newspaper 'le temps' Translation error : 'dans la semaine' instead of 'week-end' SUISSE Same word 'météorologique' in the question and newspaper. No translation error.	Solved	43% (140)	58% (180)
B3Q2	Problem: the word 'pourcentage' is not in the question. SUISSE The word 'pourcentage' is in the question but the problem formulation of the question is different. In the Swiss version 'utilisé à diverses fins' is more complicated to understand than 'différentes utilisations'	Different	52% (113)	38% (168)
B3Q5	Problem : 'Amiens-Gare' SUISSE OK.	Solved	79% (112)	84% (168)
B3Q9	The word 'après-entretien' is missing in the sentence where the answer is. SUISSE Word 'revue' is both in the question and in the answer.	Solved	63% (112)	80% (167)
B3Q11	Problem: Different verbs in the question 'vous assurer' and in the answer 'vérifier'. SUISSE Question and answer : 'vérifier'	Solved	59% (112)	74% (166)
B3Q13	'mutation génétique' instead of 'gêne mutant' SUISSE Same problem	Not solved	58% (111)	64% (166)
B3Q15	Problem : The word 'randonnée' in the document is a distractor SUISSE Same problem	Not solved	80% (110)	81% (165)

Table A3cont. **Comparison of French and Swiss questionnaire in retest for items with a problem in French version**

Item	Problem	Using the Swiss version the problem is...	Proportion answers correct French Version 1998 (n. cases)	Proportion answers correct Swiss Version 1998 (n. cases)
B4Q2	Question: 'Citer trois situations pour lesquelles il est préférable de consulter un médecin'. In one of the answer we have the verb: 'renseigner' instead of 'consulter'. SUISSE Question et answer : 'consulter' Other Problem: question: 'Enumérez trois situations où vous devriez consulter un médecin'. The pronoun 'vous' refer to the interviewee. If it is a man it is difficult for him to answer 'if I am pregnant'. This is checked with a lower proportion of correct answers for men (44%).	Other problem	59% (123) men:62% women : 57%	54% (176) men:44% women: 62%
B4Q3	'Combien de comprimés peut on prendre au maximum en 24 heures?'. You may give two answers. SUISSE 'Quel est le nombre maximal de comprimés'	Solved	78% (123)	78% (176)
B5Q5	The indication : 'le plus important' is missing in the question SUISSE Question: 'Quelle est la chose la plus importante à observer?'OK	Solved	47% (141)	59% (193)
B5Q11	Document : the term 'Report hebdomadaire' is in the question and in the document but is difficult to understand as a total SUISSE Different problem : question : 'sommaire hebdomadaire', document : 'total' and the description of the task is less clear	Other problem	38% (138)	28% (191)
B6Q6	'Pourquoi ces dix pays'. The pronoun 'ces' refers to the previous item. SUISSE Problem of translation. The question 'Pourquoi les dix pays figurant sur le graphique ont-ils été choisis?' ommitting to precise '... choisis pour figurer sur le graphique?	Other problem	61% (122)	57% (167)
B6Q7	Problem : Michel Blanc is often acting in comedies SUISSE Same problem but the titles of the movies have been translated, then it is quite easier to decide whether it is a comedy or not.	Different	61% (122)	70% (167)
B6Q9	Problems : 1- The word 'Principal' is not translated 2- 'Quels taux..' instead of 'List all the rates' SUISSE'Enumérez tous les taux.'	Solved	43% (122)	74% (167)
B6Q11	Problem : question 'en moins de 5 ans' instead of 'en cinq ans' SUISSE : 'en cinq ans.'	Solved	62% (121)	74% (167)
B7Q10	Question : 'offre d'emploi', answer 'petites annonces' SUISSE Same problem	Not solved	74% (121)	69% (171)
B7Q11	Question : 'Nommez trois choses que vous devez mentionner' and in the answer we have the verb 'présenter' for one answer SUISSE Question and answer : 'mentionnez' helps to find one of the three answers	Partially Solved	37% (121)	38% (170)
B7Q15	Document : 'extincteur' instead of 'extincteur d'incendie' SUISSE 'Extincteur d'incendie'	Solved	76%(119)	56%(169)

Table A6.3b **Comparison of French and Swiss questionnaire in retest for items with a problem in Swiss version**

Item	Problem	Proportion answers correct French Version 1998 (n. cases	Proportion answers correct Swiss Version 1998 (n. cases)
B1Q12	Question:' 'Citez deux raisons...expliquant pourquoi il est préférable de discuter...' SUISSE 'Donnez deux raisons.. pour discuter des possibilités d'emploi' is an incorrect translation.	33% (114)	14% (187)
B5Q6	Question: '..., quelles sont les 3 questions que vous devez vous posez? Document: 'Vous devez vous poser ces trois questions.' *SUISSE* Question:' énumérez 3 points à ne pas oublier.' Document: '...Voici les trois critères dont il faut tenir compte.'. The link between question and answer is not preserved.	60% (141)	43% (193)
B1Q2	Question: '..., que peut-on faire pour y remédier ?' Document : 'Déplacer le bouton vers la droite.' *SUISSE* Question : '..., que peut-on faire pour remédier à ce problème ?' Document : '...assurez-vous que l'interrupteur econergie...'. The question ' what can we do ?' suggests an action like 'move' more than 'be sure'.	89% (115)	70% (188)

Figure A6.1 Mean number of omissions by region, France

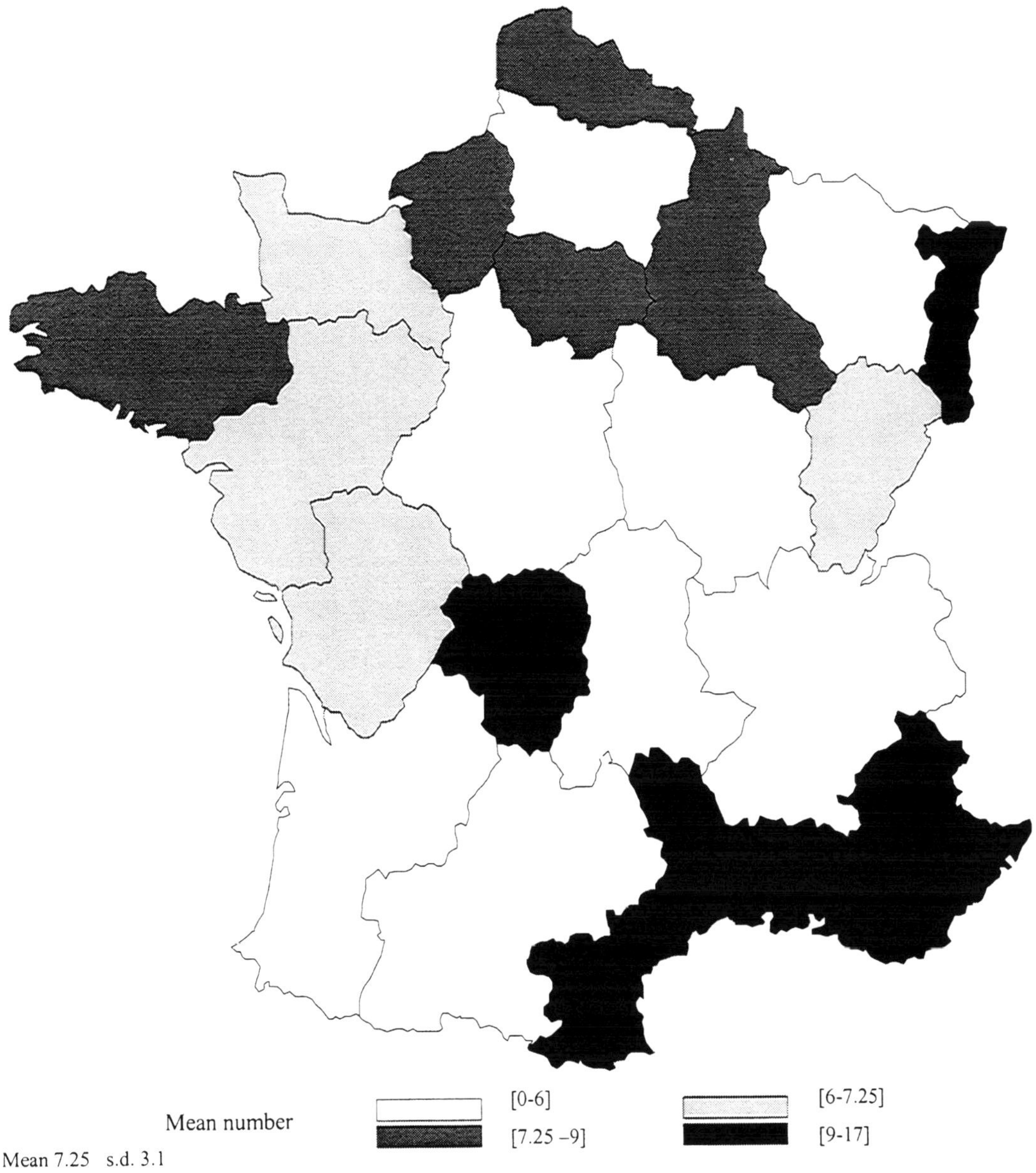

Figure A6.2 Mean number of refusals by region

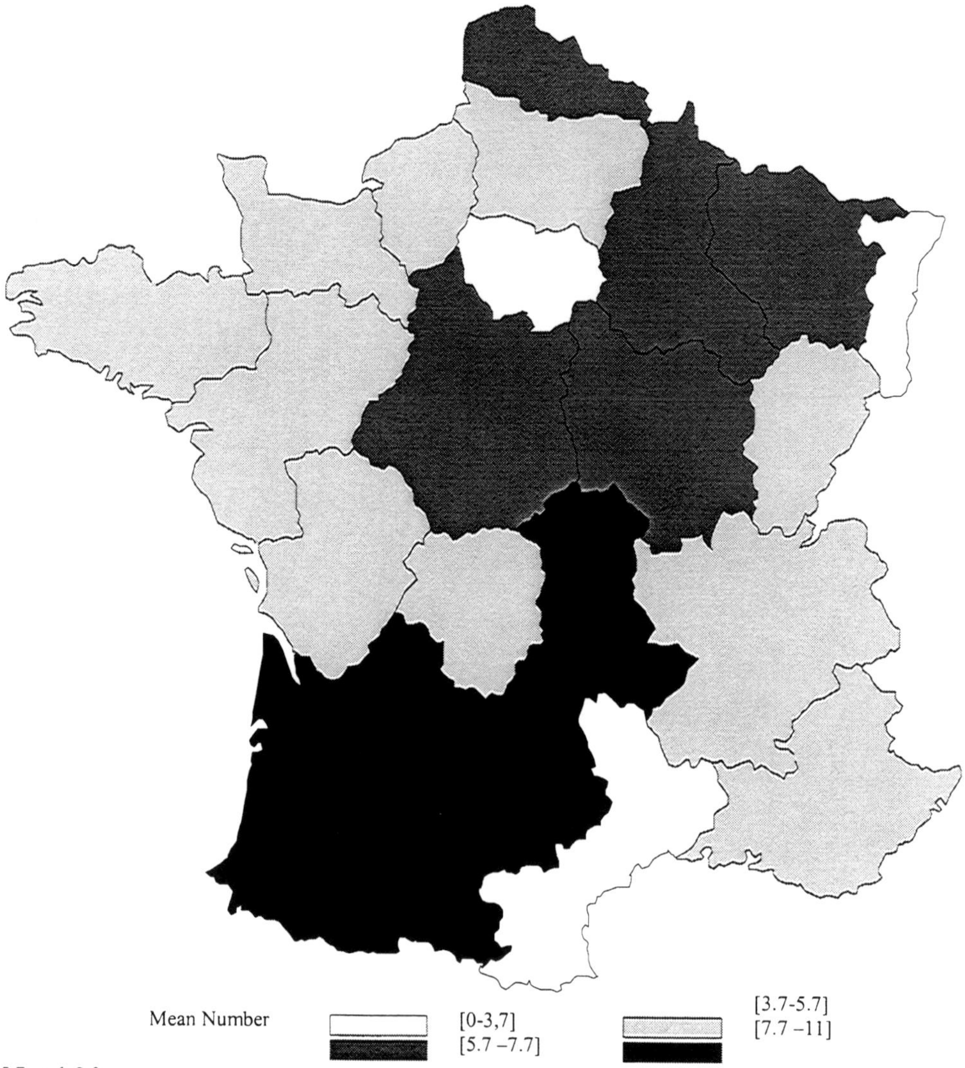

Mean 5.7 s.d. 2.0

7. How much complexity? Balancing the demands of validity and practicality in a cross-national ability survey

Patrick Heady, Office for National Statistics

7.1 Introduction

One of the major innovations of the IALS study is the way it draws on two hitherto distinct research traditions: psychometrics and survey research. The result, viewed from the perspective of people brought up in the social survey tradition is a very complex piece of work. This complexity is apparent in a number of ways.

- A lengthy piloting and consultation process is needed to design a test that will be relevant and acceptable in a range of different cultures.
- Since the test has to be administered in several different languages, rigorous controls are needed to ensure that the translations are fully comparable – not just in terms of semantic content but also in terms of a number of other features that affect the difficulty of the cognitive task.
- The complete test includes a large number of items. In order to obtain data on all of them, the items were divided into seven blocks. Each informant was asked to complete three blocks (itself a substantial task). A 'rotation' pattern ensured that each possible pairing of blocks was answered by at least some informants.
- The results are presented in terms of a set of scales whose conceptual and statistical sophistication perplexes some – otherwise highly literate and numerate – readers.

Clearly, there are good reasons for introducing each of these complexities into the design and implementation of the research. Nonetheless, it is equally true that the burdens, in organisational resources and - not least - in cost, are unusual in terms of survey research. Test procedures that are feasible in the setting of a sample of schools where all concerned are used to following the requirements of examination boards, may be much harder to organise in the less orderly context of people's homes, in which they have to be explained and administered by interviewers who may themselves be unfamiliar with the routines of this kind of test. Similarly, methods of presenting research results that are acceptable in the academic community may be considered unacceptably obscure in many parts of the heterogeneous community which is commonly interested in the results of major social surveys.

In a nutshell, the various kinds of complexity may be desirable in research terms, but they impose both organisational and practical costs. So it is natural for people coming from the social survey tradition to ask whether all the complexities of the IALS research design were strictly necessary. That is the theme of this chapter. It is divided into four main parts, dealing (in reverse order) with each of the four kinds of complexity listed above.

The analyses presented here are based on data from the first wave of IALS. This dataset covers ten different nationalities – counting French and English speaking Canadians, like French and German speaking Swiss, as distinct national groups. However, data from the USA were excluded from most of the analyses because the IALS data set for the USA contains only two blocks of IALS test items. A comparison between the full test and the simplified versions would not mean quite the same thing for the USA as in the other nine countries, for which the data set contains three blocks per person.

7.2 Ways of presenting the survey results

7.2.1 What kind of scores?

Some readers of the IALS reports have commented that the scale scores were rather abstract, and have suggested that a simpler measure – such as the number of questions answered correctly – might be easier for non-specialists to grasp. A key issue is whether results presented in such a form would distort the pattern shown by the full model-generated scores. Charts 7.1a and 7.1b compare the relative position of different countries in terms of model-derived scores (based on the total of the three different scales) with their relative positions in terms of the average number of right answers. The two charts are very similar – suggesting that the simpler measure might provide a satisfactory way of presenting the results.

Chart 7.1a: Model derived Scores

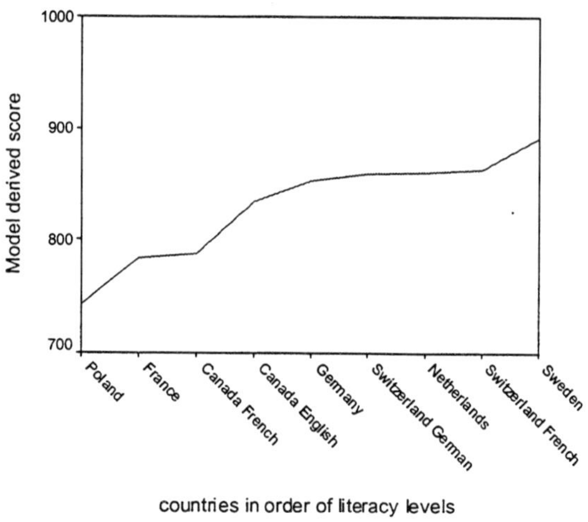

Chart 7.1b: Average number of right answers

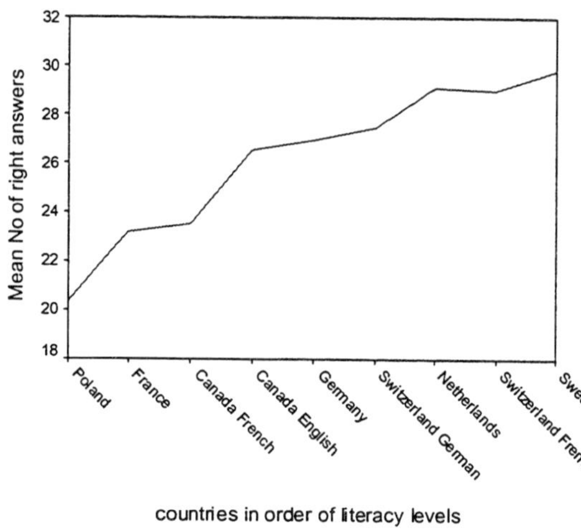

7.2.2 How many scales?

One feature of IALS is the presentation of results in terms of three different scales relating to prose, documents, and quantitative tasks – which have been identified as distinct kinds of competence on cognitive grounds. However, despite the measures' distinctness in terms of cognitive theory, individuals' scores on the three scales were very highly correlated (Table 7.1).

Table 7.1 **Correlations between scores on literacy scales (3rd plausible value)**

	Prose	Document	Quantitative
Prose	1.00		
Document	.89	1.00	
Quantitative	.86	.92	1.00

The relative distribution of scores for different countries was also very similar, though not identical (Charts 7.2a to 7.2c). This raises the question of whether it would have been enough to use a single combined scale.

Chart 7.2a: Mean prose score

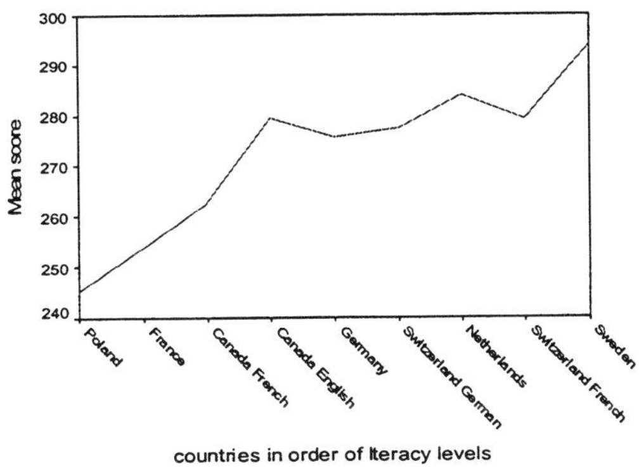

Chart 7.2b: Mean document score

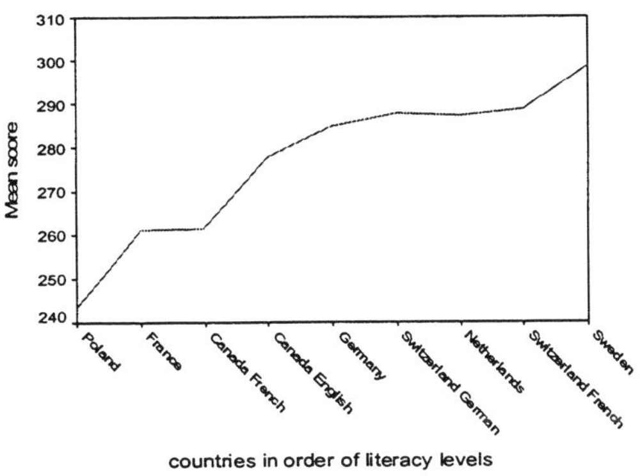

Chart 7.2c: Mean quantitative score

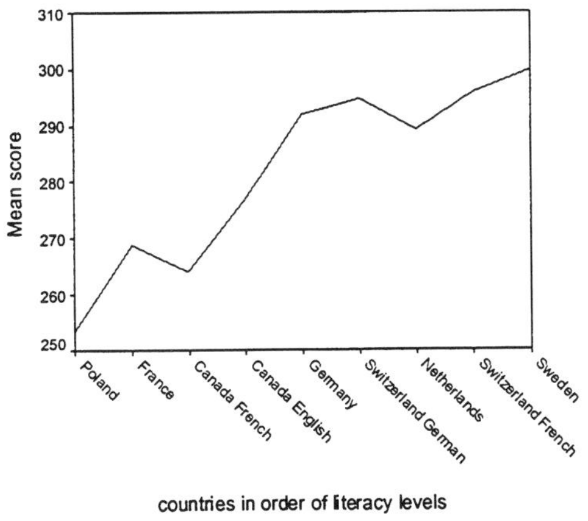

The answer depends on the purpose of the investigation. If there was an interest in testing the degree of association between the different kinds of literacy skill, then it would be essential to measure the three kinds of skill separately – even if the eventual conclusion was that they were so closely associated as to count as a single skill. For example, if one was interested in a population with relatively similar levels of overall literacy (e.g. university students) one might want to investigate whether the balance of different types of skill differed between, say, students of sciences and the humanities. Similarly, one might be interested in whether men and women had different reading habits, associated with different emphases on particular kinds of reading and comprehension skill.

However, in the case of IALS much of the interest has focused less on divergent patterns of reading skill, and more on the very substantial differences in the *overall* level of literacy – between age-groups, between socio-economic categories, between people with different amounts of schooling and, above all, between different countries. So the key issues for this chapter relate to the conceptualisation, measurement, and reporting of overall literacy levels – and of how they vary between countries.[1]

[1] Since the emphasis of this chapter is on scaling and related procedures, we have set aside questions of sampling, weighting, and even population definition. The results cited below are based on unweighted analyses that include every member of each national sample who was presented with the questions concerned.

7.2.3 Allowing for cultural bias

It is often argued that the ability to deal with each test item in a study such as IALS draws not only on literacy skills in the strict sense but also on a shared cultural background between the setters of the test and the people taking it. If this is so, one reason why people in country A might do better at the test than people in country B, might be that their culture was closer to that of the people setting the test. Perhaps, after all, the three-scale framework used by IALS is too simple, and we ought to look for additional dimensions – potentially cross-cutting the three main scales – which reflect differences in the cultural appropriateness of different items.

An alternative way of testing for cultural bias is to consider the country from which each test item originated. Since items devised in any particular country would, presumably, be compatible with its own culture, the hypothesis that the test is culturally biased leads to the prediction that survey participants will score relatively highly on those test items which were devised in their own country. In order to test this hypothesis we analysed data from four countries in our dataset which had originated questions. (USA originated 53 questions, Netherlands 22, Germany 14, and France 6. Although Canada also originated some questions, we have not included it here, since we don't know whether they originated in the anglophone or francophone communities.) This made 95 questions altogether (including a few that were dropped from the final IALS scales). For each question we calculated the average percentage of right answers taking all four countries together. We then took each country separately, and for each question subtracted the four-country average from the percentage of right answers in that particular country. In effect this difference measures how well people in that country answered that question relative to people in the other three countries. We then compared the mean value of this difference for those questions originating in the country concerned, with the mean value of the difference for questions originating in other countries – to see whether people performed better (relative to respondents in other countries) on questions that had originated from within their own national culture. Table 7.2 gives the results.

Table 7.2: **Comparison of questions originating in each country with questions originating in other countries**

	Mean value for questions originating in that country		Mean value for questions originating in other countries	
	Mean	*Number of questions*	*Mean*	*Number of questions*
USA	3.4	*53*	3.0	*42*
Netherlands	1.6	*22*	2.5	*73*
Germany	4.8	*14*	4.0	*81*
France	-10.8	*6*	-9.6	*89*

The figures provide no evidence of an originating-country effect. It is however possible – but no more than possible - that some effects of this kind could have been eliminated at the pilot stage. If so, this could be interpreted in two distinct ways – as the elimination of cultural bias (see Beaton, chapter 4 in this report) or as the consistent imposition of a particular cultural norm, with an inherent bias against countries that did not share that aspect of culture (see Goldstein, chapter 5). Though this issue is potentially important, we cannot pursue it further using the data available here.

7.3 The possibility of simpler test design

7.3.1 *Sampling error and inter-item variability*

There is of course a rich literature on the relation between test design and the precision of estimates. Here I wish only to comment on how precision relates to two very basic features of test design: the number of items in the test, and the size of the sample of individuals who take the test.

In very rough terms one can think of the error in the estimates as the sum of two components: the error associated with the choice of a particular sample of respondents – what survey analysts think of as sampling error – and the error associated with the choice of a particular set of test items.[2]

In thinking about the number of items it is useful to get back to basics, and ask ourselves what we need the items for. We can do so by considering a slightly simplified version of the measurement task – which nevertheless brings out the main issues involved. Suppose that we categorise questions into 5 levels of difficulty. To start with, we will suppose that all questions in a given category are of exactly the same level of difficulty.

If the purpose is to obtain accurate assessments of each individual's ability level (as it would be in the case of college entrance examinations) then we need to allow for the fact that any particular person will get some items of a given difficulty right and others wrong. So we need several questions of roughly the same difficulty to make an assessment of whether that particular person has the skills needed to deal with material at this level. The problem is that there is an element of chance about the way she happens to answer any one particular question. Using just one question, we make the measurement with a high standard error. However, by using four questions and averaging the score, the standard error would be reduced by half. If we took nine questions, the standard error would only be one third of its value in the single-question case – and so on.

If the purpose is to assess the distribution of literacy skills in a whole country – or in an age group or social class category – what we probably want to know is how often the country's inhabitants answer questions at each of the five levels correctly. Since we will be putting the questions to a large sample of people in each country, we can – given our assumptions - obtain precise estimates of these proportions by setting respondents a test containing just one question in each difficulty category. To see why this is so, let us suppose that on average, people in country A answer category 3 questions correctly 50 percent of the time. If we tested 2,500 inhabitants of the country, chosen at random, put the same question to all of them, and worked out the proportion who got it right, then the standard error of that proportion – calculated using the appropriate formula, namely

$$SE(\hat{p}) = \sqrt{\frac{p(1-p)}{n}}$$

would be only 1%. For values of p greater or less than 0.5, the standard error would be lower – so the proportions of right answers to questions in the other difficulty categories would be estimated even more accurately.

Of course, this example is not entirely realistic. For one thing, the sample would probably not be chosen using simple random sampling. It is also unrealistic to assume that all questions in

---

[2] Strictly speaking, one can only add variances, or other kinds of squared errors.

a given category are equally difficult. However, choosing the representative question for each category from about the middle of its difficulty range could circumvent that difficulty. The really crucial assumption is that the relative difficulty of the questions is the same for each of the populations being compared. It is generally agreed that item difficulty may vary between individuals and social groups according to the familiarity of the subject matter and the presentational context. The key issue here is whether items also vary in difficulty between different countries

To investigate this issue, I have taken the 15 items in block 1. (Table 7.3 gives the number of informants in each country who were asked to complete this block, and the overall proportion of right answers to each question – non-answers being counted as incorrect).

Table 7.3a **Number of informants who were asked to complete block 1 – by country***

Poland	987
France	1,094
Canada French	588
Canada English	1,437
Germany	890
Switzerland German	511
Netherlands	1,276
Switzerland French	553
Sweden	1,435
TOTAL	8,771

*These figures represent about 43% of the sample completing the main test in each country

Table 7.3b **Proportion of correct answers to each item in block 1**

Q1	.70
Q2	.78
Q3	.73
Q4	.71
Q5	.50
Q6	.63
Q7	.62
Q8	.43
Q9	.62
Q10	.76
Q11	.30
Q12	.31
Q13	.76
Q14	.63
Q15	.71
BASE	8,771

Charts 7.3a to 7.3o show how the patterns of right answers vary from country to country. In the charts the countries are listed from left to right in order of their overall IALS literacy scores. The questions are presented in order of increasing difficulty – starting with question B1Q2, answered correctly by 78% of respondents in the nine countries, and ending with B1Q11 answered correctly by just 30%.

If the assumption of equal relative difficulty is true, the charts for items of roughly equal difficulty should be similar. In fact they differ quite a lot – suggesting that the relative difficulty of items does vary between countries.

Chart 7.3a: Block 1 question 2

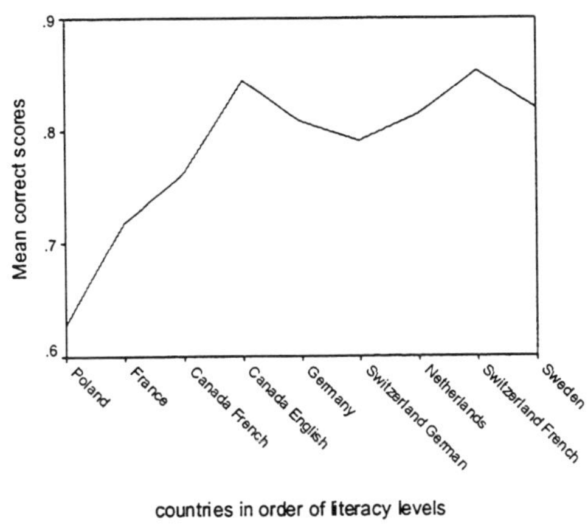

Chart 7.3b Block 1 question 13

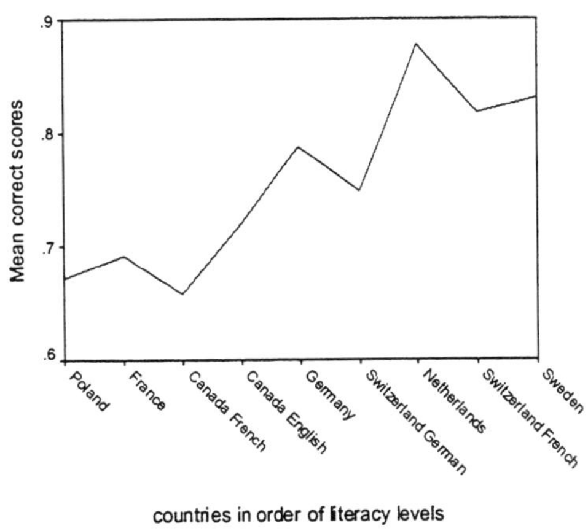

Chart 7.3c: Block 1 question 10

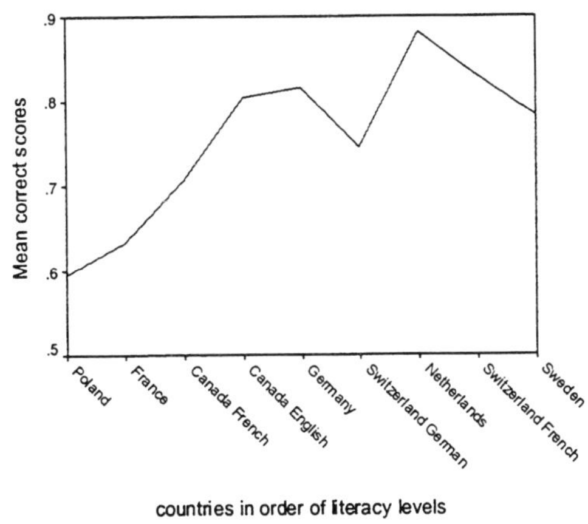

Chart 7.3d: Block 1 question 3

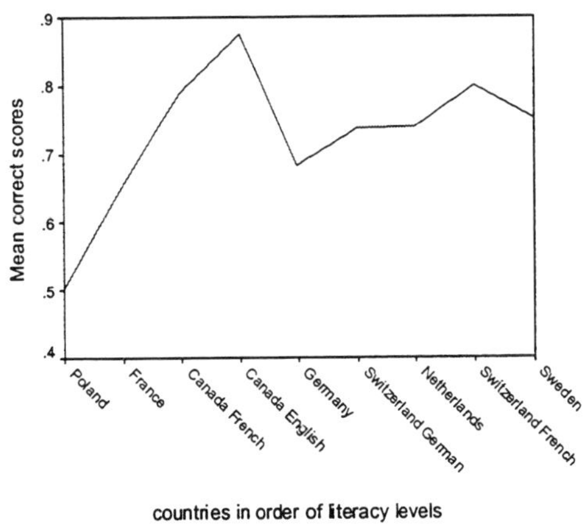

Chart 7.3e: Block 1 question 15

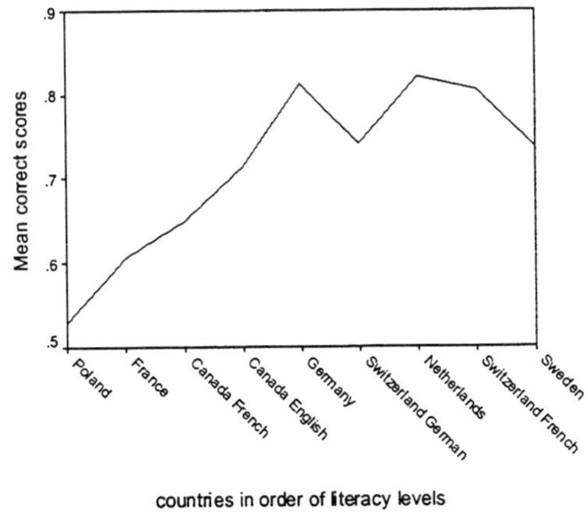

Chart 7.3f: Block 1 question 4

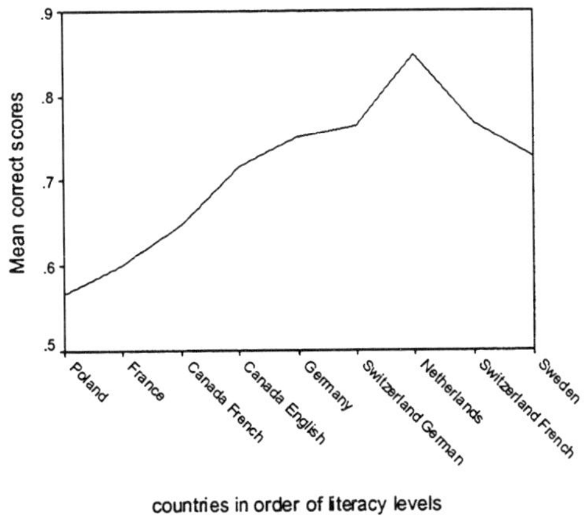

Chart 7.3g: Block 1 question 1

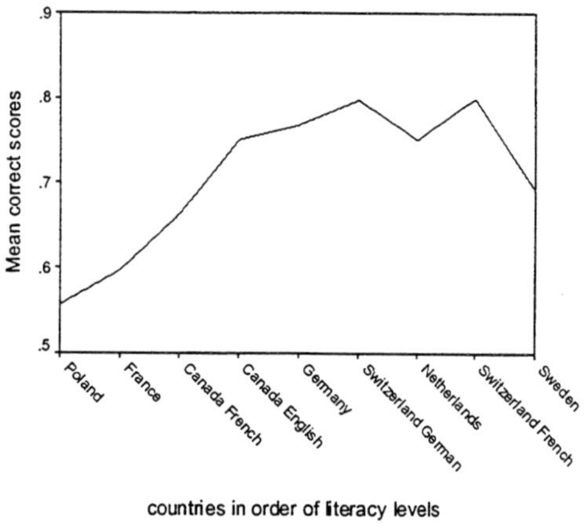

Chart 7.3h: Block 1 Question 6

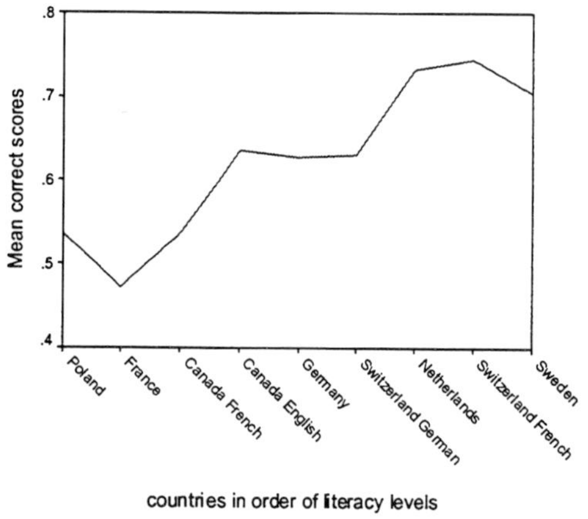

Chart 7.3i: Block 1 question 14

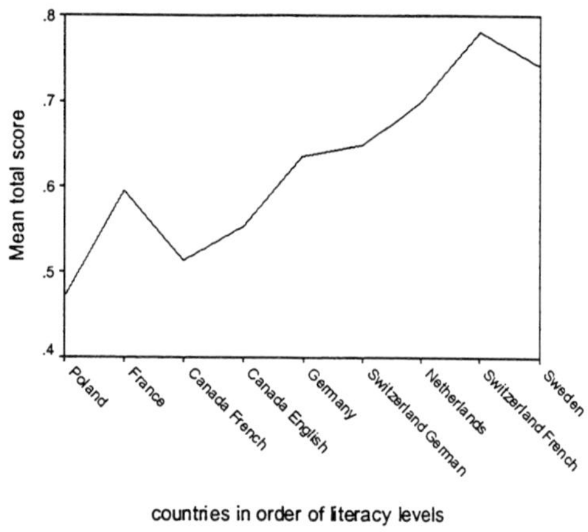

Chart 7.3j: Block 1 question 9

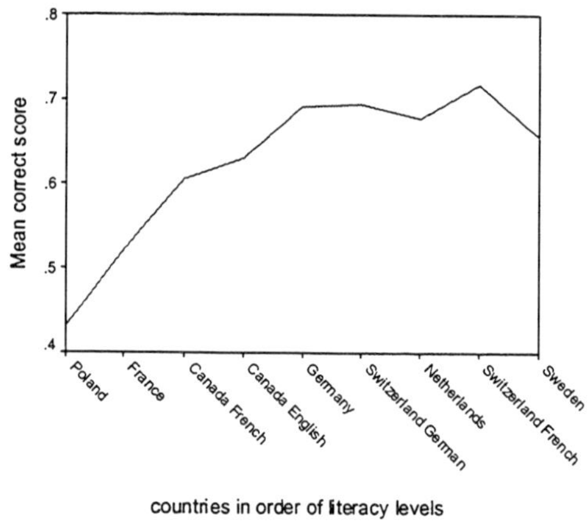

Chart 7.3k: Block 1 question 7

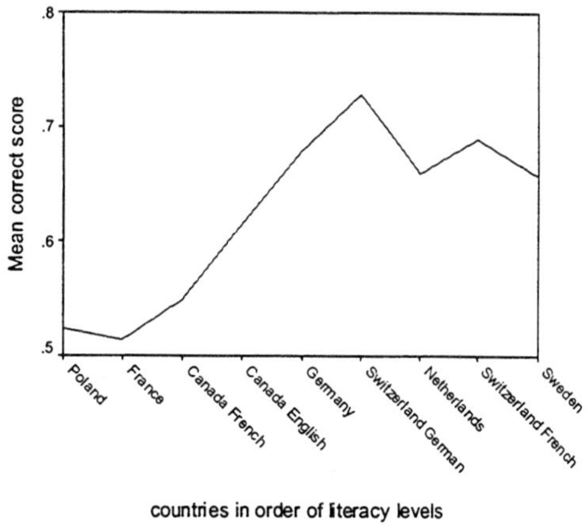

Chart 7.3l: Block 1 question 5

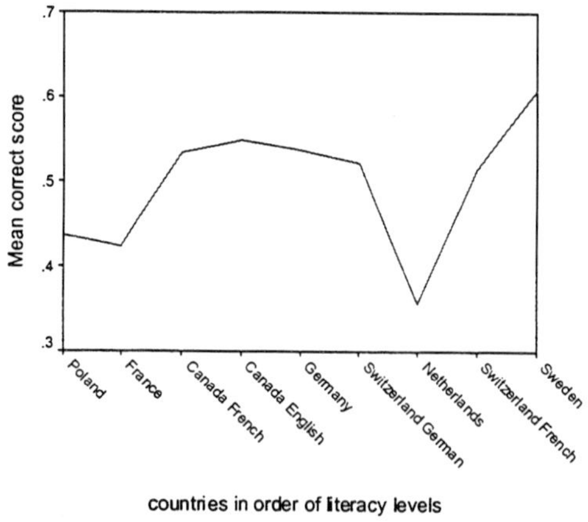

Chart 7.3m: Block 1 question 8

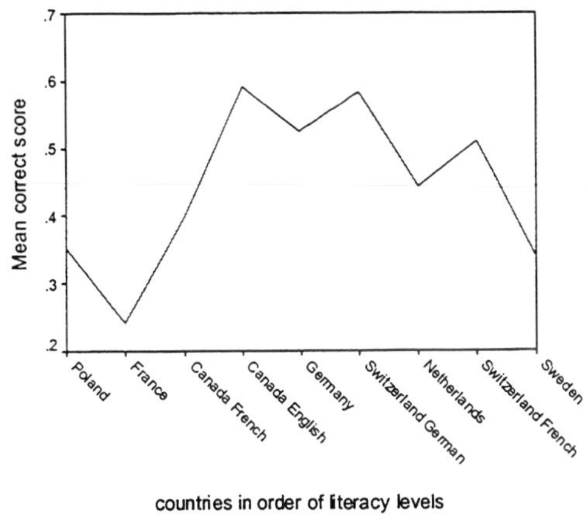

Chart 7.3n: Block 1 question 12

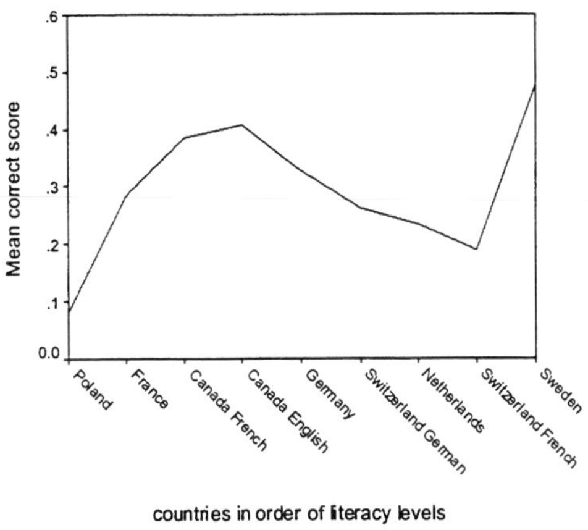

Chart 7.3o: Block 1 question 11

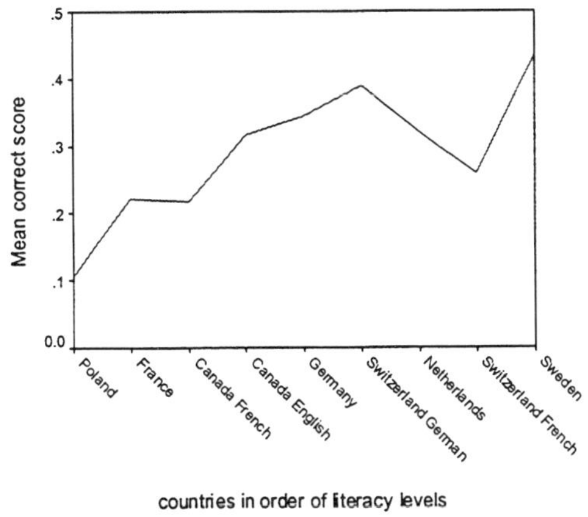

7.3.2 Scale scores and item variability

We need some way of estimating what proportion of each country's respondents one would have expected to answer each question correctly – given the apparent differences in overall literacy skills between the countries. This could be used to produce a more specific estimate of the extent of the inter-country variation in the relative difficulty of items. In order to obtain some approximate predictions I have used the multi-level modeling package MLwiN[3] to fit a modified Item Response Theory (IRT) model to the data. The model we have chosen is a version of the Rasch model – which is the simplest of the commonly used IRT models. The Rasch model aims to predict the probability that a particular individual will answer a particular question correctly by estimating two parameters. One of these parameters reflects the literacy skill of the person concerned, while the other reflects the difficulty of the question. In order to estimate the probability of a right answer, you simply subtract value of the question parameter from the person's ability score. This means (as common sense suggests) that the more skilled the person, the more likely she is to answer the question correctly, while the harder the question the less likely she is to get it right. (To be strictly accurate what the difference of the two parameters predicts is not the probability of a correct

[3] See Goldstein H et al. 1998 A User's Guide to MLwiN. Multilevel Models Project. London University, Institute of Education.

answer but the 'logit' of the probability – the logarithm of the odds of a correct answer. But, although this is an important technical point, it does not affect the essential rationale of the model.[4]). The way this particular version of the Rasch model has been set up in MlWin enables us to allow for the variability in the data due to:

- differences in overall literacy levels between countries,
- the specific difficulty level of each question,
- random variation in individuals' literacy levels (the degree of variability is assumed to be the same in each country – though this variation takes place around different national averages),
- and also random variation in the answers given to each question by people of the same overall literacy level.[5]

The results are set out in Table 7.4. The table includes parameter estimates for each country (except English-speaking Canada, which was taken as the baseline) which can be interpreted in much the same way as the average scale scores in IALS. It also includes a score for ten of the questions. (Question 1 was taken as the baseline, and another four questions were excluded because they showed unusual inter-country distributions. I will return to this point below.)

In order to investigate the possibility of inter-country variation in item difficulty, we have modified the Rasch model, by assuming that item difficulty may vary randomly between countries. For the sake of simplicity we have assumed – to start with – that the inter-country variability was the same for each item.

The additional variance due to this item/country interaction – 0.039 for each question (estimated with a standard error of 0.007) - is highly statistically significant. To get a feel for how large it is, we can convert it to a standard deviation by taking the square root. The result – 0.197 – can be interpreted as an approximate indication of the average amount by which the score of each country might be expected to differ from its true underlying score if the assessment were based on just that one question.[6]

---

[4] For an explanation of this and some other IRT models see Benjamin D.Wright (1997) A history of social science measurement. Educational Measurement: Issues and Practice 16(4) 33-45.

[5] The Rasch model does not make these allowances in quite such a sophisticated way as the IALS model - which also includes slope parameters indicating how powerful each item is as a measure of literacy level. We don't think this simplification will have affected the main conclusions of the analysis that follows, but would welcome comments on the point.

[6] Strictly speaking, this would only be true if the sample in each country were large enough to for random between-person variance to be ignored. More realistically, adding another question makes it possible to estimate each person's literacy level more accurately, and so reduces the variance of the estimate of the average national literacy level as well.

Table 7.4[7] **Rasch model: parameter estimates**

	Parameter estimates	*Standard error of estimate*
Parameter Values		
(1) Fixed effects		
Baseline (Canada E, Q1)	0.936	*0.098*
Country Effects		
Poland	-0.716	*0.102*
France	-0.479	*0.101*
Canada (f)	-0.346	*0.108*
Germany	0.184	*0.104*
Swiss (g)	0.149	*0.111*
Netherlands	0.378	*0.100*
Swiss (f)	0.357	*0.110*
Sweden	0.200	*0.099*
Question effect		
Q2	0.403	*0.101*
Q4	0.021	*0.100*
Q6	-0.380	*0.100*
Q7	-0.394	*0.100*
Q9	-0.386	*0.100*
Q10	0.272	*0.101*
Q11	-1.837	*0.100*
Q13	0.264	*0.101*
Q14	-0.371	*0.100*
Q15	0.041	*0.100*
(2) Variance parameters		
Answer level variance	$\pi(1-\pi)$	
Person level variance	1.482	*0.029*
Item/country interaction	0.039	*0.007*

As we have already mentioned, the model measures each country's score on the logit scale (which is a transformation of the simple proportions of right answers, which we were discussing above). The scores themselves range from –0.716 in the case of Poland to +0.378 in the case of the Netherlands – a range from top to bottom of 1.094. This is much larger than the standard deviation of each question's difficulty level. So we can conclude that, even if we based the literacy assessment on a single question, we would be unlikely to make a mistake about the relative position of countries at the top and bottom of the literacy range. However, we would be very likely to make mistakes about the rankings of countries with similar underlying literacy levels (for instance Germany, German Switzerland, and the Netherlands) – since the measurement error, using just one question, would be greater than the underlying differences we were trying to assess.

7.3.3 *The feasibility of mini-scales*

Another advantage of calculating the between-country variance in item difficulty is that we can estimate how much we can improve it by increasing the number of test items. If we use four items, we can halve the standard error due to question variation – bringing it down to 0.099. With 9 questions it reduces to 0.066. With 11 questions – the number used in our

[7] The model was fitted by first-order marginal quasi-likelihood. See Goldstein et al. (p101) and also Goldstein H 1995 Multilevel Statistical Models. London:Edward Arnold (pp98-101).

model – we should be able to obtain quite a good estimate of the relative literacy levels of different countries. This suggests that a simple scale based on the number of right answers to a block of 15 or so items would be a good deal better than a measure based on just one test item.

But just how good would a simple block-total scale be? Remember that it would include a few items (excluded from our Rasch model) which differed radically from the overall pattern. It should also be borne in mind that there is likely to be some covariance between test items based on the same text – which would reduce somewhat the precision of the overall score. In the end, the only way to be sure how well these simple block-total scales would perform is to compare them with the overall scale derived from the full IALS procedure (i.e. with the overall total score shown in chart 7.1a). In order to compare like with like, the comparison needs to be restricted to those respondents who actually answered the block concerned.

These comparisons are presented in charts 7.4a-n, and are broadly encouraging. In five of the seven cases the simple block-total score produces virtually the same pattern of inter-country differentials as the full IALS score. In the other two cases (blocks 2 and 4) the block-total score produces a rather less smooth progression from least to most literate, but the main shape of the overall pattern is nevertheless preserved. We can conclude from this that a scale based on the total scores for a single block might not always provide an adequate picture of inter-country literacy differentials. However, a relatively small enhancement, such as taking the total number of right answers for *two* blocks, probably would produce a scale that was virtually as good as the full IALS score as an indicator of the overall pattern of inter-country literacy differentials.

Block 1

Chart 7.4a

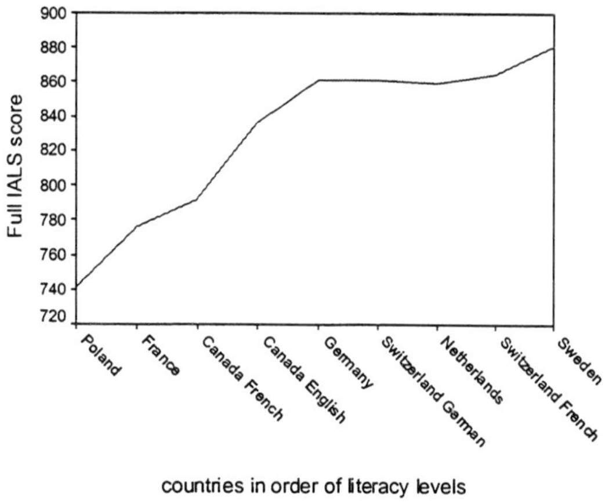

Chart 7.4b

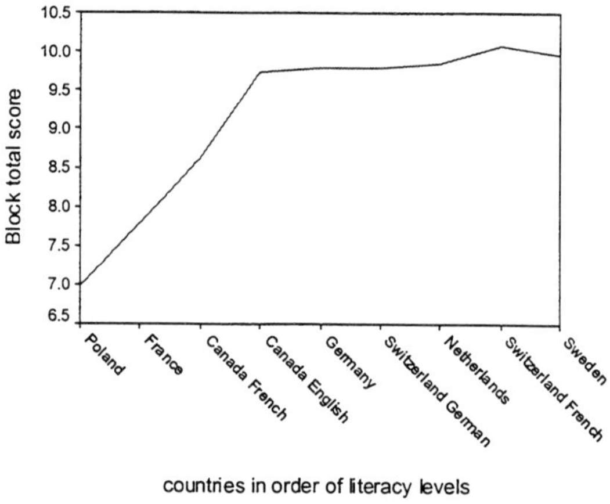

Block 2

Chart 7.4c

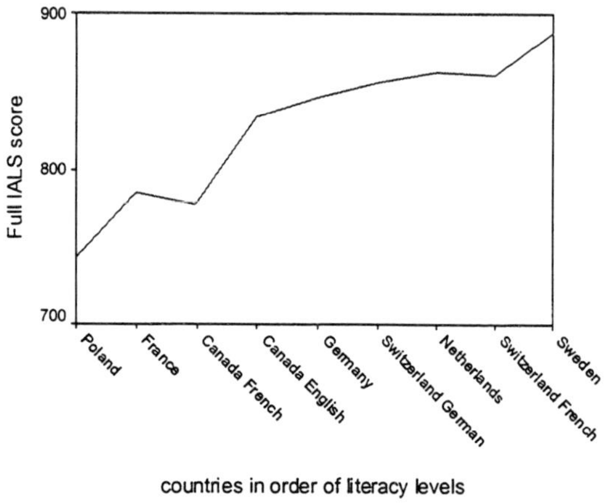

Chart 7.4d

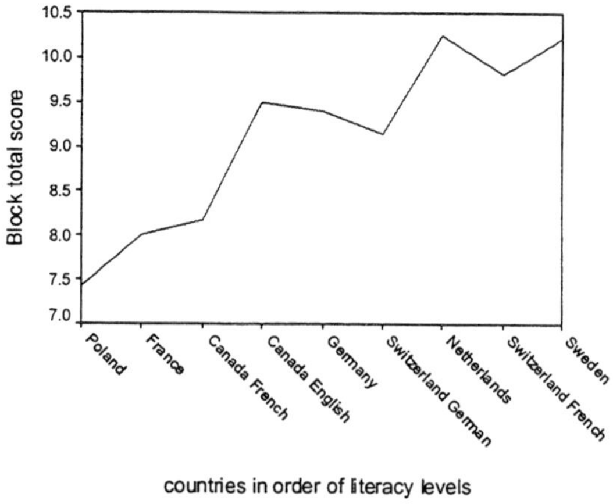

Block 3

Chart 7.4e

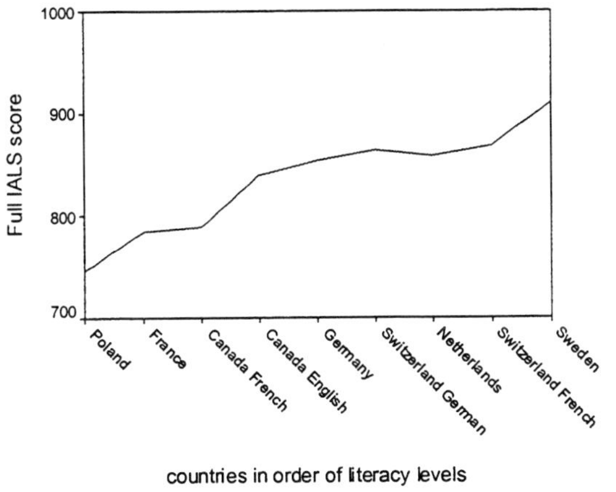

Chart 7.4f

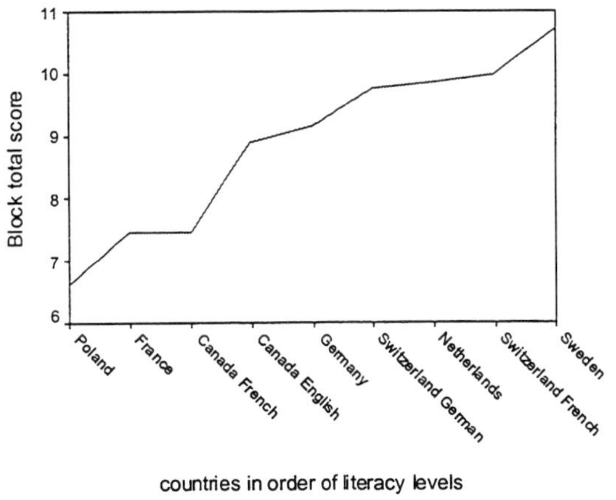

Block 4

Chart 7.4g

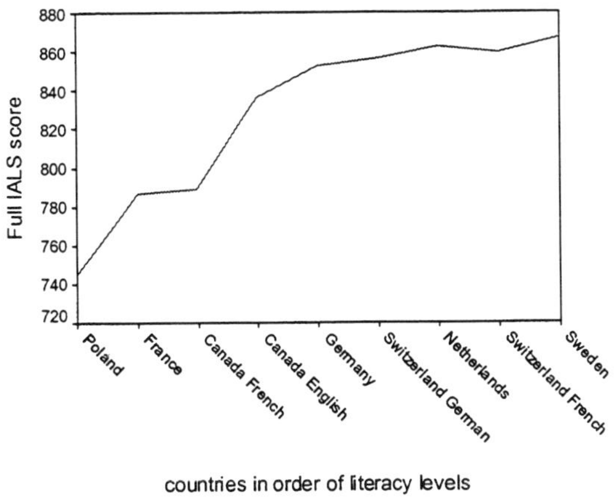

Chart 7.4h

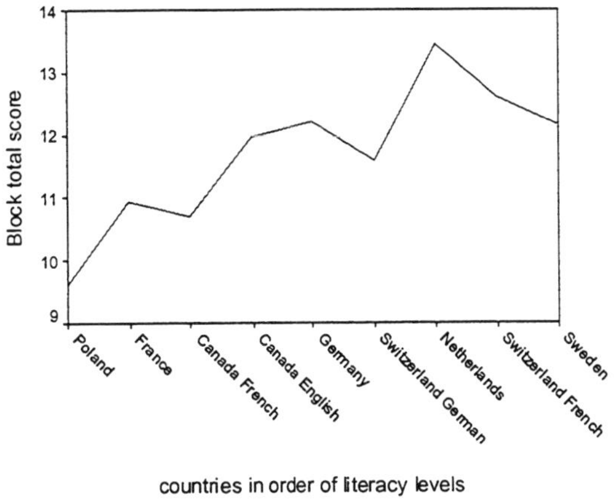

Block 5

Chart 7.4i

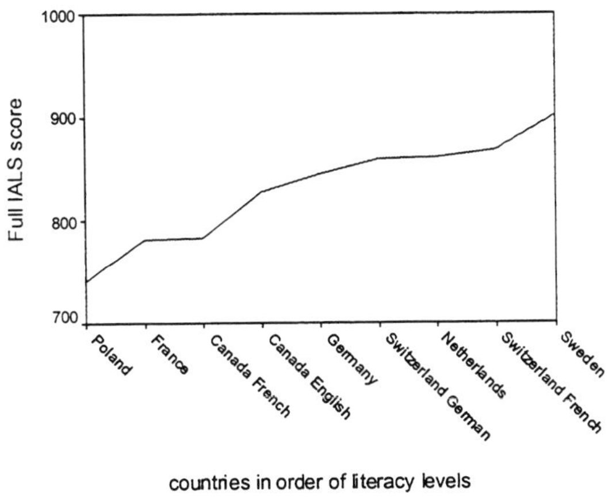

Chart 7.4j

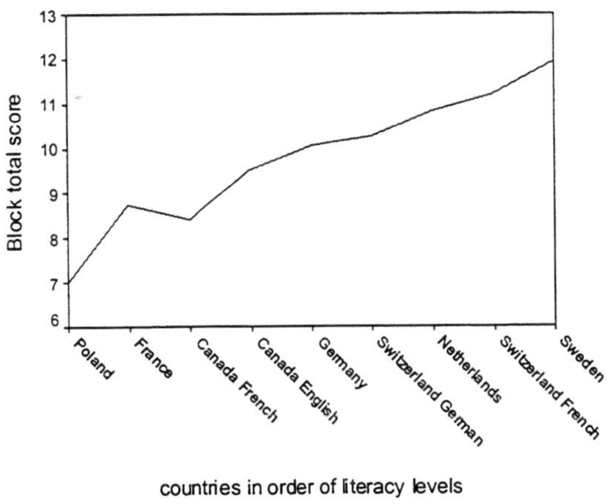

Block 6

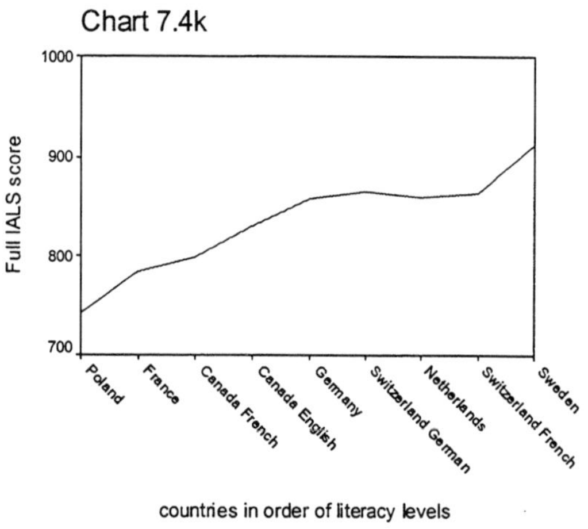

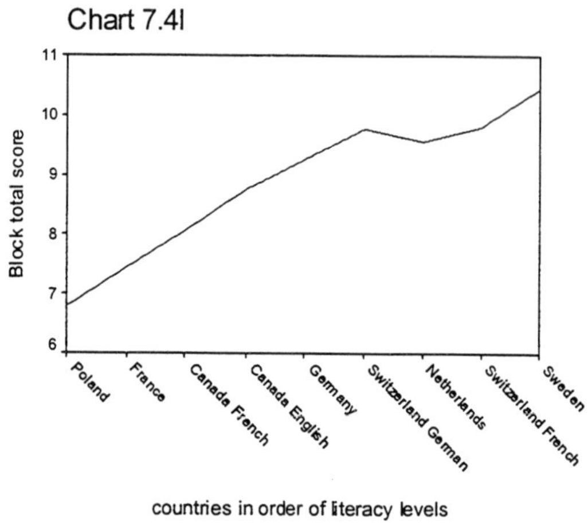

Block 7

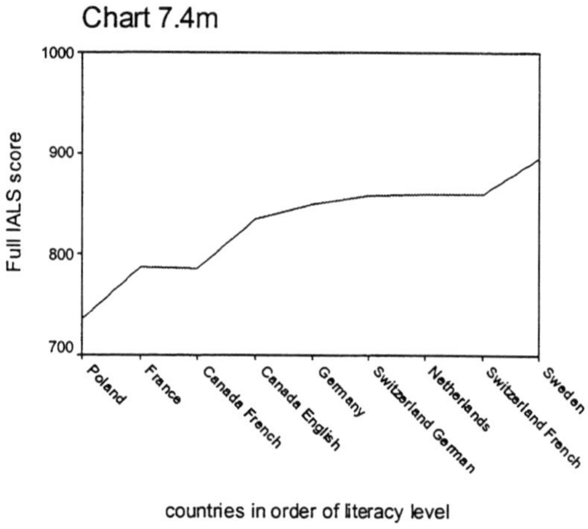

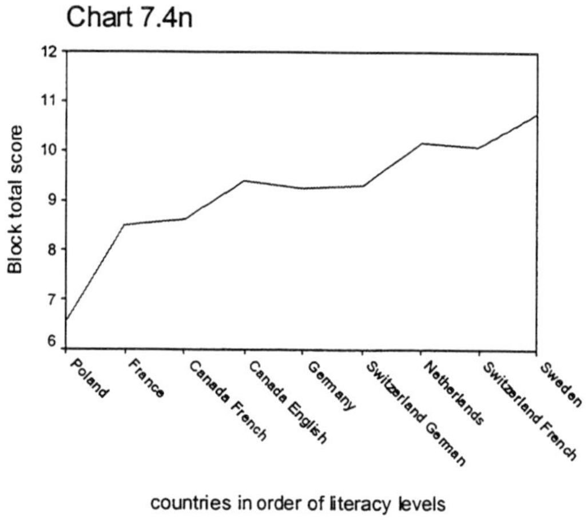

7.4 Translation effects

7.4.1 How we checked the translation

The final aspect of the secondary analysis reported in this chapter was a check on the translation. It complements the work done by Guerin and Blum, in two ways:

- By including more countries
- By seeing whether problem questions can be identified *ex ante* as well as *ex post.*

The check was carried out at the London University Institute of Education. Two bilingual people, with experience of exam setting, assessed the "prose literacy" test items, for each of the following countries:

- France
- French Switzerland (assessed by the same pair as the French test)
- Germany
- Poland
- Sweden.

The items which were rejected altogether at the main IALS analysis stage were not included in this exercise, but items assigned country-specific parameters were left in.

The check was blind – in so far as the checkers did not know which items their country had performed relatively well or badly on. Nor were the assessors told which countries had performed better or worse than expected – except in the case of France, which one of the assessors was already aware of.

The assessors compared the version in the country concerned, with the version used in English-speaking Canada – which was implicitly treated as a kind of standard. This procedure corresponded to the final stages of the sequence of translation actually used when setting up IALS. For IALS items from all countries were all translated into American English and then that version (in either its Canadian or US form) was used as the basis for further translations into the languages of each of the participating countries.

The two checkers in each team worked independently – following an initial half-day briefing. They were provided with a standard questionnaire to complete about each item, with the correct answer, with a note of the points which the IALS team considered essential to preserve when doing the translation, and with some documentation explaining the rationale of the test procedure. Among the questions asked were whether the translation had affected the specificity of either the question or the key information in the text, and whether the translation had affected the ease with which the question could be matched with the key information in the text. Other questions asked whether there was any outright error in the translation, and whether the item was culturally appropriate. A final question asked for the assessor's own evaluation of the overall ease or difficulty of the question concerned – and this is the measure which has been used in the following analysis of the results.

7.4.2 How to read the tables

The units in each table are the 34 questions that were covered in our evaluation exercise. The variable entitled *relative performance* was calculated by taking the percentage of correct answers to the particular question in the country concerned, and subtracting from it the percentage of correct answers to that question in English-speaking Canada. *Assessor 1* and *2* refer to ratings given to each question by the assessors of the translation of questions for each particular country. A score of 1 meant that the question was judged to be harder in the translated version than in the version for English-speaking Canada. A score of 2 meant that they were judged to be equally difficult, and 3 meant that the translated version was judged to be easier.

Tables 7.5 and 7.6 correlate the judgements of the assessors with each other, and with the differential in the proportion of correct answers compared to English-speaking Canada. They thus enable us to see how closely our assessors' judgements of each question's relative difficulty corresponded to the question's real relative difficulty – as shown by the percentage of respondents getting the item right in each country. For any particular question, the point that matters is not whether Germans (or whoever) answered it right more or less often than Canadians, but which questions the Germans did best at (relatively to the Canadians) and which they did worst at. If they did best at the questions which our assessors said were easier in the German version, and worst at those which our assessors said were harder, then this confirmed our assessors' judgement that the translation had indeed affected the difficulty of the questions.

Table 7.7 looks in a little more detail at the judgements made by one of the assessors for each country – namely the assessor whose judgement of translation problems was most closely borne out by the comparisons of the proportions of right answers. It shows the differential between the country concerned and Canada in the percentage of right answers for each of three categories of question – those thought by the assessor to harder, equally difficult, or easier than their Canadian versions.

The results in Tables 7.5 and 7.7 are based on all the items included in the prose scale. The results in Table 7.6 exclude those items assigned country-specific parameters in either English-speaking Canada or the country concerned.

7.4.3 The results

The results in Table 7.5 are based on all the items included in the prose scale. They confirm that a considerable degree of translation bias did remain in the final IALS dataset – even after some items had been rejected from the analysis. Of the ten sets of translation judgements (two for each of five countries) nine were positively correlated with the actual differentials in question performance. Three of the correlations (for one assessor in each of France, French Switzerland, and Poland) were statistically significant in their own right.

Table 7.5 **Translation effects on items in the prose literacy scale – correlations with rater assessments, including all items used in the scale**

	Relative performance	Assessor 1	Assessor 2
German translation			
Relative performance	1.00		
Assessor 1	.26	1.00	
Assessor 2	.12	.47*	1.00
French translation			
Relative performance	1.00		
Assessor 1	.42*	1.00	
Assessor 2	.12	.21	1.00
French Swiss translation			
Relative performance	1.00		
Assessor 1	.38*	1.00	
Assessor 2	.17	.55**	1.00
Polish translation			
Relative performance	1.00		
Assessor 1	.13	1.00	
Assessor 2	.40*	.31	1.00
Swedish translation			
Relative performance	1.00		
Assessor 1	-.27	1.00	
Assessor 2	.23	-.22	1.00

* Significant at the 0.05 level (2-tailed) **Significant at the 0.01 level (2-tailed)

I would like to comment on some interesting features of these results – but, before doing so, it is necessary to issue a warning about the dangers of over-interpretation. The half-day's training that we gave to our assessors was not enough for them to become fully expert in the aspects of translation that might affect the difficulty of the respondents' task. This lack of expertise is reflected in the relatively low correlation between the judgements of each pair of assessors. It is also reflected by some evident misjudgments shown in Table 7.7. Thus, taking the two questions which the German assessor had judged more difficult as a result of translation, we see that the test respondents had done them just as well (relatively to their Canadian counterparts) as the 24 questions which the assessor thought unaffected by the translation. Even more strikingly, the French assessor identified only one question that had become more difficult as a results of translation (the figures in Table 7.7 show that it became much more difficult), even though the findings of Blum and Guerin demonstrate that a much higher proportion of items in the French questionnaire had been made more difficult by the translation. These problems mean that we cannot use the findings of this test to make a quantitative assessment of the extent of translation bias for any particular country.

Nevertheless we can assess the extent to which the assignment of county-specific item parameters managed to reduce the bias. Table 7.6 removes the items concerned from the analysis (effectively what happens to these items in the intercountry comparisons carried out by IALS). The result weakens the association between assessors' judgements and differential item performance considerably, but does not eliminate it altogether. It is reasonable to assume that the effect of special parameters in the main IALS analysis was similar.

The other interesting point is the direction of the translation biases our assessors discovered (and which were confirmed by the relative performance of respondents in the countries concerned). Translation bias often made the question *easier*. (In fact this effect is commoner in Table 7.7 than the opposite and more expected effect – but the quality of our data is not good enough to enable us to conclude that helpful mistranslations really outnumber ones that make the task more difficult.) The explanation for this initially surprising result is that translation biases did not only result from semantic errors (which would indeed be expected to make the questions more difficult) but also from more subtle changes which affected the ease with which the question could be matched to the appropriate information in the text. A semantically equivalent translation might well be easier than the original if, for instance, it used precisely the same wording in the question as in the target text - although the original had phrased the question differently from the target text.

Table 7.6: **Translation effects on items in the prose literacy scale – correlations with rater assessments, excluding items with country specific parameter estimates (in either the country concerned or English-speaking Canada)**

	Relative performance	Assessor 1	Assessor 2
German translation			
Relative performance	1.00		
Assessor 1	.34	1.00	
Assessor 2	.23	.50*	1.00
French translation			
Relative performance	1.00		
Assessor 1	.22	1.00	
Assessor 2	-.11	.07	1.00
French Swiss translation			
Relative performance	1.00		
Assessor 1	.35	1.00	
Assessor 2	.19	.61**	1.00
Polish translation			
Relative performance	1.00		
Assessor 1	.11	1.00	
Assessor 2	.47*	.09	1.00
Swedish translation			
Relative performance	1.00		
Assessor 1	-.25	1.00	
Assessor 2	-.10	-.28	1.00

* Significant at the 0.05 level (2-tailed)

**Significant at the 0.01 level (2-tailed)

Table 7.7 **Translation effects on items in the prose literacy scale – relative performance in relation to best rater assessment, including all items used in the scale**

	Harder		**No difference**		**Easier**	
	Mean r.p.	*No of questions*	*Mean r.p.*	*No of questions*	*Mean r.p.*	*No of questions*
Germany – Assessor 1	-6.5	*2*	-7.4	*24*	1.0	*6*
France – Assessor 1	-45.0	*1*	-17.6	*31*	-11.5	*2*
French Switzerland – Assessor 1	-12.2	*5*	-4.3	*25*	-2	*2*
Poland – Assessor 2	-	-	-20.6	*22*	-11.4	*9*
Sweden – Assessor 2	.2	*5*	3.2	*26*	6.7	*3*

7.5 Conclusions – and some issues relating to the test development process

Preceding sections of this chapter have shown that it would be possible to simplify both the design of the test and the presentation of the results while still preserving some of the main features of the results identified by the full IALS procedure. On the other hand the procedures used to verify the full comparability of translations need to be tightened still further.

However, these conclusions were all based on analyses using a dataset based on test procedures that had already been piloted. Might the test development and piloting procedures themselves be simplified, and what would happen if this were done? The answer is that we simply do not know, because many of the specifics of the IALS development process have not been made public. It might be the case (as Goldstein argues in this volume) that the test-construction process over-rode important cultural differences – producing an apparent, rather than real, absence of cultural bias. If Goldstein is right, a simplified test construction process might well result in a richer data set, in which questions subject to different patterns of cultural bias still remained. A more complex set of scales – based perhaps on a multi-dimensional version of IRT - would probably be needed to capture these patterns. In order to estimate these scales reliably a more extensive bank of test items might also be needed.

Beaton also would agree that piloting was needed to weed out discrepant items (whether the discrepancy reflected cultural or any other factors) but he would see these as particular factors obscuring a few underlying dimensions of literacy. In that view, the effect of not piloting would be to include more irrelevant noise in the tests. As a result the number of items needed for a reliable result might be increased, but an unpiloted test would still not be multi-dimensional in the sense expected by Goldstein.

In order to resolve these issues, it is to be hoped that future cross-national ability studies will report more fully on the details of their development and piloting processes, and will make their pilot datasets available for independent analysis.

However, the question of how many dimensions a test should ideally measure is distinct from the question of whether the main lines of information captured by a specific test could have been captured and reported in a simpler way. As already indicated, in the case of IALS the answer to this second question seems to be 'Yes'.

8. Taking part in IALS – the respondent perspective

Ann Bridgwood, Monique Laouénan & Åsa Ericson

8.1 Introduction

The first step in the retest project was to carry out qualitative research to provide greater insight into the experience for respondents of taking part in a survey like IALS. The aims of this research were to:

- explore attitudes to survey research, including respondents' reactions and attitudes to the IALS assessment and their understanding of what was expected of them;
- examine levels of personal motivation for literacy tests, including the level of commitment respondents felt towards the task and their views on incentives, in the context of an interview in the home;
- investigate the nature of cultural differences in approaches to surveys and tests, in order to provide a basis for the development of the interview component of the retest project;
- identify how items were understood, processed and answered; and
- inform the overall design of the retest project.

8.2 Methodology and sample

The qualitative research took place in October-November 1997 in countries that had taken part in IALS; France, Great Britain and Sweden. Each of the three participating countries selected 15 former IALS respondents and 15 new respondents to take part in the qualitative research. The two groups were broadly similar in age, sex, educational level and economic activity status in the three countries, with the exception that in Britain, twice as many women as men took part (Tables 8.1 – 8.3).

A letter was sent to sampled addresses prior to fieldwork. Interviewers made appointments by telephone and confirmed them on the day before the interview.

Former IALS respondents were asked to complete a shortened version of the background questionnaire, and the same IALS booklet they completed last time. New respondents were given the full IALS background questionnaire and a booklet selected at random to complete. While respondents were completing the booklets, interviewers filled in an observation sheet, noting progress with the tasks, any audible or visible reactions and any interruptions. Respondents were stopped after they had spent 40 minutes on the booklet and were then interviewed in depth about the survey and their approaches to completing the booklet. Interviewers used a qualitative interview probe list to structure this qualitative part of the interview. The probe list covered respondents' memories of IALS (for former IALS respondents), their reasons for taking part, their views on the advance letter, their understanding of the term 'literacy', their overall impressions of the booklet, how they approached completing it, which questions they found easy or difficult, its length, motivation and incentives. The discussions were recorded on tape and later transcribed for analysis.

When considering the results of the qualitative research, it is important to remember that former IALS respondents had agreed to take part in both the original survey and the follow-up qualitative survey, and that their attitudes may be systematically different from those who refused to take part at either stage. In addition, comments were made in response to prompts from interviewers, and would not necessarily have been made spontaneously.

Table 8.1 **Sample for cognitive and attitudinal research: Great Britain**

Characteristic	IALS respondents	New respondents	Total
Sex	*Number of respondents*		
Male	6	4	10
Female	8	11	19
Age			
16-25	5	5	10
26-44	5	6	11
45 and over	4	4	8
Economic activity			
Working	11	9	20
Unemployed	2	2	4
Economically inactive	1	4	5
Educational level			
No further education	9	6	15
Further education	4	4	8
University	1	5	6
Total	14	15	29

Table 8.2 **Sample for cognitive and attitudinal research: Sweden**

Characteristic	IALS respondents	New respondents	Total
Sex	*Number of respondents*		
Male	7	6	13
Female	8	9	17
Age			
16-25	4	4	8
26-44	7	7	14
45 and over	4	4	8
Economic activity			
Working	13	11	24
Unemployed	1	3	4
Economically inactive	1	1	2
Educational level			
No further education	5	3	8
Further education	5	9	16
University	4	3	7
Total	15	15	30

8.3 Attitudes towards survey research

Respondents' perceptions of the aims of the survey, and their understanding of what they were doing and why, may have had a bearing on their approach to the task. It was also important to explore whether any elements of the survey procedures may have affected respondents' motivation or performance.

8.3.1 Respondents' recall of IALS

Former IALS respondents were asked what they remembered about the survey. IALS fieldwork was conducted in France and Sweden in 1994 and in Britain in 1996. Because respondents were trying to remember experiences of 2-4 years previously, there may have been some problems of recall. It was therefore not surprising that about half of French and Swedish respondents either did not remember taking part or only had vague memories of the survey. In Britain, in contrast, most people could remember something about the survey and the booklet, although overall memories of IALS were very vague. When prompted with the booklet, some had no specific memories; others remembered it as a range of reading or mathematical tasks.

Table 8.3 **Sample for cognitive and attitudinal research: France**

Characteristic	IALS respondents	New respondents	Total
Sex	*Number of respondents*		
Male	6	8	14
Female	9	7	16
Age			
16-25	2	3	5
26-44	9	7	16
45 and over	4	5	9
Economic activity			
Economically active	10	10	20
Economically inactive	5	5	10
Educational level			
Primary	4	6	12
O level and over	11	7	18
Total	15	15	30

Those French respondents who had positive memories of IALS said it was an interesting or varied survey, although others thought the task booklet was long and difficult. This assessment may have been influenced by just having completed a booklet.

British respondents remembered that it was an international survey on literacy, carried out on a cross section of people, was confidential, involved doing some 'questions' or 'exercises', and that they received a pen for taking part.

Most Swedish respondents vaguely remembered having done something concerned with reading, writing and/or testing or that the purpose of the IALS was to study reading comprehension or similar matters. A few had no idea what the survey was about, with only one spontaneously mentioning the international aspect. Almost all the Swedish respondents were positive about their participation. A few were more neutral. No one made negative statements.

8.3.2 Perceptions of what the survey was about

In France, the purpose of the survey was not always clearly understood by those who had taken part in IALS in 1994 and, for many, there was a discrepancy between their expectations and their experiences. Many respondents were expecting the survey to be about coping with different situations in their daily lives, perhaps because its title was 'Savoir-faire dans les situations de la vie quotidienne', but the questions did not seem to relate to this. Some thought it would be a survey of opinions, an impression that may have been generated because the fieldwork was carried out by an organisation which mainly does opinion and consumer surveys. Some saw it as an evaluation of their abilities or as a test, particularly as the booklets resembled tests that they had done at school.

In Britain the survey was seen by the majority of respondents as being about education, or about the skills based on the written word which are needed for daily life and society. These were perceived as important because literacy was believed to be necessary to improve the quality of life. When asked what they meant by 'literacy' most respondents made reference to reading and writing. Some mentioned comprehension of the written word; a few thought it meant the basic skills required in daily life or the ability to read items such as leaflets and government forms. One or two mentioned Mathematics, but this may have been prompted by doing the booklet.

Most respondents in Sweden thought it was a survey looking at reading, writing and arithmetical abilities, or something to do with school. Some respondents found it hard to give a definition of literacy, mentioning dyslexia, reading and writing problems, or the social problems of poor reading.

In summary, IALS was seen in Britain and Sweden as a survey about literacy, which was broadly interpreted as reading and writing skills, or about education. In France, there was confusion about the purposes of the survey, with the references to daily life, and the expectation that opinions were being sought, being at odds with the school-like 'tests' which respondents were asked to complete.

8.3.3 Reasons for agreeing to participate in IALS

Former IALS respondents in all three countries were asked why they had agreed to participate in the survey. It should be noted that this was not asked at the time of the original interview; respondents' answers are therefore a reconstruction of their feelings rather than a contemporaneous report. Not surprisingly, individuals' reasons varied. In France, they included curiosity, a sense of civic duty, wanting to make a contribution to national education and having the time to take part.

In Britain too, duty, curiosity and interest played a part, as well as a wish to help the survey organisation and the interviewers achieve their objectives. There was a belief in Britain that it is important to address literacy and, in Sweden, that lots of people are poor readers, which puts them at a disadvantage in a society in which many tasks require literacy. Respondents in both countries felt that information is needed if things are to change or the educational system improved. Some understood that it was important for the survey to reach every type of person and that it allowed information to be collected about international standards and thus comparisons to be made between countries.

8.3.4 The advance letter

Letters were sent to respondents prior to both the original IALS fieldwork and the qualitative fieldwork. Letters were signed by the Ministry of Education (in 1994 only) in France, by the Field Officer (the office-based interviewer supervisor) in Britain and by the project manager in Sweden. Some concern was expressed following IALS that the signatory to the letter may have influenced respondents' attitude and approach to the survey, and particularly to the literacy assessment.

Letters sent out before the qualitative fieldwork reminded former IALS respondents about the survey, gave all respondents some results from IALS and sought their co-operation for the qualitative research. As part of the debriefing, respondents were asked for their reactions to the letter sent out prior to IALS. Some did not remember it at all. No particular importance was attached to the signatory in any of the three countries; a few people in Britain would have preferred a known figure, such as a government Minister, to sign it, but this was only after prompting. Some French respondents thought that having the letter signed by the Ministry helped; others thought it would put people off. Some in France felt the letter was most useful if it arrived shortly before the interview, while some Swedish interviewees thought it contained too little information about the purposes of the study and the process by which they had been selected.

8.4 Completing the booklet

One of the aims of the qualitative research was to provide infromation on the range of respondent understanding of items in the booklet and how they processed and answered the tasks. This would have been shaped by a combination of factors: respondents' perceptions of the content and purposes of the survey, the booklet itself, their experience of completing both this particular booklet and similar ones in the past, and an assessment of their own ability and knowledge. This is a complex cognitive process that is likely to affect both motivation and performance, and the different strands cannot be disentangled in such a small sample. Respondents' comments can, however, offer some insights.

8.4.1 Overall assessments of the booklet

Respondents in all three countries likened the booklet to a school test or examination; for some French respondents, in particular, it evoked memories of being at school and of failure. This may have been strengthened by the fact that the name of the Ministry of Education was printed on every page of the booklet albeit in very small print at the bottom of each page. Some respondents in all three countries expected trick questions; in France, because it is usual to have them in school tests; in Britain and Sweden because some questions were seen as 'too easy' or, in Britain, as a check to see whether people were reading the questions or following the instructions properly. Interviewers in Britain specifically told respondents, if they asked, that there were no trick questions.

Overall assessments of the booklet varied. One or two highly educated French respondents were not sure what the test was about; whether it was a magazine-type questionnaire, a psychological assessment or a test of abilities. This lack of clarity made respondents nervous about the booklet, and unsure about how to approach it. British and Swedish respondents who felt positive about the booklet said it was enjoyable, interesting with a good variety of tasks and challenging, even though it required a lot of work (Sweden) or could be tiring (Britain). Other negative comments were that it was long, difficult, tedious, frustrating, stressful, or that tasks lacked clarity and included ambiguous question wording or material.

8.4.2 Approaches to completing the booklet

Respondents in the three countries adopted a variety of approaches to completing the booklet. In France, those who were least involved in the task tended to do it as quickly as possible, even if this meant making errors; while those who saw it as a challenge read the questions first then searched the text for the answers, concentrated on writing with care, and erased mistakes. Those who were strongly reminded of school tests tended to start quickly in a panic then slow down and start reading and re-reading more carefully. This group also tried to answer easy questions first. Respondents who felt they understood the aims and purposes of the survey and took the booklet very seriously tried to work out the most efficient way of proceeding quickly. This usually involved reading the questions followed by selective reading of the text to answer them. This group tended to answer questions in the order they appeared in the booklet.

In Britain, respondents could be grouped into two broad categories. One group thought the objective was to finish the booklet quickly, answering as many questions as possible at the expense of accuracy. This group did not check their answers and tended to make 'educated guesses' rather than spending time working out the exact answer. The other group thought it was more important to answer accurately at the expense of not completing the booklet. The approach of this latter group was to work slowly and methodically, taking time to check their answers.

In Sweden most respondents started from the beginning, and worked their way through the end of the booklet. Some started by reading the texts and then answered the questions; others read the questions before reading the text. Some respondents did the booklet as quickly as possible and found it 'a bit stressful'. Others said they hurried, and would have gone back if they had the time. Nobody wanted to stop before they were asked to, although some did skip a few questions, with the intention of going back to them.

8.4.3 Different types of question

Most French respondents reported feeling more comfortable with items familiar to them through their home or working life (which may relate to their expectation of the survey being about 'daily life'), such as the items about choosing a car seat for children, refrigerators, swimming pool opening times, recipes, the weather and employment. Unfamiliar items, such as those on disposable nappies, were seen as difficult and lacking relevance for those who do not have daily experience of these things; similarly the questions on applying for a job were perceived as unfamiliar to those who are not in this situation. A few, however, saw the more unfamiliar items as a challenge and as an opportunity to learn something new. The bus timetable was thought to be old-fashioned and difficult to consult. The questions on frozen embryos made some respondents uncomfortable.

In Britain, some respondents indicated a preference for questions that had a clear right or wrong answer. A number, including those who did well (using a simple measure of the number of correct answers), disliked long texts and wordy sentences or complained about the presentation of some of the charts, with the item on clock radios being the most disliked. Several respondents commented that some questions were ambiguous and open to interpretation, with no right or wrong answer, and that it was irritating having to locate answers in continuous prose, especially for the item on frozen embryos.

In Sweden, quite a few respondents were surprised to find calculation tasks. Most thought some tasks resembled everyday or working life; they could see the relevance of being able to fill in forms, read advertisements, warranties, instructions for choosing a car seat for children, or a weather map. Some felt positive towards easy tasks, or towards topics which they had a personal interest in, such as the item on flowers. Very few found questions which were not relevant to Sweden.

8.4.4 Ease or difficulty of questions

Many respondents in all three countries did not like and/or found items requiring calculations difficult. In France, these items reminded people of difficulties they had experienced at school, whereas in Britain items requiring percentages to be estimated were avoided by those who 'knew' they could not do them without a calculator. Some Swedish respondents would have liked to have been told about the quantitative items before they started work on the booklet.

A few highly educated French respondents thought the booklet did not go beyond an easy school evaluation, whereas those who were already ill-at-ease about tackling the booklet found it daunting when it began with difficult tasks such as those on choosing a car seat for children, or disposable nappies. In Britain, those with the highest scores (total number of right answers) were most likely to find it easy, while respondents who said they found it difficult (although they did not always do badly) said they could not always understand the questions or were confused by the material, for example, for the item on clock radios. Among those who found the booklet neither easy nor difficult, a few initially felt panicked, but relaxed once they started work. No particular type of question was found to be easy or difficult in Sweden, although it was recognised that some questions required more work than others to answer.

8.4.5 Use of prior knowledge

Although all the information required to answer the questions was contained in the test booklets, some British respondents drew on prior knowledge to speed up their search of the material or to double check their answers. Some disagreed with the information given in some texts, based on their own knowledge and experience of the topic, but could see this was not important as it was their skill in using the texts that was being tested. Others used their own knowledge to answer the questions rather than the information provided in the test wishing to demonstrate what they knew, for example in deciding the quantity of eggs to use for 6 people in a recipe for scrambled eggs. This was sometimes at odds with the answer provided in the text and resulted in respondents answering the question incorrectly. The question was 'How many eggs *should* you use' (with the implied understanding of 'according to the recipe' whereas some respondents chose to answer about how many eggs *they would use* if they were making the recipe for 6 people. The interaction of the need for prior knowledge and the possibility of trick questions is demonstrated on the question on distances between towns on a mileage chart for Mexico. The town names were unfamiliar to respondents such as Tecoman, Manzanillo and Zamora. The instruction to respondents was "to use the table.. showing distances between cities in Mexico….." Some respondents wondered whether these cities were actually cities in Mexico of whether they were in some other country. The suspected that since they didn't know if they were in Mexico that this might be a trick question. Respondents felt at a disadvantage if they lacked knowledge of the topics.

In summary, there was a widespread perception in all three countries that the booklet was a test, which coloured respondents' expectations and how they approached it. For those with bad memories of school, it created some anxieties. Although most people recognised that it was a survey, many also felt that they personally were being judged and that their knowledge was being tested. The distinction between whether the respondent felt their skill (of handling printed material) or their knowledge was being tested is important. Familiarity, context and relevance were all seen as aiding comprehension and the likelihood of getting an item right, although what is familiar and relevant varied for different countries and for different groups of people within each country.

Respondents in all countries felt that more complex questions were more difficult, particularly those which required the extraction of material from a long text or that a judgement be made. Easy questions were not always liked, however, because they made some respondents feel uneasy and some respondents were suspicious thinking they must be missing something and that it couldn't be that simple. Perceptions of booklets or individual items as easy or difficult were shaped by respondents' educational levels or by an assessment of their own abilities (which was sometimes at odds with their actual performance). The ideal appeared to be tasks which stretched people to some extent, but did not require them to struggle too much.

8.5 Motivation

One of the main aims of the qualitative research was to examine levels of personal motivation for literacy tests in the context of an interview in the home. As part of the debriefing, interviewers therefore asked respondents about a number of factors which may have affected their motivation.

8.5.1 Commitment to the task

Almost everyone appeared to be trying hard - or as respondents often put it, 'to the best of my ability'. In Britain there were a number of key indicators that people were trying hard, such as largely unbroken concentration; re-reading questions to clarify them when they got stuck; re-reading the material when the answer was not obvious; checking answers; or seeing difficult questions as a challenge and spending more time on them. Some respondents said, however, that in 'real life' they would usually skim read or give up.

Respondents were asked how they felt when asked to stop working on the booklet after 40 minutes. Although some people in all three countries felt relieved, most were disappointed because they wanted to finish. This included some of those who felt relieved. Almost all wanted to go back to try the answers they had skipped and intended to return to later. For those who felt anxious about the booklet, being stopped made them feel a 'failure' that they had not completed it 'on time'; they thought others would have completed it more quickly.

8.5.2 Time pressures

Those who had taken part in IALS previously had an expectation of how long it would take to complete the booklet and reported feeling less pressure than last time. Some said they deliberately worked more slowly this time. Among new respondents, some were able to make an assessment of the likely time needed for the booklet from the time the interviewer had suggested they set aside for her visit. In France, respondents who understood the purpose of the survey, understood that it took time to complete assessments of this nature. Some Swedish respondents would have liked a clear indication so they could plan their time. Respondents were not always sure whether it was most important to complete the booklet accurately, even if this meant taking a long time, or whether speed was most important, even at the expense of accuracy.

Factors which contributed to a sense of time pressure in Britain included personal pressure to complete the booklet as quickly as possible, or a belief that the interviewer's time was limited. In France, those with unhappy memories of school tests believed that others would complete it more quickly. Those who did feel under some time pressure thought it had a mostly negative effect. In Britain for example, this could be seen in the following ways.

- general rushing, at the beginning or close to the perceived time limit for fear of not finishing;
- hurrying through and quickly finding an answer;
- poor concentration;
- accidentally missing a double page;
- making more guesses;
- deciding to discontinue checking answers;
- reading too fast and having to reread;
- using a strategy that was not their preferred or usual one: e.g. skimming when they preferred to read carefully; and
- giving summary answers to questions when they would have preferred to give fuller answers.

In Sweden, some respondents found the perceived time pressure stressful, and would have liked to go back to check some of their answers.

The effect of speed over accuracy in terms of getting a question right or wrong varies depending on the subtleties of the question. In the question on why impatiens are good plants to have one of the target responses is that they "produce flowers almost all year long". In order to be marked correct the respondent needed to include the word 'almost' so that being economical with the answer and saying 'they produce flower all year' would not have been sufficient to count towards a correct answer. This item was dropped from the analysis as the item was inconsistent across countries.

8.5.3 Incentives

No incentives were used in either IALS or in the qualitative work in Britain and France. In Sweden, respondents were given a gift voucher at both stages as had been done in IALS. Respondents in all three countries were asked what effects they thought incentives would have on performance. It should be noted that this was a hypothetical question in France and Britain, and that it was asked of people who had just participated in the research without an incentive.

The idea of an incentive payment provoked surprise when mentioned in France, as a reward is not usually given for participation in a survey. Respondents did not reject the idea in principle, and expressed a preference for a gift rather than money.

Respondents in Britain felt that a small payment in cash or a gift voucher might have encouraged some people to participate in the survey. One or two said an incentive payment might have improved their performance, they would have felt it was more important and taken longer over some questions. Some respondents who found the booklet tedious thought that a payment might have stopped them skipping or giving up on questions. More important than incentives were a personal sense of pride from answering correctly, and wanting to avoid feeling 'like an idiot'. Respondents also thought it was important to do well for the sake of the survey; doing the booklet properly would make the survey more valid and meaningful and the data would be more accurate.

Quite a few Swedish respondents thought incentives made no difference, although they appreciated the voucher as a token for participation. The amount was of minor importance. No one thought the incentive made them perform better.

8.5.4 The international dimension of IALS

Most French respondents were not impressed by the international aspect of the survey, and were aware of it only through a number of items dealing with 'foreign' subjects such as the text on nappies which was clearly from a Dutch newspaper and which discussed environmental concerns in the Netherlands. Exceptions were those who participated in the study from a sense of civic duty; for this group, the international dimension added weight and seriousness to the survey.

The majority of people in Britain were aware that international comparisons were being made of the survey results. A minority thought it had an effect on their personal performance, with more thinking it might help encourage others to participate if they knew about the international dimension. A few were deterred by the idea of a 'league table', while others wanted to belong to a country which performed well.

Most Swedish respondents were aware that IALS was an international survey, and that comparisons were being made between countries. They thought it would have made no difference if only Sweden had taken part; the survey would still have been important.

8.5.5 Feedback of results

In all countries, people were interested in receiving feedback from the survey. In France, for example, two people remembered having asked the interviewer for feedback on the survey, and being disappointed not to receive any. Respondents wanted to know:

- how they personally had done on the assessment;
- how the survey results from IALS were being used by governments to help plan the education system; and
- how their country compared with others that took part in the survey.

8.5.6 Interviewer effect

One concern was whether the presence of the interviewer affected respondents' attitudes to and performance on the assessment. Caution must be exercised when interpreting these comments, as respondents may not have wished to cause offence to the interviewer by admitting that he or she disturbed them. In all three countries, the majority said they were undisturbed by his or her presence, particularly if they were concentrating hard and/or absorbed in the task. Those who did feel put off by the interviewer, either felt self-conscious when struggling with a question, less relaxed or even intimidated by the interviewer (Britain), felt nervous or preferred to do the test in peace and quiet (Sweden) or were anxious about the booklet and saw the interviewer as a teacher or surveillance figure (France). Some respondents were curious about what the interviewer was doing during the interview, and some did not wish to disturb him or her by, for example, asking for a newspaper when it was required for a question.

In summary, respondents, on the whole, took the survey seriously and were committed to doing well. Time pressures were perceived as having largely negative effects. Perceptions of the importance of the international dimension varied.

8.6 Conclusions

The qualitative research identified the range of experience of respondents which was not uniform. It also provided some clear conclusions for subsequent stages of the retest project and for literacy surveys in general. The overall response to the survey was positive; where its purpose had been clearly explained to them, respondents could see the need to carry out such surveys if literacy levels were to be improved.

The research identified a need to:

- outline the purposes and aims of the survey clearly to respondents,
- explain that the booklet was assessing respondents' skills, not their knowledge,
- explain that the survey aimed to measure literacy at a societal level, not to test respondents at an individual level (although this is difficult for people to understand),
- give respondents an idea of the range of tasks included in the booklet, including pointing out that there are tasks involving calculations,
- give clear guidance on how to tackle the booklet; for example, on whether accuracy is more important than speed, and
- explain to respondents that there is no time pressure, and that they can take as long as they like over the booklet.

There was little evidence that incentives could be used to improve effort. Respondents wanted feedback from the survey; promising in the advance letter that they would get some results from IALS or from previous similar surveys might help to increase participation. Many of the findings from the attitudinal and cognitive work were built into the design of the field test and of the main fieldwork for the retest project. In particular, respondents' comments were used to inform the design of the Best Practice protocols, and the content of the debriefing interview.

9. Results of the field trial

9.1 Introduction

The results of the qualitative research described in chapter 8 indicated that increased information about how to complete the booklet and more feedback such as providing the respondent with summary results could improve motivation and performance. There appeared however, to be little evidence that a financial incentive would also have this effect. As part of the developmental process, a field trial was carried out to test whether increased information and/or an incentive payment was associated with improved performance on the test.

Most of the literature on the effect of incentives is focused on the use of incentives to increase survey response. Some studies have shown that the impact of incentives for increasing response varies across groups, for example, hoseholds from lower socio-economic groups and large families. There is less consensus however on the impact of incentives on the quality of data. The main areas where the data quality may be affected are by respondents changing behaviour (particularly important for expenditure surveys), by eliminating bias although some feel that incentives may simply change the type of bias, and by affecting the quality of responses. There is some evidence that incentives improve the completeness resulting in fewer missing items and improve the accuracy of information provided[1].

In IALS 2 countries had offered incentives to respondents, Sweden and Germany. From a study conducted in the US the effect of incentives in the National Adult Literacy Survey (NALS) showed that incentives increased response rates to the survey particularly among certain groups, for example, those with low educational attainment and ethnic minorities[2]. The effect of the greater participation of these groups in literacy surveys is to increase the precision of the population estimates of literacy levels. As there is a strong relationship between educational attainment and literacy proficiency, low response among these groups could lead to an overestimation of the literacy skills of the population depending on how non-response is catered for.

9.2 Design and Methodology

9.2.1 Sample

In Great Britain, Sweden and France, the sample was drawn from former IALS respondents who had completed enough of the booklet in IALS to have a score calculated rather than imputed and who had agreed to a recall. Those who demonstrated literacy skills at the highest level (Level 5) were excluded, as they had no room for improvement. In Portugal, the sample was drawn from former PALS respondents in the region of Lisboa e Vale do Tejo. Individuals with the lowest literacy level in PALS (Level 0) were excluded as they had not completed any of the test quoting literacy related reasons and therefore there was no item data available for them from 1994.

---

[1] Dodd, Tricia. Incentive payments on social surveys: a summary of recent research in *Survey Methodolgy Bulletin* No. 43 July 1998, 23-27. ONS.
Willimack, D.K. et al. Effects of prepaid non-monetary incentives on response rates and response quality in face to face surveys in *Public Opinion Quarterly*, 59, 78-92. 1995.
Allen, R. Providing incentives to survey respondents. *Perspective from the United States Department of Agriculture – National Agriculture Statistics Service: Paper to the Symposium on respondent Incentives in Federal Surveys,* Cambridge, Mass. October 1-3, 1992.
Groves, R and Couper, M. Nonresponse in Household Interview Surveys. Wiley: New York, 1998.

[2] Berlin, M., Mohadjer, L., Waksberg, J., Kolstad, A., Kirsch, I., Rock, D., and Yamamoto, K. 'An experiment in monetary incentives', *Proceedings of the Section on Survey Research Methods*, American Statistical Association, pp. 393-398. 1992.

To study the effect of giving an incentive and/or increasing information, the sample was assigned to the four groups shown in the following figure. In order to ensure that each group had roughly the same characteristics, they were matched on age, sex, literacy level, educational level and employment status.

Figure 9.1: Formulation of treatment groups

Treatment groups	**Increased information**	**No increased information**
Voucher	Group A	Group B
No voucher	Group C	Group D

In each country the sample was selected to achieve 48 interviews. This resulted in 49 interviews in Britain, 48 in France, 44 in Portugal and 42 in Sweden.

9.2.2 Fieldwork

Fieldwork took place in Britain, Sweden and France in late January/early February 1998 and in Portugal in April 1998. A training meeting for scorers was held in London in February and the booklets from Britain, Sweden and France were scored at the same location to ensure consistency. Because of the different timetable in Portugal, the Portuguese booklets were scored separately.

Respondents were asked to complete a shortened version of the background questionnaire and the same test booklet as in the original IALS survey. Respondents were given the same booklet to control for the different compositions of the booklets in terms of item difficulty and context. The qualitative research found that although people were told to take as long as they liked, they still felt under time pressure when completing the booklet. To ensure that they felt less time pressure in the field trial, respondents were asked to allow two hours for the interview and were given, as in IALS, an unlimited amount of time to complete the booklet. They were also re-assured that the interviewer was not pressed for time. When respondents had completed the booklet, the interviewer conducted a debriefing interview, which asked the respondent about motivation, effort and attitude to the test. Interviewers also provided some feedback to researchers by written comments and in discussion at a debriefing session.

A further objective of the field trial was to test the feasibility of going back to respondents and asking them to redo the assessment. In all countries there were some problems in tracing those who had moved in the intervening period. Movers created a more scattered sample and so added to the costs. Those who agreed to take part again did so for a variety of reasons – a sense of public duty, for the sake of the interviewer, they felt it was worthwhile research or were pleased to be asked again.

9.3 Additional information

In Great Britain, Sweden and Portugal but not in France, all groups were sent an advance letter. In Britain, respondents in groups receiving extra information (groups A+C) were sent two booklets with their advance letter – the ONS publication 'Adult literacy in Britain - Summary' which summarised the UK findings from the 1996 survey and contained an international table and an OECD summary of IALS which included the UK results. All other respondents in Britain were given a copy of the summary 'Adult Literacy in Britain' at the end of the interview. In Sweden, they received a one page press release summarising the results of the 1994 Swedish study, with their advance letter. In Portugal, respondents received a summary of the results of the 1994 PALS survey. In France, the OECD booklet (French version) summarising the results of IALS was handed to respondents before the interview.

This booklet did not include any results for France as the French IALS data had never been published. When respondents in the extra information groups had finished the background questionnaire they were given some guidelines on what to expect from the test booklet and how best to approach completing it.

9.4 Incentives

In all countries, incentive payments in the form of a voucher were made to respondents in Groups A and B. Those in group A also received extra information (summary results and guidelines) but those in group B only received the voucher. In Britain, respondents were given a £20 voucher. In Sweden, they had a choice between a voucher worth 200 Swedish crowns (around £15) for either flowers or cinema tickets. In France, respondents were given a voucher for 200 French Francs (around £20). In Portugal, respondents received a voucher worth 3,000 Escudos (about £10) for savings certificates. A voucher of the same value as in the other countries was viewed by the researchers in Portugal to be too high given income levels in Portugal. The voucher of 3,000 PTE was deemed to be roughly equivalent in terms of effect to those offered in the other countries. The voucher was given to respondents after the background questionniare, and before they started the booklet and if they were in Group A, before guidelines for completing the booklet were introduced to them. Interviewers made it clear to respondents that the voucher was in recognition of their time spent on the booklet.

9.5 Items correct and attempted

Table A shows that respondents in Britain and France who participated in the field trial, attempted on average more items than respondents in Sweden (39 in Britain, 37 in France and 34 in Sweden). Respondents in France however, had on average fewer items correct than those in Britain but a similar number to those in Sweden (33 in Britain, 28 in Sweden, 27 in France) and more than those in Portugal (18). The Portuguese booklet was however shorter than in other countries; with only 33 items compared with an average of 45 items in IALS.

Table 9.1. **Average number of items correct and number correct and attempted – IALS and field trial for respondents who participated in the field trial**

	GB		**Sweden**		**France**		**Portugal**	
	IALS	**Field trial**	**IALS**	**Field trial**	**IALS**	**Field trial**	**PALS**	**Field Trial**
Mean Number of items correct	27	33	25	28	21	27	17	18
S.d.	8	7	11	11	12	10	10	9
Mean number of items attempted	34	39	29	34	29	37	-	-
S.d.	7	3	12	10	12	8	-	-
Base	*49*	*49*	*42*	*42*	*48*	*48*	*44*	*44*

1 In Portugal, if for any non-literacy related reason the interview was not completed, the respondent was excluded from the sample so the Portuguese data refers to the number of items correct as a proportion of the total number of items

In Britain, Sweden and France, respondents who participated in the field trial attempted more items on average than when they took part in IALS. They also had on average, more items correct in the field trial than in IALS (in Sweden the difference was not statistically significant). In Portugal, there was no significant difference in the number of items respondents had correct in the field trial and when they took part in PALS.

Table 9.2 shows that there was no evidence in any country that extra information or a financial incentive improved a respondent's performance as measured by either the number of items which they got correct or the number attempted.

In Portugal, it was also found that there was no evidence of an association between the incentives and performance on the test. There was however an interesting effect of incentives on the decision to participate. Response rates in Portugal were recorded separately for each group and showed that in group A (voucher plus information) a 100% response rate was achieved; group C (information only) 83%; group B (voucher only) 64%; group D (neither voucher nor information) the lowest response rate of 61%. This is in line with other research on the effect of incentives.

Table 9.2 **Average number of items correct and number correct as a proportion of items attempted by treatment group for respondents who participated in the field trial**

	GB, Sweden, France				Portugal			
	Voucher & information	*Voucher only*	*Informati on only*	*IALS style*	*Voucher & information*	*Vouche r only*	*Informati on only*	*IALS style*
								mean
Number of items correct	29	30	29	29	17	18	19	20
S.d.	10	8	11	10	10	9	19	20
Number of items attempted								
S.d.	38	38	37	36	-	-	-	-

9.6 The debrief interview

9.6.1 Financial incentive

In Britain, results from the debriefing interview with respondents and feedback from interviewers suggested that paying a financial incentive might improve response among some groups who would not otherwise participate (lower income, younger people) but did not improve respondent motivation. In Sweden it was found that giving extra information was more successful in increasing motivation than a financial incentive. In France, there was no evidence that either the financial incentive or additional information increased motivation or commitment.

In Portugal, respondents who received vouchers for savings certificates said that this type of incentive had no impact whatsoever on the number of correct answers they gave. Once they had agreed to take part in the survey, they made the greatest possible effort to do as well as they could. They thought that the value of the savings certificates (3,000 PTE) did not adequately compensate them for the time spent on the booklet. Nevertheless when group C, who were only given extra information, were asked the effect that receiving vouchers for savings certificates would have on participation in this type of research, they said that it would be a good way of compensating people for the inconvenience caused and the effort they made. Civic awareness and collaboration with the National Statistics Institute also proved to be important factors for participating in this type of research.

9.6.2 Views on extra information and completing the booklet

Britain

The booklets summarising results had a mixed reception. Some found them interesting, some complained that they were too many statistics in them and some treated them as junk mail. The OECD booklet was not well liked. Interviewers suggested that something simpler and bolder would be more appropriate. For people not in the groups receiving extra information, the booklets which were given to them at the end of the interview were nevertheless appreciated.

There was no indication that the guidelines had any effect for example on the use of prior knowledge or the perception of trick questions. Some respondents complained that there was too much to read in the guidelines.

Most respondents said that they tried their best when completing the booklet. They thought it was very important to finish the booklet and to answer correctly. They were motivated by personal satisfaction and a desire to make the survey accurate. Most were aware of the international aspect of the study, which was communicated to them through the advance letter, the summary booklets and the interviewer's introduction. Many said that this made it a more important survey. Interviewers felt that respondents were more relaxed and felt less time pressure than in IALS. They generally finished within 5-10 minutes (either shorter or longer) of their IALS time.

Sweden

In Sweden, respondents had a positive attitude to participating in the survey. They found the assessment booklet easy and interesting. The majority thought it was important to do all the booklet and to be careful and accurate. Although they felt some time pressure, this was not so great as to make them hurry or be careless. Only one respondent thought there were any trick questions in the test.

France

In France, respondents who agreed to participate in the field trial were already fairly committed to the task. Although many felt that the guidelines and summary booklet did not change their level of commitment, they felt they had helped to clarify what the survey was about. Most respondents wanted more explanation of why they were doing the survey again. Presentation of the purpose of follow-up survey was more problematic in France as the summary booklets used did not contain any French results. French respondents were more likely to say that they were uneasy with the test booklet than their counterparts in other countries and were more likely to leave questions unanswered and to think there were trick questions.

Portugal

Respondents in Portugal thought that the information booklet fulfilled its informative function well, particularly regarding literacy levels in Portugal. The found some aspects of the guidelines surprising and unexpected, such as the statement that there were no 'trick' questions in the booklet. This alerted them to something they had not thought about and sensitised them to the possibility that there might have been trick questions and made them apprehensive about the assessment.

10. Methodology of the follow-up survey

10.1 Aims of the follow-up survey

The follow-up survey was the largest single strand in the IALS review. The design of the follow-up survey evolved over the life of the project taking into account initial research into some of the areas of interest. In particular, it took account of the results from the qualitative research reported in Chapter 8 and secondary analysis undertaken by Blum and Guerin on the effect of translation (Chapter 6). The aims and structure of the follow-up survey are outlined in Chapter 1. Four countries took part in the follow-up survey. France, Great Britain, Sweden and Portugal. France, Sweden and Great Britain had taken part in IALS in 1994 and 1996. The follow-up survey involved re-interviewing IALS respondents and asking them to repeat the IALS assessment. A split sample design was used, one part of the sample having the survey implemented in the same way as in IALS and the second part of the sample changing those aspects that were identified as constituting unnecessary variation in survey practice. The IALS or replicate part of the sample would give a measure of the effect of the passage of time or what happens on two separate occasions and the second part of the sample, the Best Practice treatment would measure the impact, if any, of changing the survey protocols.

In Portugal respondents from the 1994 Portuguese Adult Literacy Survey were (PALS) were re-interviewed and asked to repeat the PALS assessment in 1998. The IALS survey was then carried out a new sample in Portugal as a follow-up to the Labour Force Survey (Chapter 13).

This chapter outlines the sample design, response, fieldwork protocols, scoring and data processing procedures used for the follow-up survey.

10.2 Sample design

In Great Britain, Sweden and France the sampling frame for the follow-up survey was the list of respondents who had participated in IALS and had completed enough of the assessment booklet to have a score calculated rather than imputed[1]. In Portugal, the sampling frame consisted of people who had taken part in PALS in 1994 and who had completed a booklet.

The process by which samples were selected varied between countries. In Sweden, the existence of a Population Register meant that it was possible to identify most of the people who had died, emigrated or moved since IALS and to exclude them from the sampling frame before the retest sample was chosen. In the other countries, it was not until interviewers called at an address that it became known that respondents had moved or died. The Swedish Population Register also meant that the current address of most of the people who had moved house since their IALS interview was known. Elsewhere, there was often no forwarding address and it was not always possible to trace people.

As the analysis of the follow-up survey would focus on the two data points for each individual rather than trying to produce population estimates it was not so critical that representative samples be achieved. The follow-up survey was limited in size and even if representative samples could be achieved the small number of cases would be too few to support re-estimation. Given the time difference between the two interviews (4 years in

---

[1] In IALS where a respondent had not completed at least five items on each literacy scale their proficiency values were estimated. Different imputation procedures were used depending on whether the non-completion of the assessment was reported to be for literacy-related reasons such as language problems or for non literacy-related reasons such as not having any more time to spend on the interview. Those who had not done enough of the booklet to have their score calculated were excluded from the retest as there would be insufficient information on their proficiency from the first survey to make interpretation meaningful.

France, Sweden and Portugal) it was always going to be a challenge to trace people from the first survey. Although every effort was made to achieve representative samples it was more important that sufficient cases were achieved. Each country therefore had a target for the number of interviews which were to be achieved in the IALS and Best practice treatment groups (IALS and PALS in Portugal), the rationale for which is outlined in Chapter 1. The target numbers are shown on Figure 10.1.

Figure 10.1 **Target number of interviews for the follow-up survey**

Treatment	GB	Sweden	France	Portugal
IALS – Replicating IALS as carried out in each country	300 IALS respondents doing IALS test	300 IALS respondents doing IALS test	300 IALS respondents doing IALS test	300 PALS respondents doing PALS test
Best Practice: Translation rules/guidelines presentation advance letter	300 IALS respondents doing IALS test	300 IALS respondents doing IALS test	500 IALS respondents doing Swiss French test	1200 (new sample) respondents doing IALS test

Judgements had to be made about expected response rates and levels of attrition to estimate the number of cases to be issued to interviewers to ensure sufficient completed interviews.

10.2.1 Sweden

In Sweden, in addition to the 3% who did not complete very much of the booklet 16% of the 2,858 IALS respondents were excluded from the sampling frame because they had died or emigrated (2%), lived North of Falun in Dalarna (about 300 kilometres north of Stockholm) (9%), had done incomplete interviews in 1994 (3%) or had participated in the qualitative research or in the pilot (3%). The remaining 2,132 respondents were stratified by age (16-35, 36-45 and 46-65) and by literacy level. Using a random start, a systematic sample was chosen within each of these strata to ensure that the retest sample had the same age and literacy profile as 1994 IALS respondents.

10.2.2 Britain

In Britain, the sampling frame for IALS was the Postcode Address File and 3,811 interviews were conducted of which 3,320 provided usable booklets for scaling purposes (87%). For the follow-up survey eligible respondents from IALS in adjacent postal sectors were grouped together to make a sufficient workload for interviewers. The groupings tried to ensure a mixture of rural and urban areas and a geographical spread across England, Wales and Scotland. A few respondents were excluded because they lived in very remote areas. Depending on the size of the grouping, each interviewer was asked to achieve 8 or 15 interviews. Using a random start, the required number of respondents was chosen systematically from the total number of eligible respondents in each area. The other respondents were held in reserve; interviewers were asked to contact them only if they failed to achieve their target number of interviews.

10.2.3 France

In France, 2996 respondents took part in IALS in 1994 and 2,530 (85%) provided sufficiently complete booklets to be used in scaling. As in other countries those who did not complete enough of the booklet to be usable were excluded, as were respondents who were approached to take part in the qualitative research or in the pilot. Unlike Sweden there was no means of identifying those who had moved or died in the 4 years since the first interviews so a large number of people were untraceable. The sample size in France required for the follow-up survey was also larger than in Sweden or Britain so all the eligible addresses were used.

10.2.4 Portugal

In Portugal, the PALS interviews in 1994 were carried out in the mainland only; Madeira and the Azores were excluded. Respondents for the follow-up survey were selected from those who took part in PALS in 1994; those at the lowest level of literacy in 1994 were excluded from the sampling frame.

Because high levels of non-response were anticipated, one or two substitutes with the same characteristics were selected for each sampled individual. In total, 1060 individuals were selected for PALS. Substitution was used when sampled individuals could not be located, when they refused to take part, were unable to respond or did not complete at least one third of the questions in the background questionnaire, the core booklet and the test booklet. Interviewers called at a total of 718 addresses.

A two-stage sampling procedure was used for Portuguese IALS respondents, who were selected from the responding sample of the Portuguese Labour Force Survey (LFS). The LFS in Portugal usually achieves response rates of 91% - 92%. At the first stage, one sixth of the responding sample from the LFS was selected, and stratified according to their highest level of educational attainment. Individuals were randomly selected within each stratum from statistical sections (approximately 300 dwellings; some remote areas with very small populations were excluded). In order to ensure that sufficient items were completed for scaling, the sample was weighted towards more highly educated respondents; 10% of the IALS sample were drawn from the group which had completed primary education, and 45% each from those who had completed first level of secondary education and the second level of secondary education or higher.

Because high levels of non-response were anticipated, one or two substitutes with the same characteristics were selected for each sampled individual. In total, 3020 individuals were selected for IALS. Substitution was used when sampled individuals could not be located, when they refused to take part, were unable to respond or did not complete at least one third of the questions in the background questionnaire, the core booklet and the test booklet. Interviewers called at a total of 2,083 addresses for the IALS interview.

10.3 Response

The aim of the follow-up survey was to achieve sufficient interviews and completed test booklets for analysis and scaling purposes, rather than to achieve a specific response rate. Although the data on response supplied by the participating countries were classified in as similar a way as possible, the different methods of selecting the sample in each country and national differences in defining response, mean some caution must be exercised when comparing countries.

In Britain, of the 1,230 respondents whom interviewers tried to contact, 50% completed the interview and test booklet, 24% could not be contacted, and 26% refused to take part.

In France 50% agreed to take part including partial interviews and a third of those approached refused to take part.

In Sweden, of the 910 sampled respondents whose address was known, 63% completed the interview and test booklet. Fourteen per cent could not be contacted, 23% refused to take part and 1% could not be interviewed because of illness or health problems.

In Portugal a high proportion of 1994 PALS respondents had moved house since the first interview; 45% of sampled individuals could not be located. Among those who were located, 71% completed the interview and test booklet, 11% started but did not complete the interview, and 7% could not be contacted, while 4% refused to take part. In the IALS sample in Portugal 64% of respondents agreed to co-operate, combined with response to the LFS this gives a response rate of 59%.

Table 10.1 **Response to the follow-up survey**

	France		Britain		Sweden		Portugal PALS		IALS	
	n	%	n	%	n	%	n	%	n	%
Number sampled	2194		1557		951		1060		3020	
Cases issued	2097		1236		951		718		2083	
Died, emigrated, moved, no forwarding address	568		6		24		319		128	
Eligible sample	1529	100	1230	100	910	100	399	100	1955	100
Complete interviews	722	47	612	50	569	63	284	71	1203	62
Incomplete interviews	49	3					43	11	35	2
Non-contact	225	15	296	24	129	14	29	7	456	23
Refusal	509	33	322	26	205	23	17	4	261	13
Unable to interview					7	1	-	-		
Other	24	2					26	6		

10.4 Characteristics of the samples

Tables 10.2-10.4 show some of the characteristics of the samples in the different countries for the full IALS sample and for the two parts of the follow-up survey.

Table 10.2 **Characteristics of the IALS and retest samples: France**

Characteristic	IALS 1994	Best Practice 1998	IALS 1998
Sex	*Percentage of respondents*		
Male	45	46	41
Female	55	54	59
Age			
16-24	17	11	10
25-34	26	16	19
35-44	24	27	30
45-54	15	22	20
55 and over	18	23	22
Economic activity			
Working	56	61	59
Unemployed	10	7	6
Economically inactive	33	32	35
Educational level			
Second level, first or lower	29	21	21
Second level, 2nd stage	43	44	44
Third level	29	35	35
Base	2996	422	300

Table 10.3 **Characteristics of the IALS and retest samples: Sweden**

Characteristic	IALS 1994	Best Practice 1998	IALS 1998
Sex	*Percentage of respondents*		
Male	49	43	49
Female	51	57	51
Age			
16-24	20	11	7
25-34	21	22	19
35-44	21	19	26
45-54	22	23	26
55 and over	16	26	22
Economic activity			
Working	68	71	80
Unemployed	6	7	6
Economically inactive	26	22	14
Educational level*			
Second level, first or lower	27	42	46
Second level, 2nd stage	43	27	26
Third level	24	31	28
Base	2645	333	233

* 4% of cases were not definable by level

There was no significant difference in the sex breakdown of the the Best Practice and IALS samples. It should be remembered that the time lapse between the original and the retest interview means that there is a shift in age. The elapsed time between interviews differed between countries, four years in France and Sweden and two years in Britain. In Britain and in France, a lower proportion of the retest than of the original IALS sample was qualified to Lower Secondary Level; 21% in France and 36% and 37% in Britain, compared with 29% and 56% respectively in IALS. This is to be expected as those who did not complete enough of the IALS booklet at the first interview were not eligible for the follow-up survey and these were predominantly those with lower levels of education (see Chapter 11).

A different pattern was evident in Sweden, with a higher proportion of the retest sample than of the 1994 sample being classified to both the lowest and highest of the three categories. Respondents qualified at the second level, second stage were under-represented in 1998, compared with 1994.

Table 10.4 **Characteristics of the IALS and retest samples: Britain**

Characteristic	**IALS 1996**	**Best Practice 1998**	**IALS 1998**
	Percentage of respondents		
Sex			
Male	45	44	47
Female	55	56	53
Age			
16-24	12	7	7
25-34	25	18	21
35-44	23	30	25
45-54	20	23	24
55 and over	20	21	23
Economic activity			
Working	69	76	72
Unemployed	7	2	6
Economically inactive	24	22	22
Educational level			
Second level, first or lower	56	37	36
Second level, 2nd stage	19	23	29
Third level	25	40	35
Base	3811	307	305

Table 10.5 **Characteristics of the IALS and PALS samples: Portugal**

Characteristic	**PALS 1994**	**PALS 1998**	**IALS 1998**
	Percentage of respondents		
Sex			
Male	49	48	48
Female	51	52	52
Age			
16-24	19	12	34
25-34	20	18	20
35-44	21	20	18
45-54	18	22	17
55 and over	22	28	11
Economic activity			
Working	60	66	62
Unemployed	8	5	8
Economically inactive	32	29	29
Educational level			
Second level, first or lower	75	78	58
Second level, 2nd stage	13	12	23
Third level	12	10	19
Base	2449	265	1238

Tables 10.5 compares key characteristics of the sample achieved in the follow-up survey in Portugal with the PALS 1994 survey. Differences in the education and age distributions for PALS and the follow-up sample in Portugal reflect the fact that those who did not complete any of the booklet in the original PALS survey were excluded from the follow-up. These were predominantly at the lower education levels.

10.5 Fieldwork procedures

Prior to the start of fieldwork, interviewers in all countries were required to attend a face-to-face training session. Advance letters were sent to respondents reminding them of their participation in IALS and asking them whether they would be willing to take part in the follow-up study. Interviewers followed this letter by telephoning to make an appointment where possible. Fieldwork took place in summer 1998. In France and Portugal, where the sample size was increased over the original design, it was necessary to extend the original fieldwork period to maximise the number of cases available for analysis.

Respondents were asked a shortened version of the IALS background questionnaire. In Britain and in Portugal, this part of the interview was carried out using computer-assisted personal interviewing (CAPI); in France and Sweden; paper and pencil questionnaires were used.

In France, Britain and Sweden, respondents were given an assessment booklet which had one Block in common with the booklet which they completed for IALS; thus, for example, respondents who did Booklet 1 for IALS (containing Blocks 1, 2 and 4) were given Booklet 5 (containing Blocks 5, 6 and 1); those who did Booklet 2 for IALS did Booklet 6 for the retest and so on. Apart from in Sweden, respondents were not asked to complete a core booklet, as only those who had successfully completed the core in IALS were eligible for the retest.

As in IALS, Swedish respondents were given a token for a film or for flowers worth 100 SEK (about £7-8). Interviewers were allowed to mention this token when arranging a time for the interview.

While respondents were working on the booklet, interviewers filled in an observation sheet, noting any disturbances or indications that respondents were having difficulties. When the booklet was complete, interviewers carried out a short debriefing interview (reported in Chapter 12). The different stages of the interview are summarised in Figure 10.2.

Figure 10.2 **Fieldwork procedures**

Background questionnaire
(Shorter version of IALS questionnaire, 15 mins)

↓

Core Booklet (Sweden and Portugal only)

↓

Test Booklet
(one Block in common with IALS, unlimited time)

↓

Qualitative debrief interview
(20 minutes)

Plus
Interviewer observation of respondent during assessment
Calls and outcome information for responders and non-responders

10.5.1 Differences between IALS and Best Practice

As outlined in Chapter 1, the sample in the three countries that did an IALS follow-up was split between the two treatments, IALS and Best Practice. The definition of 'Best Practice', however, differed between countries. Because of the concerns which had been raised about the translation of IALS items into French, Best Practice respondents in France were given the Swiss French version of the booklets, which had been used for IALS in Switzerland in 1994. The Swiss French booklets also did not have the name of the French Ministry of Education printed on each page, as the IALS booklets did, which had been identified as a possible negative factor nor did they include any additional materials or questions.

In Britain, France and Sweden, Best Practice the protocols for the introduction and administration of the booklet were changed. Interviewers were issued with guidelines to read to the respondent about how to approach it and what was expected. The procedures for administering the Booklet in IALS were very directive; as respondents finished a page interviewers were supposed to say 'Now turn over to page X'. Anecdotal evidence suggests that interviewers found this rather artificial and often abandoned this 'interview' method of adminsitration part way through the booklet once they were sure the respondent had understood the layout of the booklet. The IALS method of administering the assessment was used in the IALS part of the follow-up survey. For the Best Practice sample an 'invigilation' style adminstration was used, so that once interviewers had explained the key points about completing the booklet respondents were left to work their own way through it.

Best Practice respondents were sent a set of summary results from IALS with their advance letter.

10.5.2 The PALS follow-up survey

The PALS was carried out in 1994 and the main features of PALS are outlined in Chapter 13. PALS used a similar conceptual framework to IALS but was simpler in its implementation. It did not use a spiral design and there was only one main booklet, which was completed by all respondents. Although the PALS included prose, document and quantitative type tasks, these were reported in a single scale, rather than as three separate scales, as was the case in IALS. There was no imputation for missing data in the follow-up survey. Some results from PALS were sent out with advance letters for both PALS and IALS samples; interviewers for both samples were also given guidelines on how to administer the booklet.

10.6 Scoring

In order to ensure that the same standards were applied across time and across countries it was very important to try and achieve consistency between scorers and to ensure that the scoring guides were applied in a consistent way. For IALS one or more people from each participating country attended a training session for scorers, then trained a team within their own country. Each country was required to double score (blind) a proportion of booklets to ensure consistency between scorers. In addition to consistency within national teams it was important to establish that the scoring was consistent across countries. In order to do this, where language permitted, booklets from one country were sent to another for blind scoring. Where there was no other country with the same language, a second team was established in that country and trained separately.

The national project managers for the follow-up survey in Britain, France and Sweden attended a training session in March 1998 for countries participating in the Second International Adult Literacy Survey (SIALS). Each national project manager then trained a team of scorers in their own country; the Portuguese team leader participating in the UK scoring training. Core booklets in IALS are scored by interviewers during the interview to determine whether the respondent is given the main Booklet; Portuguese and Swedish interviewers, as is the practice in IALS, therefore scored them during the interview. A centralised office-based team in all four countries scored the main booklets.

10.6.1 Scoring complexity

The booklets completed by respondents were scored, using a scoring guide, and keyed. The scoring and keying was done in all countries in a single operation using a shared Computer Assisted Data Input (CADI) system. The scoring of most of the test assessment items was straightforward. Of the 114 items about two thirds are closed questions where it is clear that the answer is either correct or incorrect. For example some of the questions ask the respondent to underline a sentence in the stimulus material. Given rules about what constitutes a sentence and the allowable overspill at either end it is clear whether the respondent has marked the correct part of the text or not. Similarly, the answer to 'what can be done to remedy moisture on the outside of a refrigerator?' is ''Move the energy switch to the right', which is easy to score. These types of questions are subject to very little ambiguity and a high degree of consistency can be achieved.

Other questions are not so easy to mark. These are usually questions where the respondent has to write out a longer answer such as listing three reasons for using disposable nappies, or two examples of what one should do to prevent fire. In scoring these questions the scorer has to make a judgement about whether the respondent's answer is sufficient to qualify as correct. The potential for introducing errors and inconsistencies in scoring and the interaction of scoring and proficiency estimates is discussed in Chapter 11.

10.6.2 Quality control procedures

Any answers which were difficult to score were flagged, and discussed at regular meetings of the scoring teams; those which could not be resolved were e-mailed for review to the IALS co-ordinators and the resulting adjudications were circulated to all four countries. Items requiring judgements to be made by respondents and scorers, such as the examples given above, were more likely than others to be 'flagged' as difficult to score and formed the bulk of the queries sent for adjudication. Thus, for example, the items on disposable nappies (B1Q4-6), frozen embryos (B2Q7), job interviews (B3Q7-9), one and five-year warranties for refrigerators (B4Q7), choosing car seats for children (B5Q3-6) regularly featured in team discussions ain the items sent for arbitration.

In line with the standard quality checking procedures required for IALS a proportion of booklets were double marked. Discrepancies were investigated and, where necessary, booklets were rescored for the relevant items.

10.7 Data processing

As noted earlier, respondents to the retest were asked a shortened version of the IALS background questionnaire. Data files were formatted to the SIALS record layout. In order to comply with the SIALS formats information from the original IALS background questionnaire was carried forward with the new interview data after fieldwork was completed. This caused the flow of the questionnaire to be inconsistent for some cases required some extra editing to ensure that the data went through the flow and continuity checks. In order to ensure continuity in statistical procedures Educational Testing Service (ETS), who scaled and analysed the IALS data, undertook the scaling of the follow-up survey and scaled the IALS data for Portugal.

Table 10.6 **Mean time spent on task booklet in minutes and percentiles 1998 by treatment group and country**

	GB		Sweden		France		Portugal
	BP	**IALS**	**BP**	**IALS**	**BP**	**IALS**	
				minutes			
Mean time (m)	56	55	61	59	59	61	85
5th percentile	33	31	30	29	31	33	40
25th percentile	44	43	51	45	45	46	61
75th percentile	65	67	70	70	70	75	100
95th percentile	88	89	95	88	98	95	150
Correlation time with:			*Correlation co-efficient*				
Prose	-.077	-.078	-.085	-.073	.145	.028	.018
Percent correct	-.015	.034	.117	.203	.163	.095	.044
Base	*128*	*131*	*133*	*109*	*190*	*119*	*492*

10.8 Time spent on the booklet

Respondents were told they could take as much time as they needed to complete the booklet however from the qualitative research (chapter 8) we know that many respondents calculate an expected time from the information provided by the interviewers on how long the whole process might take. On average respondents spent about an hour on the booklet, except in Portugal, where the average time taken was 85 minutes. There was no difference in average time taken between IALS and Best Practice samples in 1998. Table 10.6 also shows the spread of test time duration in the follow-up survey which was similar between Best Practice and the IALS style sample. There was little association between the time spent on the booklet and the outcome in terms of literacy score with correlation co-efficients around 0.1 for most.

The IALS Technical Report discusses the possibility that the time taken to do the booklet might be an indicator of motivation. It argued that the evidence did not support this hypothesis, rather that the length of time taken to do the booklet was likely to be associated with ability. Those countries with the lowest overall scores also recorded the longest average test times[2]. This view would appear to be confirmed by the relatively low literacy skills in Portugal and the fact that they took on average longer than other countries. Although the Technical report shows that the French had the longest time in 1994, it does not indicate whether any adjustment was made for the presence of the additional Block[3]. Table 10.7 shows the mean average time spent on the booklet in 1994 for Britain and France. In the 1994 IALS Sweden did not record the time taken to complete the booklet. The French appear to have taken longer in 1994 than in 1998, but this is because the 1994 French booklet contained four, rather than three Blocks. There was only weak association between literacy (whether scaled score or percent correct is used) and the time spent on the assessment.

Table 10.7 **Booklets used for scaling: Mean time spent on task booklet 1994/6 in minutes and percentiles by treatment group (1998) and country**

	GB			**France***		
	All	**BP**	**IALS**	**All**	**BP**	**IALS**
			minutes			
Mean time (m)	54	55	59	75	79	77
5th percentile	24	30	30	29	41	39
25th percentile	43	43	45	59	61	60
Median	54	51	56	75	77	75
75th percentile	65	63	70	92	92	94
95th percentile	90	95	92	125	112	123
Correlation time with			*Correlation co-efficient*			
Prose	.132	.120	.132	.97	.066	.215
Document	.146	.141	.142	.101	.074	.237
Quantitative	.151	.164	.158	.107	.089	.257
Percent correct	.216	.180	.225	.205	.242	.344
Base	*3340*	*307*	*305*	*2250*	*422*	*300*

* The french booklet included additional questions in IALS

2 Jones S. 'Incentives and the motivation to perform well' in *Adult Literacy in OECD countries: technical report on the first International Adult Literacy Survey*. Washington: National Centre for Education Statistics 1998.

3 In IALS, countries had the option of including additional test items in the booklet as long as they were placed at the end. It is difficult to estimate how much this would increase the average time taken to complete the booklet. The additional Block included in France had 16 questions based on 6 texts.

11. Literacy measures at two points in time

11.1 Introduction

This chapter describes the findings of the follow-up survey of IALS respondents and looks at the effect of introducing 'Best Practice' on the performance of respondents on the assessment. The follow-up survey or retest was conducted in Great Britain, France and Sweden. Previous chapters of this report have set out the developmental process and the decisions on the final design and a fuller description of the methodology of the research is given elsewhere in this report (Chapter 10). By way of providing context for the results from the follow-up survey the distribution of literacy in the three countries as found in IALS and the amount of data that was usable from the interviews in the different countries are described.

In 1998, 612 respondents to IALS in Great Britain, 566 in Sweden and 722 in France were re-interviewed[1]. These respondents had previously been interviewed in 1994 in France and Sweden and in 1996 in Great Britain. Prior to the 1998 survey, qualitative work was undertaken to find out what influenced respondents to take the study seriously and how they approached it. As a result, the follow-up survey was divided into two halves, assigned randomly. One half (the IALS style or 'replicate' sample) had the survey administered in the same way as in 1994/6. The design of the other half (the 'Best Practice' sample) was formed on the results of the qualitative work reported elsewhere in this report (Chapter 8), on the review of the survey practice (Chapter 2) and on concerns about how the translation of the IALS assessment used in France might have impacted on the difficulty of some of the questions (Chapter 6). To control for this, respondents in the French Best Practice sample in 1998 did the version/translation of the IALS assessment used in the French speaking part of Switzerland[2].

The follow-up survey was essentially testing two main hypotheses. The first hypothesis being tested was that improved performance on the literacy assessment could be achieved from the respondent by increasing their engagement in the task through a series of measures, defined during the course of the project as 'Best Practice'. In each country the survey was carried out by the same fieldwork organisation as had done IALS and there was also some continuity of staff in each country in the research teams involved. The control group (IALS style sample or replicate sample) had the survey administered in the exact same way (or as close to as possible) in the retest as in the original IALS. This group serve as the base measure for what happens to the performance of individuals in the intervening time or how individuals might performance on an assessment at any given two points in time. Our expectation would be that there would be some skill gain or skill attrition in the intervening period. Skill gain could be due to improvement simply because they had done a similar test before, because they simply performed better on a different day, because they were trying harder or because their skill had improved in the interveing period. In addition to that skill acquisition or attrition there would be a performance dividend from following best practice. This would result in a higher average increase in score for those in the treatment group (best practice) than for those in the control group.

The second hypothesis was that there were differences in engagement in the tasks between different regions of Europe, particularly between the North and the South or Mediterranean

[1] Portugal was not included in the IALS retest as IALS had not been carried out there before this project. A retest of Portugal's own literacy survey (PALS) was carried out and a Portuguese IALS; these are reported in Chapter 13.

[2] In considering how to best correct for the translation issue two main options were considered – use another French language version of the assessment (either the version used in Switzerland or the version used in Canada) or attempt to adapt the French version of the assessment as used in France to make the problems identified more consistant with the other versions. This would have meant that an untried version of the assessment was being used in the French Best Practice sample. On balance it was decided best to use a version of the assessment that had already been used elsewhere and for which the results were available for a population. The Swiss version of the assessment was deemed to be more suitable for use in France.

countries. If this were true then we might expect to see the patterns of results in Sweden and Britain being similar with those in France and Portugal sharing similarities also but different from the pattern in the two Northern countries.

There are several ways of analysing the results of the retest data; comparing the original and the retest data at the level of items, at individual level and at population level. All these views of the data add more to our knowledge and understanding about how tests perform in practice. Because it is important to understand how the individual questions build up to the summary statistics this chapter follows that pattern. It starts with analysis first from the perspective of how individuals respond to the different questions in the assessment (sections 11.6) and then moves on to looks at two different summaries of the assessment data (section 11.8), a crude and simple summary measure, the proportion of items in the booklet answered correctly and the standard IALS measure produced from statistical models (IRT or 'scaling', see Chapters 3 & 4 for a discussion of IRT). The formulation and review of the hypotheses being tested are discussed in section 11.9.

Performance on items (answering them correctly) is however inextricably linked with scoring issues. The extent to which an item behaves reliably and consistently, by individuals over time and across countries may be as much a factor of the stability and consistency (or lack of it) in the application of the scoring criteria as it is of the item or the individual's proficiency or ability. As a result the analysis at item level in the first part of this chapter includes a review of scoring issues in IALS as encountered in the retest project (section 11.5).

Figure 11.1 **Prose literacy level by country**

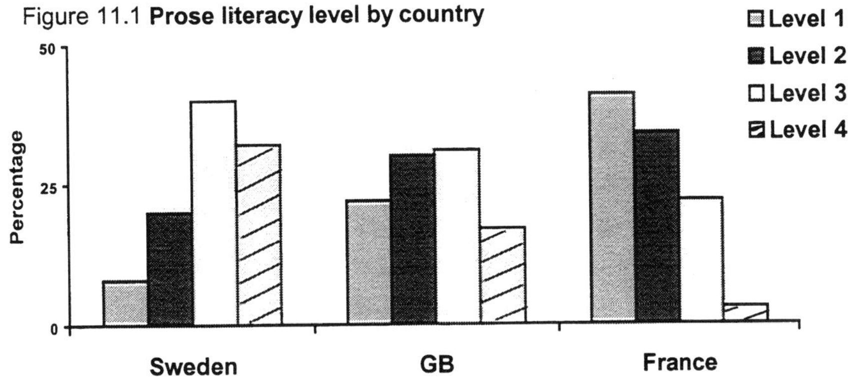

11.2 Adult literacy in France, Sweden and Britain

The distribution of prose, document and quantitative literacy skills differ between countries. Some countries had very skewed distributions across the different skill levels with the majority of the population at either the lower or upper end of the distribution. Other countries had more centrally distributed skill levels with only small proportions performing at the upper or lower levels and the majority of the population performing in the middle skill levels. Some countries had a more uniform distribution with relatively equal proportions at each level. The countries that took part in the retest all had different literacy profiles. According to IALS only 8% of the population aged 16-65 in Sweden are at the lowest literacy level, Level 1, on the prose scale compared with 22% of the same population in Great Britain and 41% in France. In both Britain and Sweden there was little difference between the 3 literacy scales in the proportion of the population estimated to be at the lowest literacy level. In France however a higher proportion were at Level 1 on the Prose scale than at the same level on the Document scale or on the Quantitative scale . In France, 41% of the population were estimated at Level 1 on Prose literacy compared with an estimate of 36% at this level on the Document scale and 33% on the quantitative scale. This is similar to differences found in other countries with a large proportion at the lower end of the distribution.

Table 11.1 **Literacy level by country**

	Level 1		Level 2		Level 3		Level 4/5		Total	Mean	Base
France	%	*s.e.*	%	*s.e.*	%	*s.e.*	%	*s.e.*	%		
Prose literacy	41	*0.8*	34	*0.8*	22	*0.8*	3	*0.2*	**100**	*233*	*2996*
Document literacy	36	*0.8*	32	*1.0*	26	*0.6*	6	*0.4*	**100**	*239*	*2996*
Quantitative literacy	33	*1.0*	30	*0.9*	28	*0.7*	9	*0.5*	**100**	*245*	*2996*
Great Britain											
Prose literacy	22	*1.0*	30	*1.3*	31	*1.2*	17	*0.8*	**100**	*267*	*3811*
Document literacy	23	*1.0*	27	*1.0*	31	*1.0*	19	*1.0*	**100**	*268*	*3811*
Quantitative literacy	23	*0.9*	28	*1.0*	30	*0.9*	19	*1.0*	**100**	*267*	*3811*
Sweden											
Prose literacy	8	*0.5*	20	*0.6*	40	*0.9*	32	*0.5*	**100**	*301*	*2645*
Document literacy	6	*0.4*	19	*0.7*	39	*0.8*	36	*0.6*	**100**	*306*	*2645*
Quantitative literacy	7	*0.4*	19	*0.6*	39	*0.9*	36	*0.7*	**100**	*306*	*2645*

In all three countries the three domains were highly correlated with the correlation in Britain and France being very similar and with slightly weaker correlations in Sweden.

Table 11.2 **Correlations of three domains in each country**

	France			Sweden			GreatBritain		
	Prose	**Doc**	**Quant**	**Prose**	**Doc**	**Quant**	**Prose**	**Doc**	**Quant**
Prose	1			1			1		
Doc	.950	1		.872	1		.946	1	
Quant	.928	.964	1	.813	.952	1	.912	.960	1

That there should be such a difference between these countries in the proportion of the population at Level 1 seemed implausible. One explanation offered is that the literacy distribution is merely a reflection of the different structure or composition of the populations in the different countries in terms of the characteristics that are know to be correlated with literacy such as age and education. Table 11.3 shows the age of the population in the three countries around the time of IALS, which have similar distributions. Of the poulation aged 15-64 about a fifth in each country are in the youngest age-group, 15-24. When holding age constant, and looking at education within age-group the countries are again relatively similar in the proportion of each age-group who have attained at least upper secondary education. Figure 11.2 shows that among those in the youngest age group (25-34) in each country a similar proportion had attained at least upper secondary education, 84% in France, 85% in Sweden and 86% in Britain. There were differences between countries among the two oldest age groups in the proportion who had reached this level of education. In France only 41% of those in the oldest age-group, 55-64 had attained this level of education compared with 52% of the same age-group in Sweden and 58% in Britain. Among those aged 45-54 Sweden and Britain had similar proportions educated to this level (69%) compared with 60% of the same age group in France.

Table 11.3 **Population aged 15-64: Age-group by country (1995)**

	France	Sweden	GB
Age		%	
15-24	20	19	21
25-34	22	25	23
35-44	21	21	23
45-54	22	20	18
55 –64	15	15	15
Total	**100**	**100**	**100**

Figure 11.2 **Percentage who had attained at least upper secondary education by age-group and country**

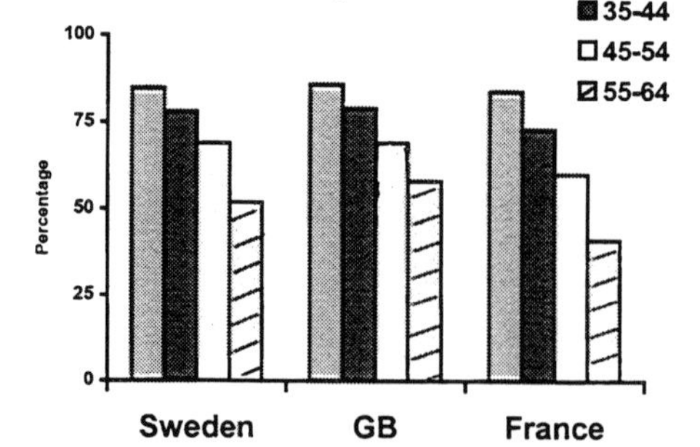

The findings in IALS also do not fit with earlier studies on student attainement. For example in a 1960 study of reading comprehension among school children aged 13/14 the 12 participating countries were placed in the following order: Yugoslavia, Scotland, Finland, England and Wales, the US, Switzerland, West Germany, Sweden, France, Israel, Belgium and Poland. This cohort would be aged 37/38 at the time of IALS in 1994. In simlar studies in 1971 the rank position of England and Sweden was not consistent across the age groups tested (9,13/14 and 15/16)[3].

11.2.1 Literacy skills and age

Among the youngest age group (16-25) in both Britain and France the proportion estimated to be at Level 1 and Level 2 combined on the document scale are relatively similar. Just over half of those aged 16-25 in France (52%) were at Level 2 or lower as were 45% of the same age-group in Britain while only one fifth of those in Sweden were at this level (20%). Otherwise the relative performance of the three countries is the same in each age-group with France always having larger proportions of the population estimated to be at Level 1 or Level 2.

Figure 11.3 **Percentage of each age-group performing at literacy Levels 1 and 2 on the document scale**

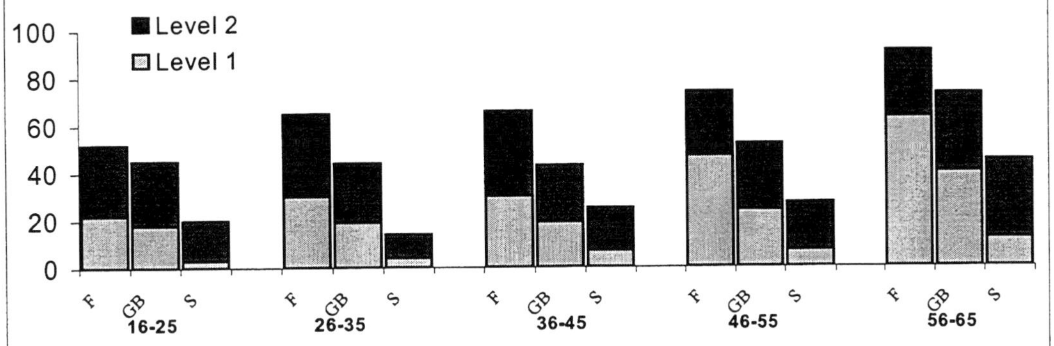

11.2.2 Literacy skills and education

In all countries those with more education tended to perform at higher literacy levels on all three scales. The relationships however are different across countries. In addition to there being differences between countries in the educational attainment of the population there are also differences between countries in the estimated literacy proficieny as measured in IALS at any given level of education. Figure 11.4 shows the proportions at each literacy level on the prose scale for each level of educational attainment in a selection of countries in addition to the three in the follow-up survey. In most countries the majority of those at the lowest educational level, primary education or lower are at Level 1. At the next level of education in both France and Poland the majority are estimated at Level 1 while those with the same level of education in Britain, French speaking Switzerland and Germany are mostly at literacy Level 2. The same is true at each level of education where the proportion in France and Poland estimated to be at the lower literacy levels is always substantially higher than in the other countries.

[3] Foshay, A.W., Thorndike, R.L., Hotyat, F., Pidgeon, D.A. and Walker, D.A. (1962). *Educational Achievements of Thirteen-year-olds in Twelve Countries.* Hamburg: UNESCO Institute for Education.
Thorndike, R.L. (1973). *Reading Comprehension Education in Fifteen Countries.* Stockholm: Almqvist and Wiksell.

Figure 11.4 **Prose literacy level by highest level of educational attainment and country**

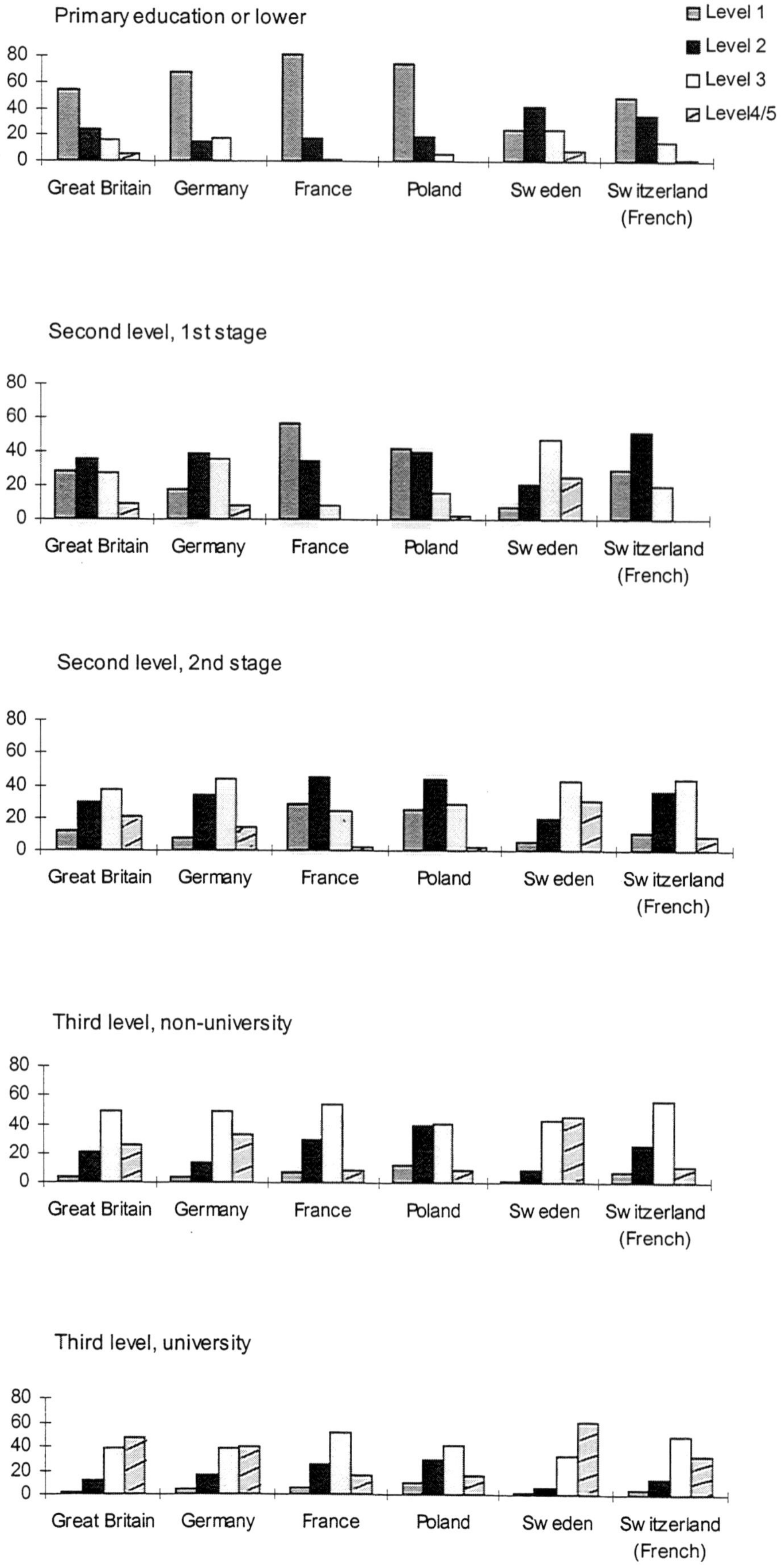

Although there is an incremental shift in literacy level for each education level in France even at the highest education level the proportion of the population estimated to be at the two highest levels combined (Level 4/5) on the quantitative literacy scale is still substantially lower than in either Sweden or Britain. In France a third of those with University education are estimated to be at Level 4/5 on the quantitative scale compared with over half of those in Britain and almost two thirds of Swedes with the same level of education (Table 11.4).

Table 11.4 **Quantitative literacy level by highest level of educational attainment level (ISCED) and country**

		Level 1		Level 2		Level 3		Level 4/5		Total
Quantitative literacy		%	*s.e.*	%	*s.e.*	%	*s.e.*	%	*s.e.*	%
France	Primary education or lower	72	*2.1*	22	*2.3*	6	*1.0*	0	*0.2*	**100**
	Second level, 1st stage	48	*3.7*	33	*3.7*	17	*2.7*	2	*0.6*	**100**
	Second level, 2nd stage	19	*1.3*	36	*1.3*	36	*1.3*	8	*1.2*	**100**
	Third level, non-university	4	*0.9*	24	*1.4*	47	*3.1*	24	*2.2*	**100**
	Third level, university	5	*0.8*	18	*1.5*	44	*1.6*	32	*1.9*	**100**
Great Britain	Primary education or lower	50	*3.8*	33	*3.9*	14	*2.8*	3	*2.0*	**100**
	Second level, 1st stage	30	*1.2*	32	*1.5*	29	*1.4*	9	*0.8*	**100**
	Second level, 2nd stage	13	*1.6*	27	*2.3*	36	*2.0*	24	*2.4*	**100**
	Third level, non-university	7	*1.6*	22	*2.4*	41	*2.7*	29	*2.9*	**100**
	Third level, university	3	*0.8*	12	*1.4*	29	*2.6*	56	*2.7*	**100**
Sweden	Primary education or lower	22	*2.1*	32	*1.6*	35	*2.2*	11	*1.5*	**100**
	Second level, 1st stage	7	*1.2*	21	*2.7*	41	*2.4*	31	*2.2*	**100**
	Second level, 2nd stage	5	*0.6*	18	*0.6*	42	*1.1*	35	*1.2*	**100**
	Third level, non-university	1	*0.4*	15	*2.2*	39	*2.7*	46	*2.8*	**100**
	Third level, university	1	*0.7*	6	*2.2*	29	*2.2*	64	*3.4*	**100**

s.e. = Standard error of the estimate. The reported sample estimate can be said to be within 2 standard errors of the true population value with 95% confidence

11.3 IALS in France, Sweden and Britain

The IALS survey was carried out in France and Sweden in 1994 and in Great Britain in 1996. The response rates in each country were 55%, 60% and 68% respectively. Table 11.5 shows the distribution of the total sample in each country by age and education both before and after weights were applied. There are a couple of things that are notable about the samples. First is the high proportion of the sample in Sweden for whom it was not possible to classify education compared with the other two countries. For only 1% of cases in France and for no cases in Britain was it not possible to assign an education code. In both France and Britain the youngest age group were under represented in the sample. In France those with lower education were underrepresented while those with higher education were overrepresented. In Sweden the effect of weighting on both of these variables was minimal which would not normally be expected with a response rate of 60%. As the IALS methodology produces estimates at the population level rather than individual level it was a requirement of IALS that countries weight and gross their data to known population estimates. For some countries this is not standard practice on samples as small as the IALS. The characteristics used for weighting varied between country. In Britain, age, sex and educational attainment levels were used for reweighting to known population characteristics in addition to weights to take account of unequal probabilities of selection from choosing only one person per household and for over sampling in Wales and Scotland. In France, weights were based on six characteristics, household size, number of eligible household members, education, community size, age, sex and occupation. In Sweden estimates were referenced to region, education, age and sex.

Table 11.5 **IALS sample characteristics in Britain, France and Sweden**

	France	Sweden	GB	France	Sweden	GB
		Unweighted			Weighted	
Age		%			%	
16-25	19	22	14	22	22	20
26-35	27	21	26	24	21	23
36-45	23	21	22	22	22	22
46-55	15	21	19	15	19	19
56 -65	16	14	18	17	16	16
Total	**100**	**100**	**100**	**100**	**100**	**100**
Education level						
Education not definable by level	1	4	..	2	4	..
Primary education or lower	15	12	5	20	13	6
Second level, 1st stage	14	15	50	18	15	55
Second level, 2nd stage	42	45	19	42	45	20
Third level, non-university	10	13	11	7	13	8
Third level, university	19	11	14	11	11	11
All	**100**	**100**	**100**	**100**	**100**	**100**
Base	*2996*	*2645*	*3811*	*2996*	*2645*	*3811*

In IALS status codes are used for the main elements of the survey, the background questionnaire, the core booklet and the main task booklet. The codes are intended to identify the presence of a booklet and the extent to which the booklet is complete. From Table 11.6 below there would appear to be differences in how the outcome codes were applied. In the 1996 survey the outcome codes for the main assessment booklets were

- Attempted every question (completed)
- Omitted some questions but attempted at least one question on each page (partially completed)
- Failed the core booklet
- Left at least one page blank or refused the booklet altogether (refused).

This final code was problematic since it effectively combined a ‘refusal’ and a ‘partially completed’ booklet. Interviewers, certainly in Britain, had to be convinced that this was a legitimate code to use even when someone had actually completed most of the booklet but had simply left out a page, sometimes by accident. Comparison of the distribution of these codes in the three countries points to some inconsistencies in their application.

Table 11.6 **Status codes for main assessment booklet in 1994/6**

Outcome code	**France**	**Sweden**	**GB**
		%	
Completed booklet	56	95	48
Partially completed	30	0	18
Respondent refused main booklet	7	1	30
Refusal on behalf of respondent	0	-	0
Failed core task booklet	4	1	1
Literacy related reasons	**2**	**0**	**2**
Language difficulties	2	-	1
Reading /writing difficulties	0	-	1
Learning disability	0	-	0
Mental/Emotional condiiton	0	0	0
Mental dvelopment problem	0	0	0
Non literacy related reasons	**0**	**2**	**1**
Hearing impairment	0	-	0
Visual impairment	0	0	0
Physical disability	0	0	0
Other disability	0	0	0
Other unspecified	-	2	0
Total	**100**	**100**	**100**
Base	*2996*	*2645*	*3811*

Using an alternative classification based on the presence or absence of booklet data we still find differences between countries. Figure 11.5 shows the data yield from respondents for the main assessment booklet using two different measures, the proportion of respondents who appear to have attempted the booklet indicated by the presence of some booklet data[4] (ignoring the different scales) and the proportion of interviews that yielded a booklet that was sufficiently complete to be used in the scaling of the data which takes into account the pattern of responses on the different scales. The definition used for including a case for scaling is that the respondent must have attempted at least 5 items on each scale[5]. This includes the recoding of omitted items to incorrect or not reached depending on their position and the pattern of responses around them. Omitted responses in IALS are defined as any missing responses that occur before a valid response. Not reached responses are consecutively missing responses at the end of a block. The IALS technical report shows no significant correlations for any of the literacy scales between the mean proficiency estimate and the mean responses omitted (page 184). Almost all (97%) of the respondents in Sweden completed sufficient amounts of the booklet for the booklet to be used in the scaling process compared with 88% of respondents in Great Britain and 84% of respondents in France. The two measures pick up mostly the same cases so the adjustments for not-reached items do not seem to have a large impact on the interpretation of the data yield.

Figure 11.5 **Percentage of usuable booklets by country**

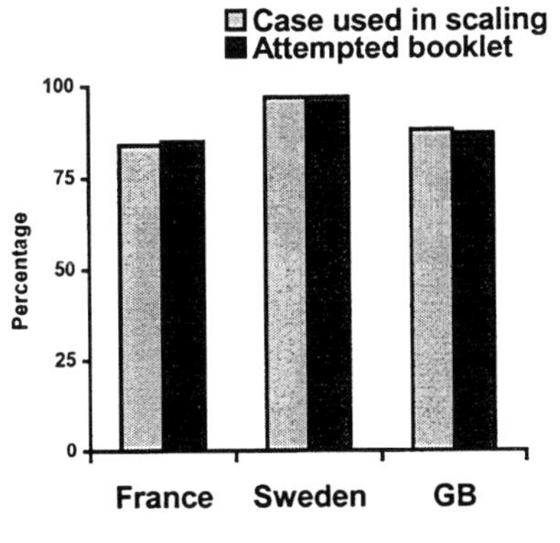

Table 11.7 shows the proportion of those at each literacy level (using the first plausible value for prose literacy) and education level who had attempted at least some of the booklet although not

[4] Cases where the number of omitted items (code 0) equals the number of items in the booklet and cases where the booklet data was set to system missing were defined as not having attempted the booklet. Although the presence of a code 0 on a file should indicate theat the person started the booklet where all the codes are 0 it is possible that this is due to variation in scoring practice between countries. Given that there is no evidence on these booklets that the respondent attempted any items in the booklet it is assumed that the booklet has not been attempted.

[5] IALS Technical report p.77

necessarily enough to be usable for scaling purposes. The pattern of respondents attempting the booklet is quite different in Sweden compared with both Britain and France. In Sweden, even those at the lower levels of educational attainment attempted to complete a booklet. Among those with primary education or lower 90% in Sweden attempted the booklet compared with 68% and 64% of those with the same level of education in Britain and France respectively. In both France and Britain the pattern of respondents being more likely to attempt the booklet with increased education levels is similar. Of those educated to second level, first stage, 83% attempted the booklet in both countries rising to 90% and over among those educated to second level, second stage or higher. If the reason for attempting or not attempting the booklet is literacy related then the pattern in Sweden is consistent with the high levels of literacy reported through IALS. In all countries those estimated to be at the lowest literacy level were less likely than others to have attempted a booklet, 67% of the population at Level 1 prose in Britain, 67% in France and 73% in Sweden. When the presence of assessment data is compared with whether the cases are used for scaling in both Sweden and France the same cases are being identified. In Britain, a small number of cases appear to have no data but were included in the scaling process. This may have been due to the fact that in Britain those items that had been dropped from the scaling in the first round of IALS were not scored as the data would not be used. This may have affected the identification of cases which provided assessment data.

Table 11. 7 **Presence of booklet data in IALS by literacy level, education level and country**

	France	Sweden	GB
Prose		% who attempted booklet	
Level 1	69	73	67
Level 2	93	98	88
Level 3	94	99	94
Level 4	93	100	96
All	**85**	**97**	**87**
N. of attempted booklets	**2556**	**2577**	**3306**
N. of booklets used for scaling	**2530**	**2573**	**3340**
Education level			
Education not definable by level	11	96	..
Primary education or lower	64	90	68
Second level, 1st stage	83	97	83
Second level, 2nd stage	90	99	92
Third level, non-university	94	100	94
Third level, university	93	99	95
All	**85**	**97**	**87**
Base	***2996***	***2645***	***3811***

Since the cases used for scaling purposes and those where there is an indication of the respondent attempting the booklet are virtually the same the second of these measures is used. Table 11.8 shows the mean number of questions answered correctly, omitted, attempted, answered wrongly (including crossed out or struck through) and the mean proportion of questions in the booklet answered correctly. Each respondent in IALS is only asked to answer a subset of the total test so the calculation of a simple percent correct will not reflect the variations in the booklets that the respondents received.

On each of these measures Sweden stands out from the other two countries with higher average proportion of answers correct, fewer skipped items and fewer wrong items. Some booklets from the first IALS were rescored by the 1998 scoring teams and this is discussed later in this chapter in the context of test completeness.

Table 11.8 **Those who attempted booklet: mean number of questions omitted, correct, attempted and wrong, IALS 1994/6**

	France	Sweden	GB
		Mean	
Number correct answers	23.2	32.1	26.7
Number of questions attempted	35.2	37.8	36.6
Number of questions omitted	6.3	3.8	4.9
Proportion correct	55.7	77.3	64.4
Number of answers wrong	12.0	5.6	9.9
N. of attempted booklets	**2556**	**2577**	**3306**

11.4 Extending the scoring rubric

The scoring categories for the follow-up survey were extended from those used in IALS. In IALS only three categories of response were coded for the booklets– code 0 (item not answered, i.e. left blank), code 1 (item answered correctly) and code 7 (any other response including incorrect response). The scoring therefore did not distinguish between a wrong answer where the respondent attempted the question but got it wrong and questions where the respondent crossed out or struck through the question or answer space. Both of these would have received a score of 7. The assumption was made that if someone struck through a question then it indicated that they had read it and rejected it and were not able to do it. This assumption carries through in how the data summarization treats such answers. The scaling procedure took account of non-response and missing data in various ways. Where items were omitted they were counted as wrong answers depending on the pattern of responses in the block[6]. Some concerns were expressed about whether this was an entirely valid assumption. This also raised the question as to what extent there were inconsistencies between countries and between sweeps of the survey in the extent to which countries/interviewers were following the guidelines and protocols about instructions to the respondent on how to fill in the booklet. We were aware that interviewers found the administration procedure awkward and artificial and many departed from the prescribed format in favour of 'invigilation methods' rather than 'interviewing' while the respondent completed the asssessment.

In the 1998 follow-up survey, in order to examine the extent to which items had been skipped or crossed out more detail was coded about such answers. In an ideal world the actual response the respondent wrote would be captured so that analysis of frequently occurring incorrect answers could be carried out. This however would add substantially to the costs of scoring and data capture. In the Best Practice sample respondents who skipped questions were encouraged by the

Codes used in follow-up survey

Code 0. Item not attempted

Code 1. Correct answer

Code 3. Skipped, marked with a question mark

Code 5. Skipped, crossed out or marked don't know.

Code 7. Other response (i.e. wrong answer given)

Code 9. Booklet abandoned

interviewer to indicate that they had read the question by marking it in some way. They were asked to put a question mark if they intended to come back to that question and another mark such as a cross, when they had read a question and decided to skip it. This extra information about

[6] Yamamoto, K .and Irwin S Kirsch. Proficiency Estimation *in Adult Literacy in OECD Countries, Technical Report of the first International Adult Literacy Survey*. Washington: NCES 1998.

skipped questions was coded to give some further insight into how frequently questions were skipped and for what reason. If a respondent abandoned completing the booklet, a separate code was used indicating that no further questions in the booklet were answered.

For each person in the follow-up survey there are two sets of booklet data[7]. From those booklets for each person there is possibly 5 different sets of data. For some respondents the original IALS booklet has been scored 3 times and the retest booklet twice. The score information available is:

Score 1	**1994/6 booklet scored by 1994/6 team**
Score 2	**1994/6 booklet second scored by 1994/6 team**
Score 3	**Retest booklet scored by 1998 team**
Score 4	**Retest booklet second scored by 1998 team**
Score 5	**1994/6 booklet scored by 1998 team**

11.5 Response to questions at two points in time

In 1998, respondents participating in the follow-up survey were asked to complete an IALS booklet. Each booklet contained three of the seven IALS blocks. In the 1998 retest, one of the three blocks completed by a respondent was exactly the same as a block completed by them in 1994/6. This enables comparison of the stability of the performance of individuals faced with the exact same questions but on two different occasions some years apart. For the French sample this can only be compared for the replicate sample group as the Best Practice sample received a different version of the booklet.

How a respondent answers a particular question on a given day will vary and so the relationship between an individual doing the same question on two different occasions should not be expected to be perfect. An individual with high literacy skills may answer a relatively easy question incorrectly through lack of care, miscalculation etc. but would be expected to answer it correctly most of the time. Similarly an individual with poor skills may have answered correctly, on a particular day, by chance or through familiarity, a difficult question but in general would be expected to answer questions of a similar difficulty incorrectly most of the time. Higher levels of consistency in answering questions right or wrong can be expected on questions at the extremes of the scale, most people answering the very easiest questions correctly and the most difficult questions wrongly on both occasions. Consistency between how the question is answered on the two occasions will depend on the item and on the ability of the individual. In addition, the consistency with which the answers are scored on the two occasions will have an impact on the level of agreement.

There was variation between items in the level to which performance on the two occasions agreed, with some items having a very high level of agreement, over 90% and other questions with much lower levels. One could expect that the level of agreement would be higher, for items at both ends of the scale. In Britain the time difference between the first and second time the respondent completed the common block was shortest and so might be expected to be more protected from possible learning affect or changes in ability than in the other countries.

The possibility for interaction of ability, item difficulty and ease of scoring is best illustrated by example.

Block 1 question 2 is a document task at Level 2. It is easy to score with little or no judgement being required of the scorer. In Great Britain the agreement between first and second attempt of this question was 93%. Block 1 question 4 is a quantitative task at Level 3 (difficulty level of 289). It is very easy to score, either the person calculated and entered the correct number or they

[7] Those who did not complete a booklet were not eligible for inclusion in the follow-up survey.

did not and it agreed between the first and second attempt in 84% of cases. Most of the discrepancy between both answers to the same question in these cases therefore is likely to reside with the respondent rather than with inconsistency in scoring, so that on one occasion they calculated the answer correctly and on another they didn't.

However the agreement level on other quantitative literacy items of a similar difficulty varies. Block 2 question 4 is also a Level 3 (315) quantitative item for which the agreement level was 67% while a more difficult quantitative item, block 2 question 5 (Level 5, 408) had an agreement level of 66%.

For other questions the poor levels of agreement observed may be due to the subtleties of the tasks. For example, Block 6 question 10 is a quantitative Level 4 task (348) which is very simple to score with no judgement required on the part of the scorer. The respondent is asked to 'calculate the total amount of money you will have if.....'. To get a correct mark the respondent must identify the two amounts and then do the calculation. The task however is subject to misinterpretation by respondents and is mistakenly understood or interpreted by some respondents that the two pieces of information need not be added together. So while many respondents correctly identified the two amounts they simply gave the answer 'x + y'. These responses are coded as incorrect as they had not completed the task by working out the sum of the two amounts. This is the sort of lack of precision easily made if reading quickly or carelessly or is open to interpretation as to whether expressing the two amounts without doing the calculation is equivalent to 'the total' or may be influenced by interpretation of what is required.

Block 1 question 5 is a prose Level 3 task which is very difficult to score with the scorer having to apply a complicated rule and to make a judgement on the equivalence of the answer to the requirements of the scoring guide. The agreement between responses to this question on the two occasions in Great Britain was only at the 50% level. Other items that had particularly low levels of agreement are characterised by either difficulty or subtlety of the task or difficulty of scoring, or both.

Overall, the average agreement between answers to the same question at two different points in times 1994/6 (score 1) and 1998 (score 3) was higher in Sweden and Great Britain (74% and 72% respectively) than in France (62%). Although there were items in all countries that had very low levels of agreement the overall level of disagreement was very high (more than 50%) for 18 items in the replicate sample in France (doing the same French version of the assessment) but for only two item in Great Britain and three in Sweden.

Table 11.9 **Common block: Agreement[1] between response in 1994/6 (score 1) and 1998 (score 3)**

Item	Scale /Level	GB	Sweden	France *
Block 1		% in agreement		
Q1	D3	76	62	42
Q2	D2	93	87	60
Q4	Q3	84	78	63
Q5	P3	50	51	40
Q6	P3	74	80	51
Q7	Q3	63	68	65
Q9	Q3	68	72	74
Q10	P2	89	85	81
Q11	P5	50	55	60
Q13	D2	84	93	72
Q14	Q3	56	77	70
Q15	Q2	77	88	70
Base		*82*	*94*	*43*
Block 2		% in agreement		
Q1	P2	57	91	79
Q3	P2	84	98	79
Q4	Q3	67	68	60
Q5	Q5	63	55	54
Q6	P4	66	52	54
Q7	P4	60	38	50
Q8	D3	48	53	50
Q9	Q2	77	79	71
Q10	D3	64	69	48
Q111	D2	88	89	71
Q112	D3	72	91	52
Q113	D2	88	94	62
Q114	D1	90	89	71
Q115	D2	62	75	67
Base		*91*	*80*	*52*
Block 3		% in agreement		
Q1	Q3	80	72	67
Q2	D4	52	48	42
Q3	Q3	82	82	52
Q5	D2	78	89	61
Q6	Q2	74	85	58
Q7	P3	53	65	54
Q8	P4	56	61	39
Q9	P3	63	76	48
Q11	P3	70	80	61
Q12	P3	74	68	61
Q13	P3	82	52	42
Q14	Q4	70	48	58
Q15	P2	82	65	39
Base		*98*	*54*	*33*

Item	Scale /Level	GB	Sweden	France *
Block 4		% in agreement		
Q1	P1	98	96	92
Q2	P2	71	84	64
Q3	Q2	85	75	72
Q4	D3	65	73	51
Q5.1	D3	64	59	45
Q5.2	Q3	55	68	55
Q6	P3	46	86	49
Q7	P3	60	60	47
Q9	Q3	63	58	49
Q10	Q3			
Q11	Q3	71	68	74
Q121	D2	83	84	85
Q122	D2	90	67	64
Q123	D1	91	80	81
Q124	D1	90	84	87
Q125	Q2	90	75	85
Q126	Q1	91	71	85
Base		*86*	*97*	*47*
Block 5		% in agreement		
Q1	P1	89	98	84
Q2	P2	89	96	64
Q3	P2	82	88	64
Q4	P4	59	47	60
Q5	P3	52	68	42
Q6	P3	58	61	58
Q7	D2	85	91	80
Q8	D3	70	81	69
Q9	Q3	81	81	56
Q10	D3	74	69	49
Q12	D3	70	70	53
Q13	Q4	70	63	56
Q14	Q3	75	65	53
Q111	Q4	64	54	47
Q112	Q4	68	49	49
Q114	D3	66	70	56
Base		***80***	*57*	***45***
Block 6		% in agreement		
Q1	P1	92	98	94
Q2	Q3	80	79	65
Q3	Q2	73	98	74
Q4	D1	89	94	80
Q5	Q3	75	75	54
Q6	D3	72	78	70
Q7	P2	81	85	70
Q8	P3	69	79	48
Q9	D2	73	85	63
Q10	Q4	55	61	57
Q11	D3	71	76	56
Base		*75*	*85*	*46*

Table 11.9 continued **Common block: Agreement[1] between response in 1994/6 (score 1) and 1998 (score 3)**

Item	**Scale /Level**	**GB**	**Sweden**	**France ***
Block 7		% in agreement		
Q1	D1	86	97	87
Q2	Q2	76	81	74
Q3	D2	77	89	71
Q4	D2	76	76	74
Q5	Q3	60	66	45
Q6	Q3	59	58	64
Q7	D4	56	65	64
Q8	D3	66	75	68
Q9	D5	54	58	58
Q10	P2	71	73	61
Q11	P4	58	52	58
Q13	P1	86	91	81
Q14	P3	62	63	61
Q15	P2	78	80	68
Base		*96*	*93*	*31*
All Blocks		**72**	**74**	**62**

*In the case of France the two parts of the retest sample were given different translations/ versions of the test so only those in the replicate or IALS style sample received the exact same version of the questions as the last time.

[1] For comparability between years, codes 0 and 9 were combined on the extended scoring rubric (to compare with code 0 on the original); codes 3,5,7 were combined on score 3 (to compare with code 7 on score 1).

11.5.1 Interaction of proficiency and scoring

The two items that had such low level of agreement in Great Britain serves as useful illustrations of how scoring contributes to the analysis of response agreement. Block 4 question 6 is one where the British scoring team had difficulty in establishing consistency within the team as it was felt that the scoring guide did not allow for the most common answer which the team considered to be correct. The question asked,

> *"What can you do to establish that your refrigerator is still covered by warranty".*

The relevant passage in the text in the British version was

> *'Save proof of original purchase date such as your sales receipt or credit card slip to establish warranty period'.*

The scoring guide allowed to be scored as correct the following answers; 'sales receipt', 'credit card slip' or 'proof of original purchase date'. Additional information that could be supplied but was not required was 'Save' in front of any of the answers. Respondents who said 'check your sales receipt' or 'check date on receipt' were to be scored as incorrect. In Britain these were commonly occuring answers. British scorers argued that what the person could legitimately do to establish warranty was not to 'save' the receipt, they would have needed to have done that at the time of the purchase. What they should do, now that the fridge is faulty, is to check the date of purchase on their receipt saved from when they bought it. While this may seem rather pedantic it is sometimes difficult for scorers to rigidly follow a scoring guide which they believe does not encompass all the right answers even though they believe it is being scored in the same way in all the other countries.

Table 11.10 **French IALS retest: tems with a level of agreement below 50% - responses to questions in 1994 and 1998 (respondents who attempted item)**

Item	Item scale and level	Correct 94/6, incorrect 98	Incorrect 94/6, correct 98	Correct both years	Incorrect both years	Total
		%	%	%	%	
B1Q5	P3	42	14	17	28	100
B1Q1	D3	45	10	24	21	100
B5Q111	Q4	35	14	30	22	100
B5Q5	P3	30	19	32	19	100
B3Q9	P3	19	29	29	38	100
B4Q9	Q3	18	30	42	10	100
B3Q15	P2	46	0	29	25	100
B2Q10	D3	16	30	46	7	100
B4Q6	P3	15	30	20	35	100
B7Q5	Q3	17	26	52	4	100
B4Q7	P3	32	10	47	10	100
B3Q8	P4	23	18	27	32	100
B5Q112	Q4	15	26	45	14	100
B5Q10	D3	18	21	39	21	100
B3Q13	P3	9	30	30	30	100
B4Q51	D3	12	24	54	9	100
B3Q2	D4	10	24	33	33	100
B6Q8	P3	29	0	44	26	100

Items are ordered by proportion who answered differently on the two occasions

The second item in Britain with poor agreement is Block 2 question 8 where the respondent had to circle the area on a map showing where according to the weather forecast heavy rain was expected. This is an item which the inter-country rescore in 1996 found that Britain was out of line with its second marker. This should in principle be an easy item to mark, either the respondent has circled the relevant area or they have not. The difficulty in scoring this item pertained to how big the circle could be and still be marked correct. Most respondents might assume that they would not be penalised for the fact that they have large handwriting or are generous underliners or circlers. Two approaches can be adopted, a) that the centre of the circle is the area indicated so long as the circle does not encompass huge tracts of the map or b) that the circle must only cover the area concerned, i.e. it must not touch any other area of weather marking such as the snow area. In the refinement process in the 1996 round of IALS it was agreed that the second view should be taken in scoring this item and it is one of the items that Britain had to go back and rescore for all booklets in the 1996 survey following the adjudication on the inter-country rescore. British scorers were allowing too large a circle compared with the scorers in the other country.

For both the items that had poor agreement in Britain it is possible to explain why that might be so and both reasons centre on the consistency and reliability of the scoring rather than on the performance of the respondent.

The reason for the high level of disagreement in France was investigated. Just over half of the items with a high level of disagreement were those for which concerns had been expressed about the possible effect of translation[8]. It was also found that in 1998 respondents were more likely to give a response, either correct or incorrect rather than skipping or omitting for these items in 1998 than in 1994. As the drift from invalid to valid response contributed to the level of disagreement, respondents not giving a response in either year were eliminated from the calculation of level of agreement. Table 11.10 shows the effect of basing the level of agreement only on those who gave a valid response in both years. For seven of these eighteen items, the largest contribution to disagreement was amongst those who gave a correct response in 1994 but an incorrect response in 1998. This warranted further investigation

[8] See Chapter 6

11.5.2 Scoring and scoring drift

Scorers from Sweden, France and Britain attended the scorer training provided for the Second IALS (SIALS) which was scheduled for around the same time as the follow-up survey. In all countries there was some continuity in the scoring team between IALS and the follow-up survey. Feedback from all teams following attendance at the scorer training suggested that scoring guidance had drifted between the first time they had scored IALS and the follow-up survey. As part of the procedures for the follow-up survey a sample of assessment booklets from the 1994/6 IALS for those respondents who participated in the follow-up survey were re-scored by the scorers in 1998. This would enable the detection of any scoring drift or bias between the two different rounds of the survey. The number of booklets from the original IALS re-scored in 1998 was 560 in Great Britain, 172 in Sweden, and 388 in France.

Table 11.11 **Agreement between scoring teams in 1994/6 and 1998: rescore of IALS booklets by retest scoring team[1]**

Block 1	GB	Sweden	France
	% in agreement		
Q1	92*	91*	68*
Q2	100	96*	92*
Q4	100	99	100
Q5	82*	51*	63*
Q6	98	92*	97
Q7	98	99	97
Q9	99	96	97
Q10	99	100	97
Q11	98	85*	94*
Q13	97	99	99
Q14	100	99	97
Q15	99	100	98
Base	*241*	*79*	*153*

Block 2	GB	Sweden	France
	% in agreement		
Q1	93*	99	94*
Q3	99	100	95*
Q4	99	100	100
Q5	96	99	99
Q6	94*	-	91*
Q7	89*	85*	86*
Q8	67*	-	93*
Q9	99	97	97
Q10	98	100	97
Q111	100	96*	97
Q112	96*	90*	94*
Q113	100	97	97
Q114	100	96*	97
Q115	96	99	98
Base	*235*	*71*	*181*

Block 3	GB	Sweden	France
Q1	99	94*	98
Q2	92*	88*	91*
Q3	98	95*	98
Q5	82*	94*	75*
Q6	100	100	98
Q7	94*	85*	88*
Q8	83*	88*	90*
Q9	91*	96*	84*
Q11	97	99	90*
Q12	99	94*	97
Q13	97	90*	63*
Q14	99	100	99
Q15	96*	-	91*
Base	*234*	*72*	*170*

Block 4	GB	Sweden	France
Q1	98	99	100
Q2	92*	92*	95*
Q3	99	100	100
Q4	94*	88*	89*
Q6	90*	97	76*
Q7	90*	84*	91*
Q9	100	99	98
Q11	100	97	99
Q51	94*	95*	98
Q52	94*	93*	99
Q121	100	97	98
Q122	97	91*	99
Q123	97	99	99
Q124	98	100	99
Q125	99	96*	98
Q126	99	97	99
Base	*234*	*76*	*161*

Block 5	GB	Sweden	France
	% in agreement		
Q1	98	100	99
Q2	98	100	99
Q3	98	100	99
Q4	86*	85*	93*
Q5	96*	98	93*
Q6	90*	89*	79*
Q7	100	98	99
Q8	94*	92	99
Q9	98	98	98
Q10	93*	87*	91*
Q12	99	98	98
Q13	98	100	99
Q14	98	100	98
Q111	69*	74*	64*
Q112	98	100	82*
Q114	99	100	87*
Base	*239*	*53*	*162*

Block 6	GB	Sweden	France
	% in agreement		
Q1	99	100	96*
Q2	100	100	99
Q3	100	100	98
Q4	100	99	99
Q5	100	98	97
Q6	96	90*	94*
Q7	99	100	99
Q8	99	94*	97
Q9	96	98	98
Q10	95	98	98
Q11	96	98	98
Base	*228*	*84*	*172*

Table 11.11 cont. **Agreement between scoring teams in 1994/6 and 1998. Rescore of IALS booklets by retest scoring team**

Block 7	**GB**	**Sweden**	**France**
		% in agreement	
Q1	100	99	99
Q2	98	99	98
Q3	99	100	99
Q4	99	99	99
Q5	98	96	98
Q6	98	98	98
Q7	99	100	98
Q8	98	99	96*
Q9	98	91*	98
Q10	94*	86*	95*
Q11	92*	89*	94*
Q13	99	100	98
Q14	93*	75*	69*
Q15	97	98	92*
Base	*263*	*81*	*162*

* Items with more than 3% of scores 1 and 5 in disagreement

[1] For comparability between years, codes 0 and 9 were combined on score 5 (to compare with code 0 on score 1); codes 3,5,7 were combined on score 5 (to compare with code 7 on score 1)

Overall, the level of agreement between the two teams of scorers in each country was high - 96% in Great Britain, 95% in Sweden and 94% in France. While many items were agreeing at the 100% or the 99% level (in line with the results from the inter-rater study on IALS[9] some items were found to have very poor inter-rater reliability between the two waves of the survey. These were investigated further. In IALS when the score by the original team (score 1) differed from the score by the retest team (score 5) by more than 3%, scores were defined as asymmetric e.g. a response was scored as correct in the original score but as incorrect in the re-scoring or vice versa. These items are marked by an asterisk in Table 11.11. Items which were asymmetric in all countries, are shown below in Table 11.12 along with information about the difficulty of the items and a judgement as to the difficulty of scoring. Overall the direction of the discrepancies was for these items to have been coded as correct by the scorers in 1994/6 but as any other response including incorrect by the 1998 scoring team.

To those familiar with IALS scoring, there were no surprises in the items found to be assymetric. They were typically those that were either a) difficult to score in terms of having to make a judgement about the equivalence of the respondents answer to the scoring guide or b) where difficulties had been experienced in maintaining consistent application of the scoring guide. As part of the scoring process adjudications were made on an ongoing basis on responses where an argument could be made for it to go either way. During this process the interpretation of the scoring guides and the treatment of contradictory or complementary information given in the response were refined. The aim in the retest was to try and score in a manner consistent with the original IALS scoring as implemented in that particular country to illiminate scoring effect from the differences in the proportion correct on particular items. Because of the continual refinement of the scoring guide and its interpretation through the adjudication process it was difficult to recapture exactly the scoring procedure from the original IALS. In all countries there was some continuity in personnel between the scoring of the original IALS and the follow-up survey. During the scorer training and subsequently in the actual scoring there was anecdotal evidence that certain items were being scored in a slightly different way in all countries between the two rounds of the survey and also between countries. This could have been individual scorer differences or team differences. The investigation of the items with poor agreement between the 1994/6 and 1998 scorers raised a new set of concerns about the scoring of the items and about the implementation of the scoring guidelines between rounds of the survey. Because of the fact that two versions of the test were being used in the French retest and the large number of items that

[9] see IALS Technical report p.87

were assymetric particular attention was paid to investigating the scoring issues within the French sample. In the rescoring of the original IALS booklets in France by the 1998 scoring team (score 5) 26 items were identified as problematic indicating systematic drift in application of scoring procedures.

Table 11.12 **Items for which scoring over time was inconsistent in all countries**[1]

Items	Text	Scale and Level	Ease of scoring
B1Q1	Fridge warranty	Document level 3	Difficult
B1Q5	Nappies	Prose level 3	Very difficult
B2Q7	Embryos	Prose level 4	Very difficult
B2Q8	Weather report	Document level 3	Difficult
B2Q112	Employment application	Document level 3	Moderately difficult
B3Q2	Oil use charts	Document level 4	Difficult
B3Q5	Bus timetable	Document level 3	Very easy
B3Q7	Job interview pamphlet	Prose level 3	Moderately difficult
B3Q8	Job interview pamphlet	Prose level 4	Very difficult
B3Q9	Job interview pamphlet	Prose level 3	Very difficult
B4Q2	Pain reliever label	Prose level 2	Moderately difficult
B4Q4	Copying form	Document level 3	Moderately difficult
B4Q7	Refrigerator warranty	Document level 3	Moderately difficult
B5Q4	Car safety seat	Prose level 4	Very difficult
B5Q6	Car safety seat	Prose level 4	Moderately difficult
B5Q10	Fireworks chart	Document level 3	Difficult
B5Q111	Hours worked	Quantitative level 4	Easy
B7Q10	Contacting employer	Prose level 2	Moderately difficult
B7Q11	Contacting employer	Prose level 4	Moderately difficult
B7Q14	Fire safety tips	Prose level 3	Item dropped

1 defined as a difference of more than 3% between scores 1 and 5

11.5.3 Resolving scoring drift

The first step in this investigation was to list, for all respondents, the verbatim responses to each of the 26 items with a discrepancy in how their response to their original IALS booklet was scored by the 1994/6 scoring team and the 1998 scoring team The aim was to adjudicate as to whether the item should have been scored as correct or incorrect according to the scoring guidelines. The adjudication of the French items was carried out by the scorers from the 1998 British scoring team and the results were then reviewed by scorers at Statistics Canada. The overall conclusion of this investigation was that in France, booklets were scored to stricter standards in 1998 than in 1994. On some of these items there was clear evidence of a systematic difference in scoring between the two rounds of the survey in line with the earlier anecdotal evidence from scorers.

Consider again the example of the question on the fridge warranty. This item had poor agreement statistics in both France and Great Britain on the common block, that is the block that was answered by respondents on both occasions. The investigation of the scoring of the French item showed that the French scoring in 1998 was more in line with how the item was being scored in Great Britain, that is that merely answering 'checking' or 'looking' at the date of purchase on the till receipt was scored as wrong. When the French booklets from 1994 were re-examined answers which said 'check the till receipt' or 'look at the receipt' were accepted as correct in 1994.

The investigation also showed that the scoring guidelines were not being applied correctly to all items. For example, Block 3 question 13 required respondents to underline a sentence in a newspaper article which specified how two explorers traveled across Antarctica. The scoring guide rules on underlining of sentences allows answers to be marked as correct if they underline any part of the relevant sentence even if they do not underline the actual exact words and so long as they underline no other sentence. In France in the 1994 survey however respondents were marked as having given an incorrect answer if they did not underline the actual words, even if they had underlined another part of the correct sentence and no other. It was also discovered that whereas the scoring guide specified that questions which had been left blank in a form (B5Q11), indicating for example a respondent's availability for employment should be scored as incorrect (score=7) rather than blank (score=0), in France these questions were scored as blank so that comparison of the unadjusted raw score could be misleading. This type of discrepancy is of little consequence as this would have been taken account of in the treatment of missing item data within matrix questions as part of the scaling.

Table 11.13 **Proportion of questions answered correctly before and after re-scoring – France 1998 booklets**

Item	Description	Before re-scoring	After re-scoring
		% correct	
B1Q1	Refrigerator problem	48	75
B1Q5	Nappies	26	55
B2Q7	Newspaper article – embryos	25	30
B3Q9	Post interview review	50	71
B3Q13	Newspaper article – gene defect linked to allergies	49	59
B3Q15	Newspaper article – how explorers traveled across Antarctica	63	77
B4Q6	Refrigerator warranty	48	64
B7Q14	Fire safety tips	35	56

For almost all of the items affected the 1998 French scoring team were in line with the scoring team in Britain. The interrater study at the time of IALS across countries found high average levels of agreement with up to 11 items being asymmetric involving the French scoring team recoring other countries but only 1 item asymmetric in French booklets being rescored by another country[10]. The number of assymetric items was higher among the French speaking scoring teams than among the other languages and may be a consequence of the different versions of the assessment in use. In scoring, some of the problems in the translation of the version of the assessment used in France were being addressed. Among the French speaking scoring teams in IALS the assymetry was in one direction only and was not replicated in the reciprocal rescore. The IALS technical report concludes that this may have been due to a single scorer rather than systematic differences in scoring within the teams. The technical report (p.88) says that the inter-country rescore can 'identify poorly constructed items, ambiguous scoring criteria, erroneous translations of items or scoring criteria, erroneous printing of items or scoring criteria, scorer inaccuracies, and, most important, situations in which one country consistently rates a certain response as being correct while those in another country score the same response as incorrect.'

Establishing exact consistency in scoring between countries is clearly not easy to achieve on something as large and complex as IALS. The extent to which the inter-country rescore in IALS was used for all the above objectives is not clear. However the poor agreement on some items between the French rescore and the British scoring suggests that there may have been some scoring drift between the 1994 and 1996 rounds of the survey, or at least between Great Britain and France. It is possible that France was out of line with scoring in the first IALS but more likely is that the countries that took part in 1996 were over zealous in the application of the scoring guide to the strict letter of the law having taken on board the questions over the comparability of IALS. In the 1996 survey the inter-country rescore did not include any countries that took part in the 1994 survey and so while the scoring may have been internally consistent within the 1996 group of countries it may have some inconsistencies with the 1994 countries.

On the basis of these findings, it was decided, as mentioned earlier, that the drift between 1994 and 1998 scoring needed to be addressed and that all 1998 French booklets should be re-scored for the eight items shown in Table 11.13 to anchor them firmly back onto the 1994 scoring standards. The reasons for this are that each of these items had a high level of disagreement, a drift in scoring mostly in one direction and a relatively high number of cases were affected. The nature of the discrepancies is illustrated in Table A11.7 in the appendix to this chapter. This is the same procedure as used in IALS after the inter-country rescore identified the cause of asymmetric items. The outcome of the rescoring was that the score on the 1998 retest booklets on these eight items was changed for 44% of cases. The majority of changes involved re-scoring an item as correct when it had been scored as incorrect in 1998. After re-scoring, the proportion of

[10] see IALS technical report page 87

correct responses increased for all eight items when the 1994 standard of scoring was applied in 1998 to the retest booklets. The overall effect was that in France, the average number of items correct on the retest booklet (score 3) when 1994 scoring standards were applied increased from a mean value of 26 to 27 but continued to remain lower than in either Great Britain or Sweden (mean values of 31).

Table 11.14 **Proportion of respondents who answered items correctly (1998) by type of sample (weighted[1])**

Item	Scale / Level	GB BP	GB IALS	Sweden BP	Sweden IALS	France BP	France IALS	Portugal
					% correct			
Block 1								
Q1	D3	88	82	73	72	74	75	61
Q2	D2	97*	90	91	94	67	87**	67
Q3	Exc.	95*	87	87	91	81	75	60
Q4	Q3	91	90	89	91	79	80	70
Q5	P3	56**	40	40	38	52	61	26
Q6	P3	79	69	83	85	65	63	32
Q7	Q3	81*	70	75	75	54	61	56
Q8	Exc.	78*	65	46	45	43*	29	35
Q9	Q3	80	70	76	75	63	61	63
Q10	P2	93	91	94	97	79	82	66
Q11	P5	50	49	44	49	24	39**	23
Q12	Exc.	50	47	57	50	12	31**	14
Q13	D2	88	83	96	94	83	96**	66
Q14	Q3	80	78	86	83	75	74	42
Q15	Q2	87	85	86	85	61	78**	61
Base		*128*	*131*	*133*	*109*	*190*	*119*	*493*
Block 2								
Q1	P2	81	72	95	93	71	78	56
Q2	Exc.	31	29	21	24	31*	21	15
Q3	P2	94	98	97	98	88	82	67
Q4	Q3	72	69	67	75	63	57	52
Q5	Q5	27	30	32	36	23	25	26
Q6	P4	59	51	70	73	44	35	31
Q7	P4	22	17	25	27	27	28	12
Q8	D3	39	39	44	47	55	39	42
Q9	Q2	86	83	90	92	80	75	68
Q10	D3	77	74	78	87	64	65	48
Q111	D2	96	98	99	99	81	92**	74
Q112	D3	80	85	92	96	67	86**	63
Q113	D2	94	98	98	97	87	88	80
Q114	D1	94	98	99	98	89	92	80
Q115	D2	78	79	89	89	82	86	70
Base		*125*	*122*	*151*	*107*	*182*	*143*	*466*
Block 3								
Q1	Q3	84	77	84	89	75	69	59
Q2	D4	65	60	60	67	36	49*	32
Q3	Q3	85	84	86	88	72*	59	60
Q4	Exc.	98**	89	98	97	87**	66	70
Q5	D2	92	86	95	96	82	76	69
Q6	Q2	91**	78	85	90	74*	62	54
Q7	P3	74	68	68	72	62	67	42
Q8	P4	62**	45	67	76	47	47	35
Q9	P3	78	73	78	84	78**	61	48
Q10	Exc.	24	15	34	44	3	8	5
Q11	P3	89	81	87	91	73**	55	55
Q12	P3	69	65	73	77	53	56	39
Q13	P3	90*	82	76	64	62	59	55
Q14	Q4	61	63	53	62	55	54	37
Q15	P2	93	94	88	86	86	88	71
Base		*137*	*148*	*134*	*95*	*170*	*117*	*500*

Table 11.14 cont. **Proportion of all respondents who answered items correctly (1998) by type of sample (weighted[1])**

Item	Scale /Level	GB BP	GB IALS	Sweden BP	Sweden IALS	France BP	France IALS	Portugal
Block 4					*%correct*			
Q1	P1	98	98	99	100	92	99**	89
Q2	P2	71	67	87	91	51	58	47
Q3	Q2	85	92	83	86	74	79	56
Q4	D3	63	52	80	71	45	42	21
Q5 .1	D3	74	64	57	60	50	51	31
Q5 .2	Q3	61	57	64	70	55	60	45
Q6	P3	58	58	93	97	58	66	55
Q7	P3	57	62	55	65	53	56	43
Q8	Exc.	86	79	80	84	69	84**	49
Q9	Q3	75	77	76	74	53	58	58
Q10	Q5	28	19	19	23	11	9	5
Q11	Q3	87	86	72	77	67	79	60
Q12.1	D2	94	94	93	94	84	97	80
Q12.2	D2	88	92	83	83	80	84	74
Q12.3	D1	91	89	89	88	89	93	80
Q12.4	D1	95	98	92	92	96	99	74
Q12.5	Q2	87	85	90	85	88	95*	78
Q12.6	Q1	92	93	88	89	89	96	70
Base		*129*	*135*	*141*	*103*	*178*	*123*	*494*
Block 5								
Q1	P1	99	99	99	100	89	91	84
Q2	P2	94	98	97	99	84	87	77
Q3	P2	84	84	91	95	85	77	60
Q4	P4	43	48	50	60	32	40	23
Q5	P3	76	76	73	77	56*	45	42
Q6	P3	67	65	57	69	40	55**	31
Q7	D2	94	92	91	94	81	82	78
Q8	D3	79	71	79	80	53	66*	62
Q9	Q3	86*	76	79	83	68	72	60
Q10	D3	78	79	73	79	42	49	35
Q11.1	Q4	65	56	55	53	27	37	41
Q11.2	Q4	56	49	60	57	48	57	23
Q11.3	Exc.	53	49	65	66	51	63*	26
Q11.4	D3	67	60	69	69	57	68*	37
Q12	D3	71	71	68	70	52	62	43
Q13	Q4	58	46	57	61	34	38	30
Q14	Q3	74	70	73	70	52	59	36
Base		*136*	*122*	*134*	*101*	*196*	*145*	*497*
Block 6								
Q1	P1	96	95	98	97	90	89	88
Q2	Q3	75	70	81	88	68	68	59
Q3	Q2	88	85	97	97	79	78	76
Q4	D1	97	93	96	99	92	93	79
Q5	Q3	90*	80	82	88	72	66	58
Q6	D3	89*	80	89	94	59	59	46
Q7	P2	88	82	89	89	66	60	52
Q8	P3	80	83	86	91	48	46	37
Q9	D2	84	80	87	94	75**	40	52
Q10	Q4	61	49	61	77*	48	39	14
Q11	D3	78	72	78	83	72	66	41
Q12	Exc.	64	59	51	60	55	69*	61
Q13	Exc.	85	91	94	95	78	83	66
Base		*128*	*123*	*126*	*69*	*170*	*125*	*503*

Table 11.14 cont. **Proportion of all respondents who answered items correctly (1998) by type of sample (weighted[1])**

Block 7		GB BP	GB IALS	Sweden BP	Sweden IALS	France BP	France IALS	Portugal
					%correct			
Q1	D1	99	100	96	98	95	97	91
Q2	Q2	90*	79	87	86	72	80	65
Q3	D2	92	90	92	97	85	87	80
Q4	D2	86	85	86	89	80	76	68
Q5	Q3	69	70	60	71	57	58	18
Q6	Q3	73	64	64	68	56	63	22
Q7	D4	61	53	68	74	51	55	31
Q8	D3	78	85	75	84	70	73	45
Q9	D5	28	29	39	49	6	16**	6
Q10	P2	91**	78	78	88*	66	71	57
Q11	P4	59	55	41	46	36	35	15
Q12	Exc.	77	69	61	70	59	66	37
Q13	P1	97	96	99	100	95	95	84
Q14	P3	79	70	60	66	50	64*	15
Q15	P2	90	93	94	96	55	75**	59
Base		*123*	*131*	*162*	*115*	*174*	*125*	*448*

[1] Data was weighted after eight items (B1Q1, B1Q5, B2Q7, B3Q9, B3Q13, B3Q15, B4Q6, B7Q14) had bee re-scored for France (see section 11.5 of this chapter)
*significant at the 0.05 level ** significant at the 0.01 level

11.6 Individual items – correct and incorrect answers

Table 11.14 shows the percentage in each country who answered each item correctly in the 1998 retest for the two parts of the sample. In Great Britain, for about two thirds of the items overall, a higher proportion of respondents in the Best Practice sample gave a correct answer than in the IALS or replicate sample. For some items the difference between the two parts of the sample answering a question correctly in Britain is quite large although because of the small sample sizes most of these differences were not significant. For about a third of items the difference in the proportion correct was greater than 5 percentage points. Unlike in France, both parts of the sample in Britain were completing the exact same versions of the assessment.

Table 11.15 shows those items where the largest differences were observed in Britain. Many of the questions were quantitative items. From the qualitative work we know that many people reported making educated guesses on some of the quantitative questions rather than working out the exact answer since this is what they would do in real life. In the Best Practice protocol it was impressed on respondents that accuracy was important and that it was more important to get it right rather than to do it quickly. The higher proportion of correct responses on these types of questions may therefore be due to effect of the more detailed explanations about how the assessment works.

The other questions where there was a large difference in percent correct between the two groups were questions where the respondent had to write out an explanation or to enumerate reasons. For many of these questions it is easy for respondents to get a wrong score if they do not supply sufficient information. The example quoted earlier in this chapter in the section on scoring illustrates this point. In the question on the refrigerator warranty the respondent is asked to 'List two things....'. The target text which contains the answers consists of a list of four bullet points. Reference to one of the bullets points is not a valid answer so the respondent has to correctly identify which bullet points contain the required answer. Two of the answers possible contain multiple conditions:

- Door may have been left ajar or package may be holding door open.
- Too frequent and too long door openings

The scoring guide accepts the two elements in the first bullet point (differentiated by the use of 'or') as acceptable answers. Answering 'Door left ajar' and 'Package holding door open' would be sufficient to meet the criteria of 'List two things'. For the second bullet point in the target text the two parts are conjoined. Answering 'Too frequent opening' or 'Too long opening' would not constitute sufficient detail for one of the two required reponses. The respondent must give both parts of the point to have this point attributed as one of the two things to be listed. Many respondents when anwering fall foul of this subtle distinction. By being more careful or by paying more attention to detail as they are encouraged under the Best Practice protocol may mean that people are giving fuller answers and thus not inadvertently getting questions wrong through carelessness.

Table 11.15 **Items where largest differences between Best Practice and IALS sample were observed in proportion correct in Britain.**

Item	Scale[1] / Level	Problem	Best Practice	IALS
			% correct	
B3Q8	P4	Q. Describe in your own words the differences between the panel interview and the group interview. This is a question which many people get wrong because they are not sufficiently specifi or full in their answers. It is also one of the most difficult items to score consistently	62**	45
B1Q5	P3	Q. List three reasons why the letter writer prefers to use disposable rahter than cotton nappies. This question is difficult to score and again many people do not provide sufficient infromation or summarise the information into general comments like 'environmental reasons' which is not acceptable as a credit toward the three reasons.	56**	40
B3Q6	Q2	Q. How many minutes does it take to get from Springfield to Queen Elizabeth Gardens on a Sunday morning. This question involves identifying the two times in the bus timetable and doing a calculation.	91**	78
B7Q10	P2	Q. According to the pamphlet, which three types of information can you expect to see in a job advertisement.	91**	78
B6Q10	Q4	Q. Using the infromatino in the table, calculate the total amount of money you will have if you invest £100 at a rate of 6% for 10 years. The most common wrong answer on this question is where respondents have correctly identified the amoun but fail to realise that the amount needs to be added on to the amount invested.	61	49
B5Q13	Q4	Q. Calculate the total number of kilometers travelled in a trip from Guadalajara to Tecoman and then to Zamora. This question involves the identification of the two distances from a mileage chart and to be added together.	58	46
B1Q7	Q3	Q. How many quadrillion BTU of primary energy does Canada produce more than it consumes. This involves the identification of information from two tables and subtracting them	81*	70
B4Q4	D3	Q. Suppose the annual budget statement will be 105 pages and you need to distribute 300 copies. Would Quick Copy do this job? Explain your answer. This involves relating the conditions in the request form to the question condition and judging the correct outcome.	63	52
B7Q2	Q2	Q. Calculate the percentage of men in the teaching profession in Italy. The respondent has to identify the percentage of women teachers in Italy and subtract from 100.	90*	79
B1Q9	Q3	Q. Calculate the total amount of energy in quadrillion Btu consumed by Canada, Mexico and the United States. The respondent has to identify the thre amound and do the calculation.	80	70
B4Q3	Q2	Q. What is the maximum number of tables that can be taken in 24 hours? This question requires the identification of the number of tablets per time period an dthe calculation of how many of those time periods are in 24 hours.	85	92

*significant at the 0.05 level ** significant at the 0.01 level
[1]. P= Prose, D=Document, Q=Quantitative

The higher proportions correct in the Best Practice sample in Britain concur with the finding from the de-brief interview that respondents in Great Britain were more likely to say that they had tried hard to answer the questions correctly and left none unanswered if they were in the Best Practice sample.

In Sweden there were fewer differences between the Best Practice and replicate sample in the proportion who answered questions correctly. For most items the difference in the proportions of the two samples answering a question correctly was less than 5 percentage points (81 questions). Among the items where the differences were greater than 10 percentage points in favour of the replicate sample, two were quantitative items and the other was a prose item where the respondent had to list three things although for only one of these items were the differences significant.

In France quite a different pattern emerges where two different assessments were being used in the two parts of the sample. The pattern in the proportion of items correct in the two samples was very similar to that found in Britain but in the opposite direction. For one third of the items the difference between the two samples in the proportion correct was greater than 5 percentage points with those in the IALS sample (using the French version of the assessment) more likely to answer questions correctly than those in the Best Practice sample on the Swiss French version. A further 20% of the items had a similar difference between the two groups but with those answering the Swiss assessment more likely to answer them correctly. Among the 12 items which had the greatest difference in the proportion correct between the two samples where those responding to the Swiss version of the assessment were more likely to answer correctly, 3 were questions which were not used in scaling, 6 were questions where the problem in the French version was not present in the Swiss and 3 were quantitative items. See Chapter 6 of this report for a further discussion of the impact of translation.

Among those questions where the difference was in the other direction, i.e. that the proportion answering correctly was higher on the French version compared with the Swiss version the pattern is less clear cut. Among the 21 items where the difference in the proportion correct was greater than 10 percentage points 4 were items which had been dropped from the scaling. In some cases the question was easier in the French text by virtue of inclusion of direct matches with the target text or less complexity in the formulation of the question. Some of the questions where problems were identified in the French version of the assessment and which on the face of it seem to be unproblematic in the Swiss version remain unresolved. The items shown in Table 11.16 include some of the items where the proportion correct might have been expected to differ but didn't or where the proportion correct in the IALS sample was higher. This table also illustrates the nature of some of the problems that were encountered. According to the IALS measurement framework the difficulty of an item is determined by several features; the type of information, the type of match required and the plausibility of any distractors present in the text[11]. Where there is a direct match for example between the question and the text and that is the only place that such a literal match occurs then the task will be easier than if other literal matches were present. Preserving the integrity of matches across versions of the text therefore is important. The type of match required is affected by whether the task is simply to locate information, the number of pieces of information that are required, whether inferences need to be made and whether any new information is requested. Preserving the degree of specificity or vagueness of the question across versions is also important in maintaining the difficulty of the task constant or equivalent. The unwitting introduction of additional distractors or omission of existing distractors in translation or adaptation will also impact on the difficulty of the task.

---

[11] Kirsch, Irwin, Ann Jungelblut and Peter B. Mosenthal. The Measurement of Adult Literacy in *in Adult Literacy in OECD Countries, Technical Report of the first International Adult Literacy Survey*. Washington: NCES 1998. Peter Mosenthal. Defining Prose Task Characteristics for Use in Computer-Adaptive Testing and Instruction. *American Educational Research Journal*. 1998.

Table 11.16 **Items where largest differences between Best Practice and IALS sample were observed in proportion correct in France or where differences expected but not found**

Item	Scale[1] / Level	Problem	Best Practice	IALS
			% correct	
B1Q2	D2	On this question the Swiss version has more complexity in the target answer. The emphasis in the Swiss text is to 'check' rather than 'moving the switch' and the ue of English word ON is not present in the French version. Swiss verision: Assurez-vous que l'interrupteur ecoenergie est placé en position ON (a droite) French: Déplacer le bouton de l'économiseur d'énergie sur la droite.	67	87**
B7Q15	P2	Although the direct match between question and text has been preserved in the Swiss version thus solving the translation problem there is no evident explanation for the difference in performance.	55	75**
B2Q112	D3	The respondent has to fill in the availability for days of the week. In the Swiss version, as in the English version only the first letter of each day of the week is given. In the French version the days are indicated by the first three letters.	67	86**
B1Q15	Q2	No explanation evident	61	78**
B5Q6	P3	No explanation evident	40	55**
B1Q11	Q5	The French version includes a direct link with the target phrase which is not present in the Swiss version making detectino of the correct inforamtion easier.	24	39**
B7Q14	P3	Investigate further – scoring maybe? Nu. On the phone?? This question was subject to rescoring and had poor scoring conistency in all countries.	50	64*
B3Q2	D4	Different formulation of question, difficult to determine effect.	36	49*
B5Q8	D3	No explanation evident	53	66*
B4Q121	D2	Different formulation of question but no evident explanation	84	97**
B1Q13	D2	There is a direct link between the question and the answer in the French version that is not present in the Swiss version.	83	96**
B1Q1	D3	The link between question and text is weaker than in Swiss French. This question was subject to rescoring.	74	75
B1Q4	Q3	In french version the direct link between question and text is not preserved, synonym used instead	79	80
B1Q6	P3	There is a direct link between question and wrong part of text (not in others) and no direct link to the right part of the text as in other versions.	65	63
B3Q5	D2	Additional distractors are present in French version next to target answer that are not present in other versions	82	76
B3Q15	P2	Additional distractor introduced in French version. Subject to rescoring.	86	88

*significant at the 0.05 level ** significant at the 0.01 level

[1]. P= Prose, D=Document, Q=Quantitative

11.7 Test completeness

In section 11.3 we saw that the proportion of respondents providing usable booklet data in IALS varied between countries. Apart from respondents being willing or not to attempt the booklet there is the issue of the extent to which the booklet is complete. Overall, the average number of items left unanswered in the follow-up survey was fairly low in all countries. The high standard deviations however, show that there was considerable variation between items as to whether they were skipped or left unanswered. As very few respondents in any country flagged a question with a question mark indicating that they intended to return to it but failed to do so they have been combined with the crossed out code.

Respondents in France were the most likely to have skipped an item, leaving it blank, or to have crossed it out, and Swedish respondents were the least likely. In the Best Practice sample in France on average 4 items were not attempted compared with about half that in Sweden and France. Although the results for Portugal are not discussed in this chapter the pattern of booklet of completeness is included in the tables presented here for comparison purposes. Respondents in

Portugal had higher rates of item omission than any of the other countries, consistent with the literacy profile expected. It is interesting to note that the effect of Best Practice in Sweden was to reduce the proportion of complete cases compared with the IALS sample. This may be due to respondents being less likely to have a go at questions they weren't sure about. In Britain cases were more likely to be complete in the Best Practice sample. In France there was no difference between the two samples in the overall proportion of complete cases but there was a difference in whether they were struck through or left blank.

Table 11.17 **Average number of items omitted or skipped by treatment group and country 1998**

	Great Britain		Sweden		France		Portugal
	BP	IALS	BP	IALS	BP	IALS	
Items omitted							
Mean	0.5	1.3	1.8	1.5	1.2	2.6	1.7
s.d.	1.3	3.1	3.3	3.9	3.1	5.1	3.9
Items skipped							
Mean	1.4	1.5	0.5	0.2	2.7	0.9	3.2
s.d.	3.2	3.3	1.6	1.0	5.7	3.2	6.4
Total items skipped or omited							
Mean	1.9	2.8	2.2	1.8	4.0	3.5	4.9
s.d.	*3.7*	*4.7*	*3.7*	*4.0*	*6.7*	*6.2*	*7.4*
% of cases with no items skipped or omitted (0,3,5)	57	49	52	61	42	45	39
Base	*307*	*305*	*333*	*233*	*422*	*300*	*1238*

Tables A11.8 and A11.9 in the appendix to this chapter shows the ommission rate and crossed out or marked rate for each question in the retest by country and treatment group. Some questions had very high proportions of respondents rejecting the question. Many of these items were the more difficult items, particularly quantitative items which involved doing complex calculations and among prose and document items many of the questions not answered were not so much difficult as requiring fuller answers, the questions which required the respondent to list three reasons, or explain in their own words or to compare two events or objects. Some items with high omit or skip rates were clustered on the text with either particular texts proving unpopular or the last question on a particular text being left unanswered. Texts such as the text on frozen embryos and the form for the photocopy requests were particularly unpopular. Other texts were unpopular in particular countries, for example the distance chart for cities in Mexico was omitted or skipped by about a fifth to a quarter of the samples in Sweden , France and Portugal but was attempted by most people in Britain. From the qualitative research reported in Chapter 8 we know that many people reported lack of interest in and discomfort with the text on the embryos and many respondents in France thought the distance charts was a trick question in that they wondered whether these cities they were unfamiliar with were actually in Mexico at all.

11.7.1 Booklet completeness in IALS

The same extended scoring codes were used when rescoring the original IALS booklets so that distinction could be made between items answered wrongly and those where the question was crossed out. Only a sample of booklets were rescored in each country, 560 in Britain, 388 in France and 172 in Sweden. Only booklets for those in the retest were rescored and as those who had done very little of the booklet were excluded from the retest sample it means that these booklets are not representive of all the booklets. They will be most representative for Sweden where as we saw in section 11.3 most respondents completely the booklet sufficiently to be used for scaling purposes.

In Sweden the booklets were most complete with very few respondents crossing out or putting a question mark or other mark beside the question. Over half (55%) of the booklets from 1994 rescored with the extended scoring guide had no items that were crossed out or marked in any way. In Great Britain 51% of the 1996 booklets rescored did not have any questions crossed out or marked compared with 35% of the French booklets. The mean number of items skipped/crossed out was highest in France as were the number of abandoned items and was highly dispersed with a standard deviation of 5.1. The presence of marks beside questions on the booklets may of course have not been done by the respondent but by the intereviewer or the scorer, this we don't know. In Britain interviewers were specifically instructed not to put any marks whatsoever on the booklets and as scoring was done using a Computer Assisted Data Input Programme (CADI) we can be reasonably confident that the booklets are as the respondent left them. Even if the strike through was made by the scorer or interviewer the distinction between a wrong answer and skipped or omited is still valid. On the original booklets that were rescored using the extended scoring guide the mean proportion of questions answered wrongly in France and Britain dropped by 2, from 13 to 11 in France and in Britain from 9 to 7. As in the retest particular items were more likely to be omitted or skipped than others with as many as 40% of the respondents rejecting certain items in France. Again the text on the embryos and the photocopy form had high omit/skip rates as did many of the questions where fuller answers were required. Table A11.10 in the Appendix to this chapter gives the omit and skip rates for each question.

Table 11.18 **Mean number of items skipped and omited and standard deviations based on IALS booklet (1994/6) when scored using 1998 scoring codes (score 5)**

	Great Britain		Sweden*		France	
	Mean	S.d.	Mean	S.d.	Mean	S.d.
Items omited	1.8	4.0	2.0	3.4	2.5	4.6
Items marked with ?	0.3	1.3	0.0	0.0	.1	0.6
Items crossed out	1.2	3.9	0.0	0.3	2.2	5.0
Total items crossed out or ?	1.5	4.1	0.0	0.3	2.3	5.1
Abandoned items	1.1	4.9	0.2	1.5	2.0	6.8
Items wrong score 5	7.0	4.8	*	4.2	11.0	4.9
Items wrong score 1	8.9	6.4	5.5	4.1	13.0	7.5
% of cases with no items skipped or omitted (0,3,5)	51		55		35	
Base	*560*		*172*		*388*	

* some items where the answer was written on the newspaper accompanying the assessment booklet were not rescored in the Swedish booklets. The number of items affected varied depending on the composition of the booklet.

11.8 Summary measures of performance

While the previous sections have looked at the proportion who answered individual questions correctly this is difficult to assimilate into a coherent picture of overall ability. Therefore some kind of summary measure is needed to be able to get an feel for the aggregate position. In IALS the summary measure used was generated by IRT models which have been discussed in Chapters 3 and 4 of this report. In order to include a broad coverage IALS uses matrix sampling so that individuals answer different combinations of the items in the test in one of seven different booklets. An alternative measure is to use the proportion correct. As the composition of the test booklets will differ in terms of the profile of item difficulty the raw number right or percent scores are not directly comparable. IRT as a summary measure is able to overcome this problem and produce reasonably comparable scores even though the individuals have not all answered the same questions. The proportion correct is highly correlated with the scaled score and this is acknowledged in the IALS technical report "...mean proficiency values and proportion correct statistics have a strong linear relationship" (p.183) while Goldstein (Chapter 4 in this report) and Heady (Chapter 7) argue that it would be simpler, and essentially change nothing, if one reported results consisting simply of the proportion correct despite the matrix sampling. The advantages of using proportion correct are that it is quick and easy to calculate, universally understood as a measure and is cheaper than using more sophisticated models.

Table 11.19 shows the composition of the different booklets in terms of the three scales and the level of the items. As Level 1 literacy is defined negatively, in that they have failed to demonstrate the level of competency required of Level 2, there are very few items at the lowest level. Most of the items in the assessment are at Levels 2 and 3 with very few at the highest level, Level 5. In the whole test (excluding the core booklet) there are only five Prose items at Level 1 and only one Level 1 item on the quantitative scale. The balance of items across booklets is reasonably well spread so using proportion correct will not be too distorted by the varying item difficulties across the booklets.

Table 11.19 **Compostion of booklets by domain and level**

	Booklet number							
Prose	**1**	**2**	**3**	**4**	**5**	**6**	**7**	**All**
Level 1	1	1	2	3	2	2	1	5
Level 2	4	5	3	5	4	5	4	10
Level 3	4	7	8	5	5	2	8	13
Level 4	2	4	1	2	1	3	2	5
Level 5	1	0	0	0	1	0	1	1
Dropped	3	1	1	2	1	2	2	5
Document								
Level 1	3	1	3	3	1	3	1	6
Level 2	7	5	4	5	4	6	5	12
Level 3	6	7	4	7	7	6	2	13
Level 4		1	1	1	0	1	2	2
Level 5			0	1	0	1	1	1
Dropped	2	2	4	0	4	2	4	7
Quantitative								
Level 1	1	0	1	1	0	0	0	1
Level 2	4	2	4	3	2	3	3	9
Level 3	9	5	8	8	8	5	8	17
Level 4	0	4	2	3	4	1	1	5
Level 5	1	1	0	0	0	1	0	1
Dropped	0	1	0	1	1	0	0	1
Total	**48**	**47**	**46**	**50**	**45**	**43**	**45**	**114**

Table 11.20 shows the correlations between the proportion correct and the proficiency estimates for each scale for those who did attempt the booklet and who completed sufficient items for the data to be usuable for scaling. The problem remains of how to treat those who have not done very much of the booklet for non-literacy related reasons. As shown earlier, this varied considerably between countries with almost all respondents in Sweden providing sufficient data for scaling purposes. This section considers the retest data using summary measures of an individuals performance on the assessment.

Table 11.20 **Cases with sufficient data for scaling: Correlations between first plausible value for each dimension and percentage of items answered correctly – IALS**

	GB (96)	France (94)	Sweden (94)
	Percent correct	Percent correct	Percent correct
Percent correct	1.00	1.00	1.00
Prose	.894	.816	.771
Document	.908	.824	.818
Quantitative	.891	.814	.798
Base	3340	2530	2573

11.8.1 Proportion of items answered correctly

Figure 11.6 shows, for those who were re-tested in 1998, that the proportion of questions answered correctly in IALS in 1994/6 (score 1), was higher in Sweden and Great Britain than in France. In the original survey, the respondents who took part in the retest in Sweden answered on average 80% of the questions correctly compared with 77% for respondents in Britain and 65% in France. There was little difference between the two parts of the sample in the proportion of questions answered correctly.

Figure 11.6 **Mean proportion of questions answered correctly in 1994/6 by sample treatment and country**

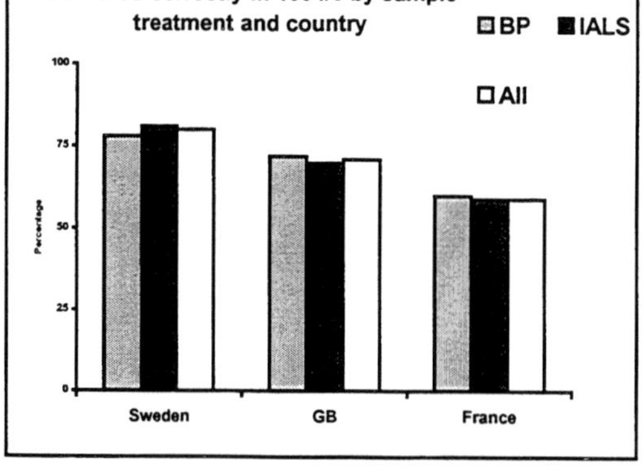

There was no significant difference in any country between the IALS and Best Practice samples in either the average number or proportion of items answered correctly. It is unlikely that the composition of the Best Practice and IALS samples affected these results, as there was no significant difference in any country between the characteristics of respondents in these two samples (see Chapter 10). This is in line with the results from analysis of the individual questions (section 11.6) where there were no systematic largescale differences between the two parts of the sample in the percentage who answered individual questions correctly. In both Britain and France the proportion of questions answered correctly increased in both parts of the sample while in Sweden the proportion decreased although these did not reach statistical significance.

Table 11.21 **Average number of items correct and proportion correct by treatment group and country in IALS 1994/6 and Retest 1998**

	Great Britain		Sweden		France	
	BP	**IALS**	**BP**	**IALS**	**BP**	**IALS**
Number of items correct						
Mean 1994/6	30	29	33	34	25	25
s.d.	9.0	8.8	7.4	6.5	9.9	10.1
Mean 1998	32	31	31	32	27	27
s.d.	7.4	8.0	8.6	8.5	9.8	9.8
Mean proportion correct						
Mean 1994	72	70	78	81	60	59
s.d.	21.2	20.9	17.9	15.0	23.5	23.9
Mean 1998	77	74	72	76	65	65
s.d.	17.8	18.7	20.1	19.8	23.4	22.8
Base	*307*	*305*	*333*	*233*	*422*	*300*

The large standard deviations indicate the degree of dispersion on the distribution. This is better illustrated in Figure 11.7 which shows the mean proportion correct and percentiles by treatment group in each country. The distribution in France extends far lower than in either Great Britain or Sweden with a long trailing tail.

Figure 11.x **Mean proportion correct and percentiles by treatment group and country 1998**

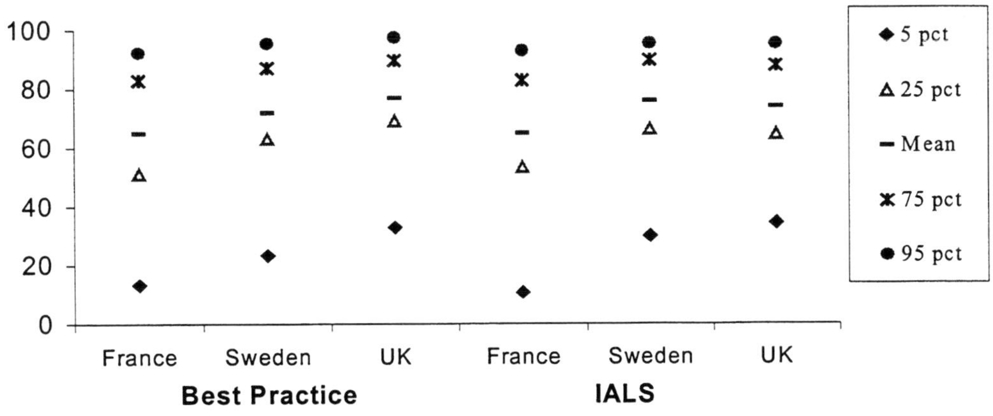

11.8.2 Scaled score

The proportion of items answered correctly is one way of summarising the item data from the assessment into an overall measure. IALS uses an alternative method of data summation, Item Response Theory (IRT) to produce an estimate of proficiency on each of the three scales. (See chapters 3 and 4 of this report for a discussion of the relative benefits and problems of different data reduction methods). In the retest the data was put through the same scaling procedure as for IALS. In order to maintain the contribution of each individual to the overall distribution at the same level as in the original IALS the same case weights were maintained. The scaling produces estimates on the three dimensions of literacy, prose literacy, document literacy and quantitative literacy for the retest samples each on a scales ranged of 0 to 500.

The following sections use the estimated proficiency levels from the scaling for each dimension.

Table 11.22 shows the correlations of the the average proificiency across five plausible values in 1994 with the average proficiency across five plausible values in 1998. The correlations are strongest in Britain which had the shortest elapsed time between first and second testing with values greater that 0.8.

Table 11.22 **Correlations between average of five plausible values in 94/6 and '98 for each dimension by treatment group and country**

	France	Sweden	Great Britain
		Correlation co-efficient	
Best Practice			
Prose	.749	.683	.814
Document	.736	.660	.800
Quantitative	.742	.655	.814
Base	*422*	*333*	*307*
IALS			
Prose	.707	.655	.803
Document	.733	.652	.801
Quantitative	.744	.636	.821
Base	*300*	*233*	*305*

In all countries, the average score of both the control group (IALS) and the treatment group (Best Practice) at the time of the original study were roughly equivalent. In both Britain and France, the Best practice or treatment group had a marginally higher but not significant mean score (3-5 points) on each scale than the replicate or IALS style sample whereas in Sweden the replicate sample had a slightly higher average score (5-8 points) than the treatment group.

Table 11.23 **Mean estimated proficiency in IALS (94/6) for each sample**

	Great Britain				**Sweden**				**France**			
	BP		**IALS**		**BP**		**IALS**		**BP**		**IALS**	
	Mean	*s.e.*	Mean	*s.e.*	Mean	*s.e.*	Mean	*s.e.*	Mean	*s.e.*	Mean	*s.e.*
Prose	289	*5.1*	286	*3.3*	308	*1.4*	312	*2.4*	252	*3.1*	247	*2.7*
Document	293	*5.7*	288	*3.7*	310	*2.7*	318	*2.9*	261	*3.4*	256	*3.2*
Quantitative	292	*5.7*	287	*3.3*	310	*2.8*	317	*3.2*	269	*3.5*	263	*2.9*
Base	*307*		*305*		*333*		*233*		*422*		*300*	

s.e. = Standard errors of the estimate.
The reported sample estimate can be said to be within 2 standard errors of the estimate

11.9 The first hypothesis – the best practice dividend

The first hypothesis being tested was that improved performance could be achieved from the respondent by increasing their engagement in the task through a series of measures, defined during the course of the project as 'Best Practice'. The control group (IALS style sample or replicate) had the survey administered in the exact same way (or as close to as possible) in the retest as in the original IALS. This group serve as the benchmark for what happens to the performance of individuals in the intervening time or how individuals might perform on an assessment at any given two points in time. Our expectation would be that there would be some skill gain or skill attrition in the intervening period or that people simply answer questions differently on two different ocassions (section 11.6). In addition to that skill acquisition or attrition there would be a performance dividend from following best practice. This would result in a higher average score for those in the treatment group (Best Practice) than for those in the control group.

11.9.1 The control group

There is no consistent pattern across the three countries in the performance of the control group. In Britain there was a small gain on the mean Prose score of 6 points, the results for the Swedish control group were identical to those the previous time on the prose scale and less than 5 points different (lower) on the other scales. The control sample in France however showed a considerable improvement in performance over the previous occasion with a gain of 16 points on the prose scale, 18 points on the document scale and 19 points on the quantitative scale.

Changes in mean score of a minor nature may have an exaggerated effect on the distribution of literacy levels if the movement is around the cusp of the levels. The assignation of scores to literacy levels is not evenly distributed along the scale of 0 – 500. The levels are defined as follows:

Level 1	**0**	**-**	**225**
Level 2	**226**	**-**	**275**
Level 3	**276**	**-**	**325**
Level 4	**326**	**-**	**375**
Level 5	**376**	**-**	**500**

It is the proportion of the population at various levels rather than mean score that is generally discussed when international comparisons are being made and certainly when results are being reported in the media. For the control group in Great Britain the gain of 6 to 9 points on the average score meant a decrease of 3% in the proportion of the replicate sample at Level 1 on each of the three scales. The case of Sweden demonstrates well the effect of averaging the scores of the population. On both document and quantitative literacy there was a decrease in mean score of 3 and 5 points respectively and this did not affect the proportion of the sub-sample at Level 1. This is hardly surprising since only a very small proportion of the population were at Level 1 on any of the scales. On the prose scale the mean score was the same for the control group on both occasions but the percentage of the sample at Level 1 decreased by 1 percentage points in 1998 over the 1994 level. At the higher literacy levels, where most of the Swedish population is distributed, 43% of the control sample were at Level 3 on the prose scale compared with 39% in 1994 with a similar reduction in the proportion of the sample at the highest literacy levels, Level 4/5 although these differences did not reach statistical significance (Table A11.11 in the appendix to this chapter).

Table 11.24 **Mean proficiency estimates and proportion at Level 1 on each scale in retest for control (IALS) sample**

	Mean proficiency estimate			Proportion at Level 1			
	1994/6	1998	Gain	1994/6		1998	
Prose				%	*s.e.*	%	*s.e.*
Great Britain	286	292	+ 5.9	11	*2.4*	8	*1.7*
Sweden	312	312	-0.4	3	*0.8*	2	*0.8*
France	247	264	+ 16.6	32	*3.1*	20	*2.1*
Document							
Great Britain	288	297	+ 9.1	12	*2.5*	9	*1.7*
Sweden	318	315	- 2.8	2	*0.4*	3	*0.9*
France	256	274	+ 18.0	27	*2.5*	17	*2.4*
Quantitative							
Great Britain	287	295	+ 7.4	13	*2.2*	10	*1.7*
Sweden	310	305	- 4.8	3	*0.5*	3	*1.4*
France	263	282	+ 18.9	24	*2.1*	16	*2.4*

s.e. = Standard errors of the estimate.
The reported sample estimate can be said to be within 2 standard errors of the estimate

In France, where there was the greatest increase in mean score in the control group the proportion of the population at Level 1 decreases by 8 to 12 percentage points. Almost a third of the control group were at Level 1 on the prose scale in the 1994 survey compared with one fifth in the 1998 survey. Similarly, 17% of the control sample were at Level 1 on document literacy in 1998 compared with 27% of the same sample at that level in 1994.

Despite the increase in scores in Great Britain and France, in 1998, Swedish respondents in the control sample, had on average a higher mean score on all three scales than in either Great Britain or France:

- Prose literacy - mean score of 312 in Sweden, 292 in Great Britain, 264 in France
- Document literacy – mean score of 315 in Sweden, 297 in Great Britain, 274 in France
- Quantitative literacy – mean score of 312 in Sweden, 295 in great Britain, 282 in France

Figure 11.7 **Control sample: Mean estimated proficiency 1998 on each scale by country**

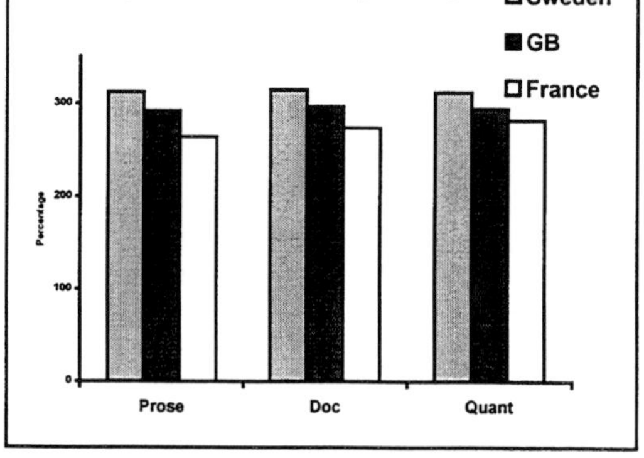

Table 11.25 shows the difference in mean proficiency values for key characteristics. There were differences between countries in how different sub-populations in the control sample performed on the two occasions. There was little difference between men and women in any of the countries in their mean score. Among the different age groups however in Sweden older people tended to have a lower score on the retest than on the original booklet but these differences were small . This was also the case in Britain for the prose and document scales. In France the oldest and youngest age groups had significantly higher mean scores. The oldest age groups had the biggest gain over their previous score, particularly those aged 46-55 who gained 27 points on their average prose proficiency level and 36 points on their average quantitative score. In France the mean score of those in the youngest age group 16-25 increased 27 points on prose, 31 points on document and 39 points on quantitative scale.

In Britain and Sweden the only group showing a gain were those with upper secondary education. In France these were the group that showed the highest gain.

For the control group the hypothesis so far holds true for only Britain and France (see chapter 13 for Portugal). The results for Sweden could indicate a 'ceiling effect' and that these people were already completely engaged in the tasks in the original study and therefore performed at their best with no room for improvement. Of all countries that took part in IALS Sweden had the highest mean score. It must be remembered that the retest sample is a sample of those who had agreed to take part in the original IALS and also agreed to a follow-up interview so are a self-selected goup who are well disposed to participating in this type of survey. Response rates to the original study also varied considerably between countries. The large increase in the mean score in the control sample in France could indicate that certain groups were poorly engaged in the original study and simply took it more seriously since we had gone to the trouble of going back to them. Compared with Britain this result might not necessarily be so surprising since there was longer elapsed time between first and second test, and if distance between tests resulted in learning rather than attrition then the results for the control group in France could simply reflect the bigger time difference. The lack of any change in Sweden over the same time period makes this explanation seem implausible.

The interaction of scoring and proficiency also needs to be kept in mind. Although every effort was made to standardise scoring across countries and across time not all items were readjusted following the inter-rater checks between waves. In France, the rescore increased the proportion who answered the question correctly for those items that were rescored. As only those most seriously affected were adjusted the retest results may underestimate the improvement in score.

However, the scoring in France IALS was found to be out of line with the scoring in IALS in Britain and so the 1994 results may be an underestimate of the proficiency compared with the distribution in Great Britain however France may be in line with the scoring in the other countries in the first round of IALS.

Table 11.25 **Difference in mean proficiency estimate of control sample between 1994/6 and 1998 on each literacy scale by sex, age group and education level**

	Prose			**Document**			**Quantitative**		
Sex	**Sweden**	**France**	**GB**	**Sweden**	**France**	**GB**	**Sweden**	**France**	**GB**
Male	2.2	16.8	4.4	-0.5	14.9	7.8	-2.3	16.0	4.9
Female	-3.2	16.6	7.5	-4.9	20.7	10.8	-6.9	21.2	10.3
Age Group									
16-25	5.9	27.3	13.8	5.2	30.9	14.0	4.0	38.7	14.1
26-35	2.1	17.4	-7.2	-1.8	16.3	-3.1	-4.2	15.8	-5.2
36-45	9.6	5.8	12.6	5.8	5.0	18.8	2.2	4.8	16.3
46-55	-10.2	26.7	12.8	-9.5	34.6	7.4	-11.6	36.2	15.5
56-65	-5.3	19.1	3.4	-8.8	22.0	4.9	-13.8	12.0	-1.7
Education Level									
Primary education or lower	*1.5*	16.8	*[-49.2]*	*-2.1*	18.0	*[-56.7]*	*0.3*	13.0	*[-42.9]*
Lower secondary level	-7.3	12.9	-0.7	-13.2	10.9	-1.7	-14.1	7.8	-1.3
Upper secondary level	21.9	10.3	9.7	17.6	8.3	15.2	16.1	10.3	6.2
Third level, university	-6.9	3.8	-2.5	-4.7	11.0	4.8	-9.7	13.7	2.6

11.9.2 The Best Practice sample

According to the hypothesis that was being tested we have so far found that the difference between first and second assessment under near identical conditions has produced different results in each country. The expected effect of introducing Best Practice, i.e. changing elements of the presentation, administration and questions to greater or lesser degrees would be a performance 'dividend'. This would result in a higher average score for those in the treatment group (Best Practice) than for those in the control group.

Figure11.8 **Difference in mean score of Best Practice over IALS by scale and country**

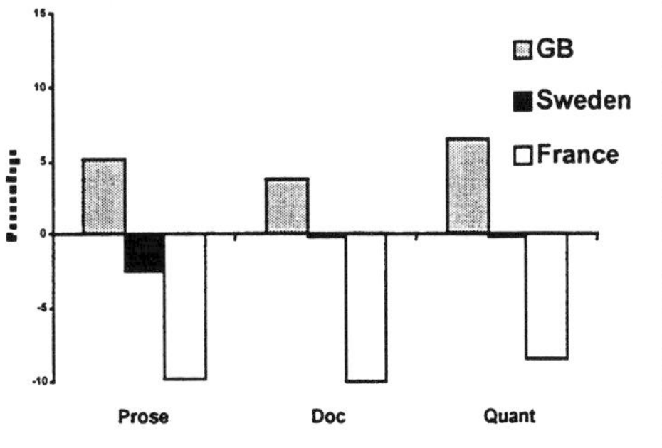

The data for Great Britain shows this expected relationship. Within the control group there was an increase of 6 – 9 points between their performance in 1996 and in 1998. The treatment group however showed a gain in average score of between 11 and 14 points, representing a gain over the control group of 4 to 7 points. As the time difference between test and retest in Britain was shorter than in the other two countries and as the differences between control and treatment conditions were less than in other countries we might have expected to find similar patterns of differences between control and treatment groups in the other countries. These differences would be expected to be greater reflecting the increased time differences between test and retest and the greater differences between control and treatment conditions, particularly in France where more aspects of the survey (including the version of the assessment used) were changed.

The results however do not fit the expected pattern. In Sweden there was no noticeable difference between control and treatment group and the average score reduced over time. Within the control group there was no difference in the average score on the prose scale and a decrease of 5 points on the quantitative scale. A similar decrease was found on the quantitative scale in the treatment group in Sweden. This could indicate as in the control group that the Swedish sample was suffering from a ceiling effect and were already performing at their best.

In France a totally different picture emerges. The average score of the control group increased by 17 to 18 points. Within the Best Practice sample, where the respondent completed the Swiss French version of the assessment, the improvement in average score was less than that in the control group, an increase of 7 to 10 points. This is in line with the reported average number correct.

Table 11.26 shows the difference in mean score for document literacy when taking literacy level as measured by the first plausible value in 1994 into account. The numbers in the cells are very small particularly in the lowest literacy level in Sweden. In France those at the lowest literacy level on the document scale showed the greatest improvement, 41 points in the IALS replicate sample. In Great Britain those at the lowest literacy level gained 30 points in the replicate sample and 38 points in the Best Practice sample.

Table 11.26 **Difference in mean proficiency estimate between 1994/6 and 1998 on the document scale by document literacy level in 1994**

	Best Practice			**IALS**		
Document literacy level 1994 (plausible value 1)	**France**	**Sweden**	**Great Britain**	**France**	**Sweden**	**Great Britain**
Level 1	16.3	[27.1]	38.2	41.1	[32.2]	29.9
Level 2	14.5	13.1	26.4	19.7	16.2	21.9
Level 3	0.3	0.1	11.9	3.2	0.2	4.2
Level 4/5	-40.7	-28	-10.3	-15.6	-25.7	-10.7
Bases						
Level 1	*80*	*12*	*27*	*69*	*4*	*35*
Level 2	*152*	*63*	*71*	*101*	*40*	*80*
Level 3	*152*	*121*	*128*	*106*	*87*	*117*
Level 4/5	*38*	*137*	*81*	*24*	*102*	*73*
Total	*422*	*333*	*307*	*300*	*233*	*305*

11.9.3 Differences within groups - Best Practice

As in the control sample there were differences within groups in the change in performance although some of these groups are very small and not statistically significant. In France, men in the Best Practice sample gained 4 to 7 points between first and second assessment. The gain for women was greater than men on all three scales but on quantitative literacy was double that for men and on document was three times the gain for men. In Britain the largest gain for men was on the prose scale.

In France those aged 46-55 showed the largest gain over their mean score in '94, and increase of 18 to 20 points on each scale. In Sweden there was no consistent pattern within the different age groups and in Britain the those aged 36-45 had the least gain in mean score. The oldest age group in Britain showed the largest increase, almost 25 points on the prose scale.

In France those with primary education had the greatest increase in mean score, 18 points on prose and 21 points on document scale. In Sweden those with upper secondary level had an increase in mean score of 5 to 9 points while those with lower secondary educaiton had a reduction of 11 to 13 points. In Britain there was little difference by educational attainment level with all groups gaining in the retest.

The gain of best practice over the control sample does not fit with the hypothesis as formulated. It has earlier been described how the proportion of respondents answering correctly on individual items was going in both directions between the two French versions used, sometimes favouring the French version of the assessment and sometimes favouring the Swiss French version (see also Chapter 6).

Table 11.27 **Mean proficiency estimates and proportion at Level 1 on each scale in IALS and retest for best practice sample**

	Mean proficiency estimate			Proportion at Level 1			
	1994/6	1998	Gain	1994/6		1998	
Prose				%	*s.e.*	%	*s.e.*
Great Britain	289	300	+ 11.0	10	*2.5*	6	*2.0*
Sweden	308	305	-2.8	4	*0.7*	4	*0.6*
France	252	259	+ 6.8	28	*2.5*	23	*2.5*
Document							
Great Britain	293	306	+ 12.8	10	*2.8*	5	*1.6*
Sweden	310	308	- 2.9	5	*0.8*	4	*0.8*
France	261	269	+ 8.0	23	*2.5*	20	*2.2*
Quantitative							
Great Britain	292	306	+ 13.9	10	*2.8*	6	*2.0*
Sweden	310	305	- 4.9	5	*1.0*	4	*0.6*
France	269	280	+ 10.4	18	*2.1*	16	*2.2*

Table 11.28 **Difference in mean proficiency estimate of best practice sample between 1994/6 and 1998 on each literacy scale by sex, age group and education level**

	Prose			Document			Quantitative		
Sex	Sweden	France	GB	Sweden	France	GB	Sweden	France	GB
Male	-4.8	5.6	14.6	-5.2	4.2	15.1	-5.9	7.2	15.5
Female	-1.1	7.8	7.2	-0.9	11.5	10.6	-4.1	13.3	12.4
Age Group									
16-25	-4.4	7.6	8.8	-3.1	7.3	13.5	0.5	18.0	10.4
26-35	-6.3	0.5	14.8	-7.8	3.8	16.2	-15.4	1.9	16.6
36-45	2.3	6.5	2.8	6.4	8.3	3.5	5.0	12.1	7.7
46-55	-3.4	18.0	10.4	-4.1	19.6	14.9	-5.7	20.7	17.0
56-65	2.3	6.0	24.5	-1.1	6.4	23.8	-6.2	-1.1	19.7
Education Level									
Primary education or lower	0.4	18.0	*[-5.5]*	0.1	20.9	*[11.7]*	-2.8	13.0	*[16.8]*
Lower secondary level	-13.3	-3.8	6.9	-11.4	-3.2	8.1	-12.7	-1.1	9.8
Upper secondary level	8.9	1.7	7.8	7.8	-1.6	8.7	4.8	3.6	10.7
Third level, university	-8.9	-7.8	4.2	-9.5	-1.1	5.5	-11.6	1.5	2.9

Many of these characteristics are interrelated. To take account of these relationships mulit-variate analysis was carried out on the proportion correct including country, age, sex, education level, treatment (Best Practice or IALS) and literacy as measured in the first survey (again using proportion correct. Only in the UK is there a significant effect for Best Practice. There was found to be no gender effect. (data not shown)

11.10 Differences in improvement between countries or pairs of countries

The second hypothesis was that there were differences in engagement in the tasks between different regions of Europe, particularly between the North and the South or Mediterranean countries. If this were true then we might expect to see the patterns of results in Sweden and Britain being similar as well as those in France and Portugal.

If the pair of hypotheses were true then the expected pattern would be as follows. In each country there would be a small increase in average score in the control group reflecting the fact that people had already taken part in IALS and might therefore approach the booklet differently. There would be an additional increase in the best practice sample reflecting the increased application or engagement in the tasks that was encouraged by best practice. The increase in Best Practice over and above the control sample would be of the same order in the two northern european countries (Sweden and Britain) and the increase in the other pairs of countries would be even greater.

In each country a different pattern emerged between the control sample and the best practice. It Sweden there was no change over time and this was the same in both parts of the sample. In Britain there was an increase in mean performance in the control sample and a larger increase in the Best Practice sample. In France there was a large increase in the mean proficiency of the control sample with a smaller improvement in the Best Practice sample. In Portugal (see chapter 13) there was a small improvement in the mean proficiency estimate (number of correct answers[12]) in the retest sample. For the retest sample in Portugal the mean number of questions answered correctly was 13.7 in the first survey in 1994 compared with an average of 14.3 when retested in 1998.

Far from being a pattern of pairs of countries the pattern is more that one country, Sweden, stands out as being different from the others both in terms of literacy profile and in how the survey was received by respondents. There are similarities between France, Britain and Portugal although in different directions and to different degrees in the improvement over time and in the completeness of the assessments.

11.11 Conclusions

The follow-up survey has provided interesting and sometimes surprising data in that some of the findings are contrary to expectations and along the way some new issues emerged or became more prominent. Although the analysis of the retest has only addressed some of the issues we hope that the data will be used by other resesarchers to shed further light on how surveys such as IALS can be improved in future.

11.11.1 Differences between two points in time

In both the control sample and in the treatment group complex interactions were observed and no consistent pattern was evident across countries in the skill measures taken at two points in time. Both snapshots are subject to error and some of those sources of error have been investigated but others remain. The results from the follow-up survey show that Britain is the only country where the findings were in line with the hypothesis being tested, that is that the profile for any population at two given points in time would differ depending on when, where and how the picture was taken. By controlling for some of the aspects thought to influence the respondent engagement in the assessment a performance dividend would be observed. France showed a similar pattern but in a different direction with a greater improvement in the control sample than is the treatment sample. There was significant improvement in mean score among particular groups of the population. There is no obvious explanation as to why the improvement using the Swiss version of the assessment was less than that using the French version. Both versions of the assessment had some questions which were problematic in comparison with the English version but the French version was most affected.

Although we did not set out to re-estimate the French sample (that would have required a much larger sample) the improvement in France in both parts of the sample is greater than in any of the other countries. Given that follow-up surveys were done in four countries and four different patterns emerged one is tempted to think that one would find as many patterns as countries had a follow-up survey been done in all countries that took part in IALS.

The complexity of the data at item level and the interaction of ability, the questions and the survey process are difficult to disentangle. While the consistency of both the version of the assessment used and the scoring reliability in France have been reviewed the other countries have not been subject to the same degree of inspection. The non-sampling error in these countries therefore is unknown. There was considerable variation at item level between countries in the same direction as the overall summary measures.

[12] Total number of questions in assessment was 33.

11.11.2 Differences in scoring.

The need to stabilise scoring is paramount in order to minimise the interaction of proficiency and scoring. The scoring of booklets is a source of survey error that can be improved. Depending on how the scoring is organised there can be several layers of possible sources of error, in particular variability between scorers and errors in data capture. We have seen from the analyses here that this is not easy to achieve.

In reviewing the scoring of the follow-up survey systematic differences were found to exist between countries. While the most serious of these were rescored it does indicate how vulnerable the scoring is to changes over time and to differences in interpretation between countries. Alternative methods to paired inter country rescores, often organised within language groups may help minimise the contribution of scoring to total survey error or at least share that error across all countries thus taking it out of between country differences.

11.11.3 Data completeness

There appear to be differences between countries in how the survey is approached by respondents. Sweden stands out among the countries involved in the follow-up survey in the application of respondents to the tasks presented as evidenced by the compliance with the request to complete a booklet. Completion of the assessment is not only to do with literacy levels as in Sweden even those with poor literacy skills seem to have made every effort to complete the assessment. In surveys which aim to measure something as intrinsic to each individual as their literacy proficiency then every effort must be made to maximise data from the respondent and to encourage respondents to try their best to answer accurately. We have seen from the analysis at item level that it possible to reduce the item non-response through the implementation of such measures as formed part of the Best Practice at least in some countries. It is useful to be able to distinguish between different types of wrong anwers and future surveys of this type might consider capturing this distinction. There were differences between countries in the attitudes reported to the booklet and perhaps this also needs to be taken into account into estimating proficiency in future surveys of this type.

Appendix

Tables A11.1 – A11.12

Table A11.1 **Percentage who have attained at least upper secondary education (ISCED 3) by age group and country**

Country	**Age-group**			
	25-34	35-45	45-54	55-64
	Percentage who have attained ISCED 3			
France	84	73	60	41
Great Britain	86	79	69	58
Sweden	85	78	69	52

Table A11.2 **France: IALS literacy level by sex**

	Level 1		**Level 2**		**Level 3**		**Level 4/5**		**Total**	**Mean score**	***Base***
Sex	%	s.e.	%	s.e.	%	s.e.	%	s.e.	%		
										Prose literacy	
Men	44	1.5	32	1.5	21	1.1	3	0.3	100	229	*1343*
Women	39	0.8	35	1.0	22	0.8	4	0.4	100	237	*1653*
Total	41	0.8	34	0.8	22	0.8	3	0.2	100	233	*2996*
Document literacy											
Men	36	1.4	31	1.0	27	0.9	6	0.6	100	240	*1343*
Women	37	1.2	32	1.4	24	0.6	6	0.3	100	238	*1653*
Total	36	0.8	32	1.0	26	0.6	6	0.4	100	239	*2996*
Quantitative literacy											
Men	31	1.7	29	1.3	29	1.5	12	0.9	100	249	*1343*
Women	35	1.0	31	1.3	27	0.6	7	0.5	100	241	*1653*
Total	33	1.0	30	0.9	28	0.7	9	0.5	100	245	*2996*

s.e. = Standard errors of the estimate. The reported sample estimate can be said to be within 2 standard errors of the estimate

Table A11.3 **IALS literacy level by age and country**

		Level 1		Level 2		Level 3		Level 4/5		Total	Mean score	Base
Age group		%	s.e.	%	s.e.	%	s.e.	%	s.e.			
Prose literacy												
France	16-25	27	2.7	35	2.7	32	2.4	6	0.5	100	254	581
	26-35	34	2.0	38	2.4	25	1.4	3	0.4	100	242	796
	36-45	36	2.5	36	1.8	24	2.3	3	0.6	100	239	688
	46-55	51	2.5	30	2.2	17	2	3	0.5	100	220	438
	56-65	67	2.1	27	2.3	5	0.7	1	0.3	100	194	493
Great Britain	16-25	17	1.7	30	2.4	33	2.7	20	1.8	100	274	*549*
	26-35	18	1.5	29	2.0	34	2.0	19	1.5	100	275	*991*
	36-45	17	1.3	29	2.3	33	2.2	21	1.6	100	277	*844*
	46-55	22	2.6	29	2.7	35	2.4	14	1.3	100	264	*724*
	56-65	39	2.2	37	2.2	19	1.5	6	1.2	100	236	*703*
Sweden	16-25	4	1.0	17	1.5	40	2.0	40	1.4	100	312	*575*
	26-35	5	0.8	14	1.5	39	2.5	42	2.9	100	313	*562*
	36-45	7	0.7	20	1.4	42	1.3	32	1.1	100	300	*563*
	46-55	8	1.4	22	1.7	42	1.9	28	2.5	100	296	*562*
	56-65	16	2.5	33	1.8	35	2.1	16	2.4	100	276	*382*
Document literacy												
France	16-25	22	3.3	30	2.9	38	2.7	11	1.3	100	266	581
	26-35	30	1.7	35	1.1	28	1.6	7	0.5	100	249	796
	36-45	30	2.0	36	2.2	29	2.3	5	0.7	100	246	688
	46-55	47	1.3	27	2.8	21	2.1	4	0.8	100	224	438
	56-65	63	3.0	28	3.3	8	0.9	1	0.4	100	195	493
Great Britain	16-25	18	1.8	27	1.9	34	2.4	22	2.0	100	276	*549*
	26-35	19	1.6	25	2.2	32	1.8	23	1.6	100	278	*991*
	36-45	19	1.7	24	2.3	32	2	24	1.8	100	278	*844*
	46-55	24	2.3	28	1.7	31	2.9	16	1.6	100	264	*724*
	56-65	40	2.4	33	2.3	21	1.3	6	1.0	100	233	*703*
Sweden	16-25	3	0.8	17	1.9	40	1.5	41	1.6	100	314	*575*
	26-35	4	0.9	10	1.2	38	2.7	48	3.7	100	320	*562*
	36-45	7	0.5	18	1.6	40	1.7	35	1.6	100	305	*563*
	46-55	7	1	20	1.8	43	2.5	30	2.1	100	302	*562*
	56-65	12	1.8	33	1.8	36	2.3	19	19	100	234	*382*
Quantitative literacy												
France	16-25	23	3.1	30	2.8	35	1.7	12	1.1	100	262	581
	26-35	27	1.8	31	1.2	30	1.5	13	0.8	100	256	796
	36-45	28	1.8	33	2.8	30	2.5	10	1.3	100	254	688
	46-55	39	1.7	27	1.9	26	2.5	8	1.3	100	233	438
	56-65	56	2.8	27	3.0	15	1.1	2	0.4	100	206	493
Great Britain	16-25	22	1.7	29	2.5	33	2.4	16	2.1	100	265	*549*
	26-35	20	1.7	28	2	30	2	23	1.6	100	277	*991*
	36-45	19	1.2	24	2	32	1.9	25	1.5	100	279	*844*
	46-55	24	2.3	26	2	33	2.8	17	1.7	100	266	*724*
	56-65	35	2.3	34	2.5	23	1.8	8	0.9	100	240	*703*
Sweden	16-25	5	0.7	18	1.8	39	2.2	38	1.9	100	309	*575*
	26-35	4	1	14	1.9	36	1.4	45	2.7	100	317	*562*
	36-45	7	0.6	16	1.4	41	1.5	35	1.5	100	307	*563*
	46-55	6	1.1	20	1.5	40	1.9	34	1.9	100	307	*562*
	56-65	13	2.1	27	2.7	38	2.5	23	2.3	100	285	*382*

se = Standard errors of the estimate. The reported sample estimate can be said to be within 2 standard errors of the estimate.

Table A11.4 **France: IALS literacy level by highest level of educational attainment and sex**

	Level 1		Level 2		Level 3		Level 4/5		Total	Mean score	*Base*
Prose literacy	%	s.e.	%	s.e.	%	s.e.	%	s.e.	%		
Men											
Primary education or lower	84	3.2	14	2.8	2	1.1	0	0.0	100	164	*183*
Second level, 1st stage	59	5.7	33	4.5	8	2.4	0	0.3	100	210	*171*
Second level, 2nd stage	35	2.3	43	3.0	20	2.3	2	0.5	100	240	*593*
Third level, non-university	9	3.1	29	3.4	54	2.0	8	1.7	100	280	*127*
Third level, university	6	1.7	24	4.2	55	2.6	15	2.7	100	291	*250*
Total	41	0.8	34	0.8	22	0.8	3	0.2	100	233	*1324*
Women											
Primary education or lower	80	3.9	19	4.0	1	0.6	0	0.0	100	179	*258*
Second level, 1st stage	55	4.7	37	4.5	8	2.4	0	0.0	100	217	*235*
Second level, 2nd stage	22	1.9	47	1.6	28	1.2	2	0.4	100	255	*674*
Third level, non-university	6	1.8	30	5.4	54	5.9	10	2.3	100	286	*162*
Third level, university	6	1.8	25	2.3	49	2.6	20	1.7	100	292	*308*
Total	44	1.5	32	1.5	21	1.1	3	0.3	100	229	*1637*
All											
Primary education or lower	82	2.1	17	2.1	2	0.6	-	-	100	172	*441*
Second level, 1st stage	57	2.8	35	2.5	8	1.5	0	0.2	100	214	*406*
Second level, 2nd stage	29	1.1	45	1.5	24	1.4	2	0.3	100	247	*1267*
Third level, non-university	8	1.4	29	3.1	54	2.8	9	1.5	100	283	*289*
Third level, university	6	1.0	25	2.9	52	2.2	17	1.5	100	292	*558*
Total	39	0.8	35	1.0	22	0.8	4	0.4	100	237	*2961*
Document literacy											
Men											
Primary education or lower	78	4.2	19	3.1	4	1.7	0	0.0	100	168	*183*
Second level, 1st stage	50	5.2	31	3.4	17	4.6	2	1.0	100	222	*171*
Second level, 2nd stage	24	1.6	42	1.9	29	1.9	5	1.1	100	256	*593*
Third level, non-university	7	2.2	22	3.1	60	5.7	11	2.7	100	288	*127*
Third level, university	5	1.7	16	3.5	54	4.3	26	3.0	100	303	*250*
Total	36	1.4	31	1.0	27	0.9	6	0.6	100	240	*1324*
Women											
Primary education or lower	80	3.9	19	4.0	1	0.5	-	-	100	173	*258*
Second level, 1st stage	51	4.2	39	4.0	10	2.3	-	-	100	216	*235*
Second level, 2nd stage	20	1.9	39	1.8	36	1.3	6	0.7	100	262	*674*
Third level, non-university	7	1.7	34	2.2	43	2.9	16	2.0	100	287	*162*
Third level, university	6	1.8	26	2.7	44	3.1	24	2.3	100	294	*308*
Total	37	1.2	32	1.4	24	0.6	6	0.3	100	238	*1637*
All											
Primary education or lower	79	2.2	19	2.1	2	0.8	0	0.0	100	170	*441*
Second level, 1st stage	51	2.8	35	2.7	13	2.4	1	0.5	100	219	*406*
Second level, 2nd stage	22	1.2	40	1.4	32	1.0	5	0.7	100	259	*1267*
Third level, non-university	7	1.8	28	1.7	52	2.8	14	1.2	100	288	*289*
Third level, university	5	1.0	21	2.4	49	2.9	25	2.3	100	298	*558*
Total	36	0.8	32	1.0	26	0.6	6	0.4	100	239	*2961*

Table A11.4 cont. **France: IALS literacy level by highest level of educational attainment and sex**

	Level 1		**Level 2**		**Level 3**		**Level 4/5**		**Total**	**Mean score**	***Base***
Quantitative literacy	%	s.e.	%	s.e.	%	s.e.	%	s.e.	%		
Men											
Primary education or lower	70	4.1	21	3.8	8	1.7	1	0.5	100	175	*183*
Second level, 1st stage	44	7.0	33	4.7	20	5.7	4	1.2	100	228	*171*
Second level, 2nd stage	19	2.0	37	2.2	34	2.8	10	1.8	100	266	*593*
Third level, non-university	4	1.6	19	3.5	50	4.9	27	3.5	100	300	*127*
Third level, university	4	1.8	13	2.0	45	2.5	38	2.7	100	311	*250*
Total	33	1.0	30	0.9	28	0.7	9	0.5	100	245	*1324*
Women											
Primary education or lower	74	2.9	22	3.1	4	1.4	0	0.0	100	176	*258*
Second level, 1st stage	51	4.5	34	4.1	15	2.3	0	0.0	100	218	*235*
Second level, 2nd stage	19	2.0	36	2.2	38	1.5	7	1.4	100	264	*674*
Third level, non-university	4	1.2	28	3.4	45	3.6	22	3.2	100	294	*162*
Third level, university	5	1.6	25	2.3	44	2.9	26	1.9	100	296	*308*
Total	31	1.7	29	1.3	29	1.5	12	0.9	100	249	*1637*
All											
Primary education or lower	72	2.1	22	2.3	6	1.0	0	0.2	100	176	*441*
Second level, 1st stage	48	3.7	33	3.7	17	2.7	2	0.6	100	223	*406*
Second level, 2nd stage	19	1.3	36	1.3	36	1.3	8	1.2	100	265	*1267*
Third level, non-university	4	0.9	24	1.4	47	3.1	24	2.2	100	297	*289*
Third level, university	5	0.8	18	1.5	44	1.6	32	1.9	100	303	*558*
Total	35	1.0	31	1.3	27	0.6	7	0.5	100	241	*2961*

s.e. = Standard errors of the estimate. The reported sample estimate can be said to be within 2 standard errors of the estimate

Table A11.5 **France: IALS literacy level by economic activity status**

Economic activity status	**Level 1**		**Level 2**		**Level 3**		**Level 4/5**		**Total**	**Mean score**	***Base***
	%	s.e.	%	s.e.	%	s.e.	%	s.e.	%		
Prose literacy											
Working	38	1.1	35	1.4	24	1.0	4	0.3	100	238	*1688*
Employed	65	3.6	28	4.1	6	1.0	1	0.4	100	196	*309*
Student	14	3.3	34	3.9	42	3.2	9	1.8	100	272	*307*
Inactive	52	2.1	33	1.8	14	1.3	1	0.3	100	216	*692*
Total	41	0.8	34	0.8	22	0.8	3	0.2	100	233	*2996*
Document literacy											
Employed	32	0.7	34	1.3	28	1.2	6	0.4	100	246	*1688*
Unemployed		3.6	27	3.7	11	1.7	0	0.4	100	196	*309*
Student	9	2.9	27	2.8	47	3.3	17	2.4	100	287	*307*
Inactive	49	3.0	31	3.1	17	1.2	3	0.5	100	219	*692*
Total	36	0.8	32	0.9	26	0.6	6	0.4	100	240	*2996*
Quantitative literacy											
Employed	28	0.9	30	1.7	30	1.4	12	0.7	100	255	*1688*
Unemployed	52	3.1	24	3.2	20	2.6	3	0.8	100	212	*309*
Student	13	3.2	28	3.2	44	2.5	16	2.5	100	280	*307*
Inactive	46	3.2	31	3.1	18	1.3	4	0.8	100	219	*692*
Total	33	1	30	0.9	28	0.7	9	0.5	100	245	*2996*

s.e. = Standard errors of the estimate.
The reported sample estimate can be said to be within 2 standard errors of the estimate

Table A11.6 **France: IALS literacy level by frequency of reading newspapers and magazines**

	Level 1		**Level 2**		**Level 3**		**Level 4/5**		**Total**	**Mean score**	***Base***
Frequency of reading	%	s.e.	%	s.e.	%	s.e.	%	s.e.	%		
Prose literacy											
Daily	38	1.4	35	1.8	23	1.2	4	0.3	100	238	*1384*
Weekly	39	2.2	36	1.4	22	1.3	4	0.3	100	236	*1169*
Monthly	41	3.3	30	3.2	24	1.3	4	1.3	100	237	*214*
Several times a year	47	3.5	28	3.7	21	3.3	4	1.9	100	225	*104*
Never	80	6.8	16	6.2	4	2.3	0	0	100	155	*117*
Total	41	0.8	34	0.8	22	0.8	3	0.2	100	233	*2988*
Document literacy											
Daily	35	1.5	31	1.3	27	0.5	7	0.8	100	244	*1384*
Weekly	33	2.1	35	1.7	26	1.3	6	0.4	100	244	*1169*
Monthly	37	3.5	28	3.2	27	3.0	8	2.1	100	244	*214*
Several times a year	39	5.1	31	3.9	24	4.4	7	1.9	100	234	*104*
Never	75	6.4	19	4.4	6	2.6	0	0.0	100	152	*117*
Total	36	0.8	32	1.0	26	0.6	6	0.4	100	239	*2988*
Quantitativ e literacy											
Daily	30	1.2	30	0.8	30	1.1	10	0.9	100	252	*1384*
Weekly	31	2.0	32	1.5	28	1.1	10	0.7	100	248	*1169*
Monthly	33	3.0	26	4.0	27	3.1	13	1.5	100	247	*214*
Several times a year	39	6.3	28	4.7	26	4.3	7	1.8	100	234	*104*
Never	72	5.8	16	3.5	12	4.5	0	0.5	100	154	*117*
Total	33	1.0	30	0.9	28	0.7	9	0.5	100	245	*2988*

s.e. = Standard errors of the estimate.

The reported sample estimate can be said to be within 2 standard errors of the estimate

Table A11.7 **Nature of discrepancies in scoring: France**		
Item	**Discrepancy**	**Number of discrepancies**
B1Q1 Refrigerator door	In 1994, respondents only had to say the door was left open too long or opened too frequently; in 1998, they had to specify both.	51
B1Q2 Energy saver switch	In 1998, but not in 1994, this item was marked wrong if 'Not unusual during period of high humidity' was included in the answer because it was seen as contradictory.	13
B1Q5 Three reasons for using disposable nappies	In 1994, but not in 1998, minimally correct answers such as 'happier baby' or 'bags of clothes' were accepted as correct.	56
B2Q1 Impatiens: what do the smooth leaf surface and stems suggest?	In 1994, but not in 1998, minimally correct answers such as 'needs water' were accepted as correct. 'Sensitive to cold' and 'tropical origin' were accepted as complementary in 1994, but not in 1998.	10
B2Q3 Impatiens: subject to cold	'Stems will rot' was accepted as complementary in 1994, but marked wrong in 1998.	7
B2Q6 Embryos: what the Australians did	No clear pattern of discrepancies.	6
B2Q7 Embryos: give two examples	In 1994, but not in 1998, minimal responses such as 'dead husband', 'legal case', 'sperm of dead husband' were accepted as correct.	21
B3Q2 Oil charts	No clear pattern of discrepancies.	14
B3Q7 Job advertisement	In 1994, but not in 1998, anything from the first two paragraphs, such as 'products manufactured', 'services provided', or 'would you be replacing someone or is it a new position?' was accepted as correct.	19
B3Q8 Group versus panel interview	No clear pattern of discrepancies. Some respondents were marked more leniently in 1994 than in 1998, others more strictly.	17
B3Q9 Post interview debrief	In 1994, answers such as 'Know your strong points' were accepted as correct, whereas in 1998 respondents had to specify that applicants had to learn from the debrief for future interviews.	26
B3Q11 Bicycle: saddle	In 1994, but not in 1998, 'foot on pedal' was accepted as correct if other relevant information was given.	17
B3Q13 Allergy sufferer	This item was incorrectly translated as 'herite de la mere allergique'. Allowance was made for this in 1994, but not in 1998.	59
B3Q15 Explorers	The scoring guide was applied incorrectly in 1998. Respondents who had not underlined '95-day walk' but who had underlined another part of the correct sentence, were marked wrong.	11
B4Q4 Photocopy form	In 1994, but not in 1998, 'more than the maximum' was accepted as correct.	14
B4Q6 Warranty: establishing validity	In 1994, 'check the receipt' was accepted as correct, whereas in 1998, respondents had to specify 'keep the receipt'.	36
B4Q7 Warranty: 1/5 year difference	No clear pattern of discrepancies.	12
B5Q4 Child seat	No clear pattern of discrepancies.	11
B5Q6 Child seat: three things to keep in mind	Some answers were marked more leniently and others more strictly in 1998 than in 1994. In 1994 'age of child' was accepted without weight or height, but 'fits my car', was not accepted. Respondents had to specify the front or back of the car.	33
B5Q10 Fireworks	In 1994, 'proportional' and 'parallel' were accepted as correct, whereas in 1998, respondents had to specify that both sales of fireworks and injuries had increased.	13
B6Q1 Recipe	In 1994, but not in 1998, 'acidity' or 'because of acidity' were accepted as correct.	6
B7Q11 Post interview	No clear pattern of discrepancies.	7
B7Q14 Fire precautions	In 1994 respondents only had to write 'Know the telephone number of the fire brigade'; in 1998, they had to specify that the number should be kept on the telephone.	47
B7Q15 Fire in cars	The scoring guide was interpreted too strictly in 1998; 'extinguisher in car' was not accepted as correct.	9

Table A11.8 **Proportion of respondents who omitted questions in retest (1998) by type of sample and country (score 3)**

Item	Scale / Level	GB BP	GB IALS	Sweden BP	Sweden IALS	France BP	France IALS	Portugal
Block 1		*% omitted*						
Q1	D3	1	..	2	..	..	2	4
Q2	D2	1	1	1	3	2	..	4
Q3	Exc.	1	2	1	1	..	..	1
Q4	Q3	2	5	2	1	1	3	2
Q5	P3	2	5	2	2	3	4	4
Q6	P3	4	7	8	7	6	11	5
Q7	Q3	1	2	1	4	2	8	3
Q8	Exc.	2	4	3	4	3	9	6
Q9	Q3	2	4	3	4	3	10	4
Q10	P2	2	3	3	2	1	4	5
Q11	P5	3	4	5	4	5	6	8
Q12	Exc.	6	6	8	8	8	11	13
Q13	D2	5	3	1	1	..	2	1
Q14	Q3	..	5	2	1	1	6	6
Q15	Q2	..	3	4	3	..	3	3
Base		*128*	*131*	*133*	*109*	*190*	*119*	*492*
Block 2		**BP**	**IALS**	**BP**	**IALS**	**BP**	**IALS**	
Q1	P2	1	1	1	3	6	5	5
Q2	Exc.	1	3	1	2	7	14	8
Q3	P2	1	..	1	1	3	4	3
Q4	Q3	1	2	2	2	..	4	2
Q5	Q5	3	3	6	8	3	9	6
Q6	P4	5	4	4	3	9	10	9
Q7	P4	4	8	15	11	8	20	11
Q8	D3	4	6	1	..	7	10	8
Q9	Q2	3	4	2	1	2	8	5
Q10	D3	3	3	1	1	3	6	5
Q111	D2	..	..	3	1	2	5	3
Q112	D3	1	..	3	1	2	5	3
Q113	D2	1	..	3	1	2	5	3
Q114	D1	..	..	3	1	2	5	3
Q115	D2	2	3	3	1	2	5	3
Base		*125*	*122*	*151*	*107*	*182*	*143*	*465*
Block 3								
Q1	Q3	3	3	5	2	2	10	4
Q2	D4	4	6	14	7	8	16	7
Q3	Q3	2	4	8	3	2	15	4
Q4	Exc.	..	4	..	..	1	3	2
Q5	D2	..	4	1	..	2	4	3
Q6	Q2	..	4	1	..	1	3	2
Q7	P3	..	2	2	..	1	4	3
Q8	P4	..	5	11	4	5	15	6
Q9	P3	..	5	10	5	2	9	4
Q10	Exc.	..	4	3	1	1	5	2
Q11	P3	..	5	4	1	3	6	3
Q12	P3	..	5	3	2	3	9	4
Q13	P3	2	3	5	1	2	5	4
Q14	Q4	2	3	8	3	4	9	5
Q15	P2	2	3	6	2	6	11	6
Base		*137*	*148*	*134*	*95*	*170*	*117*	*497*

Table A11.8 cont. **Proportion of respondents who omitted questions in retest (1998) by type of sample and country (score 3)**

Item	Scale /Level	GB BP	GB IALS	Sweden BP	Sweden IALS	France BP	France IALS	Portugal
					% omitted			
Block 4								
Q1	P1	1	4	..	..	2	2	..
Q2	P2	1	4	1	..	2	2	1
Q3	Q2	1	4	1	..	1	2	1
Q4	D3	5	7	10	17	5	14	8
Q5 .1	D3	3	13	12	15	15	15	10
Q5 .2	Q3	5	13	13	15	14	15	10
Q6	P3	2	3	1	2	4	4	2
Q7	P3	2	3	5	3	2	6	3
Q8	Exc.	2	3	..	1	2	2	2
Q9	Q3	..	4	1	1	2	4	3
Q10	Q5	2	5	14	14	11	18	8
Q11	Q3	..	4	1	2	2	4	3
Q12.1	D2	1	1	1	1	2	1	2
Q12.2	D2	1	2	1	1	2	1	2
Q12.3	D1	..	1	1	1	2	1	2
Q12.4	D1	..	1	1	1	2	1	2
Q12.5	Q2	..	1	1	1	2	1	2
Q12.6	Q1	..	1	1	1	2	1	2
Base		*129*	*135*	*141*	*103*	*178*	*123*	*493*
Block 5								
Q1	P1	1	1	1	..	3	6	5
Q2	P2	..	1	1	..	3	4	4
Q3	P2	..	..	2	2	1	1	2
Q4	P4	2	2	8	10	4	14	10
Q5	P3	..	1	3	1	3	10	7
Q6	P3	..	2	4	1	4	7	8
Q7	D2	..	..	1	1	1	1	1
Q8	D3	1	1	2	1	3	2	3
Q9	Q3	..	..	1	1	3	3	3
Q10	D3	1	2	6	6	3	13	8
Q11.1	Q4	6	9	5	14	1	7	10
Q11.2	Q4	2	4	5	10	1	7	10
Q11.3	Exc.	2	3	5	10	1	7	10
Q11.4	D3	3	3	5	10	1	7	10
Q12	D3	1	..	8	7	1	6	3
Q13	Q4	1	4	15	12	4	10	8
Q14	Q3	..	2	14	13	2	10	6
Base		*136*	*122*	*134*	*101*	*196*	*145*	*496*
Block 6								
Q1	P1	2	2	1	1	1	2	1
Q2	Q3	2	2	1	1	2	..	1
Q3	Q2	2	2	1	1	1	..	..
Q4	D1	..	2	2	..	1	2	2
Q5	Q3	..	2	2	..	5	5	3
Q6	D3	1	6	2	4	2	8	4
Q7	P2	..	2	2	1	3	7	3
Q8	P3	1	5	2	1	4	9	6
Q9	D2	2	6	5	4	1	5	7
Q10	Q4	2	4	6	7	7	5	9
Q11	D3	2	4	8	9	4	8	10
Q12	Exc.	1	3	1	1	..	3	1
Q13	Exc.	..	2	1	3	1	3	2
Base		*128*	*123*	*126*	*69*	*170*	*125*	*502*

Table A11.8 cont. **Proportion of respondents who omitted questions in retest (1998) by type of sample and country (score 3)**

		GB		Sweden		France		Portugal
		BP	IALS	BP	IALS	BP	IALS	
Block 7		*% omitted*						
Q1	D1	..	..	1	1	..	1	1
Q2	Q2	..	3	3	4	4	3	3
Q3	D2	..	1	1	1	..	2	2
Q4	D2	1	1	2	3	1	5	4
Q5	Q3	..	3	7	10	8	14	6
Q6	Q3	1	3	10	10	5	7	5
Q7	D4	..	5	2	6	1	5	3
Q8	D3	..	4	11	10	5	9	7
Q9	D5	..	5	6	5	3	7	5
Q10	P2	2	2	10	6	4	10	6
Q11	P4	1	3	9	7	2	10	8
Q12	Exc.	1	7	22	15	3	6	9
Q13	P1	1	2	2	..	..	..	1
Q14	P3	1	2	2	..	1	2	3
Q15	P2	1	3	6	2	3	1	7
Base		*123*	*131*	*162*	*115*	*174*	*125*	*487*

Table A11.9 **Proportion of respondents who crossed out questions in retest (1998) by type of sample and country (score 3)**

Item	Scale / Level	GB BP	GB IALS	Sweden BP	Sweden IALS	France BP	France IALS	Portugal
Block 1				*% skipped*				
Q1	D3	..	2	..	..	3	2	4
Q2	D2	..	1	..	..	4	2	3
Q3	Exc.	..	1	..	..	3	1	2
Q4	Q3	2	1	..	..	4	1	4
Q5	P3	1	1	..	..	6	2	6
Q6	P3	1	1	..	..	3	1	4
Q7	Q3	5	6	..	..	8	3	9
Q8	Exc.	3	7	..	..	8	2	9
Q9	Q3	6	8	1	..	8	3	10
Q10	P2	2	2	..	..	9	2	7
Q11	P5	2	3	..	..	13	2	12
Q12	Exc.	6	5	1	..	20	3	20
Q13	D2	1	1	..	..	3	1	2
Q14	Q3	3	2	..	..	8	3	11
Q15	Q2	1	2	..	..	6	3	8
Base		*128*	*131*	*133*	*109*	*190*	*119*	*492*
Block 2		**BP**	**IALS**	**BP**	**IALS**	**BP**	**IALS**	
Q1	P2	2	3	1	..	8	2	9
Q2	Exc.	5	9	1	..	6	4	14
Q3	P2	2	2	..	..	3	2	7
Q4	Q3	1	2	..	..	2	2	7
Q5	Q5	9	11	3	..	8	6	14
Q6	P4	5	3	..	1	2	1	6
Q7	P4	20	15	3	5	13	5	22
Q8	D3	1	3	..	..	3	1	3
Q9	Q2	5	2	..	..	7	2	7
Q10	D3	2	3	..	..	5	2	5
Q111	D2	1	0	..	..	2	..	4
Q112	D3	1	0	..	..	2	..	4
Q113	D2	1	0	..	..	3	..	4
Q114	D1	2	0	..	..	3	..	4
Q115	D2	1	0	..	..	3	1	4
Base		*125*	*122*	*151*	*107*	*182*	*143*	*465*
Block 3								
Q1	Q3	7	9	2	..	8	3	9
Q2	D4	10	13	1	1	15	5	16
Q3	Q3	7	5	1	..	7	3	7
Q4	Exc.	1	1	..	..	4	4	4
Q5	D2	2	1	..	..	5	3	4
Q6	Q2	1	1	..	..	5	3	6
Q7	P3	2	1	..	..	5	3	6
Q8	P4	6	2	..	..	8	4	12
Q9	P3	4	0	..	..	7	3	10
Q10	Exc.	..	3	1	..	3	3	5
Q11	P3	..	1	..	..	4	4	7
Q12	P3	..	3	..	..	2	1	4
Q13	P3	2	1	1	1	6	3	9
Q14	Q4	4	8	2	..	9	5	13
Q15	P2	1	0	1	..	3	1	6
Base		137	148	134	95	170	117	497

Table A11.9 cont. **Proportion of respondents who crossed out questions in retest (1998) by type of sample and country (score 3)**

Item	Scale /Level	GB BP	IALS	Sweden BP	IALS	France BP	IALS	Portugal
					% skipped			
Block 4								
Q1	P1	..	..	..	..	1	..	2
Q2	P2	..	..	1	..	2	1	3
Q3	Q2	..	..	..	..	1	..	2
Q4	D3	9	19	4	2	15	5	19
Q5.1	D3	12	16	4	3	14	2	15
Q5 .2	Q3	14	15	4	3	15	2	15
Q6	P3	..	2	..	..	5	2	2
Q7	P3	..	1	1	..	7	2	5
Q8	Exc.	..	..	1	..	5	2	3
Q9	Q3	..	2	1	..	7	1	6
Q10	Q5	11	13	4	3	..	6	16
Q11	Q3	..	1	1	..	7	2	7
Q12.1	D2	1	..	..	..	1	..	4
Q12.2	D2	1	..	..	..	1	..	4
Q12.3	D1	1	..	..	..	2	..	4
Q12.4	D1	1	..	..	..	2	..	4
Q12.5	Q2	1	..	..	..	2	..	4
Q12.6	Q1	1	..	..	..	1	..	4
Base		*129*	*135*	*141*	*103*	*178*	*123*	*493*
Block 5								
Q1	P1	1	..	..	..	2	..	3
Q2	P2	1	..	..	..	3	1	3
Q3	P2	..	1	..	1	1	1	5
Q4	P4	5	9	3	2	9	3	17
Q5	P3	1	3	1	1	5	3	9
Q6	P3	3	3	2	1	10	3	14
Q7	D2	1	1	..	..	4	1	3
Q8	D3	1	1	..	..	6	1	3
Q9	Q3	2	1	..	..	5	2	4
Q10	D3	8	12	5	2	16	4	14
Q11.1	Q4	9	10	5	1	10	2	13
Q11.2	Q4	9	12	6	1	11	3	14
Q11.3	Exc.	9	12	5	1	10	2	14
Q11.4	D3	8	12	6	1	11	2	14
Q12	D3	7	6	3	3	15	2	7
Q13	Q4	10	10	6	5	19	4	13
Q14	Q3	11	11	9	5	25	4	16
Base		*136*	*122*	*134*	*101*	*196*	*145*	*496*
Block 6								
Q1	P1	1	..	..	..	1	..	1
Q2	Q3	..	..	..	..	1	1	1
Q3	Q2	1	..	..	..	1	1	2
Q4	D1	..	1	2	..	1	1	4
Q5	Q3	1	2	1	..	2	2	6
Q6	D3	5	3	3	..	6	3	8
Q7	P2	4	2	..	..	7	2	7
Q8	P3	5	2	..	..	8	3	11
Q9	D2	8	8	2	..	6	4	17
Q10	Q4	8	8	1	..	8	6	17
Q11	D3	7	11	4	..	9	10	21
Q12	Exc.	2	2	..	..	5	..	3
Q13	Exc.	2	3	..	..	5	..	3
Base		*128*	*123*	*126*	*69*	*170*	*125*	*502*

Table A11.9 cont. **Proportion of respondents who crossed out questions in retest (1998) by type of sample and country (score 3)**

		GB BP	IALS	Sweden BP	IALS	France BP	IALS	Portugal
Block 7					*% skipped*			
Q1	D1	2	..	..	..	2	..	3
Q2	Q2	4	5	1	1	12	2	8
Q3	D2	2	1	..	..	4	..	2
Q4	D2	1	2	..	..	5	1	7
Q5	Q3	6	8	1	2	16	5	9
Q6	Q3	7	7	3	..	12	8	8
Q7	D4	3	5	1	1	7	2	9
Q8	D3	11	8	3	2	14	9	16
Q9	D5	4	6	2	3	11	4	13
Q10	P2	2	3	3	1	8	6	12
Q11	P4	3	7	3	..	10	5	16
Q12	Exc.	10	11	3	3	10	7	19
Q13	P1	2	..	..	..	2	..	2
Q14	P3	2	..	1	..	4	..	4
Q15	P2	2	2	1	..	8	3	9
Base		*123*	*131*	*162*	*115*	*174*	*125*	*487*

Table A11.10 **Proportion of respondents who omitted or crossed out questions in IALS (1994/6) by country (score 5)**

Item	Scale / Level	GB Omit	GB Skip	Sweden Omit	Sweden Skip	France Omit	France Skip
				Percentage			
Block 1							
Q1	D3	2	..	3	..	5	3
Q2	D2	2	..	1	..	3	4
Q3	Exc.	2	..	1	..	4	2
Q4	Q3	2	..	4	..	5	5
Q5	P3	3	2	4	..	7	6
Q6	P3	6	2	5	..	12	7
Q7	Q3	5	6	3	..	10	6
Q8	Exc.	5	6	9	..	7	5
Q9	Q3	6	6	6	..	14	5
Q10	P2	4	2	5	..	9	8
Q11	P5	8	5	8	..	14	13
Q12	Exc.	11	7	13	..	20	20
Q13	D2	1	..	1	..	1	1
Q14	Q3	4	4	4	..	3	3
Q15	Q2	4	2	3	..	3	5
Base		*241*	*241*	*79*	*79*	*153*	*153*
Block 2							
Q1	P2	3	3	3	..	8	6
Q2	Exc.	9	6	4	..	14	11
Q3	P2	6	3	3	..	6	6
Q4	Q3	1	4	3	..	3	3
Q5	Q5	9	7	9	2	6	9
Q6	P4	3	3	1	..	12	4
Q7	P4	11	14	28	..	17	14
Q8	D3	4	1	1	..	4	1
Q9	Q2	4	3	3	..	5	4
Q10	D3	5	2	3	..	4	3
Q111	D2	2	1	..	..	6	4
Q112	D3	3	2	..	..	5	4
Q113	D2	2	1	..	..	5	4
Q114	D1	2	1	..	..	5	4
Q115	D2	2	1	..	..	5	4
Base		*235*	*235*	*71*	*71*	*181*	*181*
Block 3							
Q1	Q3	4	6	4	..	9	12
Q2	D4	11	8	15	..	18	16
Q3	Q3	6	5	4	..	10	11
Q4	Exc.	2	1	1	..	4	4
Q5	D2	2	1	1	..	3	3
Q6	Q2	2	1	1	..	4	4
Q7	P3	3	3	..	..	5	5
Q8	P4	8	6	14	..	12	9
Q9	P3	8	3	7	..	9	12
Q10	Exc.	3	2	..	..	4	4
Q11	P3	4	2	1	..	5	5
Q12	P3	5	2	3	..	6	2
Q13	P3	2	3	4	..	5	4
Q14	Q4	3	4	6	..	9	6
Q15	P2	3	2	..	..	5	2
Base		*234*	*234*	*72*	*72*	*170*	*170*

Table A11.10 cont. **Proportion of respondents who omitted or crossed out questions in IALS (1994/6) by type country (score 5)**

Item	Scale /Level	GB Omit	Skip	Sweden Omit	Skip	France Omit	Skip
		Percentage					
Block 4							
Q1	P1	1	..	..	..	3	..
Q2	P2	2	..	3	..	3	1
Q3	Q2	2	..	1	..	3	..
Q4	D3	9	12	25	..	14	15
Q5.1	D3	15	11	28	..	17	14
Q5 .2	Q3	15	12	26	..	17	14
Q6	P3	5	1	..	..	10	4
Q7	P3	5	3	9	..	10	6
Q8	Exc.	4	..	4	..	7	3
Q9	Q3	2	2	1	..	6	4
Q10	Q5	12	13	18	..	14	12
Q11	Q3	3	2	5	..	5	6
Q12.1	D2	..	1	..	..	1	1
Q12.2	D2	..	1	..	..	1	1
Q12.3	D1	..	..	..	..	1	1
Q12.4	D1	..	..	..	..	1	1
Q12.5	Q2	..	..	..	..	1	1
Q12.6	Q1	..	..	..	..	1	1
Base		*234*	*234*	*76*	*76*	*162*	*162*
Block 5							
Q1	P1	2	1	..	..	1	..
Q2	P2	2	1	2	..	1	..
Q3	P2	3	1	..	..	4	..
Q4	P4	13	3	8	..	14	6
Q5	P3	8	1	2	..	9	6
Q6	P3	8	3	..	..	10	5
Q7	D2	0	1	..	..	1	2
Q8	D3	2	..	2	..	0	2
Q9	Q3	3	1	..	..	1	3
Q10	D3	6	5	6	..	11	11
Q11.1	Q4	6	7	8	..	7	6
Q11.2	Q4	5	7	8	..	7	6
Q11.3	Exc.	5	7	8	..	7	6
Q11.4	D3	5	7	8	..	7	6
Q12	D3	4	5	8	2	6	7
Q13	Q4	8	7	15	2	10	9
Q14	Q3	9	9	17	2	10	14
Base		*239*	*239*	*53*	*53*	*163*	*163*
Block 6							
Q1	P1	1	1	1	..	1	2
Q2	Q3	1	1	1	..	1	2
Q3	Q2	1	1	1	..	1	2
Q4	D1	1	..	1	..	4	..
Q5	Q3	2	1	1	..	5	2
Q6	D3	4	6	2	..	7	8
Q7	P2	1	1	2	..	5	9
Q8	P3	4	5	4	..	8	11
Q9	D2	6	7	4	..	2	5
Q10	Q4	7	5	4	..	4	6
Q11	D3	9	10	5	..	8	14
Q12	Exc.	3	3	..	..	2	6
Q13	Exc.	3	2	1	..	2	6
Base		*228*	*228*	*84*	*84*	*172*	*172*

Table A11.10 cont. **Proportion of respondents who omitted or crossed out questions in IALS (1994/6) by type country (score 5)**

		GB		Sweden		France	
		Omit	Skip	Omit	Skip	Omit	Skip
Block 7				*Percentage*			
Q1	D1	1	1	..	..	1	3
Q2	Q2	5	7	4	..	4	7
Q3	D2	4	3	1	..	1	4
Q4	D2	1	2	3	..	1	4
Q5	Q3	7	9	5	1	6	11
Q6	Q3	5	8	5	1	4	9
Q7	D4	6	5	9	..	5	8
Q8	D3	8	10	14	..	11	12
Q9	D5	9	7	19	..	7	10
Q10	P2	4	5	12	..	9	8
Q11	P4	5	7	10	..	7	7
Q12	Exc.	8	11	21	1	12	8
Q13	P1	2	..	1	..	1	..
Q14	P3	3	1	1	..	1	1
Q15	P2	4	4	4	..	9	5
Base		*263*	*263*	*81*	*81*	*163*	*163*

Table A11.11 Proportion of control sample at each prose literacy level in IALS (1994) and retest (1998)

Prose	**Level 1**		**Level 2**		**Level 3**		**Level 4/5**		**Total**	***Base***
Great Britain	%	*s.e.*	%	*s.e.*	%	*s.e.*	%	*s.e.*		
1996	11	*2.4*	29	*3.3*	38	*2.8*	22	*2.1*	100	*305*
1998	8	*1.7*	24	*2.3*	45	*2.9*	23	*2.4*	100	*305*
Sweden										
1994	3	*0.8*	18	*1.1*	39	*3.3*	40	*2.3*	100	*233*
1998	2	*0.8*	17	*2.2*	43	*3.0*	37	*2.6*	100	*233*
France										
1994	32	*3.1*	37	*3.4*	27	*3.0*	4	*1.3*	100	*300*
1998	20	*2.1*	38	*2.1*	33	*1.9*	8	*1.5*	100	*300*

Table A11.12 **Proportion of best practice sample at each prose literacy level in IALS and retest**

Prose	**Level 1**		**Level 2**		**Level 3**		**Level 4/5**		**Total**	***Base***
Great Britain	%	*s.e.*	%	*s.e.*	%	*s.e.*	%	*s.e.*	%	
1996	10	*2.5*	26	*2.3*	40	*2.5*	24	*3.2*	100	*307*
1998	6	*2.0*	20	*2.2*	44	*2.3*	30	*3.0*	100	*307*
Sweden										
1994	4	*0.7*	19	*1.8*	42	*1.9*	34	*2.0*	100	*333*
1998	4	*0.6*	21	*1.6*	45	*1.5*	31	*2.0*	100	*333*
France										
1994	28	*2.5*	40	*2.0*	28	*1.6*	4	*0.7*	100	*422*
1998	23	*2.5*	39	*1.2*	32	*1.9*	6	*1.1*	100	*422*

12. Debriefing Interview

12.1 Introduction

One of the difficulties in addressing claims of cultural and societal differences after the results of the first round of the International Adult Literacy Survey (IALS) was published in 1995 was that no information was available on the conditions under which the respondent did the assessment or what the experience was like for them. The qualitative research had identified the range of respondent experience and some information had been gleaned from the pilot survey on the physical conditions under which the respondent completed the test (see chapters 8 and 9 of this report). In the re-test it was decided to include a short debriefing interview (about 10 minutes) after the respondent had completed the booklet. This would serve two purposes – to give the respondent an opportunity to discuss the booklet and to collect data on what was going on during the assessment. This chapter describes the findings from this de-brief interview. In addition to the debrief interview, interviewers were asked to complete questions on the test conditions. To help them answer these questions interviewers completed detailed observation sheets while the respondent worked on the booklet. The detailed qualitative data from these observation sheets is not reported here but would be interesting to look at at a future time.

When making comparisons between the countries that took part it is important to remember that the sample design was not exactly the same in each country. In Great Britain, Sweden and France, the sample was split. One part of the sample (the IALS style or the replicate sample) had the survey administered in exactly the same way as it was administered in that country in IALS (1994 in France and Sweden and 1996 in Britain) with the addition of the debriefing questions. The design of the second part of the sample (the Best Practice sample) was based on the results of qualitative work which was undertaken to find out what influenced respondents to take the study seriously and how they approached the assessment. The differences in protocol between the IALS or replicate sample and the Best Practice sample varied between countries. The aim was to develop as standard a procedure as possible that was feasible in all countries (or that would be adhered to in all countries) thus reducing any unnecessary variation. The largest difference between the two samples was in France where in addition to changes to the introductions, explanations and guidelines the Best Practice sample were given the version of the assessment developed and used on the French speaking population in Switzerland rather than the version used in France. In Portugal, because they had not taken part in IALS a different research design was implemented (see Chapter 1). A sample of those who took part in the Portuguese Adult Literacy Survey in 1994 were re-interviewed in 1998. A new sample was selected using the Labour Force Survey as a sampling frame and these respondents were interviewed and tested using the IALS background questionnaire and assessments. The IALS in Portugal used the principles identified as Best Practice and included the debrief questions. Only those in the Portuguese IALS sample had a de-briefing interview.

The sample size in all countries is small, particulary in some groups e.g. those aged under 26 in Great Britain. Where this occurs, the data should be interpreted with caution.

12.2 Overview of findings

- British and French respondents were the most likely to say that they found the booklet easy and Portuguese respondents were the least likely (45% of British, 44% of French, 37% of Swedish and 28% of Portuguese).

- Portuguese respondents were the most likely to have found the booklet interesting – about three-quarters did so compared with nearly two-thirds of British and Swedish and over a half (56%) of French respondents.
- Although 84% of French respondents said that they tried very hard to answer correctly, they were the least likely to say that it was very important to answer correctly and to the best of their ability (70% in Great Britain, 50% in Sweden, 33% in Portugal, 30% in France).
- British and Portuguese respondents were the most likely to have found the booklet challenging (72% and 66% respectively) compared with 41% of French and 32% of Swedish respondents.
- About six out of ten British and Swedish but fewer French (49%) and Portuguese (43%) respondents answered all the questions.
- British and Swedish respondents were the most likely to think that the length of the booklet was about right (70% and 73% respectively). Most (83%) Portuguese respondents thought that the booklet was too long.

Table 12.1 **Respondent opinion on what it was like to complete the booklet**

	Great Britain	Sweden	France	Portugal
		percentage of respondents		
Found booklet easy	45	37	44	28
Found booklet interesting	64	63	56	74
Tried very hard to answer correctly	74	47	84	59
Very important to answer correctly	70	50	30	33
Found booklet challenging	72	32	41	66
Answered all the questions	62	61	49	43
Length of booklet about right	70	73	58	17

- Although there were differences between countries in the responses to most questions, the pattern was not systematic. With some exceptions however, responses were associated with sex, age and educational attainment. For example, men, those aged 26-45 and the better educated were more likely to say they found the booklet easy, less challenging and to have answered all the questions; but women were more likely to have found it interesting.
- In Great Britain, respondents were less likely to have found the booklet difficult and more likely to have tried hard to answer the questions correctly and left none unanswered if they were in the Best Practice sample. In other countries, no clear differences emerge between the IALS and Best Practice samples.

Whilst the respondent was working on the booklet, the interviewers observed that:

- British respondents were the most likely to be disturbed (50% of British, 44% of Swedish and French and 40% of Portuguese).
- There were more likely to be other people around in Portugal than in other countries (58% in Portugal, 43% in Great Britain, 35% in Sweden, 31% in France).
- The length of the booklet, time pressure and the presence of other people were all mentioned more frequently in Portugal (by 54%, 17% and 10% respectively) than elsewhere as factors which affected the respondent's work.
- The majority of interviewers did not think that their presence affected the respondent (89% in Great Britain, 92% in France, 98% in Sweden).
- Only 40% of French and Portuguese, 38% of Swedish and 30% of British respondents asked the interviewer for their support or point of view whilst working on the booklet.

Table 12.2 **Interviewer assessment of environment for working on the booklet by country**

	Great Britain	Sweden	France	Portugal
	percentage of respondents			
Disturbed whilst working on booklet	50	44	44	40
Other people around	43	35	31	58
Affected by length of booklet	3	8	12	54
Affected by time pressure	8	4	13	17
Affected by presence of other people	2	2	4	10
Not affected by interviewer's presence	89	98	92	-
Asked interviewer for support or point of view	30	38	40	40

12.3 Views on ease or difficulty of booklet

When asked for their views on how easy or difficult they found the booklet, British and French respondents were the most likely to say they found it easy (45% of British, 44% of French, 37% of Swedish and 28% of Portuguese). Only 4% of British, 3% of Swedish and 6% of French and Portuguese found it very easy. The Portuguese were the most likely to say they found the booklet difficult (27% compared with 19% of Swedish and British and 14% of French). In Great Britain but in neither Sweden nor France, respondents in the IALS sample were more likely than those in the Best Practice sample to have found the booklet difficult (25% compared with 13%).

In Great Britain, men were more likely than women to have found the booklet easy. In both Great Britain and Sweden, the respondents most likely to have found the booklet easy were those aged 26-45 and the better educated. In Portugal and in France, the better educated the respondent, the easier they found the booklet but there were no further differences by sex or age. These characteristics are described in more detail below. (Tables in the appendix to this chapter).

Table 12.3 **Views on ease or difficulty of booklet by treatment group and country**

	Very easy	Quite easy	Neither easy nor difficult	Quite difficult	Very difficult	Total	*Base*
			%				
Great Britain							
IALS	4	37	34	23	2	100	*305*
Best Practice	4	44	38	12	1	100	*305*
Total	4	41	36	17	2	100	*610*
Sweden							
IALS	3	36	44	16	1	100	*233*
Best Practice	2	33	44	18	2	100	*332*
Total	3	34	44	17	2	100	*565*
France							
IALS	3	38	46	10	2	100	*287*
Best Practice	7	38	40	13	2	100	*419*
Total	6	38	42	12	2	100	*706*
Portugal							
IALS	6	22	45	20	7	*100*	*1222*

Great Britain

- Men were more likely than women to have found the booklet easy (52% compared with 39%).
- Half of those aged 26-45 found the booklet easy, which was a higher proportion than in other age groups. Those aged 46 and over were the most likely to have found it difficult (25%). Those aged under 26 were the most likely to have found it neither easy nor difficult (43%).

- Views on the ease of filling in the booklet were strongly associated with educational attainment – ranging from 36% of those who had attained lower secondary education to 65% of those who had attained higher education.

Sweden

- Men were more likely than women to have found the booklet easy (40% compared with 35%).
- Those aged 26-45 were the most likely to have found it easy (44% compared with 36% of those aged 16-25 and 30% of those aged 46 and over).
- There was a strong association between those who thought the booklet easy and level of educational attainment – ranging from 20% of those with primary education or less, to 56% of those who had attained higher education (level 3 or university).

France and Portugal

Of the characteristics, which were analysed for French and Portuguese respondents, only the level of education that they attained was associated with how easy or difficult they found the booklet. The proportion who found the booklet easy increased:

- In France, from 26% of those with primary education or less to 67% with higher education.
- In Portugal, from 12% of those with primary education or less to 49% with higher education.

12.4 How interesting respondents found the booklet

Portuguese respondents were the most likely to have found the booklet interesting – about three-quarters (74%) did so compared with nearly two-thirds of British and Swedish and over half (56%) of French respondents. Eighteen per cent of the Portuguese found it very interesting but 6% found it boring. In comparison, fewer British, Swedish and French respondents found the booklet very interesting (13%, 8% and 5% respectively). Eighteen per cent of French, 14% of British and 10% of Swedish found it boring.

In Great Britain, Sweden and France, those least likely to find the booklet interesting were in the highest education group (level 3 or university) and there is an indication that women were more likely than men to find the booklet interesting. These characteristics are described in more detail below (see tables in appendix to this chapter). Amongst Portuguese respondents, there was no strong association between interest in the booklet and their socio-demographic characteristics.

Great Britain

- Women were more likely than man to have found the booklet interesting (68% compared with 59%).
- Interest in the booklet increased with age. Four per cent of those aged 16-25 found it very interesting, rising to 15% of those aged 46 and over.
- Nearly a quarter (22%) of respondents aged under 26 found the booklet quite boring.
- Interest was related to educational attainment. The proportion who found the booklet interesting decreased from 68% of those who had attained lower secondary education to 57% who had attained higher education. Nearly a quarter (22%) of respondents in the group with the highest level of education found the booklet boring.

Sweden

- 11% of those aged 46 and over found the booklet very interesting compared with 5% of younger respondents.

- The proportion who found the booklet interesting decreased from 68% who had attained primary education or lower to 58% with higher education.
- There is an indication that women were more likely than men to find the booklet interesting (64% compared with 61%) but the difference was not statistically significant.

Table 12.4 **How interesting respondents found the booklet by treatment group and country**

	Very interesting	Quite interesting	Neither interesting nor boring	Quite boring	Very boring	Total	*Base*
Great Britain	%						
IALS	12	53	20	13	2	100	*305*
Best Practice	13	50	23	12	2	100	*305*
Total	13	51	22	12	2	100	*610*
Sweden							
IALS	8	54	25	11	1	100	*233*
Best Practice	8	55	28	8	1	100	*332*
Total	8	55	27	9	1	100	*565*
France							
IALS	5	52	27	15	2	100	*291*
Best Practice	6	50	26	15	4	100	*419*
Total	5	51	26	15	3	100	*710*
Portugal							
IALS	18	56	20	4	2	100	*1221*

France

- Women were more likely than men to find the booklet interesting (59% compared with 53%).
- Those least likely to find the booklet interesting had attained higher education (level 3 or a university education).

Portugal

- Amongst the Portuguese, only the following characteristics were associated with interest in the booklet.
- The youngest age group (16-25) were the most likely to find the booklet interesting (80%).
- Respondents who had only attained primary level or less were the most likely to say they found the booklet neither interesting nor boring (30%).

12.5 How challenging respondents found the booklet

Nearly three-quarters of British, two-thirds of Portuguese but only 41% of French and 32% of Swedish respondents found the booklet challenging. Respondents in Sweden were more likely (52%) than those in other countries to say that they did not find the booklet either challenging or unchallenging. French respondents were amongst the most likely to have found the booklet easy and least likely to have found it challenging (40%).

In Great Britain, France and Portugal, women were more likely than men to find the booklet challenging. In Great Britain and Sweden, those with the highest level of education were the least likely to find it challenging. In Great Britain and France, older respondents were the most likely to find the booklet challenging, whereas in Portugal, younger respondents were the most likely to find it challenging. These and other characteristics of respondents, which were only found in one country to be associated with whether they found the booklet challenging, are described below, (see appendix).

Great Britain

- Women were more likely than men to find the booklet challenging (75% compared with 69%) were and twice as likely to have found it very challenging (16% compared with 8%).
- The proportion who found the booklet very challenging increased with age from 8% of those aged 16-25 to 15% of those aged 46 and over.
- Those with higher education were the least likely to find it challenging. About a quarter (26%) did not find it challenging.

Table 12.5 **How challenging respondents found the booklet by treatment group and country**

	Very challenging	Somewhat challenging	Neither challenging nor unchallenging	Somewhat unchallenging	Very unchallenging	Total	*Base*
Great Britain	%						
IALS	16	59	13	10	2	100	*305*
Best Practice	9	61	15	13	1	100	*305*
Total	12	60	14	12	2	100	*610*
Sweden							
IALS	4	26	53	15	3	100	*230*
Best Practice	5	27	52	13	3	100	*332*
Total	5	27	52	14	3	100	*562*
France							
IALS	9	33	16	24	16	100	*291*
Best Practice	10	30	21	20	19	100	*419*
Total	10	31	19	22	18	100	*710*
Portugal							
IALS	13	53	27	5	2	100	*1221*

Sweden

In Sweden only the respondent's education was associated with whether they found the booklet challenging.

- Those with the highest level of education were the least likely to have found the booklet challenging – 29% did not find it challenging and a further 52% found it neither challenging nor unchallenging.

France

- Women were more likely than men to find the booklet challenging (45% compared with 35%).
- Young people, aged 16-25, were the least likely to find it challenging.

Portugal

- Women were more likely than men to have found the booklet challenging (68% compared with 62%).
- Younger respondents were the most likely to have found it challenging – ranging from 68% of those aged 16-25 to 59% of those aged 46 and over.
- Respondents who had attained only primary education or less were the least likely (55%) to find the booklet challenging, but 37% found it neither challenging nor unchallenging.

12.6 How hard respondents tried to answer questions correctly

Eighty four per cent of French, 74% of British, 59% of Portuguese and 47% of Swedish respondents said that they tried very hard to answer the questions correctly. In Great Britain, respondents in the Best Practice sample were more likely than those in the IALS sample to have tried their best to answer correctly (79% compared with 69%). In Sweden and France, there was no significant difference between the two types of sample in how hard they tried to answer correctly.

Only the following characteristics were significantly associated with how hard respondents tried. (Tables A12.1 to A12.2)

Table 12.6 **How hard respondents tried to answer the questions correctly by treatment group and country**

	Tried my best/ very hard	Tried quite hard	Other	Total	*Base*
Great Britain		%			
IALS	69	29	2	100	*305*
Best Practice	79	20	1	100	*305*
Total	74	25	1	100	*610*
Sweden					
IALS	45	50	5	100	*233*
Best Practice	48	46	6	100	*330*
Total	47	48	5	100	*563*
France					
IALS	85	13	2	100	*291*
Best Practice	83	16	1	100	*416*
Total	84	15	2	100	*707*
Portugal					
IALS	59	34	7	100	*1222*

Great Britain

- About three-quarters of those aged 26 and over said that they tried their best. In comparison, only half of those aged 16-25 tried their best but 43% tried quite hard.

Sweden and Portugal

Women were more likely than men to have tried their best to answer the questions correctly (52% compared with 42% in Sweden; 62% compared with 57% in Portugal).

France

- Eighty five per cent of those aged 16-25 and 88% of those aged 26-45 tried very hard.
- Those aged 46 and over were more likely than younger respondents to have tried quite hard (19%) and less likely to have tried very hard (79%).
- Those with primary education or lower were more likely than respondents with more education to have tried quite hard (24%) but less likely to have tried very hard (72%). Over 80% with at least lower secondary education tried very hard.
-

12.7 Importance to respondents of answering correctly

There was a marked difference in attitude between Britain, Sweden and Portugal on the one hand and France on the other with regard to respondent attitude to the importance of answering the questions correctly or to the best of one's ability. In Great Britain, Sweden and Portugal, nearly all respondents said that it was important to answer each question correctly or to the best of their ability (98% in Great Britain, 96% in Sweden, 90% in Portugal). In France, about three-quarters said that it was important to answer correctly and a quarter considered it not very important or not at all important to answer correctly. Opinion on whether answering correctly was *very* important differed by country (70% in Great Britain, 50% in Sweden, 33% in Portugal, 30% in France).

Eighty four per cent of British, 70% of Swedish, 66% of French but only a third of Portuguese respondents thought that it was important to answer correctly for the personal challenge. Portuguese respondents were more likely than those in any other country to think it was important to answer correctly because of the importance of the survey and the need for it to be accurate (61% compared with about a quarter in Great Britain and Sweden and only 3% in France). In Great Britain, Sweden and France up to three responses to this question were coded, whereas in Portugal, only one response was coded.

In all countries, the importance of answering the questions correctly and the reasons given were in general, similar for people with different demographic characteristics (see appendix).

Table 12.7 **Importance to respondent of answering each question correctly or to the best of their ability by treatment group and country**

	Very important	Quite important	Not very/ at all important	Total	*Base*
			%		
Great Britain					
IALS	68	29	2	100	*305*
Best Practice	71	26	3	100	*305*
Total	70	28	2	100	*610*
Sweden					
IALS	48	48	5	100	*231*
Best Practice	52	44	4	100	*329*
Total	50	46	5	100	*560*
France					
IALS	32	43	24	100	*290*
Best Practice	29	49	22	100	*416*
Total	30	46	24	100	*708*
Portugal					
IALS	33	57	10	100	*1220*

12.8 Whether any questions were left unanswered

About six out of ten British and Swedish but fewer French (49%) and Portuguese (43%) respondents got to the end of the booklet and answered all the questions. A further 46% of French, 44% of Portuguese, 37% of British and 13% of Swedish respondents got to the end but did not answer all the questions. Swedish respondents were the least likely to get to the end of the booklet (26% compared with 13% of Portuguese and only 1% of British).

In Great Britain, those in the Best Practice sample were more likely than those in the IALS sample to have answered all the questions (68% compared with 57%). In Sweden, the reverse appears to be true but the difference was not quite statistically significant.

The routing to these questions was not the same in all countries. In Sweden and Portugal, all respondents including those who said that they answered all questions, were asked whether they got to the end of the booklet. In Great Britain and France, only those who left questions unanswered were asked if they got to the end. For the purpose of this analysis, it has been assumed that British and French respondents who answered all questions, also got to the end of the booklet.

About one in five Portuguese and Swedish respondents did not get to the end of the booklet because they felt tired. A further 14% of Portuguese and 10% of Swedish respondents said that the booklet took too long. Also mentioned frequently by Portuguese respondents were that they had other things to do (16%), couldn't concentrate (15%) or thought they had done enough (8%). Six per cent of Swedish and 5% of Portuguese respondents did not like the subject of the study.

In Sweden, up to three responses to this question were coded, whereas in Portugal only one response was coded. The number of British and French respondents who answered this question was too few to analyse.

Table 12.8 **Why it was important that each question was answered correctly or to the best of respondent's ability by treatment group and country**

	Personal challenge/ satisfaction	Survey is important/ survey accuracy	Other	*Base*
	% of respondents who said very or quite important			
Great Britain				
IALS	78	31	5	*298*
Best Practice	90	20	4	*296*
Total	84	25	5	*594*
Sweden				
IALS	73	23	10	*225*
Best Practice	69	29	10	*324*
Total	70	26	10	*549*
France				
IALS	66	3	31	*268*
Best Practice	66	3	31	*384*
Total	66	3	31	*652*
Portugal				
IALS	32	61	6	*1100*

In Great Britain, Sweden and France, up to three responses to this question were coded, whereas in Portugal, only one response was coded

Table 12. 9 **Whether answered all questions and got to end of booklet by type of sample and country**

	Got to end				
	Answered all	Some un-answered	Did not get to end	Total	*Base*
	%				
Great Britain					
IALS	57	43	-	100	*298*
Best Practice	68	32	1	100	*296*
Total	62	37	1	100	*594*
Sweden					
IALS	64	14	22	100	*225*
Best Practice	58	13	29	100	*324*
Total	61	13	26	100	*549*
France					
IALS	49	46	5	100	*268*
Best Practice	48	46	5	100	*384*
Total	49	46	5	100	*652*
Portugal					
IALS	43	44	13	100	*1100*

In all countries, men and those with a higher level of educational attainment were the most likely to have answered all the questions. In Great Britain, Sweden and France, younger respondents were the most likely to have answered all the questions. These characteristics are described in more detail below. (see appendix)

Great Britain

- Men were more likely than women to have answered all the questions in the booklet (74% compared with 52%).
- Respondents aged 26-45 and over were the most likely to have answered all the questions (67%).
- Answering all the questions in the booklet was associated with educational attainment – increasing from 43% of those who had attained lower secondary education to 85% of those who had attained higher education.

Table 12.10 **Reasons for not getting to end of booklet by country**

	Great Britain	Sweden	France	Portugal
	% of respondents who did not get to end of booklet			
Had other things to do	[0]	4	[10]	16
Took too long	[0]	10	[12]	14
Felt tired	[0]	22	[5]	21
Could not concentrate	[0]	-	[6]	15
Got irritated	[0]	4	[4]	4
Thought had done enough	[0]	-	[0]	8
Did not like subject of study	[1]	6	[3]	5
Other	-	58	[1]	17
Base	*[3]*	*143* [1]	*[35]*	*158* [2]

1 Percentages for Sweden add to more than 100 because some respondents gave more than one reason (up to 3 responses were coded)

2 Percentages for Portugal add to 100 because only one reason was coded

Sweden

- Men were more likely than women to have answered all the questions (71% compared with 52%)
- About two-thirds of respondents aged under 46 answered all the questions compared with 55% of older respondents.
- Answering all questions was related to educational attainment - increasing from 24% of those who had attained primary or less to 85% of those with higher education .

France

- Men were more likely than women to have answered all the questions (54% compared with 45%).
- Two-thirds of respondents aged 16-25 answered all the questions, compared with less than half in other age groups.
- Answering all questions was related to educational attainment – increasing from 22% of those who had attained primary education or less to 73% of those who had attained higher education (level 3 or university).

Portugal

- Men were more likely than women to have answered all the questions (46% compared with 39%).
- Answering all questions was related to educational attainment – increasing from 24% of those who had attained primary or less to 73% of those who had attained higher education.
- There was no association between the age of the respondent and whether they answered all the questions.

12.9 Opinion on the length of the booklet

Respondents in Britain, France and Sweden were more likely than repondents in Portugal to have found the length of the booklet acceptable. About seven out of ten respondents in Great Britain and Sweden and nearly six out of ten in France thought that the length of the booklet was about right. Only 17% of Portuguese considered the length of the booklct to be about right while 84% of Portuguese respondents thought it was long or too long.

From the pilot carried out in Portugal (see Chapter 13) respondent burden was clearly a bigger issue than it had been for example in Britain. This was thought to be due to the relatively low levels of education in Portugal. Table A12.7 shows that this view about the length of the booklet was true for all levels of educational attainment. The Portuguese were also the least likely to have got to the end of the booklet and answered all the questions. (data not shown) In Great Britain, respondents in the Best Practice sample were more likely than those in the IALS sample to think that the length was about right (73% compared with 66%).

Table 12.11 **Opinion on length of booklet by treatment group and country**

	Too long	Long	About right	Total	*Base*
Great Britain		%			
IALS	18	16	66	100	*304*
Best Practice	14	12	73	100	*305*
Total	16	14	70	100	*609*
Sweden					
IALS	9	16	75	100	*226*
Best Practice	10	18	72	100	*318*
Total	9	18	73	100	*544*
France					
IALS	15	29	56	100	*287*
Best Practice	12	29	59	100	*409*
Total	13	29	58	100	*696*
Portugal					
IALS	41	42	17	100	*1222*

In both Sweden and France, there was no significant difference in opinion between respondents in the two types of samples.In all countries, differences in opinion on the length of the booklet, between respondents with different demographic characteristics, were not significant.

12.10 Motivation

When making international comparisons on motivation, it should be remembered that in Great Britain and Sweden, all respondents were asked 'what do you think motivated you when you worked through the booklet? and up to three responses were coded in answer to this question. In Portugal all respondents were asked this question but only one response was coded. In France the question was preceded by 'did you try as hard as possible to answer the questions in the booklet?'. Only those who said 'Yes' were asked 'what motivated you to try hard?' and up to three responses were coded.

Just over two-thirds of British respondents compared with 41% in Sweden, 35% in France, 17% in Portugal said that they were motivated by a sense of personal challenge as they worked through the booklet. French and Swedish respondents were more likely (45%) than those in either Portugal (34%) or Great Britain (14%) to be motivated because they wanted the study to be accurate. Portuguese respondents were the most likely to say that they were motivated because they wanted the results to be as good as possible (22%) or because they had been told that it was an important study (22%). In Sweden, Great Britain and France, around one in ten were motivated because they had been told it was an important study and a similar proportion wanted the results for their country to be as good as possible.

Table 12.12 **What respondents thought motivated them when they worked through the booklet by country**

	Great Britain	Sweden	France	Portugal
		%		
Sense of personal challenge	68	41	35	17
Wanted study to be accurate	14	45	45	34
Wanted results to be as good as possible	8	11	9	22
Told it was an important study	10	9	10	22
Other	12	7	6	5
Base	*609*	*549*	*630*	*1223*

1 Percentages for Great Britain, Sweden and France add to more than 100 as some respondents mentioned more than one motivation. In Portugal only one motivation was coded.

In Great Britain, those in the IALS sample were the most likely to be mainly motiv ated because they wanted the study to be accurate (21% compared with 14% in the Best Practice sample). Whereas in the Best Practice sample, the main motivation was most likely to be a sense of personal challenge (65% compared with 56%). In Sweden, not all respondents were asked for their main motivation. This question was not asked in France and Portugal. (Data not shown)

12.11 Feelings on finishing booklet

When making international comparisons on how respondents felt when they finished the booklet, it should be remembered that in Great Britain, Sweden and France, up to three responses were coded, whereas in Portugal only one response was coded.

When asked how they felt on finishing the booklet, British respondents were more likely than those in other countries to say that they were relieved (55% compared with 39% in France, 28% in Portugal, 21% in Sweden). In all countries, respondents frequently mentioned that they were glad to get it over with (30% in Great Britain, 28% in Portugal, 26% in France, 25% in Sweden). Twenty eight per cent of British and 23% of Swedish but only 14% of Portuguese and 12% of French respondents were generally satisfied with their own efforts.

Swedish respondents were the most likely to say that they were disappointed with the content of the booklet (34% compared with only 2% or less in other countries). Sixteen per cent of Swedish and 15% of French respondents reported no feelings on completing the booklet, a higher proportion than in either Great Britain (3%) or Portugal (4%).

Table 12.13 **Feelings on finishing booklet by country**

	Great Britain	Sweden	France	Portugal
		%		
Relieved	55	21	39	28
Tired	10	10	6	12
Glad to get it over with	30	25	26	28
Disappointed about content of booklet	2	34	1	2
Generally satisfied with own efforts	28	23	12	14
Somewhat satisfied with own efforts	9	2	5	*
Not very satisfied	*	*	*	2
Curious to know his/her results	7	2	8	8
Booklet ok - as expected	4	8	1	1
No feelings	3	16	15	4
Other feelings	14	2	11	-
Base	*609*	*559*	*705*	*1226*

1 Percentages for Great Britain, Sweden and France add to more than 100 as some respondents mentioned more than one motivation. In Portugal only one motivation was coded.

In Great Britain, those in the IALS sample were more likely than those in the Best Practice sample to have felt tired when they finished the booklet (13% compared with 7%). In Sweden, those in the Best Practice sample were the most likely to have felt relieved when they finished (25% compared with 15% in the IALS sample).(Data not shown)

12.12 The environment for working on the booklet

While respondents worked on the booklet, the interviewer observed how they approached it, the things that they asked about, remarked on, or what disturbed them. The findings from the interviewers' observation reports are described below.

In Great Britain, Portugal and France, the respondent was most likely to work with the booklet in the living room (79%, 64% and 62% respectively). In Sweden, just over a half (53%) worked in the kitchen and about a quarter worked in the living room.

Table 12.14 **Where respondent workded on booklet by country**

	Great Britain	Sweden	France	Portugal
			%	
Living room	79	26	62	64
Study or office	4	2	4	7
Kitchen	11	53	23	9
Elsewhere	6	19	12	20
Base	*611*	*553*	*658*	*1157*

A half of all British, 44% of Swedish and French and 40% of Portuguese respondents were disturbed whilst working on the booklet. Telephone calls were the reason most frequently given for the disturbance in Great Britain, Sweden and France (20%, 17% and 15% respectively). In Portugal, respondents were most frequently disturbed by the radio or TV (12%). Children calling for attention disturbed 15% of British and 8% -9% of other respondents. The doorbell or knocker disturbed 8% of British and French, 5% of Portuguese and 3% of Swedish respondents. In each country up to three responses were coded.

There were more likely to be other people around whilst the respondent was working on the booklet in Portugal (58%) than in Great Britain (43%), Sweden (35%) or France (31%). In all countries, the others present were most likely to be members of the respondent's family – their children, spouse or partner.

Table 12.15 **Whether respondent was disturbed or other people present whilst working on booklet by country**

	Great Britain	Sweden	France	Portugal
Yes, disturbed by:	%			
Telephone calls	20	17	15	10
Children calling for attention	15	8	9	9
Radio or TV	9	10	7	12
General racket	4	4	7	8
Door bell or knocker	8	3	8	5
Other	15	13	10	10
No noise disturbance	50	56	56	60
Yes, other people present				
Children	24	21	18	12
Partner or spouse	23	22	15	14
Friends or acquaintances	3	2	2	7
Others	7	-	6	32
No other people	57	65	69	42
Base	*611*	*566*	*635*	*1157*

Percentages add to more than 100 because some respondents gave more than one answer

Interviewers assessed that a variety of factors affected or limited the respondent's work with the booklet. The length of the booklet was mentioned far more frequently in Portugal (54%) than in France (12%), Sweden (8%) or Great Britain (3%). Also mentioned more frequently in Portugal and France than in other countries were time pressure (17% in Portugal compared with 13% in France, 8% in Great Britain and 4% in Sweden) and the presence of other people (10% in Portugal compared with 4% in France and 2% in Great Britain and Sweden).

Table 12.16 **Interviewer assesment of factors which affected respondent's work with the booklet by country**

	Great Britain	Sweden	France	Portugal
		%		
Time of day	5	1	5	11
Time pressure	8	4	13	17
Environment	2	1	2	4
Presence of interviewer	2	0	3	4
Presence of children	6	6	5	6
Presence of other people	2	2	4	10
Length of booklet	3	8	12	54
Other	5	1	10	34
Nothing affected respondent	67	85	47	8
Base	*611*	*566*	*626*	*1239*

Percentages add to more than 100 because some respondents mentioned more than one person

Although interviewers recorded a number of factors which they thought affected the respondent's work on the booklet. The majority of interviewers did not think that their presence affected the respondent (89% in Great Britain, 92% in France, 98% in Sweden). In Sweden, the precodes for the answers to this question were not the same as in other countries - 68% of Swedish interviewers did not think that their presence affected the respondent at all and a further 30% did not think that their presence affected the respondent too much. (Data not shown) This question was not in Portugal due to a routing error in the questionnaire.

Only 40% of French and Portuguese, 38% of Swedish and 30% of British respondents asked the interviewer for their support or point of view whilst working on the booklet.

Table 12.17 **Whether respondent asked for interviewer support or point of view by country**

	Great Britain	**France**	**Portugal**
Yes, sought help or advice	12	12	23
Yes, sought confirmation	18	28	17
No	70	60	60
Base	*611*	*640*	*1157*

	Sweden [1]
	%
Asked for help	6
Asked for confirmation	14
Asked direct question	14
Looked for reaction	10
Other	8
No	62

1 Percentages add to more than 100 in Sweden because precodes allowed for more than one type of support to be coded

Appendix

Tables A12.1 – A12.2

Table A12.1 **Respondent views on ease or difficulty of booklet by characteristics of respondent and country**

	Very easy	Quite easy	Neither easy nor difficult	Quite difficult	Very difficult	*Base*
			%			
Great Britain - Sex						
Men	6	46	33	15	1	*276*
Women	3	36	39	19	2	*334*
Age Group						
16-25	[2]	[17]	[21]	[9]	-	*49*
26-45	6	44	35	14	1	*291*
46 and over	2	38	36	22	3	*264*
Education						
Primary education or lower	-	[1]	[1]	[7]	[2]	*11*
Second level, 1st stage	1	35	37	25	3	*210*
Second level, 2nd stage	2	37	43	16	1	*158*
Third level, non-university	2	49	36	14	-	*104*
Third level, university	14	51	30	5	-	*125*
Sweden - Sex						
Men	5	35	45	14	2	*258*
Women	1	34	43	20	2	*307*
Age Group						
16-25	5	31	45	20	-	*65*
26-45	2	42	40	14	1	*236*
46 and over	2	28	47	19	3	*264*
Education						
Primary education or lower	-	20	48	24	7	*54*
Second level, 1st stage	3	24	48	24	2	*192*
Second level, 2nd stage	2	38	42	16	1	*149*
Third level, non-university	3	42	42	10	3	*76*
Third level, university	5	51	36	7	-	*94*
France - Sex						
Men	8	37	39	14	3	*308*
Women	4	39	45	11	2	*398*
Age Group						
16-25	7	39	51	2	1	*85*
26-45	4	39	45	10	2	*331*
46 and over	7	36	36	18	4	*286*
Education						
Primary education or lower	4	22	31	33	9	*90*
Second level, 1st stage	-	24	48	22	6	*54*
Second level, 2nd stage	3	36	49	11	2	*307*
Third level, non-university	8	39	51	3	-	*77*
Third level, university	12	55	30	3	-	*169*
Portugal - Sex						
Men	6	23	46	20	6	*587*
Women	5	21	44	21	8	*635*
Age Group						
16-25	6	23	48	20	3	*462*
26-45	6	20	44	21	9	*464*
46 and over	4	23	41	22	10	*296*
Education						
Primary education or lower	2	10	34	34	20	*389*
Second level, 1st stage	5	21	53	18	2	*313*
Second level, 2nd stage	6	30	49	14	1	*280*
Third level, non-university	5	29	53	11	2	*93*
Third level, university	15	34	42	9		*144*
Total	6	22	45	20	7	*1222*

Table A12.2 **How interesting respondents found the booklet by characteristics of respondent and country**

	Very interesting	Quite interesting	Neither interesting nor boring	Quite boring	Very boring	*Base*
		%				
Great Britain - Sex						
Men	11	48	23	14	4	*276*
Women	14	54	20	11	1	*334*
Age Group						
16-25	[2]	[29]	[7]	[11]	-	*49*
26-45	12	53	22	11	2	*291*
46 and over	15	48	23	12	2	*264*
Education						
Primary education or lower	[1]	[4]	[4]	[2]	-	*11*
Second level, 1st stage	17	51	20	11	1	*210*
Second level, 2nd stage	10	56	23	10	1	*158*
Third level, non-university	12	51	20	14	2	*104*
Third level, university	9	48	22	16	6	*125*
Sweden - Sex						
Men	8	53	26	11	2	*258*
Women	8	56	28	8	1	*307*
Age Group						
16-25	5	55	29	9	2	*65*
26-45	5	58	27	9	2	*236*
46 and over	11	52	26	9	1	*264*
Education						
Primary education or lower	11	57	17	13	2	*54*
Second level, 1st stage	8	55	29	7	1	*192*
Second level, 2nd stage	8	57	28	7	-	*149*
Third level, non-university	5	53	28	12	3	*76*
Third level, university	7	51	29	11	2	*94*
France - Sex						
Men	4	49	28	18	3	*308*
Women	6	53	25	12	3	*402*
Age Group						
16-25	6	56	26	11	1	*85*
26-45	5	51	29	12	3	*332*
46 and over	5	49	24	19	4	*289*
Education						
Primary education or lower	5	52	16	20	6	*92*
Second level, 1st stage	9	67	13	9	2	*54*
Second level, 2nd stage	6	52	26	13	3	*309*
Third level, non-university	3	53	25	16	4	*77*
Third level, university	3	44	37	16	1	*168*
Portugal - Sex						
Men	18	53	23	4	2	*586*
Women	18	59	18	3	2	*635*
Age Group						
16-25	18	62	17	2	1	*462*
26-45	18	56	20	4	2	*463*
46 and over	19	48	26	5	3	*296*
Education						
Primary education or lower	16	47	30	5	2	*388*
Second level, 1st stage	20	60	16	3	1	*313*
Second level, 2nd stage	18	63	14	3	2	*280*
Third level, non-university	16	56	20	4	3	*93*
Third level, university	22	55	17	5	2	*144*

Table A12.3 **How challenging respondents found the booklet by characteristics of respondent and country**

	Very challenging	Somewhat challenging	Neither challenging nor unchalleng-ing	Somewhat unchalleng-ing	Very unchalleng-ing	*Base*
			%			
Great Britain - Sex						
Men	8	61	14	15	2	*276*
Women	16	59	14	9	1	*334*
Age Group						
16-25	[4]	[30]	[3]	[11]	[1]	*49*
26-45	11	59	18	11	1	*291*
46 and over	15	61	12	11	2	*264*
Education						
Primary education or lower	[1]	[7]	[1]	[1]	[1]	*11*
Second level, 1st stage	21	62	9	7	1	*210*
Second level, 2nd stage	10	64	15	10	2	*158*
Third level, non-university	10	58	21	12	-	*104*
Third level, university	3	51	19	22	4	*125*
Sweden - Sex						
Men	3	29	51	14	4	*257*
Women	6	25	53	14	2	*305*
Age Group						
16-25	5	32	48	12	3	*65*
26-45	3	25	53	16	3	*235*
46 and over	6	27	52	12	2	*262*
Education						
Primary education or lower	9	26	53	11	-	*53*
Second level, 1st stage	6	34	48	11	2	*191*
Second level, 2nd stage	5	25	60	9	2	*149*
Third level, non-university	3	25	45	21	5	*75*
Third level, university	1	17	52	23	6	*94*
France - Sex						
Men	8	27	22	21	21	*308*
Women	11	34	17	22	16	*402*
Age Group						
16-25	9	25	26	19	21	*85*
26-45	11	32	18	22	18	*331*
46 and over	8	32	19	23	18	*290*
Education						
Primary education or lower	11	36	13	29	11	*92*
Second level, 1st stage	13	26	26	24	11	*54*
Second level, 2nd stage	12	31	18	19	20	*308*
Third level, non-university	6	31	22	23	17	*77*
Third level, university	6	29	21	21	22	*169*
Portugal - Sex						
Men	12	50	30	6	2	*586*
Women	13	55	25	5	1	*635*
Age Group						
16-25	12	56	26	5	1	*462*
26-45	12	54	27	4	2	*463*
46 and over	14	45	31	7	2	*296*
Education						
Primary education or lower	13	42	37	7	2	*388*
Second level, 1st stage	13	57	22	5	2	*313*
Second level, 2nd stage	12	60	22	4	1	*280*
Third level, non-university	8	59	26	3	4	*93*
Third level, university	15	55	23	5	2	*144*

Table A12.4 **How hard respondents tried to answer the question correctly by characteristics of respondent and country.**

	Tried my best/ very hard	Tried quite hard	Other	*Base*
		%		
Great Britain - Sex				
Men	73	25	1	*276*
Women	75	24	1	*334*
Age Group				
16-25	[25]	21	[3]	*49*
26-45	73	26	1	*291*
46 and over	79	20	1	*264*
Education				
Primary education or lower	[9]	[2]	-	*11*
Second level, 1st stage	72	26	2	*210*
Second level, 2nd stage	80	19	1	*158*
Third level, non-university	74	25	1	*104*
Third level, university	69	30	2	*125*
Sweden - Sex				
Men	42	51	7	*258*
Women	52	45	3	*305*
Age Group				
16-25	43	49	8	*65*
26-45	48	48	4	*235*
46 and over	48	46	6	*263*
Education				
Primary education or lower	46	50	4	*54*
Second level, 1st stage	43	51	5	*191*
Second level, 2nd stage	50	44	7	*149*
Third level, non-university	53	46	1	*76*
Third level, university	47	46	6	*93*
France - Sex				
Men	82	16	2	*305*
Women	85	13	1	*402*
Age Group				
16-25	85	14	1	*85*
26-45	88	12	1	*331*
46 and over	79	19	2	*287*
Education				
Primary education or lower	72	24	3	*90*
Second level, 1st stage	83	17	-	*54*
Second level, 2nd stage	85	14	1	*308*
Third level, non-university	88	12	-	*77*
Third level, university	85	12	2	*168*
Portugal - Sex				
Men	57	34	9	*587*
Women	62	33	5	*635*
Age Group				
16-25	61	34	5	*462*
26-45	59	34	7	*464*
46 and over	57	32	10	*296*
Education				
Primary education or lower	64	30	6	*389*
Second level, 1st stage	58	36	5	*313*
Second level, 2nd stage	57	36	7	*280*
Third level, non-university	53	43	4	*93*
Third level, university	59	27	14	*144*

Table A12.5 **Importance to respondents of answering correctly by characteristics of respondent and country.**

	Very important	Quite important	Not very important	Not at all important	*Base*
			%		
Great Britain - Sex					
Men	70	28	2	-	*276*
Women	70	27	2	0	*334*
Age Group					
16-25	[25]	[22]	[2]	-	*49*
26-45	73	25	1	0	*291*
46 and over	70	27	3	-	*264*
Education					
Primary education or lower	[6]	[5]	-	-	*11*
Second level, 1st stage	68	29	2	0	*210*
Second level, 2nd stage	78	20	2	-	*158*
Third level, non-university	66	32	2	-	*104*
Third level, university	66	30	4	-	*125*
Sweden - Sex					
Men	44	50	5	1	*256*
Women	56	41	3	0	*304*
Age Group					
16-25	41	53	5	2	*64*
26-45	52	44	4	-	*233*
46 and over	51	45	3	1	*263*
Education					
Primary education or lower	43	50	7	-	*54*
Second level, 1st stage	48	49	2	2	*190*
Second level, 2nd stage	55	42	3	-	*148*
Third level, non-university	49	47	4	-	*75*
Third level, university	53	41	5	1	*93*
France - Sex					
Men	28	45	20	8	*308*
Women	32	48	16	4	*400*
Age Group					
16-25	32	49	14	5	*85*
26-45	31	47	18	4	*329*
46 and over	28	45	18	9	*290*
Education					
Primary education or lower	26	50	17	6	*92*
Second level, 1st stage	33	44	17	6	*54*
Second level, 2nd stage	33	46	14	7	*308*
Third level, non-university	33	49	16	3	*76*
Third level, university	24	45	26	5	*168*
Portugal - Sex					
Men	33	56	8	2	*586*
Women	32	59	8	1	*634*
Age Group					
16-25	36	57	5	1	*462*
26-45	31	60	8	2	*462*
46 and over	30	54	13	3	*296*
Education					
Primary education or lower	29	54	15	2	*387*
Second level, 1st stage	36	59	4	2	*313*
Second level, 2nd stage	34	60	4	2	*280*
Third level, non-university	29	62	9	-	*93*
Third level, university	37	55	6	3	*144*

Table A12.6 **Whether respondents answered all questions and got to the end of the booklet by characteristics of respondent and country.**

	Got to end			
	All questions answered	Some questions answered	Did not get to end	*Base*
Great Britain - Sex		%		
Men	74	25	1	*276*
Women	52	47	0	*334*
Age Group				
16-25	[27]	[22]	[0]	*49*
26-45	67	33	0	*291*
46 and over	58	41	1	*264*
Education				
Primary education or lower	[1]	[9]	[1]	*11*
Second level, 1st stage	43	56	1	*210*
Second level, 2nd stage	67	33	-	*158*
Third level, non-university	73	27	-	*104*
Third level, university	85	15	-	*125*
Sweden - Sex				
Men	71	8	20	*254*
Women	52	17	31	*297*
Age Group				
16-25	68	11	21	*63*
26-45	66	11	23	*230*
46 and over	55	15	30	*258*
Education				
Primary education or lower	24	26	50	*54*
Second level, 1st stage	47	18	35	*186*
Second level, 2nd stage	72	10	18	*144*
Third level, non-university	70	8	22	*74*
Third level, university	85	4	11	*93*
France - Sex				
Men	54	41	5	*304*
Women	45	50	6	*400*
Age Group				
16-25	66	32	2	*85*
26-45	48	47	4	*330*
46 and over	44	50	7	*285*
Education				
Primary education or lower	22	69	9	*91*
Second level, 1st stage	26	62	11	*53*
Second level, 2nd stage	43	52	5	*305*
Third level, non-university	66	32	1	*77*
Third level, university	73	24	4	*169*
Portugal - Sex				
Men	46	42	11	*587*
Women	39	46	14	*637*
Age Group				
16-25	42	48	11	*463*
26-45	44	43	12	*464*
46 and over	42	41	18	*297*
Education				
Primary education or lower	24	54	22	*389*
Second level, 1st stage	40	48	11	*314*
Second level, 2nd stage	50	40	10	*281*
Third level, non-university	55	43	2	*93*
Third level, university	73	22	5	*144*

Table A12.7 **Respondents opinion on the length of the booklet by characteristics of respondent and country.**

	Too long	Long	About right	*Base*
Great Britain - Sex		%		
Men	17	12	70	*275*
Women	16	16	69	*334*
Age Group				
16-25	[6]	[6]	[37]	*49*
26-45	16	13	71	*291*
46 and over	18	15	67	*263*
Education				
Primary education or lower	[3]	[2]	[6]	*11*
Second level, 1st stage	17	18	66	*210*
Second level, 2nd stage	11	10	79	*158*
Third level, non-university	19	12	68	*104*
Third level, university	19	14	66	*124*
Sweden - Sex				
Men	8	17	75	*250*
Women	10	18	72	*294*
Age Group				
16-25	6	16	78	*64*
26-45	7	15	78	*229*
46 and over	13	20	67	*251*
Education				
Primary education or lower	17	31	52	*52*
Second level, 1st stage	14	21	65	*186*
Second level, 2nd stage	5	11	84	*147*
Third level, non-university	6	17	77	*70*
Third level, university	6	14	81	*89*
France - Sex				
Men	14	30	56	*301*
Women	13	28	59	*395*
Age Group				
16-25	6	29	65	*85*
26-45	12	32	56	*325*
46 and over	17	26	57	*282*
Education				
Primary education or lower	26	25	48	*91*
Second level, 1st stage	15	19	65	*52*
Second level, 2nd stage	14	30	56	*301*
Third level, non-university	9	28	63	*76*
Third level, university	5	33	62	*167*
Portugal - Sex				
Men	40	42	17	*587*
Women	42	42	16	*635*
Age Group				
16-25	37	47	16	*462*
26-45	46	38	16	*463*
46 and over	39	42	19	*297*
Education				
Primary education or lower	47	34	19	*388*
Second level, 1st stage	38	44	18	*314*
Second level, 2nd stage	38	47	15	*280*
Third level, non-university	38	52	11	*93*
Third level, university	40	45	15	*144*

13. Adult Literacy in Portugal

13.1 Introduction

Portugal occupies a central role in this study. While other countries were participating in IALS Portugal conducted its own survey of literacy among adults, the Portuguese Adult Literacy Survey (PALS)[1]. The design of the PALS literacy measurement used a similar conceptual framework of literacy as IALS but was much simpler in construction than the assessment used in the International Adult Literacy Survey (IALS).

Apart from the use of a simpler measure, Portugal was also of interest because of its location. Most of the European countries that took part in the 1994 IALS were in the North of Europe (Sweden, Netherlands, Poland, Ireland, Germany) and the two European countries that took part in 1996 were also Northern, the United Kingdom and the Flemish speaking part of Belgium. Even in the 1998 SIALS, again many of the European countries were from Northern Europe and so far Italy is the only Mediterranean country to have taken part in the IALS programme. Some of the arguments put forward about differences between survey practices focussed on perceived social and cultural differences between Northern and Southern Europe. Portugal therefore offered a unique opportunity to examine measurement in a Southern European context and to test a simple measurement tool against the more complex IALS technique.

This chapter describes the project and its implementation in Portugal, the results from the 1994 PALS study and the follow-up of those respondents in 1998 (section 13.5 and 13.6), the results from the IALS carried out in Portugal as part of this project (PIALS) and how Portugal compares with other countries that participated in IALS (section 13.8) and finally how the distribution from the two surveys compare (section 13.12).

13.2 Study design in Portugal

The design of the study in Portugal was revised several times over the course of the project to take account of changing circumstances. When the current project was initially planned, Portugal were due to participate in the 1998 Second International Adult Literacy Survey (SIALS) and the design of the project assumed the availability of an IALS distribution for adults in Portugal through SIALS. The proposed design was to re-interview the PALS respondents using a split sample design – 600 interviews with the IALS assessment and 600 repeating the PALS assessment. The sample would also be split by whatever intervention would be decided on as potentially improving motivation, i.e. Best Practice.

In late 1997 however, Portugal decided not to proceed with SIALS. This necessitated a review of the proposed study design in Portugal. In the absence of SIALS data for Portugal one option investigated was whether it would be feasible to link the measures by doing a follow-up of the 1994 PALS sample and asking them to complete either an IALS assessment booklet or a combination/rotation of IALS/PALS items. On further analysis it seemed that the educational profile of the 1994 sample looked unlikely to yield sufficient data on IALS items to allow the test to be scaled for Portugal even if the entire sample from 1994 was re-interviewed. The best way of linking the two measures would have been to ask the 1994 PALS to complete an IALS booklet and then the PALS assessment a few days later. This was ruled out on several grounds but particularly because of respondent burden. In order to scale the IALS data at least 1,200 cases of reasonably complete IALS booklets were needed and so an alternative strategy had to be invoked. Having considered a number of possibilities it was

[1] Benavente Ana, Alexandre Rosa, António Firmino da Costa and Patricia Ávila. *A Literacia em Portugal. Resultados de uma Pesquisa Extensiva e Mongráfica.* Fundação Calouste Gulbenkian e Conselho Nacional de Educação. Lisbon 1996.

decided that the only way of achieving sufficient cases to support scaling was if a straightforward IALS was carried out in Portugal alongside a follow-up of PALS. The PALS component would provide an indication of how the PALS distributions might have changed so the linking of IALS/PALS would be based around the distribution from the two (IALS/PALS) components. The design implemented in Portugal was

- a new sample of 1,200 interviews (as a follow-up to the Labour Force Survey) doing an IALS interview and booklet (PIALS)
- a sample of 300 respondents from the 1994 PALS repeating the PALS interview and assessment

The change in design in Portugal impacted greatly on the project. Several major tasks that had not been planned had to be arranged, scheduled and financed. Arrangements had to be made to translate, adapt and validate the IALS test for use in Portugal, carry out a pilot of 300 cases to ensure the items were working well and have the PIALS data scaled independently of SIALS. All these however had to be accommodated within the existing overall budget and timetable.

13.3 The Portuguese Adult Literacy Survey (PALS)

PALS was a much simpler survey than IALS, and as a result considerably cheaper to implement. The assessment comprised two booklets, a core or screening booklet containing nine items with the question asked by the interviewers, and a main booklet containing 24 tasks which the respondent was given to complete. Respondents who did not answer correctly at least five questions in the core booklet were not asked to attempt the main booklet.

The assessment used similar style items to IALS but all stimulus materials were of Portuguese origin. For example, there is an information leaflet for Codifront codeine tablets similar to the Medco aspirin stimulus in IALS. The questions asked about this text in the PALS are almost identical to those in the IALS assessment. A cognitive analysis of the tasks was carried out, using the Kirsch-Mosenthal[2] grammar, to determine the domain and difficulty or level of each task. Although the PALS included prose, document and quantitative type tasks, unlike IALS, these were reported in a single scale.

Tasks were ordered in a hierarchy by looking at the percentage of right answers, and the four levels were assigned so that, for example, Level 1 included all those who had an 80% probability of responding correctly to all the tasks at Level 1 or who answered tasks at Level 2 or higher with less than an 80% probability of success. The score was calculated as the number of correct responses. Because a large number of respondents (about 10%) had no correct answers, they were defined as Level 0. This means that Level 0 and Level 1 in PALS correspond roughly to Level 1 in IALS. Due to the low literacy profile of the Portuguese population, Level 4 was the highest level of the scale, which corresponds approximately to Level 4 and Level 5 in the IALS scale. In practice, this is not any different from most other countries where the proportion of adults at Level 5 was so small that Levels 4 and 5 were combined for reporting purposes.

13.4 Sample design of PALS

The sample for the 1994 Portuguese Adult Literacy Survey was a two-stage stratified probability sample, using the Labour Force Survey as the sampling frame. At the first stage

---

[2] Kirsch, I. Ann Jungeblut and Peter B. Mosenthal. 'The Measurement of Adult Literacy ' in *Adult Literacy in OECD Countries Technical Report on the First International Adult Literacy Survey*. National Center for Education Statistics: Washington 1998

Peter Mosenthal. Defining Prose Task Characteristics for Use in Computer-Adaptive Testing and Instruction. in *American Educational Research Journal*. 1998.

200 statistical sectors in mainland Portugal were selected, each of which contains approximately 300 dwellings. At the second stage one person per household was selected, using a combination of education level, sex, age and economic activity status. The expected achieved sample was 3,000 individuals; in the event, the achieved sample was approximately 2,500 individuals.

The data was weighted to take account of non-response bias and to known population distributions of age, sex and education level. Unlike IALS, PALS did not undertake any imputation or use statistical procedures to adjust for non-response, whether literacy related or not. Respondents were excluded from the sample if for any reason the interview was not completed due to a simple refusal to continue, or where the respondent said they were tired or had an appointment and couldn't continue. For these respondents there was no evidence that the abandonment of the interview or assessment was for literacy related reasons. However, those respondents who failed to complete the booklet due to evident literacy related reasons remained in the sample. For these respondents, who were evidently struggling with the booklet or who said they were not able to do these things, the remaining questions in their booklet were scored as wrong as it was assumed that as the booklet got progressively more difficult they would not have been able to answer the more difficult questions correctly.

The remaining area where statistical procedures might have been used to correct for potential bias is for non-response to the survey. If those who refused to participate in PALS did so for literacy related reasons then the distribution of literacy levels in PALS may be an overestimate of the literacy distribution. The extent to which the full extent of non-response is due to literacy relates is not fully known. However this applies equally to IALS where some countries had significant non-response to the survey. Methodological work on non-response to literacy surveys in the US[3] and Sweden[4] showed that increasing participation in the survey through the use of incentives may bring in more people at the lower end of the literacy scale. In Sweden, it was found that non-responders were from both ends of the literacy distribution. The treatment of non-response, both individual and at item level, is something that could be improved in future PALS surveys. The cut off point for the different levels in PALS is also only an approximation to the IALS cut off levels and therefore may also result in an over or under estimation of proficiency compared with the IALS classification.

13.5 The PALS results - 1994

In 1994 one in ten adults of working age were at Level 0 on the PALS measurement scale, having answered none of the questions in the assessment correctly. Over one third (37%) were estimated to be at Level 1, another third (32%) were at Level 2 and only 13% and 8% of the population of working age were estimated to be at Levels 3 and 4 respectively.

13.5.1 Literacy skills and age

Table 13.1 shows the distribution of literacy skills by age group in PALS. Those in the older age groups were much more likely to be at the lower literacy levels than those in the younger age groups. Almost one third (30%) of the oldest age group, 55-64 years, were at Level 0 and a further 45% were at Level 1. Among those aged 40-54, 10% were at Level 0 and again almost half (48%) were at Level 1. In contrast almost half of those in the youngest age group (15-24) were at Level 2 while very few in this age group were at Level 0, only 4%. One in ten

[3] Groves, R and Couper, M. *Nonresponse in Household Interview Surveys*. Wiley: New York, 1998.
Berlin, M., Mohadjer, L., Waksberg, J., Kolstad, A., Kirsch, I., Rock, D., and Yamamoto, K. 'An experiment in monetary incentives', *Proceedings of the Section on Survey Research Methods*, American Statistical Association, pp. 393-398. 1992.

[4] Darcovich, N et al. Non Response Bias in *Adult Literacy in OECD Countries Technical Report on the First International Adult Literacy Survey*. National Center for Education Statistics: Washington 1998

of those in the two youngest age groups (15-24 and 25-39) performed at the highest literacy level on PALS, Level 4.

Table 13.1 **Portugal: Literacy level by age group 1994**

	Level 0	Level 1	Level 2	Level 3	Level 4	Total	*Base*
Age group	%	%	%	%	%		
15-24	4	24	47	15	10	100	*491*
25-39	5	34	35	16	10	100	*737*
40-54	10	48	25	11	6	100	*687*
55-64	30	45	17	5	3	100	*534*
Total	**10**	**37**	**32**	**13**	**8**	**100**	***2449***

13.5.2 Literacy skills and educational attainment

The level of educational attainment among adults in Portugal is relatively low compared with other European countries. Whilst between a quarter and one third of the population aged 25 to 64 in Britain, Sweden and France had their highest educational attainment level as lower secondary level or lower in 1994, the equivalent percentages for other countries is higher; 55% in Greece and Ireland, 67% in Italy, 74% in Spain and 81% in Portugal. (Table 13.2)

Table 13.2 **Highest level of educational attainment (ISCED) of population aged 25-64 by country (1994)**

Country	Highest level of educational attainment: Second level, 1st stage or lower	Second level, 2nd stage	Third level, non university	Third level, university	Total
	%	%	%	%	%
Belgium	51	27	12	10	100
France	33	50	8	9	100
Germany	16	62	10	13	100
Great Britain	25	54	9	12	100
Greece	55	27	6	12	100
Ireland	55	27	10	9	100
Italy	67	26	..	8	100
Netherlands	40	38	..	21	100
Portugal	81	8	3	7	100
Spain	74	11	4	11	100
Sweden	28	46	14	12	100
Switzerland	18	61	13	8	100
Canada	26	28	29	17	100
United States	15	53	8	24	100

Source: Education at a glance OECD (1996 Paris) Table c1.2 page 35
GB figures supplied by The Scottish Office

These differences between countries in educational attainment levels around the time of PALS are not simply due to the differences in age structure of the populations; there are real differences within age groups. Spain, Portugal and Italy stand out as having relatively low levels of the population who have attained at least upper secondary education. Only 30% of those aged 25-34 in Portugal, 45% of the same group in Spain and 47% in Italy have attained this level of education. Between 84 and 90 percent of the same age group in France, Sweden, Great Britain and Germany have attained this level of education. (Table 13.3) Recent changes in the participation rate in education in Portugal will change this distribution but only very slowly. For example, by 1996[5] 32% of those aged 25-34 in Portugal had attained at least upper secondary education as had 24% of those aged 35-44, an increase of two percentage points in 2 years.

[5] *Education at a Glance Indicators 1998*. OECD 1998 Table A1.2a page 43.

Table 13.3 **Percentage who had attained at least upper secondary education (ISCED 3) by age group and country (1994)**

Country	Age-group 25-34	35-45	45-54	55-64
	Percentage who had attained ISCED 3			
Belgium	65	54	43	28
France	84	73	60	41
Germany	90	88	84	72
Great Britain	86	79	69	58
Greece	62	50	35	26
Ireland	61	47	35	27
Italy	47	41	26	14
Netherlands	69	64	54	44
Portugal	30	22	15	8
Spain	45	29	16	9
Sweden	85	78	69	52
Switzerland	89	84	79	73
Canada	82	79	70	53
United States	86	89	85	76

Source: Education at a glance OECD (1996 Paris) Table c1.2 page 36
GB figures supplied by The Scottish Office

For reporting purposes PALS classified educational attainment using categories which discriminated better in Portugal than the international classification of education attainment (ISCED) used in IALS. The classifications used equate roughly to no education (some never went to school and others did for a while but didn't complete any level of education); "básico 1" corresponds to approximately four years of education; "básico 2" to six years of education; "básico 3" to nine years of education; "secundário" to twelve years of education; and, finally, "superior" correspond to more than twelve years of education. There was a very strong relationship between literacy and education, as shown in Table 13.4. Almost half of those with the highest level of education were also at the highest literacy level (47%) as were 29% of those with secondary education and 16% of those educated to "básico 3" level. Almost all of those with little or no education were at the lower literacy levels, 95% of those with very little or no education were at Level 0 or Level 1 as were 62% of those with minimal education (básico 1).

Table 13.4 **Portugal: Literacy by level of highest qualification (PALS 1994)**

	Level 0	Level 1	Level 2	Level 3	Level 4	Total	*Base*
Level of education	%	%	%	%	%		
S/grau (none or very little)	47	48	5	-	-	100	*209*
Básico 1 (4 years)	4	58	31	5	1	99	*230*
Básico 2 (6 years)	1	26	60	10	3	100	*408*
Básico 3 (9 years)	0	9	43	32	16	100	*406*
Seundário (12 years)	-	3	27	41	29	100	*747*
Superior (more than 12 years)	-	4	21	28	47	100	*449*
Total	**22**	**22**	**30**	**31**	**17**	**122**	***2449***

13.6 The PALS follow-up survey

The second part of the design described in section 13.2 involved the a follow-up survey similar to that in the other countries involved in the project (see Chapter 11). A sample of (PALS) respondents were visited again in 1998 and asked to redo the PALS interview and assessment. Altogether 265 interviews were conducted. There were some minor differences in the way PALS was administered between 1994 and 1998, for example, in the 1998 retest some results from the original PALS were sent out with the advance letter to make a recall more plausible and acceptable to respondents. Interviewers were also given additional guidelines on how to administer the booklet. As in other countries the sample selected was not intended to be fully representative. For example, those who were at level 0 were excluded from the follow-up survey because very little data was available for them in the PALS as they might have done none or only very few questions in the assessment. The distribution of the PALS literacy level for those who took part in the follow-up survey for both years is shown below along with the distribution of the total sample in 1994.

Table 13.5 **PALS: Literacy level for PALS (1994) and retest sample (1994 and 1998) (weighted)**

		Retest sample	
Literacy Level	**1994 PALS**	**1994 PALS**	**1998 PALS**
	%	%	%
Level 0	10		
Level 1	37	43	38
Level 2	32	35	40
Level 3	13	15	15
Level 4	8	6	6
Total	**100**	**100**	**100**
Base	*2449*	*265*	*265*

The distribution of PALS literacy levels in the retest sample in 1998 and 1994 are shown in Table 13.5. At the higher literacy levels there is no change in the proportions at Level 3 or Level 4 in the retest sample between the two assessments. The main change in the retest sample was at the lower end of the literacy distribution although these were not statistically significant. The proportion of the retest sample at the lowest literacy level, Level 1, decreased from 43% in 1994 to 38% in 1998 with a corresponding increase in the proportion at Level 2. As those at the very lowest literacy level (Level 0) were excluded from the retest this may be over optimistic in terms of the whole sample.

Table 13.6 compares the unweighted PALS literacy level in 1994 with the level in 1998. Most respondents were at the same level on the two occasions. Three quarters of those at Level 1 in 1994 were also at Level 1 in 1998, and almost one quarter were now at Level 2. None of the respondents at Level 1 in 1994 had improved sufficiently to reach Level 3 or 4. The majority of those at Level 2 in 1994 (70%) were at the same skill level in 1998, just over one in ten were now at a lower skill level (12% at Level 0/1 in 1998) and 18% were at a higher literacy level. The numbers of those at Level 4 in 1994 in the sample are very small, but if Levels 3 and 4 are combined, three quarters remain within the same level and a quarter are at a lower level in 1998 than when tested in 1994.

Table 13.6 **PALS literacy level in 1994 by the level in 1998 (unweighted).**

	PALS Level 1998					
	Level 1	**Level 2**	**Level 3**	**Level 4**	**Total**	**Bases**
PALS Level 1994	%	%	%	%	%	
Level 0/1	77	23	-	-	100	*106*
Level 2	12	70	14	4	100	*89*
Level 3	-	33	56	11	100	*46*
Level 4	-	[2]	[12]	[10]	100	*24*
Total	**35**	**39**	**19**	**7**	**100**	***265***

13.7 Item performance in 1994 and 1998

Table 13.7 shows the percent correct for each item in PALS in the entire sample in 1994 and in the retest sample in both 1994 and 1998. For most items there was little difference in the proportion of respondents who answered the question correctly. Where there was a difference it was, for over two thirds of the items, that the percentage who answered the question correctly was higher in 1998 than in 1994 although for many question the differences were very small.

Table 13.7 **PALS: percent correct on each item by type of sample**

Items	Level/Scale	94 PALS all sample unweighted	94 PALS all sample weighted	94 PALS retest sample unweighted	98 PALS retest sample unweighted
		% who answered question correctly			
A11	Level 1 – P, D	79	79	88	91
A12	Level 1 - D	74	74	81	83
A22	Level 1 - P	61	59	65	71
A31	Level 1 – Q	70	70	78	79
A32	Level 1 – Q	65	64	71	74
A41	Level 1 – P	68	67	76	79
A42	Level 1 – P	60	59	62	69
A51	Level 1 – Q, D	62	60	67	70
A52	Level 2 – Q, D	50	47	53	59
B11	Level 4 – D	19	16	17	14
B12	Level 4 – D	15	14	12	10
B13	Level 2 – D	44	40	45	43
B21	Level 2 – D	43	41	43	54
B22	Level 2 – D	45	43	49	55
B23	Level 2 – D	46	44	50	48
B24	Level 3 – D	34	30	35	32
B3	Level 3 – Q	43	38	43	47
B41	Level 2 – D	51	48	52	56
B42	Level 4 – D	22	19	22	20
B51	Level 1 – Q	56	52	60	65
B52	Level 2 – Q	49	45	53	56
B53	Level 3 – Q	42	38	46	48
B61	Level 2 – P	47	43	47	52
B62	Level 2 – P	47	43	49	47
B71	Level 3 – P	36	32	36	38
B72	Level 3 – P	40	35	40	43
B73	Level 4 – P	22	18	23	22
B81	Level 4 – P	10	8	10	9
B82	Level 4 – P	10	8	10	8
B83	Level 4 - D	8	6	8	10
B91	Level 3 – Q	35	31	37	37
B92	Level 3 – Q	29	24	30	23
B10	Level 4 – Q	14	12	15	17
Base		*2449*	*2449*	*265*	*265*

The average number of items answered correctly in 1998 was slightly higher for the retest group in 1998 than for the same group in 1994. There were also differences between groups in the average number of questions answered correctly. Those in the younger age groups had a higher mean number of correct answers than those in the older age groups. (Table 13.8)

Table 13.8 **Mean number of correct answers in PALS by type of sample and age-group**

Age	PALS 94 (All)	Retest Sample –1994	Retest Sample – 1998	*Base Retest sample*
	Mean number of correct answers			
16-35	16.0	16.1	16.9	*109*
36-50	12.6	12.7	13.2	*82*
50-65	7.5	9.7	10.3	*74*
Total	**13.1**	**13.7**	**14.3**	**265**
Base	*2449*	*265*	*265*	

As one might expect the number of questions correct on the two occasions were highly correlated with a correlation co-efficient of 0.853. Figure 13.1 shows a plot of the PALS literacy measure in 1994 with that for the same people in 1998. While the measure in 1994 is a good predictor of performance in 1998 there are anomalies with some people scoring better on the exact same test in 1994 than they did in 1998. Most of this is occuring around the bottom end of the distribution. Some of this will be accounted for by non-response at individual and at item level.

Figure 13.1 **Scatterplot of number of items correct in Pals 94 and 94.**

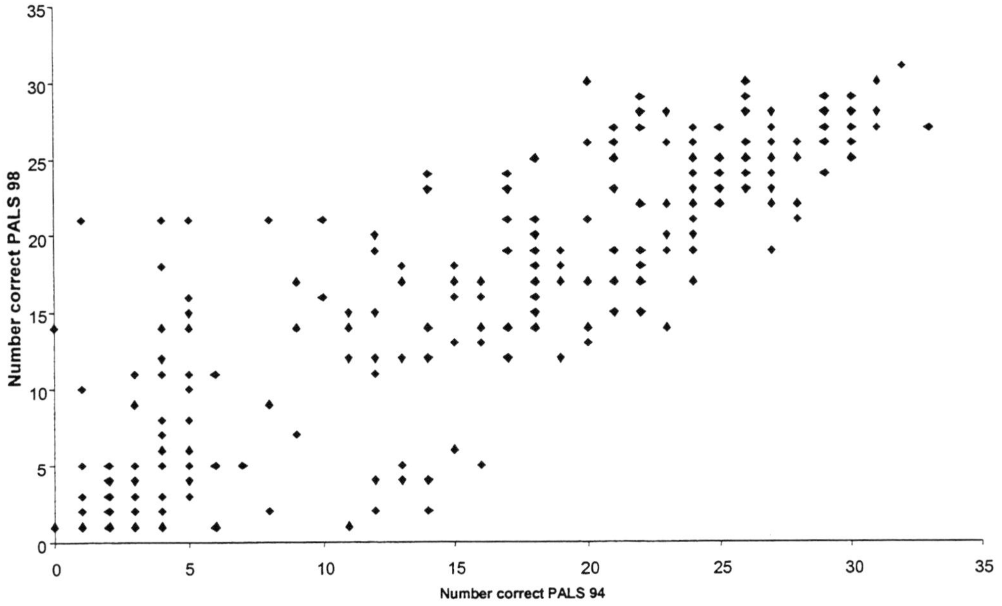

13.8 The International Adult Literacy Survey in Portugal (PIALS)

With the revised design described in section 13.2, the project effectively required an IALS to be conducted in Portugal in 1998. However this took place outside the usual IALS structure which provided guidance and explanation about exactly what was required. As a substitute for this support the GB IALS project manager (from the ONS) worked very closely with the Portuguese IALS team.

In preparation for conducting IALS in 1998, the IALS materials were translated into Portuguese. As in many of the other countries in which IALS had been carried out, the research team expressed concerns about the cultural acceptability of some of the translated items. For example, the weather map (B2Q8) used symbols which differed from those ordinarily found in Portuguese newspapers. The questions on the child's car safety seat (B5Q3-Q6) used concepts which differed substantially from a similar booklet used in Portugal for the same purpose.

13.9 Survey design - PIALS

The Portuguese IALS sample is based on a follow-up to the Labour Force Survey. In order to maximise the volume of data on the booklets, the sample under-represents the lower end of the educational distribution and over-represents those at the middle and upper education levels. The ratios are 10:45:45. A small pilot had to be carried out to test the psychometric characteristics of the PIALS test. A pilot of 300 was done in May 1998; the booklets were scored and processed and then sent to Statistics Canada and ETS for evaluation. This pilot produced little data that could be used as many people were abandoning the booklet at a very early stage. The background questionnaire used in the pilot included all the IALS core and optional questions. Following the pilot it was felt necessary to reduce the length of the background questionnaire considerably by excluding all the optional questions and by carrying forward information from the LFS interview where possible. For example, where the respondent had not changed employment between the LFS interview and the IALS interview the occupation and industry data was carried forward from the LFS.

13.10 Distribution of IALS levels

Almost half (49%) of adults in the PIALS survey were at the lowest literacy level (Level 1) on the prose and document scales and 43% were at this level on the quantitative scale. There were no significant differences in the proportions of men and women at the different levels for prose literacy. Higher proportions of women than of men, however, were at Level 1 for document and quantitative literacy. Just over a third (36%) of men were estimated to be at Level 1 on the quantitative scale compared with 50% of women.

Table 13.9 **Portugal: IALS literacy level by sex**

	Level 1		Level 2		Level 3		Level 4/5		Total	Mean	*Base*
Sex	%	*s.e.*	%	*s.e.*	%	*s.e.*	%	*s.e.*			
Prose literacy											
Men	47	*2.4*	30	*2.1*	18	*1.6*	5	*0.6*	100	227	*597*
Women	51	*2.1*	27	*1.9*	18	*0.9*	5	*0.4*	100	218	*641*
Total	**49**	***1.6***	**28**	***1.4***	**18**	***0.9***	**5**	***0.3***	**100**	**223**	***1238***
Document literacy											
Men	44	*2.6*	34	*2.5*	18	*1.0*	4	*0.5*	100	229	*597*
Women	53	*2.5*	29	*1.9*	15	*1.0*	2	*0.2*	100	212	*641*
Total	**49**	***2.1***	**32**	***1.7***	**17**	***0.7***	**3**	***0.3***	**100**	**220**	***1238***
Quantitative literacy											
Men	36	*2.7*	32	*2.5*	25	*1.9*	8	*0.9*	100	244	*597*
Women	50	*2.7*	26	*1.6*	20	*1.5*	4	*0.4*	100	219	*641*
Total	**43**	***1.9***	**29**	***1.5***	**23**	***1.2***	**6**	***0.5***	**100**	**231**	***1238***

s.e. Standard error of the estimate. The reported sample estimate can be said to be within 2 standard errors of the true population value with 95% confidence.

13.10.1 Literacy skills and age

As expected, Table 13.10 hows a strong relationship between literacy skill and age for the prose scale, with those in the youngest age group being least likely to be at the lower end of the proficiency scale on all three scales. Among those in the youngest age group, 16-25, a quarter were at the lowest literacy level on prose and document literacy compared to 41-46% of those in the next youngest age group, 26-35, and about half of those in the three oldest age groups.

Table 13.10 **Portugal: IALS prose literacy level by age group**

	Level 1		Level 2		Level 3		Level 4/5		Total	Mean score	*Base*
Age group	%	s.e.	%	s.e.	%	s.e.	%	s.e.			
Prose literacy											
16-25	25	*2.5*	37	*1.7*	28	*1.7*	10	*0.8*	100	260	*466*
26-35	46	*3.7*	25	*2.4*	22	*2.0*	6	*0.7*	100	232	*233*
36-45	59	*4.2*	23	*2.7*	14	*2.4*	4	*0.9*	100	210	*233*
46-55	55	*3.9*	32	*3.4*	11	*2.0*	2	*0.5*	100	210	*196*
56 and over	71	*4.8*	20	*3.9*	8	*2.5*	1	*0.6*	100	184	*110*
Total	**49**	***1.6***	**28**	***1.4***	**18**	***0.9***	**5**	***0.3***	**100**	**223**	***1238***

s.e. Standard error of the estimate. The reported sample estimate can be said to be within 2 standard errors of the true population value with 95% confidence.

Although these differences are large there is quite a wide margin of error around the estimates. Because they are based on a sample and on a relatively small sample size rather than the whole population they are subject to error, some of which is measurable. One measure of the precision of a survey estimate is the standard error, which allows us to estimate how close the results from this survey are likely to be to the true population value. The precision of a survey estimate is related to the variability of the characteristics of interest, in this case literacy, the size of the sample and the sample design. The larger the sample the smaller the standard error will be and the smaller the standard error the more confident we can be of the reliability of the estimates. As the size of the subgroup decreases the standard error increases, making the estimates less reliable. To illustrate the importance of taking account of such sampling error, Figure 13.2 shows the confidence intervals around the estimates of the proportion of the population at Level 1 on the prose scale for each age group. If one hundred separate samples were taken, the estimate of those at Level 1 in each age-group would fall within the ranges shown in 95 of those 100 samples.

Figure 13.2 Prose Literacy: 95% confidence intervals of estimated proportion at Level 1 by age group, Portugal

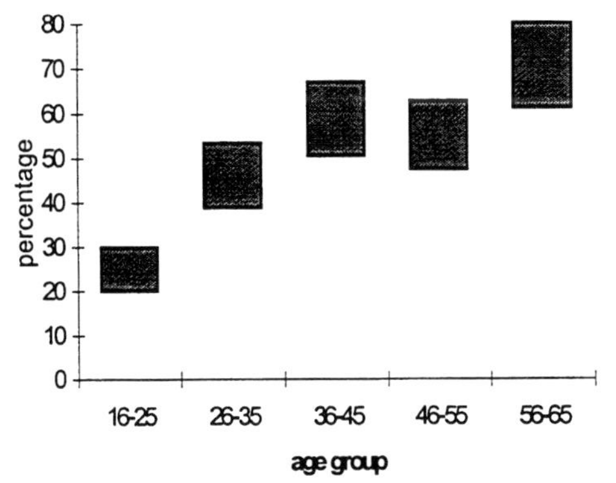

13.10.2 IALS literacy and educational attainment

In IALS the harmonised education variable used is the International Standard Classificaiton of Education (ISCED) which is a commonly used classification for making international comparisons. ISCED divides educaitonal attainment into 7 categories which span three broad levels of educaiton roughly equivalent to primary, secondary and tertiary education. In countries such as Portugal where the educational profile of the population as a whole is skewed towards the lower end of the distribution ISCED does not offer a very discrimiating classification since almost two thirds of the population are at ISCED level 1. As we have seen in section 13.5 a more usual classification used in Portugal corresponds to years of education. In this section literacy level as measured in IALS is presented using both education classifications

There was a very clear association between literacy levels and educational attainment in Portugal. Figure 13.3 shows that there was an incremental shift in the mean estimated literacy score with increasing education (ISCED). On the prose scale those with Primary education or lower had a mean estimated score of 190 compared with 267 for those with lower secondary education and 311 for those with university education. Almost three quarters (71%) of those with only primary education or lower were at Level 1 on prose compared with only 13% or fewer of those at the higher education levels (Table A13.2). Between a quarter and a third of men with any sort of third level education were at Prose levels 4/5. On the quantitative scale, 32% of those with university education and 23% of those with third level non-university education were at the highest literacy level. Among men more than one in three of those with university education were at level 4/5 on the quantitative scale.

Figure 13.3 **PIALS: mean estimated literacy score by literacy scale and level of educational attainment (ISCED)**

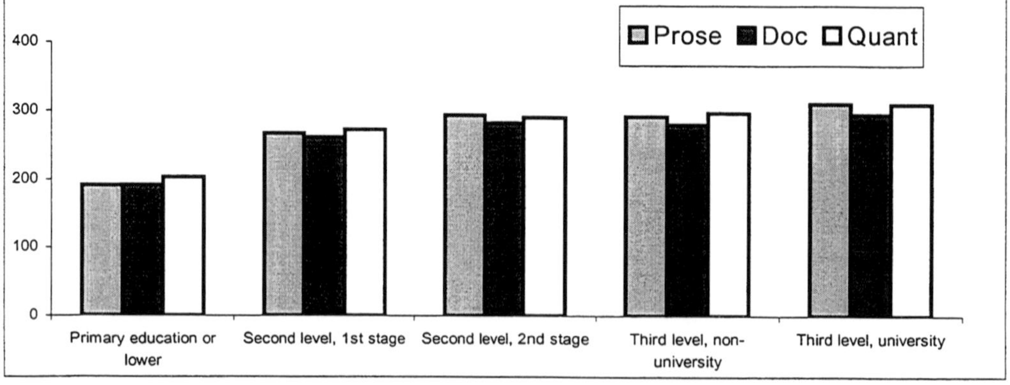

Table 13.11 shows the distribution using the more normal classification of educational attainment used in Portugal. As expected it shows a similar pattern observed above with those at the lower levels of education more likely to be at literacy Levels 1 and 2. Although literacy proficiency as measured in these surveys is strongly associated with education whichever classification is used there is a minority of people for whom it is not a good indicator of their literacy skill. A small percentage at both ends of the spectrum did not fit the expected pattern. On the prose scale 3% of those with university education were estimated to be at Level 1 as were 6% of those with third level, non-university education.

Table 13.11 **Portugal: IALS prose literacy level (first plausible value) by highest level of educational attainment**

	Level 1	Level 2	Level 3	Level 4/5	Total	*Base*
Prose literacy			%			
S/grau (none or very little)	[20]	[2]	[1]	..	100	*23*
Básico 1 (4 years)	74	21	5	..	100	*121*
Básico 2 (6 years)	53	38	9	0	100	*251*
Básico 3 (9 years)	11	53	30	6	100	*223*
Seundário (12 years)	14	37	43	6	100	*97*
Superior (more than 12 years)	4	23	53	21	100	*523*
Total	**49**	**28**	**18**	**5**	**100**	*1238*

13.10.3 IALS literacy and economic activity status

Literacy was also associated with economic activity status in Portugal as in many other countries. A higher proportion of the unemployed were estimated to Level 1 on all three literacy scales than were employed respondents. On the prose scale 47% of those in employment were estimated to be at the lowest literacy level, Level 1 compared with 60% of those who were unemployed._ Many of these characteristics are inter-related, young people being more educated and more likely to be economically active or studying.

Table 13.12 **Portugal: IALS literacy level by employment status**

Employment status	**Level 1**		**Level 2**		**Level 3**		**Level 4/5**		**Total**	**Mean**	***Base***
Prose literacy	%	s.e.	%	s.e.	%	s.e.	%	s.e.			
Working	47	2.5	29	1.9	19	1.3	5	0.5	100	225	*773*
Unemployed	60	3.1	25	3.9	13	2.1	2	0.6	100	214	*101*
Student	7	1.6	37	2.3	41	2.7	15	1.8	100	284	*216*
Economically inactive	72	3.5	22	3.4	5	0.8	1	0.3	100	184	*148*
Total	**49**	**1.6**	**28**	**1.4**	**18**	**0.9**	**5**	**0.3**	**100**	**223**	***1238***
Document literacy											
Working	47	2.9	33	2.4	17	1.1	3	0.4	100	223	*773*
Unemployed	58	5.2	26	4.0	14	3.1	2	1.0	100	219	*101*
Student	9	1.7	43	2.0	39	2.4	9	1.1	100	276	*216*
Economically inactive	72	3.0	23	2.9	5	0.8	1	0.2	100	182	*148*
Total	**49**	**2.1**	**32**	**1.7**	**17**	**0.7**	**3**	**0.3**	**100**	**220**	***1238***
Quantitative literacy											
Working	40	3.1	30	2.1	24	1.5	6	0.7	100	236	*773*
Unemployed	56	4.9	28	4.5	15	2.5	2	0.7	100	218	*101*
Student	8	1.3	37	2.9	43	2.8	12	1.2	100	281	*216*
Economically inactive	64	4.1	23	3.5	11	2.1	1	0.3	100	194	*148*
Total	**43**	**1.9**	**29**	**1.5**	**23**	**1.2**	**6**	**0.5**	**100**	**231**	***1238***

s.e. Standard error of the estimate. The reported sample estimate can be said to be within 2 standard errors of the true population value with 95% confidence.

13.10.4 Literacy skills in everyday life

Most people use literacy skills as they go about their daily life where a typical day might involve reading the newspaper, consulting a timetable to see when the next bus is going to arrive, checking food labels in the shop or supermarket, or reading instructions on how much soap powder to put in the washing machine. Respondents were asked about their use of literacy in the workplace and at home. The frequency with which respondents reported they read newspapers, magazines and books, was clearly associated with literacy levels. Among those who never read newspapers or magazines, 88% were at Level 1 on the prose and quantitative scales, with 85% at Level 1 on the document literacy scale. The corresponding proportions for those who never read books were 62%, 50% and 52%. Between a quarter and a third of of daily newspaper readers were at the lowest literacy level, Level 1, on each scale, as were approximately one in 10 of those who read books on a daily basis.

Table 13.13 **Portugal: IALS literacy level by frequency of reading newspapers and magazines**

Frequency of reading	Level 1		Level 2		Level 3		Level 4/5		Total	Mean score	*Base*
Prose literacy	%	s.e.	%	s.e.	%	s.e.	%	s.e.			
Daily	31	3.1	37	2.5	26	1.5	7	0.7	100	250	*631*
Weekly	46	2.4	30	2.4	18	1.3	7	0.7	100	233	*417*
Monthly	68	4.8	24	3.5	7	1.7	0	0.1	100	184	*73*
Several times a year	78	6.1	11	2.6	10	5.4	1	0.4	100	175	*66*
Never	88	3.6	8	2.4	3	2.4	0	0.0	100	157	*51*
Total	**49**	**1.6**	**28**	**1.4**	**18**	**0.9**	**5**	**0.3**	**100**	**223**	***1238***
Document literacy											
Daily	30	3	41	2.5	24	1.6	5	0.5	100	248	*631*
Weekly	47	2.8	32	2.4	17	1.2	4	0.5	100	226	*417*
Monthly	69	4.9	22	3.2	9	2.2	1	0.2	100	189	*73*
Several times a year	77	6.6	18	6.1	4	1.4	1	0.3	100	175	*66*
Never	85	5.6	12	4.9	3	2.4	0	0.0	100	161	*51*
Total	**49**	**2.1**	**32**	**1.7**	**17**	**0.7**	**3**	**0.3**	**100**	**220**	***1238***
Quantitative literacy											
Daily	22	2.9	38	2.5	31	2.4	8	1.0	100	260	*631*
Weekly	39	2.6	31	2.6	23	1.5	7	0.8	100	239	*417*
Monthly	66	5.5	20	3.2	13	2.9	2	0.7	100	201	*73*
Several times a year	76	6.4	11	3.1	11	5.3	1	0.7	100	180	*66*
Never	88	4.1	8	2.7	5	3.0	0	0.1	100	162	*51*
Total	**43**	**1.9**	**29**	**1.5**	**23**	**1.2**	**6**	**0.5**	**100**	**231**	***1238***

s.e. Standard error of the estimate. The reported sample estimate can be said to be within 2 standard errors of the true population value with 95% confidence.

13.11 How does Portugal compare with other countries on IALS measures

While the legitimacy of making international comparisons has been a major tenet of this study for the purposes of this analysis we report on the findings from the IALS at face value.

Figure 13.4 **Literacy level by country**

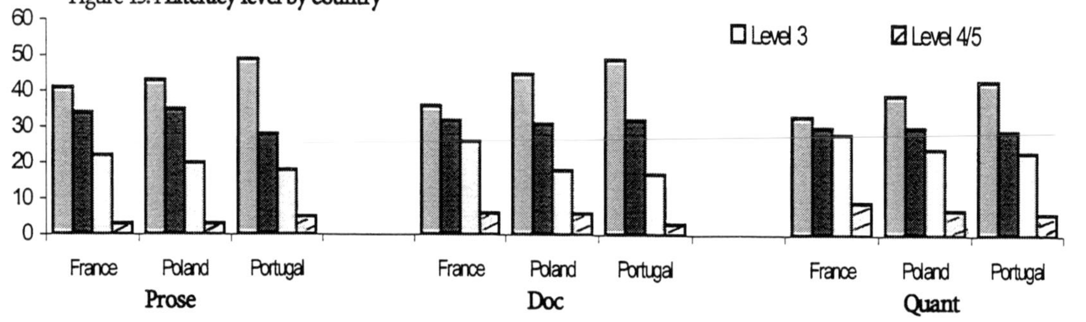

The pattern of association between estimated literacy proficiency and respondents' characteristics in Portugal is very similar to that observed in other countries which have taken part in IALS, but the distribution across literacy levels and between literacy scales varies between countries. Compared with other countries Portugal has large proportions of the population estimated to be at the lowest literacy levels. Portugal, Poland, France and Sweden, show a very skewed distribution across the different literacy levels, with the majority of the population at either the lower end or, in the case of Sweden, at the upper end of the distribution. Germany and the Netherlands, by contrast, have more centrally distributed skill levels, with the majority of the population at the middle levels. Britain, the United States and Canada have a more uniform distribution across the literacy levels; although the majority of the population was at the middle levels, there are large proportions of respondents at the highest and lowest levels.

Portugal has a very similar distribution on the prose scale across the literacy levels as Poland and France and similar distributions to Poland on the document and quantitative scale with France having lower proportions at the lower literacy levels on both these scales. Figure 13.4 shows the distribution for each scale for these three countries.

Compared with the wider range of countries Table 13.14 show literacy distributions for a number of countries for prose. Figure 13.5a 13.5b, which displays the confidence intervals around the estimates for the different countries, shows that in IALS Portugal, France and Poland had significantly higher proportions of the population at Level 1 on prose literacy, and significantly lower proportions at Level 4/5, than all the other countries.

Figure 13.5a **95% confidence intervals of estimated percentage of population at Level 1 prose scale by country**

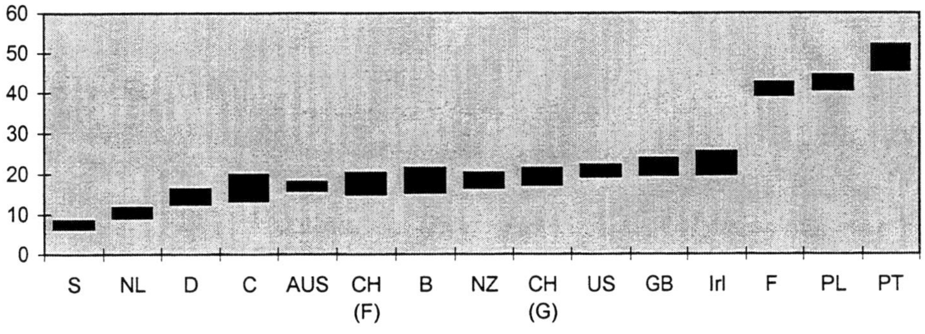

Figure 13.5b **95% confidence intervals of estimated percentage of population at Level 4/5 prose scale by country**

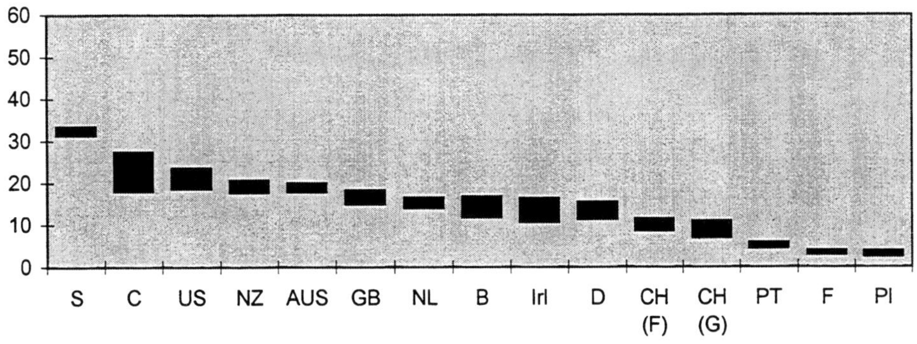

13.12 How PALS and PIALS compare

In PALS the proportion of respondents at Level 1 on prose was 47% in 1994 and the proportion of respondents in PIALS at Level 1 in 1998 was 49%. Both of these are only survey estimates of the proportion of the population at this level and as such as subject to error. From the PIALS survey we can be 95% confident that the proportion of the population aged 16-65 in Portugal at Prose level 1 in 1998 is somewhere between 41% and 44%, that is, that if we did 100 did surveys, in 95 of those surveys the proportion at Level 1 would be within that range. The results from PALS is also subject to a margin of error so that we can be 95% confident that the true value for Level 0/1 on PALS lies between 45% and 49%. Although the retest was not sufficiently large to allow re-estimation of the survey results the direction of change in the PALS retest was towards improvement in literacy score this suggests there is little difference between the two surveys.

Table 13.4 **Prose literacy level by country**

	Level 1		Level 2		Level 3		Level 4/5		Total
Prose literacy	%	s.e.	%	s.e.	%	s.e.	%	s.e.	%
Canada	17	1.6	26	1.8	35	2.4	23	2.3	100
France	41	0.8	34	0.8	22	0.8	3	0.2	100
Germany	14	0.9	34	1.0	38	1.3	13	1.0	100
Great Britain	22	1.0	30	1.3	31	1.2	17	0.8	100
Netherlands	11	0.6	30	0.9	44	1.0	15	0.6	100
Poland	43	0.9	35	0.9	20	0.7	3	0.3	100
Portugal	49	1.6	28	1.4	18	0.9	5	0.3	100
Sweden	8	0.5	20	0.6	40	0.9	32	0.5	100
Switzerland (French)	18	1.3	34	1.6	39	1.8	10	0.7	100
Switzerland (German)	19	1.0	36	1.6	36	1.3	9	1.0	100
United States	21	0.7	26	1.1	32	1.2	21	1.2	100

s.e. Standard error of the estimate. The reported sample estimate can be said to be within 2 standard errors of the true population value with 95% confidence.

PALS did not distinguish between the different dimensions of literacy covered in the IALS. It includes some questions on each dimension but not in sufficient numbers to be able to report on them separately. While the PALS and PIALS distributions are reasonably close on the prose scale in particular, the quantitative scale shows a quite different distribution with a smaller proportion of the population in Portugal at the lowest level, Level 1.

Figure 13.6 **PALS 94 and PIALS 98 literacy level**

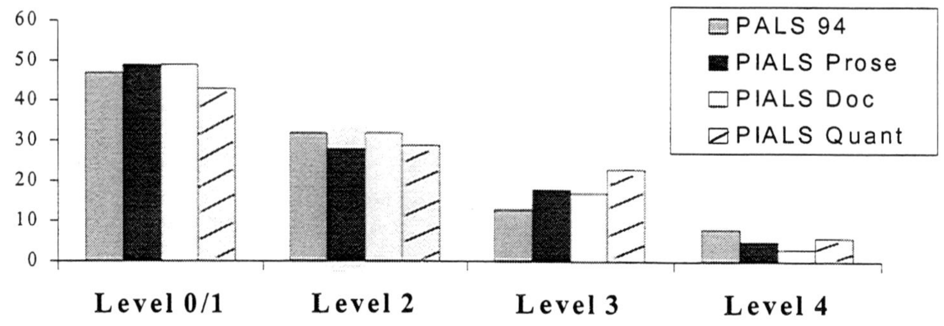

As in other countries the IALS proficiency estimate on each scale was highly correlated with the simpler summary measure proportion correct with a correlation co-efficients of 0.892 with the prose scale (first plausible value). The internal relationships within the two data sets are also similar, in the PIALS age had a negative correlation co-efficient of –0.262 with the prose scale while in PALS age and number of questions correct had a negative correlation of –0.292. Similarly, when looking at the relationship with education level the pattern is similar in both surveys. In PIALS the correlation co-efficient for prose literacy with education is 0.577 using ISCED and 0.681 using the more commonly used classification in Portugal. In the PALS data the correlation co-efficient for PALS literacy measure and the Portuguese education classification is 0.745. Within both surveys the relationships between the measure and the key characteristics of age and education level appear to be of similar order.

13.13 Conclusions

The comparison between PALS and PIALS raises a number of interesting questions. One of these is how accurate a measure is necessary. Surveys such as IALS and PALS are done to meet specific needs. One question to be asked is how sophisticated an answer is needed to the question 'How literate is our nation?" The PALS survey has produced a measure of literacy for which the distribution is reasonably close to that produced by the IALS and which has probably been just as useful to policy makers in Portugal as the IALS data has been to policy makers elsewhere. Admittedly, the PALS borrowed substantially from the conceptual developments from the US that fed in to IALS and were not in any sense starting with a blank sheet. The advantages of the simpler method of analysis however are many including transparency cost and ease of communicating what has been measured. PALS used a single booklet and a single scale and while the disadvantages of that choice are limitations on the breadth of the assessment it does mean that the measure is at the individual rather than the population level and relationships identified are not blurred or potentially spurious from the imputation procedures used in scaling. Given the other many sources of non-sampling error that can impinge on a survey of this type as seen elsewhere in this report a measure such as this may be perfectly adequate for most purposes.

The problem of the complexity of the measures produced by IALS is not insignificant. IALS uses complex procedures for imputing proficiency levels for those who have either not attempted the booklet at all or who have not done very much of the booklet. This is perfectly reasonable to do. If no adjustment were made for such cases then the literacy distribution would overestimate the true skills of the population and an unknown amount of non-response will be literacy related. The data which is used to impute proficiency estimates for those non-responders is taken from the background questionnaire on the assumption that "the missing cognitive data are similar to the observed data *when the background information is the same.*"[6]. Various things such as age, sex, ethnicity and education level are used to produce the proficiency estimates. In IALS respondents only answer a small part of the whole test and so adjustments also have to be made for the profile of tasks that the respondent has been presented with.

The IALS dataset consists of multiple plausible values. For each individual for each of the three scale a series of values are produced. This leaves the non-pyschometrician researcher with a problem. First, conceptually it is difficult to comprehend that what we have are several *estimates* of the proficiency which has embedded in it characteristics of the respondent. Respondents often ask for feedback on how they did and it seems implausible to them that their skill can not be estimated simply from what they have answered. In looking at the plausible values for individual cases there can be quite a wide range of values observed with respondents being variably at Levels 1, 2 or 3 depending on which plausible value is taken. Secondly, there is a concern that the relationships observed between background characteristics and the skills levels are enhanced or exaggerated by the IRT procedures where background characteristics are used to condition the estimates. One questions for example the validity of using multivariate techniques for example on the proficiency estimates as one is never sure how much of the perceived relationships is due to the factors in the analysis having already been taken into account in the conditioning and estimation procedures. The potential for identifying spurious relationships is a cause for concern and needs to be borne in mind when analysing this type of data set.

---

[6] Yamamoto, Kentaro and I. Kirsch. 'Proficiency Estimation' in *Adult Literacy in OECD Countries Technical Report on the First International Adult Literacy Survey*. National Center for Education Statistics: Washington 1998 p186.

Appendix tables

Tables A13.1 – A13.3

Table A13.1 **Portugal: IALS literacy level by age group**

	Level 1		Level 2		Level 3		Level 4/5		Total	Mean score	*Base*
Age group	%	s.e.	%	s.e.	%	s.e.	%	s.e.			
Prose literacy											
16-25	25	*2.5*	37	*1.7*	28	*1.7*	10	*0.8*	100	260	*466*
26-35	46	*3.7*	25	*2.4*	22	*2.0*	6	*0.7*	100	232	*233*
36-45	59	*4.2*	23	*2.7*	14	*2.4*	4	*0.9*	100	210	*233*
46-55	55	*3.9*	32	*3.4*	11	*2.0*	2	*0.5*	100	210	*196*
56 and over	71	*4.8*	20	*3.9*	8	*2.5*	1	*0.6*	100	184	*110*
Total	**49**	***1.6***	**28**	***1.4***	**18**	***0.9***	**5**	***0.3***	**100**	**223**	***1238***
Document literacy											
16-25	25	*2.9*	41	*2.1*	28	*1.8*	6	*0.7*	100	255	*466*
26-35	43	*3.7*	32	*3.4*	20	*1.6*	4	*0.8*	100	229	*233*
36-45	61	*4.3*	24	*2.7*	13	*2.1*	2	*0.4*	100	206	*233*
46-55	52	*4.9*	36	*4.7*	10	*1.7*	2	*0.5*	100	212	*196*
56 and over	73	*3.2*	20	*2.1*	6	*2.3*	0	*0.2*	100	183	*110*
Total	**49**	***2.1***	**32**	***1.7***	**17**	***0.7***	**3**	***0.3***	**100**	**220**	***1238***
Quantitative literacy											
16-25	22	*2.2*	39	*1.9*	31	*1.8*	8	*0.7*	100	261	*466*
26-35	41	*4.8*	27	*4.7*	24	*2.1*	7	*0.8*	100	238	*233*
36-45	54	*3.8*	21	*1.5*	21	*3.5*	4	*0.6*	100	217	*233*
46-55	45	*5.3*	31	*4.4*	19	*2.1*	5	*1.7*	100	228	*196*
56 and over	62	*4.3*	24	*3.3*	12	*3.0*	2	*0.8*	100	199	*110*
Total	**43**	***1.9***	**29**	***1.5***	**23**	***1.2***	**6**	***0.5***	**100**	**231**	***1238***

s.e. Standard error of the estimate. The reported sample estimate can be said to be within 2 standard errors of the true population value with 95% confidence.

Table A13.2 **Portugal: IALS literacy level by highest level of educational attainment and sex**

	Level 1		Level 2		Level 3		Level 4/5		Total	Mean score	*Base*
Prose literacy	%	*s.e.*	%	s.e.	%	s.e.	%	s.e.	%		
Men											
Primary education or lower	67	*3.3*	26	*3.0*	6	*1.7*	1	*0.4*	100	199	*202*
Second level, 1st stage	13	*1.9*	46	*2.3*	33	*3.4*	8	*2.3*	100	268	*163*
Second level, 2nd stage	4	*1.4*	30	*3.5*	47	*3.0*	19	*2.1*	100	291	*131*
Third level, non-university	6	*1.6*	14	*2.4*	48	*4.1*	32	*4.7*	100	307	*39*
Third level, university	3	*1.0*	17	*2.3*	54	*3.5*	26	*2.6*	100	307	*61*
Total	**39**	***2.9***	**32**	***2.3***	**23**	***2.2***	**5**	***0.8***	**100**	**227**	***596***
Women											
Primary education or lower	74	*3.5*	21	*2.9*	4	*1.3*	0	*0.1*	100	183	*193*
Second level, 1st stage	13	*2.8*	48	*2.8*	32	*2.4*	6	*1.5*	100	266	*157*
Second level, 2nd stage	3	*1.1*	25	*2.6*	55	*2.7*	16	*2.5*	100	294	*151*
Third level, non-university	4	*1.1*	38	*4.2*	50	*3.9*	8	*1.8*	100	282	*54*
Third level, university	0	*0.4*	13	*3.0*	50	*3.6*	36	*4.3*	100	313	*84*
Total	**40**	***2.7***	**32**	***2.7***	**22**	***1.5***	**5**	***0.5***	**100**	**218**	***639***
All											
Primary education or lower	71	*2.3*	24	*2.0*	5	*1.1*	0	*0.2*	100	190	*395*
Second level, 1st stage	13	*1.7*	47	*1.8*	33	*1.9*	7	*1.1*	100	267	*320*
Second level, 2nd stage	4	*0.8*	28	*2.3*	51	*2.2*	17	*1.9*	100	293	*282*
Third level, non-university	5	*1.0*	29	*2.3*	49	*2.8*	18	*2.4*	100	292	*93*
Third level, university	1	*0.5*	15	*1.7*	52	*3.0*	32	*3.0*	100	311	*145*
Total	**49**	***1.6***	**28**	***1.4***	**18**	***0.9***	**5**	***0.3***	**100**	**223**	***1235***
Document literacy											
Men											
Primary education or lower	62	*3.7*	32	*4.0*	6	*1.1*	0	*0.2*	100	203	*202*
Second level, 1st stage	14	*2.0*	43	*2.7*	35	*2.5*	8	*2.1*	100	268	*163*
Second level, 2nd stage	4	*1.3*	33	*3.6*	50	*3.7*	13	*1.2*	100	286	*131*
Third level, non-university	5	*1.8*	28	*3.5*	44	*4.1*	23	*5.0*	100	295	*39*
Third level, university	2	*0.5*	26	*2.7*	47	*2.3*	25	*2.9*	100	300	*61*
Total	**36**	***3.2***	**37**	***2.6***	**22**	***1.7***	**4**	***0.7***	**100**	**229**	***596***
Women											
Primary education or lower	75	*3.9*	20	*2.7*	4	*1.4*	..	*0.0*	100	181	*193*
Second level, 1st stage	21	*3.7*	52	*3.0*	25	*2.3*	2	*0.8*	100	253	*157*
Second level, 2nd stage	5	*1.1*	44	*2.9*	43	*2.6*	8	*1.7*	100	279	*151*
Third level, non-university	10	*2.5*	46	*3.6*	40	*4.5*	3	*0.9*	100	270	*54*
Third level, university	3	*1.4*	28	*3.3*	54	*3.7*	15	*2.6*	100	292	*84*
Total	**42**	***3.1***	**37**	***2.6***	**18**	***1.3***	**2**	***0.4***	**100**	**212**	***639***
All											
Primary education or lower	69	*3.0*	26	*2.6*	5	*0.9*	0	*0.1*	100	192	*395*
Second level, 1st stage	17	*1.9*	47	*1.9*	30	*1.7*	5	*1.1*	100	261	*320*
Second level, 2nd stage	5	*1.0*	39	*2.2*	46	*2.1*	10	*1.1*	100	282	*282*
Third level, non-university	8	*1.6*	39	*2.5*	42	*2.8*	11	*2.4*	100	280	*93*
Third level, university	2	*0.8*	27	*2.0*	51	*2.3*	19	*1.6*	100	295	*145*
Total	**49**	***2.1***	**32**	***1.7***	**17**	***0.7***	**3**	***0.3***	**100**	**220**	***1235***

Table A13.2 **cont. Portugal: IALS literacy level by highest level of educational attainment and sex**

	Level 1		Level 2		Level 3		Level 4/5		Total	Mean score	*Base*
Quantitative literacy	%	s.e.	%	s.e.	%	s.e.	%	s.e.	%		
Men											
Primary education or lower	52	3.9	33	3.8	14	2.0	1.4	0.8	100	219	*202*
Second level, 1st stage	10	1.8	35	3.4	42	3.3	13	2.1	100	281	*163*
Second level, 2nd stage	3	0.8	25	2.2	51	2.5	21	2.1	100	297	*131*
Third level, non-university	2	1.4	10	1.6	47	4.5	41	4.8	100	316	*39*
Third level, university	2	0.4	11	2.4	51	4.0	37	3.4	100	317	*61*
Total	**27**	**2.8**	**37**	**3.1**	**29**	**2.4**	**7**	**1.0**	**100**	**244**	***596***
Women											
Primary education or lower	71	4.2	21	2.5	7	2.4	0	0.3	100	187	*193*
Second level, 1st stage	18	3.1	42	2.4	37	3.0	3	1.0	100	261	*157*
Second level, 2nd stage	4	1.3	37	2.9	49	2.7	10	1.9	100	284	*151*
Third level, non-university	5	1.6	35	4.9	49	5.1	10	1.6	100	284	*54*
Third level, university	3	1.7	14	2.6	55	3.6	28	3.5	100	305	*84*
Total	**40**	**2.8**	**34**	**2.6**	**23**	**1.6**	**3**	**0.5**	**100**	**219**	***639***
All											
Primary education or lower	61	2.8	27	2.2	11	1.6	1	0.4	100	203	*395*
Second level, 1st stage	14	1.6	38	2.2	39	2.2	8	1.2	100	272	*320*
Second level, 2nd stage	4	0.8	31	1.5	50	1.3	15	1.3	100	290	*282*
Third level, non-university	4	0.7	25	2.4	48	3.2	23	2.6	100	297	*93*
Third level, university	2	1.0	13	1.5	53	2.5	32	2.6	100	310	*145*
Total	**43**	**1.9**	**29**	**1.5**	**23**	**1.2**	**6**	**0.5**	**100**	**231**	***1235***

s.e. Standard error of the estimate. The reported sample estimate can be said to be within 2 standard errors of the true population value with 95% confidence.

Table A13.3 **Literacy level by country**

	Level 1		Level 2		Level 3		Level 4/5		Total
	%	s.e.	%	s.e.	%	s.e.	%	s.e.	%
Prose literacy									
Canada	17	1.6	26	1.8	35	2.4	23	2.3	100
France	41	0.8	34	0.8	22	0.8	3	0.2	100
Germany	14	0.9	34	1.0	38	1.3	13	1.0	100
Great Britain	22	1.0	30	1.3	31	1.2	17	0.8	100
Netherlands	11	0.6	30	0.9	44	1.0	15	0.6	100
Poland	43	0.9	35	0.9	20	0.7	3	0.3	100
Portugal	49	1.6	28	1.4	18	0.9	5	0.3	100
Sweden	8	0.5	20	0.6	40	0.9	32	0.5	100
Switzerland (French)	18	1.3	34	1.6	39	1.8	10	0.7	100
Switzerland (German)	19	1.0	36	1.6	36	1.3	9	1.0	100
United States	21	0.7	26	1.1	32	1.2	21	1.2	100
Document literacy									
Canada	18	1.9	25	1.5	32	1.8	25	1.3	100
France	36	0.8	32	1.0	26	0.6	6	0.4	100
Germany	9	0.7	33	1.2	40	1.0	19	1.0	100
Great Britain	23	1.0	27	1.0	31	1.0	19	1.0	100
Netherlands	10	0.7	26	0.8	44	0.9	20	0.8	100
Poland	45	1.3	31	1.0	18	0.7	6	0.3	100
Portugal	49	2.1	32	1.7	17	0.7	3	0.3	100
Sweden	6	0.4	19	0.7	39	0.8	36	0.6	100
Switzerland (French)	16	1.3	29	1.4	39	1.3	16	1.1	100
Switzerland (German)	18	1.0	29	1.5	37	0.8	16	1.0	100
United States	24	0.8	26	1.1	31	0.9	19	1.0	100
Quantitative literacy									
Canada	17	1.8	26	2.5	35	2.1	22	1.8	100
France	33	1.0	30	0.9	28	0.7	9	0.5	100
Germany	7	0.4	27	1.2	43	0.8	24	0.9	100
Great Britain	23	0.9	28	1.0	30	0.9	19	1.0	100
Netherlands	10	0.7	26	0.9	44	1.0	20	0.8	100
Poland	39	1.1	30	1.2	24	0.6	7	0.5	100
Portugal	43	1.9	29	1.5	23	1.2	6	0.5	100
Sweden	7	0.4	19	0.6	39	0.9	36	0.7	100
Switzerland (French)	13	0.9	25	1.4	42	1.6	20	1.0	100
Switzerland (German)	14	1.0	26	1.3	41	1.5	19	1.3	100
United States	21	0.7	25	1.1	31	0.8	23	1.0	100

s.e. Standard error of the estimate. The reported sample estimate can be said to be within 2 standard errors of the true population value with 95% confidence.

14. Overview and recommendations

14.1 Introduction

The previous chapters in this report have outlined the programme of work undertaken as part of the EU funded review of the International Adult Literacy Survey (IALS) in the European context. The objective of the study were to review three main areas: the potential for cultural bias in large-scalc literacy surveys such as IALS; household survey methods and their application in the context of such surveys in Europe and survey methods in the context of international survey initiatives, all with the objective of establishing good practice in these areas for future similar surveys. Although the IALS was the vehicle for this study, the results are more universally applicable. IALS was a unique survey in many ways – not only was it the first time in many of the countries that participated that traditional educational testing methods were brought out of their school based environment and into people's homes, but it was also unique in its ambition. As a collaboration effort of researchers and organisations across a number of disciplines and countries it remains remarkable in its undertaking. As with all new developments there is always room for improvement. In reviewing IALS the prospect for improving future surveys of this kind, and indeed all surveys of a cross national nature has been foremost in our minds.

IALS is now coming to the close of its third wave. In 1994 nine countries took part. In 1996 a further 4 countries took part with all parties learning from the experience of those who had gone before, making improvements and refinements where necessary. At first view the schedule of countries implementing the survey over a protracted time period might have appeared problematic. Apart from the IALS estimates not being from a single point in time, preserving the assessment in tact across the waves of the survey meant that new countries would not be able to contribute items to the test and some of the items would potentially become dated. This staggered approach actually served the development of the survey well. In a relatively short space of time, only 5 years, three rounds of the survey have been scheduled, allowing a valuable opportunity to pause and review and to improve. The countries that took part in 1998 continued this process of continuous improvements, reducing further the potential for error and increasing standardisation across all aspects of the survey process. The continuous programme of IALS over three waves has provided an unprecedented opportunity to continuously improve the operation, both on the part of those organising the survey and for the individual countries taking part to test the new procedures.

The taste for such international surveys whether they be household based surveys of adults or school based assessments of pupils is unlikely to diminish, indeed, the demand for data which will support international comparisons is growing in many policy areas. We hope that this report contributes to the successful development of comparative surveys by adding to the understanding of how surveys operate in an international context. This chapter draws together the main strands of the project and summarises the key findings and recommendations.

14.2 What does it mean to be at Level 1?

IALS produces measures on three domains of literacy, Prose, Document and Quantitative literacy. Each scale ranges from 0-500 and is grouped into 5 levels, Level 1 being the lowest level and Level 5 the highest. In the debate about what constitutes sufficient literacy ability to be able to function in society there have been quite different interpretations. In the OECD reports it is suggested that anything below Level 3 is insufficient for coping with everyday life. On the other hand, in other countries the discussion has focused more on the implausibility of saying that half of the population are below the level required. Equally problematic is that between a fifth and a quarter of the population are at the lowest level,

Level 1 and for many this suggests that the levels are not sufficiently refined to distinguish between those with severe problems in using the written word and those that are not terribly proficient at it. As much of the reporting of IALS, particularly in the media focuses on those at Level 1, the lowest literacy level various mis-interpretations of what it means to be at Level 1 are evident.

The literacy measures used in IALS are intended to measure the full range of ability. The methodology used provides estimates of the skill levels of populations and not measures of the literacy ability of a given individual. Many people think that Level 1 means that these people cannot read and write. The estimation of literacy levels in IALS are defined negatively, that is, that a group is estimated to be at a given literacy Level on the basis that their responses to higher level items does not reach the required consistency (defined in IALS as 80%) for those higher levels. The following examples show sample responses from an individual who was estimated at Level 1 on prose on all plausible values.

Example A1 Block 1 Question 5

5. List three reasons why the letter writer prefers to use disposable rather than cotton nappies.

No nappies to wash

less water for washing used

no detergent required

The samples from the booklet for Example A who is representative of those at Level 1 shows his/her answers to question 5 in Block 1 and questions 1 and 2 in the same block. Question 5, on the reasons why the letter writer prefers to use disposable nappies is a Prose Level 3 item. The respondent has answered the question incorrectly. Although they have given 3 reasons they are not sufficient against the scoring guidelines. The respondent has given minimal responses in each point and the last two points quoted when combined account for only 1 argument in the scoring guide. The same respondent answered a document level 3 question correctly as shown in Example A2 question 1. Question 2 in example A2 is also answered correctly and is a document task at Level 2. In looking through the booklet from this respondent it is almost complete with two pages where there are some questions left unanswered. One of the pages concerned the questions on the longest text – the information on child safety and which contained 4 prose questions, the first question at Level 2 and the others at Level 3 and 4. The respondent answered the first question which required a relatively short answer but left the remaining questions which required longer responses unanswered. On the following page, the text consisted of a chart with information on fireworks sales and injuries. Again the respondent answered the first question (Document level 2) which required a short answer, correctly, and then left the next two questions on the page blank (Document Level 3 and Quantitative Level 3) and put a line through the final answer on the page (Document level 3). Many people assume that to be at Level 1 is to not been able to read and write. The examples for this respondent clearly show this to be a false assumption.

Example A2 Block 1 Questions 1 and 2

1. Name two things the manual suggests you check for if your frozen food develops ice crystals.

Door left ajar

Door openings too long and frequent

2 If moisture appears on the outside of the refrigerator, what can be done to remedy this problem?

Move the energy saver switch to the right

14.3 Review of IALS

In reflecting on the description of IALS as documented in the technical report the focus has been on identifying areas that could and should be improved in further initiatives of this type. Comparing literacy between different languages and cultures is extremely ambitious and it is hardly surprising that concerns have been raised about the methodology on a subject matter so important to national pride. The IALS in 1994 was the first venture of this type and was very ambitious in its undertaking. Although IALS is at least as good as similar undertakings, the debate surrounding the results from IALS has been important in underlining the need for good quality data in cross-national studies. Although much effort was put into standardising inputs such as questionnaires there is also a need to standardise the protocols and processes used. However, it is not realistic to expect that all variation can be avoided but every effort should be made to minimise the unnecessary variation in such international studies. It is important that all aspects of the survey are fully documented so that information is available to allow users to evaluate the survey quality.

The main areas which need to be addressed are sampling, response rates (individual and item), technical assistance to enable countries to meet the criteria, resourcing of national surveys, documentation and translation. Many of these have already been addressed in subsequent rounds of IALS but there is still a need to validate the background questionnaire in a cross cultural context.

14.4 Survey practice

The review of survey practices in European countries (Chapter 5 of this report) was a necessary preliminary to understanding the issue of comparability in cross-national research. Within Europe there are many surveys that produce results that are used for comparisons with other countries. For a researcher using such data there is no easy way of evaluating the methodology used and its appropriateness for that country. The metadata available is often sketchy and insufficient (for example, not providing notes on translation of questions in countries where concepts differ). In producing cross national statistics most effort is spent on harmonising the inputs and outputs of the survey process and little investment is made in terms of harmonising or standardising the survey process itself. By documenting survey practice across a number of European countries we have identified the range of practice that is currently on offer. It is clear that in some countries the possibility of optimising the implementation or design is constrained by access to a suitable sampling frame.

The review was centred on four aspects of survey practice:

- sample design and sampling procedures,
- survey experience,
- fieldwork organisation and strategies and
- survey processing.

In all of the areas reviewed different practices were encountered with countries doing things in different ways. In some areas investigated variation in IALS in how the survey was administered reflected local preferences (or indeed contractor preferences) rather than local constraints. Most of this variation is not necessary which means that it could be reduced if there is a willingness to do so. This will require compromise on all parties and can only be achieved where there is recognition of the need to standardise processes as well as inputs and outputs.

With regard to sampling design and procedures, it is possible to meet the minimum standards and requirement for probability sampling in each country if National Statistical Institutes can be involved in the survey, either by doing the whole survey or by doing the survey in co-operation with others.

When it comes to experience and expertise, public institutes seem to have greater experience in the very large and complex survey, particularly those that are continuous. Private organisations on the other hand have expertise in the smaller ad-hoc surveys with a shorter lead in and turn around time. Literacy surveys such as IALS are large or complex and ad-hoc. Public organisations have more expertise and experience with respect to data processing, coding, weighting, imputation, etc. while other institutes in most countries have specific expertise with respect to literacy. This also points to the need for collaborative efforts in staging a survey such as IALS.

There is a lot of variation between countries and between institutes within a country in terms of fieldwork and data collection procedures. This variation can and should be reduced by the use of the 'battery' of minimum measures to reduce non-response. Budget constraints should not limit the use of this battery.

In future international surveys it is best to be mindful in their conceptualisation and design of what is feasible in different countries and therefore not to set the standards unrealistically high. For example in relation to response rate it is best to encourage the use of the 'battery' and provide the necessary budgets for it and to encourage research on non-response bias than to simply set minimum targets that countries have little or no hope of achieving.

With regard to literacy surveys or any specialist topic area there is a need to ensure that all the skills required are available. From the review it is unlikely that these will be found in a single organisation as survey organisations tend to lack expertise in the specific subject matter and the particular techniques used. Institutes which have those skills tend not to have the household survey experience or expertise. It is likely therefore that consortia or partnerships will be needed to ensure the range of expertise is available. Such partnerships often experience difficulties as specific interests and priorities are difficult to manage successfully. This collaboration extends beyond national boundaries. Where organisations or countries can not source the necessary skills or experience, where for example they are departing from their standard practice in the interest of harmonising procedures then there should be a willingness to look to other countries to find the necessary input. This may also be more efficient so that rather than duplicating effort countries working together can share expertise and ensure standardisation by sharing of procedures and protocols.

14.5 Measurement and analysis tools

Over the past 30 years there have been a number of large-scale assessments carried out involving an ever growing number of countries. Many of these assessments have been carried out under two frameworks, those of the International Association for the Evaluation of Educational Achievement (IEA) and the International Assessment of Educational Progress (IAEP). Most large-scale assessments, particularly the international assessments, were restricted to student populations. The International Adult Literacy Survey (IALS) however brought together techniques from two distinct traditions, that of educational assessment and that of household surveys to bring assessment out of the classroom and into people's homes based on successful experience in the US and Canada. The introduction of measurement techniques, until now associated almost exclusively with school based surveys, into a new context, that of household based surveys, brought with it a new set of problems for many survey practitioners. These problems related to how to use and interpret the results.

The predominant assessment methodology used in international large-scale assessment is Item Response Theory (IRT) or Item Response Models (IRM). The fact that IRT has been used in all the large international assessments in recent years does not mean that it is universally accepted. Among European countries in particular the suitability and acceptability of IRT models for assessment is debated. In agreeing to participate in IALS, some countries questioned the dependence of the assessment on IRT models, a debate which appears to have been less prominent in other countries. Given that IALS was based on earlier studies conducted in the US which had used IRT and that there was little opportunity to influence the development or analysis of IALS, for many countries the debate was simply on whether to participate or not. Agreeing to participate in the study meant accepting the methodology as it stood. Countries participating in the first round in 1994 did have an opportunity to contribute items but even so most of the items came from the US or Canada where similar studies had been carried out before.

In this report we sought to present the different perspectives on the use of IRT. These are presented in chapters 3 and 4 of this report.

14.5.1 IRT models in Large-scale assessments

There are two basic assumptions underlying IRT. The first is that individuals have latent traits that are not directly observable and that the combination of the individuals' abilities and the test item properties produces the individuals' item responses under a mathematical model. It is further assumed that nothing else except random error affects the responses to items. These are quite large assumptions. Alternatively IRT can be looked at in a different way, simply as a way of expressing the probability of a student correctly answering an item given the student's ability and the properties of the item.

IRT is a means of dealing with some of the demands placed on assessments. In order to extract the most value from an assessment opportunity a broad coverage of subjects, or of topics within subjects, is often demanded. In order to meet this need matrix sampling is used so that the entire assessment is longer than any one respondent could be reasonably expected to complete. Respondents therefore take different combinations or samples of the test items. In IALS a particular form of matrix sampling is used, the Balanced Incomplete Block (BIB). This allows the possibility to estimate correlations between any two sections of the test as they are linked together in a spiral design in different combinations. Unlike assessments of individual performance at the end of a course of study or to achieve certification for proficiency in a subject the interest in large-scale assessments such as IALS is in how the skills being measured are distributed in the population and so there is no intrinsic interest or need for getting an accurate picture of an individual's competencies. So a method which gives aggregated results for the population or for sub-groups of the population should meet this need. IRT models are used to produce just such population estimates and not individual estimates.

As the composition of the test booklets will differ in terms of the profile of item difficulty the raw number right or percent scores may not be directly comparable since some assessment combinations may be more difficult than others. IRT is able to cope with this problem and produce reasonably comparable student scores even though the students have not all taken the same test.

14.5.2 Why not to use IRT

The concerns over the use of IRT in large-scale assessments such as IALS generally relate to three main aspects of their use and assumptions:

- fundamental conceptual concerns about the assumption of uni-dimensionality,
- the interpretation of the scales in terms of hierarchical levels and what those levels mean, and
- the assumption that each scale has the same meaning in each country. It is argued that separate scaling should be undertaken for each country rather than forcing the data onto a single international scale. This would not produce comparable country rankings. There is however, an argument to be made for not producing country rankings, both on measurement and survey methodology grounds but to focus on the correlates of the measures in the different countries.

14.5.3 An alternative summary measure

Since reporting of the individual items is clearly problematic in terms of presenting a coherent picture of the skills being measured then some kind of summary measure is necessary. IRT is one method of achieving this but other simpler measures could be as useful such as the proportion or number of correct responses.

One of the reported advantages of IRT is as a method of assessing Differential Item Functioning (DIF), i.e. whether an item means the same in different countries and different languages. In the paper by Blum and Guérin-Pace (Chapter 6) notable differences have been found in the translation of the IALS assessment between versions. In the case of IALS these were not identified during the scaling process and would suggest that these methods should not replace other methods of quality assuring the adaptation of test items across languages. Among those countries that took part in the original IALS France had the fewest number of items where the parameters were deemed to not fit (2). Detailed analysis of items may identify biases not detected by items which simply do not fit the expected model. A procedure based purely on IRT models could discriminate against countries which are most discrepant from this assumed common structure.

The description of what these scales mean is generally problematic. With IRT generated scales there is often an attempt to describe what it means to be at different points on the scale in terms of what people can or cannot do. This again rests on the assumption of unidimensionality with only random effects. The description of the scales on the IALS measures was developed based on detailed empirical work on the Young Adult Literacy survey conducted in the mid 1980s in the US. The anchoring procedure used response probabilities to identify examplar tasks for investigation[1]. These tasks showed characteristics which reflected different aspects of text difficulty. This work led, through further research to the development of constructs of item difficulty which seem to be solidly founded in practice. In examining the distribution of tasks incremental shifts in item difficulty values were identified which guides the partition of the scale into levels. While these levels are empirically based their value is diminished by the way the levels are distributed. Within many countries around a fifth to a quarter of the population are estimated to be at Level 1. While the assumption that these people cannot read or write is clearly wrong there is a need to further discriminate within this lowest level to identify the characteristics of tasks that show the limits of those with the very poorest skills.

14.5.4 Using data generated by IRT

Goldstein in Chapter 4 of this report considers that IRT methods are opaque and difficult to understand. The IRT method uses complex procedures for imputing proficiency levels for those who have either not attempted the booklet at all or who have not done very much of the booklet. This is perfectly reasonable to do. If no adjustment were made for such cases then the literacy distribution would potential misrepresent the skills of the population, particularly if the main reason for not doing a booklet is likely to be literacy related. The data which is used to impute proficiency estimates is taken from the background questionnaire on the assumption that "the missing cognitive data are similar to the observed data *when the background information is the same.*"[2]. Various things such as age, sex, race, education level are used to produce the proficiency estimates. This lack of transparency in how the proficiency estimates are produced is a drawback.

The resulting dataset from IALS consists of multiple plausible values. For each individual for each scale a series of values are produced. This leaves the non-psychometrically trained researcher with a problem. First, conceptually it is difficult to comprehend that what we have are several estimates of the proficiency which has embedded within it characteristics of the respondent. Respondents often ask for feedback on how they did and it seems implausible to them that their skill can not be estimated simply from what they have answered. In looking at the plausible values for individual cases there can be quite a wide range of values observed with respondents being variably at Levels 1, 2 or 3 depending on which plausible value is taken. Since they are designed to produce population estimate and not individual estimates this is not unexpected. Secondly, there is a concern that the relationships observed between background characteristics and the skill levels are exaggerated by the IRT procedures where background characteristics are used to condition the estimates. One questions the validity of using multivariate techniques for example on the proficiency estimates as one is never sure how much of the perceived relationships is due to the factors in the analysis having already been taken into account in the conditioning and estimation procedures. Of particular concern is the potential for identifying spurious relationships.

IRT is merely a tool to summarise or reduce the data into an overall measure. Goldstein argues that it would be simpler, and essentially change nothing, if the proportion correct were used. In the IALS technical report this is acknowledged "...mean proficiency values and proportion correct statistics have a strong linear relationship" (p.183) and secondary analyses by Heady (Chapter 7) confirm that overall country rankings are little affected by using such a simpler measure (number of questions correct).

---

[1] Kirsch, I. Ann Jungeblut and Peter B. Mosenthal. The Measurement of Adult Literacy. in *Adult Literacy in OECD Countries Technical Report on the First International Adult Literacy Survey*. National Center for Education Statistics: Washington 1998

[2] Yamamoto, Kentaro. Proficiency Estimation in *Adult Literacy in OECD Countries Technical Report on the First International Adult Literacy Survey*. National Center for Education Statistics: Washington 1998. p186

Given this and considering the lack of transparency in the IRT scaling procedure for IALS and the large costs involved a case could be made for not using IRT. However, given the need for maintaining continuity within series of international survey collections then it is likely that IRT will continue to be the dominant methodology used. Our main concerns are that these are used in isolation and that it is not at all transparent. We would advocate that the set of tools employed in analysing these data sets be extended to include for example more evidence of analysis for within country variation.

Regardless of the analysis tools there are other factors which must be got right before first. Even the most sophisticated statistical tools can not compensate for poor quality data. The chapter on survey practice (Chapter 5) has identified a number of areas where greater attention must be made to reduce between country variation in how the survey is implemented.

14.6 Respondent perspective

The investigations carried out as part of this project and the opportunities provided for reflection have provided interesting themes for discussion. What became clear during the initial meetings at the start of this study was how little is known about the respondent perspective in surveys. The qualitative interviewing carried out gave us a small insight into the view from where they sit. As researchers eager to have as much data as possible it is often too easy to overlook the coherence of our requests to respondents. In undertaking international surveys this is particularly important so as to try and establish a shared experience and understanding across societies, cultures and languages.

It is clear from the qualitative research that respondent experience and understanding of our requests is far from universal. There were differences within and between countries in how the respondents perceived the survey, it what they understood about its intent, in the way they responded to the demands of the survey and in their reasons for taking part. The range of within country variation is particularly interesting since it shows how even when standardised documentation and explanation is provided to respondents they select the information that is most convincing to them. Respondents had differing expectations of what the survey would be like and in some senses these expectations were self-fulfilling with people finding what they wanted in the booklets. Where people expected there to be trick questions they found examples of questions which they thought fitted that criteria.

Important lessons from the qualitative work were about the assumptions respondents make about the rules. For example, although respondents were told to take as long as they needed many were imposing time limits on themselves based on information they had assimilated about how long the whole thing might take. Such time pressure was thought to have a mostly negative effect in that respondents abandoned checking their answers or speeded themselves up in other ways.

There is also an issue about what the respondent believes is being tested, for example whether it is the ability to follow instructions, to use texts or simply to answer the questions. Following the instructions in the question does interact with the score awarded. Some respondents recognised that what was being measured was their 'skill' in dealing with documents such as those presented in the booklet. Other respondents felt that it was their 'knowledge' that was being tested and so wishing to demonstrate how much they knew answered the questions not using the text, or only partly using the text but adding their own personal answer as well. Other instances where the ability to follow the instructions was important related to questions which asked "..in your own words...". Where respondents ignored this instruction they risked getting the question wrong since verbatim transcriptions of the correct passage from the text would have counted as incorrect answers.

Regardless of whether the respondent believes their skill or knowledge is being tested their 'attitude' to the task will also play a role. In the qualitative work and in the debriefing interview to the follow-up survey there was a wide range of attitudes to the survey, from those who thought it was important to try hard, or to answer correctly to those who were quite laid back in their approach. Others considered that since the survey was about literacy in daily life then they should use the same approach as in real life, some reported that in everyday tasks they often guess or make approximations since the precision was unnecessary. The other tension was between speed versus accuracy. Many respondents made a judgement about which they thought was most important, sometimes reflecting how they were taught to approach exams in school. Although it is recognised how extremely difficult it is to get good measures of comparable attitudes across countries there were differences between countries in the attitudes displayed.

14.6.1 Financial Incentives

In the qualitative interviews the issue of financial incentives was explored with respondents which suggested that it was unlikely to impact on the commitment of participants to completing the task in hand. While many people thought it might be motivating for others they didn't think it would affect the way they had worked. This was tested in the pilot study and seemed to have little impact. Although the literature suggests that incentives can improve data quality from diary activities related to recording behaviour and usually over a protracted period of time and therefore less 'personal' than one's literacy skills there was no evidence that financial incentives could be used to enhance commitment to the exercise. Most respondents reported that they were indeed already trying their best. They were interested in knowing how they had done on the assessment and this along with additional information about how the results of the survey would be used would have been of more interest as an incentive to do well.

14.7 Literacy measures at two points in time

The follow-up survey of IALS participants was conducted in Great Britain, Sweden and France. Two hypotheses were being tested, that an improvement in performance on the test could be achieved by improving respondent commitment to the task through a series of measures defined as 'Best Practice' and that this improvement would differ between countries and between groups of countries. The survey involved going back to IALS respondents and asking them to complete another IALS assessment. The sample was split into two parts, one part, the IALS style or replicate sample had the survey administered in the exact same way as in IALS. The protocols for the second part of the sample were developed based on the qualitative work, on a review of the documentation available on how IALS was implemented across countries and an analysis of the equivalence of the assessment across various French and English versions. The differences between the two parts of the sample varied between countries. In France those in the Best Practice sample were given a different French language version of the assessment than that used in the IALS sample.

The results were analysed at individual question level and using two summary measures of proficiency, the IALS scaled estimates and the proportion of questions answered correctly. The hypothesis, if true, would suggest that there would be an improvement in performance on the assessment in the Best Practice sample over and above any changes in the IALS part of the sample. Any improvement in proficiency in the Best Practice sample can be seen as comprising the effect of Best Practice plus measurement error. Only in Britain did Best Practice have a significant impact on improving performance on the assessment. In Britain there was a small improvement in the control part of the sample and a bigger improvement in the Best Practice sample whether estimated proficiency score or proportion correct is used. In Sweden there was no difference in performance over time in either part of the sample. In France a different pattern was observed. In the control sample there was a significant improvement in the estimated proficiency in the control sample while in the Best Practice sample a smaller improvement was observed. The hypothesis was not confirmed in a general way across all countries.

The analysis of differences between countries at individual item level showed interesting variation between countries. In Britain the proportion answering an item correctly was significantly higher for about a third of the items. In Sweden there were fewer differences between the two parts of the sample in the proportions answering any given question correctly. In France the pattern was less consistent with some quite large differences observed.

In trying to establish consistency between the IALS and the follow-up survey in two other areas emerged as important, scoring and data completeness.

To establish scoring consistency within and between countries so as to minimise the contribution of scoring to survey error is important. Certain items in IALS were particularly difficult to score and required a lot of judgement on the part of the scorer making it difficult to establish consistency. During the process of the follow-up survey an in-depth investigation was undertaken on scoring reliability in France only. The scoring in the follow-up survey in France was found to be more in line with the British scoring in IALS. This showed evidence of scoring drift on some items between the IALS in 1994, the follow-up survey in 1998 and the IALS in Great Britain in 1996. IRT takes into account scoring reliability in the estimation procedure however it should be possible to improve the quality of the scoring process so that survey error is reduced.

In IALS there were large differences between countries in the data completeness, that is, the proportion of the sample who attempted a booklet and the amount of the booklet they completed. There were similarities in the levels of data completeness, given the response rates, in France, Britain and Portugal. In Sweden almost all respondents tried to do the assessment, even those at the lower literacy levels. This may be due to interviewer variability with perhaps interviewers in Sweden being more persuasive or to respondents being more co-operative or survey friendly. In the debriefing interview Swedish respondents reported attaching high levels of importance, interest, commitment and application to the request.

14.8 Simplicity and complexity

How sophisticated a measure is necessary to be able to estimate the size of the literacy problem in a given country? The answer to this will partly depend on how big the problem is considered to be. Measuring basic skills in a country which is generally thought of as being very literate will differ from countries where most of the population have little or no literacy abilities such as in some developing countries. Designing a measure which is fit for purpose depends on what that purpose is. Is a simple measure sufficient for the needs of those charged with monitoring and improving basic skills or do the three dimensions measured in IALS earn their keep?

This has been addressed through secondary analysis and through survey research in Portugal. Heady (Chapter 7) concluded from secondary analysis of IALS that it would be possible to simplify both the design of the test and the presentation of the results while still preserving some of the main features of the results identified by the full IALS procedure.

As part of this programme of research the IALS was conducted in Portugal. In 1994, at the same time as IALS, Portugal carried out a survey of adult literacy (PALS) based on the basic constructs as IALS but implemented and analysed in a simpler way. Instead of matrix sampling a single booklet was devised and instead of scaling levels were assigned to items using the conceptual framework and probabilities of answering correctly.

The PALS survey produced a measure of literacy for which the distribution is reasonably close to that produced by the IALS and for which the correlations between the measure and background characteristics are of a similar order. The advantages of the simpler method have already been mentioned. PALS used a single booklet and a single scale and while the disadvantage of that choice are limitations on the breadth of the assessment, it does mean that the measure is at the individual rather than the population level and relationships identified are not blurred or potentially spurious from the imputation procedures used in scaling to take account of the different test combinations. Given the other many sources of non-sampling error that can impinge on a survey of this type, as seen elsewhere in this report, a measure such as this may be perfectly adequate for most purposes and this simpler measure has probably been as useful to policy makers in Portugal as the IALS data has been to policy makers elsewhere.

14.9 Future international efforts

As already mentioned the demand for internationally comparable data is growing in many fields. Already there is an international survey of pupils in progress and the possibility of the International Life Skills Survey of adults. An important feature of any survey carried out in more than one country or Member State is its potential to produce unbiased weighted statistics which can be used for comparative purposes. These statistics must be robust, which requires that all stages in their collection, processing and analysis should be carried out scientifically and using best methods, harmonised as far as is practicable. A clear survey specification will help to achieve this, but it is not in itself sufficient as the *process* is as important as the specification.

Developing the instruments

In surveys such as IALS there are two sets of survey instrument, the literacy assessment itself and the background questionnaire which collects socio-demographic characteristics and will usually include additional relevant classificatory variables and behaviour. Both of these, and all the supporting documentation will need to be adapted or translated as appropriate for use in each country. For surveys such as IALS this requires considerable effort.

Some of the questions to consider when developing and adapting background questionnaires and assessment instruments are:

- whether the questions have credibility in all participating countries
- what kinds of question testing should be undertaken to ensure the relevance and acceptability of questions
- the implications, in terms of the overall shape of the questionnaire and delivery of data files, of including optional questions in different countries
- whether harmonisation within participating countries makes it difficult to include mandatory questions in the background questionnaire

Successful contribution of participating countries to the development of instruments is only likely to happen if items are adequately described in the context of the accompanying framework and this is provided to reviewers. Tight timetables work against involvement of countries in this process.

14.9.2 Translation and adaptation

Preserving the nature and difficulty of the tasks across translations is only one part of the process. It is also important to ensure that by seeking to preserve the difficulty of the task, that the authenticity of the items for certain language groups has not been affected. Question testing as part of the translation/development process is advocated as a means of validating the translation procedure in addition to standard translation management tools.

In IALS it is acknowledged that most effort went into making sure the adaptation of the literacy assessments was accurate as it was the design element which carried the most inherent risks. Guidelines were prepared on the adaptation of items for participating countries[3]. In a survey model which aims for comparability on the 'ask the same questions' model, adapting an instrument does not only involve translating the words, but also ensuring that the concepts and the task are the same. For example, where the keyword in a question was a synonym of the word used in the stimulus item in the original task, the adaptation should ensure that this is also the case when the task is translated. Failure to do this means that respondents in different countries are not being given the same task, which weakens the validity of international comparisons. Some of the problems associated with translation and adaptation in IALS are discussed in Chapter 9[4] of the IALS Technical Report and in the papers by Blum and Guérin-Pace and by Heady (Chapters 6 and 7 in this report respectively). For some items, the adaptation resulted in a different difficulty level from the original item.

How best to adapt survey instruments for survey use is problematic. Harkness[5] argues that although back translation is often taken as an indicator of quality it is one of the less recommendable procedures on both practical and theoretical grounds and a more multi-disciplinary approach is suggested. The version of the IALS assessment in France for many items does not preserve the relationship between text and task in the original. Only the French and English versions of the assessment have been looked at in detail during the course of this research and other versions of the assessment may not be truly faithful to the source version. For future surveys of this type methods need to be developed to check the translation and these should involve a multi-method approach.

14.9.3 The survey process

Both the IALS Technical Report and the external evaluators' report made recommendations for improving the survey process. The Technical Report noted that there was a lot of concern in IALS about construct validity, but that relatively little time was spent controlling the more 'pedestrian' matters of sampling and data collection. It recommended that national study teams should be required to document future rounds of IALS, and that an operations audit should be conducted just before the main study. This would enable study managers to identify changes to the survey that might compromise quality[6]. The report of the external evaluators concluded there was a need for standardisation in sampling strategies, data collection procedures, and coding and analysis procedures across countries, with best practices being established for all the components of the survey and followed in all countries[7].

Earlier chapters in this report have made further recommendations and suggestions for the minimum requirements for carrying out complex surveys, which can be used as a guide for those commissioning further surveys. These are summarised in Table 14.1, together with an indication of some of the risks associated with not being able to meet them.

---

[3] See Darcovich and Murray. in National Centre for Education Statistics. Op cit.

[4] Binkley MR and Pignal JR. 'An analysis of items with different parameters across countries' in National Centre for Education Statistics. Op cit.

[5] Harkness, J. In pursuit of quality: issues for cross-national survey research. *International Journal of Social Research Methodology Theory and Practice.* Vol 2 No 2 April-June 1999, pp125-150

[6] See Darcovich and Murray. Op Cit.

[7] Kalton G, Lyberg L and Rempp J-M. 'Appendix A: Review of Methodology' in National Centre for Education Statistics. Op Cit.

Table 14.1 **Prerequisites for carrying out complex surveys**

Prerequisite	Risks of non-compliance
Design	
• Prepare a plan for the study design for review by the project consortium.	➢ Implementation in participating countries is delayed or unsatisfactory.
• Agree in advance and document any deviations from the recommended design.	➢ Deviations are unknown. ➢ Deviations are not taken into account when results are interpreted.
• Conduct an operations audit before the start of fieldwork.	➢ Contractor lacks the capacity to carry out one or more stages of the survey.
Sampling procedures	
• A comprehensive sampling frame, with high coverage (at least 95%); its construction, coverage and exclusions to be fully documented.	➢ Inclusion possibilities or systematic exclusions not known. ➢ Biased sample selected. ➢ Systematic exclusions.
• Probability sampling to be used at all stages, i.e. sample selection probabilities should be known and every member of the target population should have a non-zero probability of being included in the sample.	➢ Inability to produce unbiased survey estimates, sampling errors and confidence intervals. ➢ Difficult to make international comparisons.
• Where multi-stage sampling is used, rules for selecting households at addresses, and individuals within households should be clearly specified.	➢ Interviewers may select the first households or people they encounter, thus biasing the sample.
• Where area sampling is used, the population size per area should be known or be able to be estimated.	➢ Impossible to calculate the probabilities of selection.
• Where telephone lists are used as sampling frames, the coverage rate should be 95% and non-listed households should not differ systematically from listed households.	➢ Biased sample is selected.
• Problematic features such as substitution should be avoided.	➢ Difficult to control practice in the field.
• Ability to calculate standard errors and weights.	➢ Standard errors and weights not correctly calculated. ➢ Survey results reported inaccurately.
• Access to survey sampling specialists.	➢ Incorrect advice may be given. ➢ Procedures may be incorrectly implemented.
Fieldwork procedures	
• Survey organisations should have recent experience of carrying out complex, face-to-face nationwide household surveys, with sample size of at least 3000 sample elements. They also must have experience of different data-collection methods (CATI, CAPI, telephone and face-to-face surveys) and be able to carry out the whole survey process	➢ Organisation will not have the resources and capacity to carry out complex surveys.
• Employ experienced interviewers, who are trained not only in interviewing, but also in doorstep sample selection procedures.	➢ Interviewers who lack the training and skills to carry out complex surveys may introduce bias by not following questioning procedures properly. ➢ Interviewers do not follow sampling rules correctly. ➢ Poor response rates.
• Interviewers to be supervised by experienced supervisors/managers.	➢ Poor monitoring and supervision of interviewers results in poor practice and response.
• Fieldwork operations to be monitored and quality checked.	➢ Problems not identified until it is too late to take remedial action.

Table 14.1 contd. **Prerequisites for carrying out complex surveys**

Prerequisite	Risks of non-compliance
Response	
• Develop a contact strategy.	➢ Interviewers do not work efficiently. ➢ Response is adversely affected.
• Reduce non-response	➢ High non-response produces biased estimates. ➢ Poor response can delay the timetable if refusal conversion is necessary.
• Some information on non-response to be collected.	➢
• An ability to assess the likely effect of non-response on survey estimates.	➢ No understanding of how non-response affects the estimates.
• An ability to assess the responding samples and results against some benchmark estimates.	➢ No information about the difference between responders and non-responders.
Data processing	
• Use experienced coders of occupation and industry.	➢ Coding is inaccurate and/or inconsistent. ➢ Difficult to make international comparisons. ➢ Plausible values may be incorrectly calculated. ➢ Covariates of literacy may not be accurately interpreted.
• Quality control procedures for occupation and industry coding.	➢ Mistakes and inconsistencies not identified.
• Fully-trained scorers/ assessors.	➢ Inconsistent and inaccurate scoring or assessments. ➢ Scales are inaccurate.
• Quality control procedures for scoring and assessment.	➢ Inaccurate and inconsistent scoring or assessments not identified.
Weighting and analysis	
• Experience of or access to methodological expertise in how to weight for selection probabilities and non-response.	➢ Inappropriate advice given. ➢ Weights not calculated correctly. ➢ Sample is described incorrectly in reports.
• Experience of or access to methodological expertise in how to calculate standard errors.	➢ Standard errors incorrectly calculated.
• Advice from specialist on appropriate analysis techniques and interpretation of data.	➢ Inappropriate techniques used. ➢ Results incorrectly interpreted. ➢ Potential of data not fully explored.
Documentation	
• All stages of the survey to be fully documented, so that assessments can be made of the effect of procedures on the survey estimates.	➢ Data cannot be interpreted or are misinterpreted. ➢ Timetable delayed while clarification is sought. ➢ Lack of clarity about whether survey was carried out on a comparable basis in all countries.

The preceding table listed some of the essential requirements for carrying out complex surveys. The following one offers further suggestions which it would be desirable to implement.

Table 14.2 **Desirables for carrying out complex surveys**

Recommended	Risks of non-compliance
• Guidelines and procedures for reducing non-response, including refusal conversion, to be provided and followed.	➢ Response targets are not met.
• Collect data on how countries obtained co-operation from respondents.	➢ Opportunities for improving response and/or survey practice may be lost.
• Reduce differences between countries in procedures for adjusting for non-response.	➢ Different practices result in response being calculated on a different basis. ➢ Different practices result in different systematic biases in response.
• Agreed policy on use of incentives.	➢ Use of incentives by some countries may affect response, approach to the task.
• Common procedures for introducing the survey to respondents.	➢ Respondents' understanding of what the survey entails may differ. ➢ Could affect response.
• Common instructions for completing any tests or assessments.	➢ Respondents' understanding of and approach to tests or assessments may differ. ➢ Could affect performance.
• Control network for complex coding.	➢ Between-country variations result in different estimates. ➢ National estimates and international comparisons are inaccurate.
• Common imputation procedures.	➢ Different procedures could result in different estimates.
• The biases likely to arise from not following recommended procedures should be clearly set out.	➢ Difficult to assess the effect on estimates.

14.9.4 Scoring

The organistion of the procedures to establish scoring consistency between countries where countries are paired based on common language does not deal with the problems of consistency across a wider range of countries.

One approach might be to treat the scoring teams in all countries as a single scoring team rather than as national teams. Instead of rescoring booklets for another country if the scoring for all countries was shared then any error is also shared and not country specific. Clearly it is difficult to imagine scorers in all countries being able to cope with all languages. A modified version of this could be practicable with countries recruiting some bi/multi -lingual scorers or organised within language groups with some countries where assessment is being conducted in more than one language completing the circle. In this way, if there were 5 English speaking countries taking part, the scoring of all their booklets would be shared across the 5 national teams as would the associated scoring error.

In addition to finding ways of minimising process variation in scoring between countries it is useful to capture more detailed information on scoring or at least to distinguish between different types of wrong answers. There is of course a trade off between using a smaller number of codes to be applied, cost and precision. This should at least be acknowledged and countries given optional additional codes to use.

14.9.5 Respondent burden

Many countries have experienced declining response rates on surveys over the past number of years. The climate for survey taking is becoming more difficult yet against growing demands for data. In the desire to have more data it is often easy to lose the perspective of what it is like for the respondent to have to sit and answer the questions we devise. The qualitative work described in Chapter 8 reinforces the need to be mindful of what the respondent understands of our requests and the plausibility of why we want their co-operation. While we may have clear ideas about how we will use the data to look at interesting relationships, the data we collect to support that may seem unconnected and irrelevant to respondents. Respondent burden and survey fatigue need to be acknowledged and attempts made to contain survey length within reasonable bounds.

Capturing more detail on scoring is in one way of providing more information about the respondent reaction to items and the assessment in general. It would also be useful to try and collect at least some information on the physical environment in which the survey was being carried out and on respondent attitude to the survey. Interviewers often reported respondents feeling stressed at the end of the interview and having to spend some time to make them feel more at ease before taking their leave. A short debriefing interview post assessment would serve this purpose while at the same time offer an opportunity for the respondent to give feedback on the experience.

14.10 Compliance

Specification of the survey design, although important and not to be neglected, still does not ensure compliance. This is a difficult issue as it cuts across a number of constraints. Where countries are paying for their own national study they will want to ensure that their national as well as international research objectives are met. This can be a source of tension. However, even where countries are not contributing to the costs it can be difficult to achieve compliance.

There may also be authoritative constraints on how certain variables are to be collected nationally. There may also be legal constraints such as data protection or confidentiality requirements which will impact on the implementation of the survey in particular countries. While some of these variations may not have an impact on the comparability it is difficult to know where to draw the line in terms of allowable variation and what threshold should be set below which the survey quality is deemed to be unacceptable.

International surveys may be organised on several different models. The relationship between those co-ordinating the survey and those taking part, both funders and implementers, will vary as does the extent to which commissioners get involved in the design and management of the survey. It is helpful if countries are explicit about their motivation for participation and about their expectations. Where there is at least a clear and shared objective non-compliance can be negotiated in terms of impact on comparability. Lack of consensus may result in different priorities being set in participating countries.

Compliance to the quality standards is also a resource issue. With new initiatives it is difficult to contain costs since in the development process the design will evolve. In costing such surveys it is difficult to see all eventualities and what the limits will be. The fear of committing to a project which could turn into a bottomless pit is rightly a concern for commissioners and practitioners alike.

While it is possible to elaborate various protocols for the translation process it is difficult to force countries to comply. The burden will be greater on some countries than on others that do not have another country who share the same language and with whom they can pool resources in translation or where multiple languages must be accommodated within a small country. Many countries will opt out of elaborate translation procedures recommended rather than required due to time and cost restraints. Where countries are submitting items in the initial trawl for questions or texts it is important that at that stage the same translation procedures are applied.

Dealing with non-compliance or unnecessary variation is problematic. If a single country is non-compliant Harkness[8] likens it to the situation of the slow, fat child when the sports team is being selected in that others will not want to use the data for comparison. The desire to have data to make comparisons drives projects to be inclusive. If sanctions, such as not reporting the data in the international report or having the data flagged in some way are to be used these need to be explicit from the start and countries need to be signed up to them. It is therefore important that the design and minimum standards are achievable so that countries are not set to fail from the start.

There is also a need for transparency to all participants in how the survey is being implemented across all countries on an ongoing basis. This creates a collective responsibility for maximising comparability. There should be no surprises for participants in the documentation of the final report which should contain full documentation on all aspects of the survey implementation.

14.11 Responsibilities of commissioners

The responsibility for delivering high quality robust data is a shared responsibility, it does not just lie with the international co-ordinator or the national survey contractor. Some of the issues relating to survey quality in studies such as IALS were due to insufficient national budgets to undertake such a complex study.

In a commissioning process, there are requirements of both the commissioning body and of the contractors. From the commissioners, contractors require timely awarding of contracts, realistic specifications and timetables and adequate resources to deliver to the required standard and these standards need to be explicitly stated at the outset.

From the contractors, the commissioners should require that a strong record in all aspects of survey research, including probability sampling, data collection, data processing and weighting; that is, that they should be able to meet the criteria set out in Table 14.1. This has cost implications, as high quality work is expensive. This needs to be borne in mind by commissioning bodies when awarding contracts as what may appear to be a cheaper proposal may not necessarily offer the best value for money. These requirements apply both to the lead organisation or consortium, and to the national project teams. Commissioners have a responsibility to ensure they themselves have those with the right knowledge and expertise to evaluate proposals and to make an informed choice of contractor with any risks identified and evaluated. Where this may not be possible due to conflict of interest in a competitive tendering process there may be a case for including representatives or experts from other countries in the evaluation panel on a reciprocal arrangement.

Ideally, commissioning bodies within each participating country would have access to a range of organisations, each of which had all the necessary resources. The review of survey practice in Chapter 5 of this report has shown that this is not always the case. Where no one organisation is able to offer all the necessary skills, an alternative would be to form consortia of organisations which, between them, have all the necessary skills and resources.

There is also a responsibility to allow an adequate timetable for the survey. There is a trade off to be made between survey quality and speed. While it can be difficult to maintain momentum on a long-term project it is counter productive to set an over ambitious timetable. A realistic time should be negotiated based on an understanding of the complexity of the project and explicitly stating the quality standards required.

---

[8] Op cit.